Library of
Davidson College

THE REVELS PLAYS

Former Editors
Clifford Leech 1958–71
F. David Hoeniger 1970–85

General Editors
E. A. J. Honigmann, J. R. Mulryne, David Bevington
and Eugene M. Waith

THE CONSPIRACY AND TRAGEDY OF CHARLES DUKE OF BYRON

Charles de Gontaut duc de Biron (1562–1602) (Archives Photographiques Larousse)

THE REVELS PLAYS

THE CONSPIRACY AND TRAGEDY OF CHARLES DUKE OF BYRON

GEORGE CHAPMAN

edited by John Margeson

MANCHESTER
UNIVERSITY PRESS
Manchester and New York

*Distributed exclusively in the USA and Canada
by* St. Martin's Press

Introduction, critical apparatus, etc.,
© John Margeson 1988

All rights reserved

Published by Manchester University Press
Oxford Road, Manchester M13 9PL, UK
and Room 400, 175 Fifth Avenue,
New York, NY 10010, USA

*Distributed exclusively in the USA and Canada
by* St. Martin's Press, Inc.,
175 Fifth Avenue, New York, NY 10010, USA

ISBN 0 7190 1545 6 *cased*

British Library cataloguing in publication data
Chapman, George, *1559?–1634*
   The conspiracy and tragedy of Charles
Duke of Byron. – (The Revels plays).
   I. Title II. Margeson, John III. Series
   822'.3   PR2447.C6

Library of Congress cataloguing in publication data
applied for

Typeset by Best-set Typesetter Ltd
Printed in Great Britain
by Bell & Bain Limited, Glasgow

TO MILLAR MacLURE
wise colleague
and generous friend

THE REVELS PLAYS

ANON. *Arden of Faversham* *The Second Maiden's Tragedy*
Two Tudor Interludes: *Youth* and *Hick Scorner*
A Yorkshire Tragedy

BEAUMONT *The Knight of the Burning Pestle*
BEAUMONT AND FLETCHER *Philaster**

CHAPMAN *Bussy d' Ambois** *The Widow's Tears*
The Conspiracy and Tragedy of Charles Duke of Byron
CHAPMAN JONSON AND MARSTON *Eastward Ho*

DEKKER *The Shoemaker's Holiday*

FARQUHAR *The Recruiting Officer*

FORD *The Broken Heart* *'Tis Pity she's a Whore*
The Lover's Melancholy

GREENE *James the Fourth**

JONSON *The Alchemist** *Bartholomew Fair**
Volpone *The New Inn* *The Staple of News*

KYD *The Spanish Tragedy*

MARLOWE *Doctor Faustus** *The Jew of Malta**
The Poems *Tamburlaine I and II*

MARSTON *Antonio's Revenge* *The Fawn* *The Malcontent*
MARSTON AND OTHERS *The Insatiate Countess*

MIDDLETON *Women Beware Women**
MIDDLETON AND DEKKER *The Roaring Girl*
MIDDLETON AND ROWLEY *The Changeling**

PEELE *The Old Wives Tale*

SHIRLEY *The Cardinal* *The Lady of Pleasure*

SKELTON *Magnificence*

TOURNEUR *The Revenger's Tragedy**

VANBRUGH *The Provoked Wife*

WEBSTER *The Duchess of Malfi** *The White Devil**

WYCHERLEY *The Country Wife*

* available in paperback

Contents

LIST OF ILLUSTRATIONS		viii
GENERAL EDITORS' PREFACE		ix
PREFACE		xi
ABBREVIATIONS		xii
INTRODUCTION		1
1	The dramatist	1
2	Date	5
3	Theatre and acting company	6
4	Censorship and the text	9
5	The text	13
6	Sources	17
7	The play	20
8	Stage history	53
	Notes	55

The Conspiracy and Tragedy of Charles Duke of Byron   63

APPENDICES		271
I	Chapman and Grimeston	271
IIA	Letter from the French ambassador, Antoine Lefèvre de la Boderie to Pierre Brulart de Puisieux, Marquis de Sillery, 8 April 1608	276
IIB	The Dobell letters	278
III	Byron and the Essex conspiracy	280
GLOSSARIAL INDEX TO THE COMMENTARY		283

Illustrations

Charles de Gontaut duc de Biron (1562–1602) (Archives Photographiques Larousse) *frontispiece*

Henri IV engraved in 1846 by R. Graves after an earlier engraving by H. Goltzius (BBC Hulton Picture Library) *page* 39

Duc de Biron as warrior in Henry IV's battles to end the civil wars and unify France (Archives Photographiques Larousse) 64

The execution of the marechal de Biron in the courtyard of the Bastille, 31 July 1602 (Archives Photographiques Larousse) 168

General Editors' Preface

The series known as the Revels Plays was conceived by Clifford Leech. The idea for the series emerged in his mind, as he explained in his preface to the first of the Revels Plays in 1958, from the success of the New Arden Shakespeare. The aim of the new group of texts was 'to apply to Shakespeare's predecessors, contemporaries and successors the methods that are now used in Shakespeare editing'. The plays chosen were to include well known works from the early Tudor period to about 1700, as well as others less familiar but of literary and theatrical merit: 'the plays included,' Leech wrote, 'should be such as to deserve and indeed demand performance.' We owe it to Clifford Leech that the idea became reality. He set the high standards of the series, ensuring that editors of individual volumes produced work of lasting merit, equally useful for teachers and students, theatre directors and actors. Clifford Leech remained General Editor until 1971, and was succeeded by F. David Hoeniger, who retired in 1985.

The Revels Plays are now under the direction of four General Editors, E. A. J. Honigmann, J. R. Mulryne, David Bevington and E. M. Waith. The publishers, originally Methuen, are now Manchester University Press. Despite these changes, the format and essential character of the series will continue, and it is hoped that its editorial standards will be maintained. Except for some work in progress, the General Editors intend, in expanding the series, to concentrate for the immediate future on plays from the period 1558–1642, and may include a small number of non-dramatic works of interest to students of drama. Some slight changes have been forced by considerations of cost. For example, in editions from 1978, notes to the introduction are placed together at the end, not at the foot of the page. Collation and commentary notes will continue, however, to appear on the relevant pages.

The text of each Revels play, in accordance with established practice in the series, is edited afresh from the original text of best authority (in a few instances, texts), but spelling and punctuation are modernised and speech headings are silently made consistent. Elisions in the original are also silently regularised, except where metre would be affected by the change; since 1968 the '-ed' form is used for non-syllabic terminations in past tenses and past participles ('-'d'earlier), and '-èd' for syllabic ('-ed' earlier). The editor emends, as distinct from modernises, his original only in instances where error is patent, or at least very probable, and correction persuasive. Act divisions are given only if they appear in the original or if the structure of the play clearly points to them. Those act and scene divisions not found in the original are provided unobtrusively in small type and in square brackets. Square brackets are also used for any other additions to or changes in the stage directions of the original.

Revels Plays do not provide a variorum collation, but only those variants which require the critical attention of serious textual students. All departures of substance from 'copy-text' are listed, including any relineation and those changes in punctuation which involve to any degree a decision between alternative interpretations; but not such accidentals as turned letters, nor necessarily additions to stage directions whose editorial nature is already made clear by the use of brackets. Press corrections in the 'copy-text' are likewise included. Of later emendations of the text, only those are given which as alternative readings still deserve attention.

One of the hallmarks of the Revels Plays is the thoroughness of their annotations. Besides explaining the meaning of difficult words and passages, the editor provides comments on customs or usage, text or stage-business – indeed, on anything he judges pertinent and helpful. Each volume contains a Glossarial Index to the Commentary, in which particular attention is drawn to meanings for words not listed in *O.E.D.*

The Introduction to a Revels play assesses the authority of the 'copy-text' on which it is based, and discusses the editorial methods employed in dealing with it; the editor also considers his play's date and (where relevant) sources, together with its place in the work of the author and in the theatre of its time. Stage history is offered, and in the case of a play by an author not previously represented in the series a brief biography is given.

It is our hope that plays edited in this fashion will promote further scholarly and theatrical investigation of one of the richest periods in theatrical history.

E. A. J. HONIGMANN
J. R. MULRYNE
DAVID BEVINGTON
E. M. WAITH

Preface

In the preparation of this volume, which was much delayed for reasons both personal and occupational, I have been given valuable help by many individuals, particularly my colleagues at Scarborough College, University of Toronto. Eleanor Irwin and John Warden answered difficult points about classical references, Patricia Vicari gave me the benefit of her wide knowledge of Renaissance learning, and Jane Abray enlightened me about aspects of contemporary politics in France and England. Judy Curtis very kindly checked and corrected my translation of the French ambassador's letter in Appendix II. I am also grateful to the Canada Council for travel grants during periods of leave and to the University of Toronto's Research Board for assistance with incidental expenses. Library staffs in Toronto and Cambridge have been consistently helpful, and other libraries and galleries in Britain, the United States and France have answered requests courteously and quickly.

Special thanks must go to my general editor, Ronnie Mulryne, for his many useful suggestions and his disarming but necessary criticism. I could scarcely have completed the edition without the help of my daughter, Sue Margeson, in proof-reading, checking and indexing.

Abbreviations

(A) EDITIONS (in chronological order)

Q1 The Conspiracie and Tragedie of Charles Duke of Byron, Marshall of France. Acted lately in two playes, at the Black-Friers. Written by George Chapman. Printed by *G. Eld* for *Thomas Thorppe*, and are to be sold at the Tygers head in Paules Church-yard. 1608.

Q2 The Conspiracie and Tragœdy of Charles Duke of Byron, Marshall of France. Acted lately in two Playes, at the Blacke-friers, and other publique Stages. Written by George Chapman. London: Printed by N.O. for Thomas Thorp 1625.

Pearson *The Comedies and Tragedies of George Chapman*, John Pearson, London, 1873.

Shepherd *The Works of George Chapman: Plays*, ed. R. H. Shepherd, London, 1874.

Phelps *George Chapman*, ed. W. L. Phelps, New York, 1895.

Parrott *The Plays of George Chapman: The Tragedies*, ed. T. M. Parrott, London, 1910.

Ray *Chapman's The Conspiracy and Tragedy of Charles Duke of Byron*, ed. G. Ray, (diss. 1966), New York, 1979.

(B) OTHER ABBREVIATIONS

Babbitt *Plutarch's Moralia IV*, ed. and trans. F. C. Babbitt, London, 1936.

Bartlett *The Poems of George Chapman*, ed. P. B. Bartlett, London, 1941.

Brooke *Bussy D'Ambois*, ed. N. Brooke (Revels edition) London, 1964.

conj. conjecture.

Consp. *The Conspiracy of Byron*.

corr. corrected sheet.

De Alexandri magni Plutarch's *De Alexandri magni virtute aut fortuna*, in *Moralia IV*, ed. F. C. Babbitt, London, 1936.

Ferguson A. S. Ferguson, 'The Plays of George Chapman', *M.L.R.*, xv (1920), 223–39.

Greg, *A Bibliography*   W. W. Greg, *A Bibliography of the English Printed Drama to the Restoration*, London, 1939, 1957.

Grimeston   *A General Inventorie of the History of France* ... trans. Edward Grimeston, London, 1607.

Herford and Simpson   *Ben Jonson*, ed. C. H. Herford and Percy Simpson, Oxford, 1925.

Iliads   *Iliads* in *Chapman's Homer*, ed. A. Nicoll, New York, 1956.

Jacquot   J. Jacquot, *George Chapman (1559–1634)*, Paris, 1951.

Koeppel   E. Koeppel, *Quellen Studien zu den Dramen*, Strasbourg, 1897.

Loane   G. G. Loane, 'Notes on Chapman's Plays', *M.L.R.*, XXXIII (1938), 248–54; 'More Notes on Chapman's Plays', *M.L.R.*, XXXVIII (1943), 340–7.

MacLure   M. MacLure, *George Chapman, a Critical Study*, Toronto, 1966.

M.L.R.   *Modern Language Review.*

M.P.   *Modern Philology.*

Parrott, 'The Text'   T. M. Parrott, 'The Text of Chapman's Conspiracy and Tragedy of Byron', *M.L.R.*, IV (1908), 40–64.

Odysseys   *Odysseys* in *Chapman's Homer*, ed. A. Nicoll, New York, 1956.

P.B.S.A.   *Papers of the Bibliographical Society of America.*

Schoell   F. L. Schoell, *Études sur l'Humanisme Continental en Angleterre à la Fin de la Renaissance*, Paris, 1926.

Schoell, 'Commonplace Book'   F. L. Schoell, 'G. Chapman's Commonplace Book', *M.P.*, XVII (1919), 199–218.

s.d.   stage direction.

S.E.L.   *Studies in English Literature.*

s.h.   speech heading.

S.P.   *Studies in Philology.*

Tilley   M. P. Tilley, *A Dictionary of the Proverbs in England in the Sixteenth and Seventeenth Centuries*, Ann Arbor, 1950.

Trag.   *The Tragedy of Byron.*

uncorr.   uncorrected sheet.

Ure   Peter Ure, 'The Main Outline of Chapman's Byron', *Elizabethan and Jacobean Drama*, ed. J. C. Maxwell, Liverpool, 1974.

Waith   E. M. Waith, *Ideas of Greatness, Heroic Drama in England*, London, 1971.

Quotations from Shakespeare's plays are from *William Shakespeare The Complete Works*, ed. Peter Alexander, London, 1951. Biblical quotations are from the Bishops Bible. Quotations from Chapman's plays are taken from Parrott's edition of 1910, except for *Bussy D'Ambois* where references are to the Revels edition, ed. Nicholas Brooke, London, 1964.

Introduction

1. THE DRAMATIST

The Conspiracy and Tragedy of Byron has often been regarded as marking some kind of turning point in Chapman's career as a dramatist. In this play he abandoned theatrical techniques and conventions he had made use of in *Bussy D'Ambois* and developed extensively philosophical themes he had already introduced in the earlier play. It seems in many respects a large step in the direction of the moral tragedies of his final period. The play also is written throughout as a dramatic poem rather than as a theatrical script: it has been variously called an epic poem, a secular oratorio, a philosophical drama. There is no prefatory polemic or learned epistle to suggest why he chose to go in a new direction in this play. The nature of the subject itself may have led him to seek an appropriate form and style, as Millar MacLure has suggested;[1] or perhaps a desire to write a 'true tragedy' in some version of the neo-classic mode, firmly based upon historical truth, and austere, high-minded and sententious in its expression. One other factor should not be neglected: this is the nature of his source, as important for him as North's *Plutarch* was for Shakespeare. *The Conspiracy and Tragedy* is a close dramatisation of Edward Grimeston's account of the rise and fall of Marshal Byron in his *General Inventorie of the History of France*. It is noteworthy that both Grimeston and the French historians from which he drew regarded the fall of the great marshal as a tragedy of heroic proportions.

Yet few would want to draw a severe boundary between *Bussy D'Ambois* and *The Conspiracy and Tragedy of Byron*. The earlier play has livelier dramatic action, a wider range of developed characters, and an emphasis on emotional conflict that is missing in its successor. However the portrait of Bussy as a powerfully independent personality is similar in many respects to the portrait of Byron, and the social order that praises, then blames the heroic individual is similarly constricting, and ultimately destructive to the individual in both plays. What marks the difference between the two tragedies is that Chapman makes Byron much more clearly the author of his own doom than he does Bussy. Moreover, the social order that defeats Byron is more obviously just and rational in its operation than is the society against which Bussy struggles. Bussy finds himself in, or rather chooses to enter, a society whose values are very ambiguous indeed. Byron's antagonist, Henry IV, is a good and wise ruler, by no means free from human weakness, but an acceptable figure of authority to the judicious observer. The values he represents are very largely affirmed at the end of the play.

Although this is not the place for a full account of Chapman's career as a poet and dramatist,[2] several questions need to be asked that are relevant to the composition of the Byron plays. First of all, there is the Essex connection. French and English commentators alike had noted the striking resemblances between the conspiracy of Essex, Earl Marshal of England, against Queen Elizabeth in 1601 and that of Marshal Byron against Henry IV a year later. Chapman himself makes several direct and indirect references to the fall of Essex in the course of *The Tragedy of Byron*. Chapman's personal connection with Essex seems to have been that of a poverty-stricken poet seeking a noble patron through the device of a flattering dedication. In 1598 he dedicated his first Homeric translations, his *Seaven Bookes* and *Achilles Shield*, to Essex, proclaiming him the 'true Achilles' whom Homer 'did but prefigure'. Though nothing seems to have come of this appeal for patronage,[3] there is little doubt that Chapman admired the valour and proud spirit of Essex, seeing him as one who exemplified 'the whole excellence of royall humanitie',[4] and that he subsequently meditated on the failure of Essex to combine wisdom with valour, in a way that gave peculiar intensity to his treatment of Byron.

Prince Henry was a patron who offered him greater encouragement and more tangible rewards: he was made 'sewer in ordinary' to the prince and was commanded by him to complete his translation of the Homeric poems. Chapman's belief in the efficacy of Homer as a guide toward virtuous and valiant action and wisdom of the loftiest kind (as the dedicatory epistles proclaim) seems to have been a prime motivation for his work as a translator. Though *The Conspiracy and Tragedy of Byron* cannot be linked in any direct way with Prince Henry – the plays are dedicated to Sir Thomas Walsingham and his young son in affectionate, almost domestic terms – nevertheless, the tone of the Prologue with its emphasis upon Byron's greatness as saviour of France and his subsequent revolt from honour suggests that in this play too he is writing a mirror for princes:

And see in his revolt how honour's flood
Ebbs into air when men are great, not good.   (*Prologue*, ll. 23–4)

INTRODUCTION 3

If Chapman was reflecting on the ambitious self-flattery of an Essex or a Byron, he was also deeply concerned with the difficult decisions faced by any prince seeking to unite virtue and political action.[5]

A further question about the background of the plays concerns Chapman's special interest in and knowledge of contemporary French affairs. There is no single important source for *Bussy D'Ambois*; for the Byron plays, he clearly used Edward Grimeston's *General Inventorie of the History of France* (1607). But in both plays, he seems to have had additional knowledge of French politics and personages, a familiarity which is mocked in the portrait of Bellamont in *Northward Ho* (acted 1605), thought by many to be a caricature of Chapman.[6] It has usually been assumed that Chapman picked up much from conversation with Grimeston who was a kinsman (Chapman's grandmother was a Grimeston)[7] and who had spent several years in France in some minor diplomatic post. Grimeston himself states in the epistle to *The Estates, Empires, and Principalities of the World* (1614) that he spent eight years in France 'for the publique service of this Estate'. Boas speculates that these eight years were immediately prior to the death of Elizabeth because of Grimeston's statement that he turned to translation when he saw 'the hopes of my service or of further imployment dead ...'. The first of his translations, 'A True Historie of the Memorable Siege of Ostend', was published in 1604.[8]

There is no evidence that Chapman himself spent any time in France, though he may have seen service in the Low Countries during the 'silent years' before 1594.[9] However there is one connection Chapman may have had with French affairs that has not, I believe, been noticed. If, as seems likely, Chapman's was the second hand in the writing of the first version of *Sejanus*, he must have worked closely with Jonson, and probably not for the first time.[10] Jonson wrote *Sejanus* while he was living in the house of Esmé Stuart, Lord D'Aubigny, who was born and educated in France and had settled in England only in 1603.[11] D'Aubigny helped Jonson and Chapman over the *Eastward Ho* difficulties in 1605: Chapman's letter to Suffolk mentions 'the lord Daubeney' as bringing them good news of the remission of part of their punishment.[12] Jonson dedicated *Sejanus* to D'Aubigny in the Folio text, and one of the Dobell letters is probably a letter of gratitude from Jonson to the same lord to thank him for 'the Noble fauoures you haue done vs'.[13]

There is also a letter in the Dobell collection addressed to Mr Crane, secretary to the Duke of Lennox, and written apparently by Chapman.[14] If the letter is genuine, Lennox was probably the patron who gave Chapman shelter at the time of the difficulties over a performance of the *Byron* plays. Lennox is addressed in the first of the commendatory sonnets appended by Chapman to his *Twelve Bookes of the Iliads* (1609). Ludovick Stuart, Duke of Lennox, was born in France, like his brother Esmé Stuart, though he spent most of his life at the court of James in Scotland and later in England.[15] He had several times been engaged upon diplomatic missions to France on James's behalf, one of them during or immediately after Byron's visit to England in 1601. It is an intriguing thought that the Stuart brothers were closely related to Henry IV's mistress, Madame d'Entragues, the Marquise de Verneuil. Their mother was Katherine de Balsac d'Entragues, the youngest sister of François de Balsac who had married Marie Touchet, mistress of Charles IX. This marriage made François stepfather and guardian of Charles's son, Charles de Valois, who is the D'Auvergne of Chapman's play. François's daughter, Henriette d'Entragues, first cousin of Ludovick and Esmé Stuart, became the mistress of Henry IV. She appears briefly in Chapman's play during the masque which reconciles queen and mistress, but the apparently lively scene of their confrontation and quarrel is known only through the objections of the French ambassador, La Boderie,[16] and did not appear in the 1608 quarto.

It is therefore within the realm of possibility that the scene which offended the French ambassador may have sprung from Chapman's conversations with D'Aubigny or members of his household at the time that he was working with Jonson on *Sejanus*, or from the household of the Duke of Lennox. Other scenes in the play for which no source has been found, usually attributed to 'common gossip', may also have their origin in Chapman's relationship with these Scottish-French patrons. One remembers as well the comic portrayal of Chapman in the guise of Bellamont in *Northward Ho* as a character who boasted constantly of his intimate knowledge of affairs in France.

In his four French tragedies, Chapman sometimes shows a knowledge of French life that goes well beyond the obvious sources of his work, where such sources exist. But there is no attempt at a realistic portrayal of the French court, rather a philosophic look at character in society and the impact of personality upon event, in a way that reflects human experience and in particular glances at English court life. His use of topical material from contemporary history in the Byron plays was no doubt designed to attract attention and interest toward its stage performance. Yet more important, the development of the Essex/Byron material into a major philosophic tragedy reveals both his interest in exploring the potentialities of the dramatic form of tragedy and his humanist ambition to make serious drama a means of pleasurable instruction, a guide to true wisdom.

2. DATE

The dating of *The Conspiracy and Tragedy of Byron* might seem to be a comparatively straightforward question, particularly when compared with the problematic dating of so many other plays of the period. The double play of *Byron* was published by G. Eld in 1608. Edward Grimeston's *General Inventorie of the History of France*, Chapman's undoubted source, was published in 1607. There was a performance of the play in March 1608 to which the French ambassador sternly objected. Hence, as Parrott argues, the play probably was written in late 1607 or early 1608.[17]

However this account neglects several points which critics have noted as possibly suggesting an earlier date for the writing and first performance of the play. First of all, there is a note in Henslowe's diary about a play called *burone* or *Berowne* which required a black satin suit and a scaffold for its production on 25 September 1602,[18] properties which inevitably have connections with the Byron known for his visit in black costume to England in 1601 and for his death on the scaffold in July 1602. However there is little or no support for the view that this was an early version of Chapman's play. A second point is that the comedy *Northward Ho* by Dekker and Webster (acted 1605) presents a dramatic portrait of a gossipy and vain author called Bellamont who claims to know intimately certain prominent courtiers in France, including Byron and 'Duke Peppernoone' and who is writing a tragedy of 'Astianax'. Many critics have taken Bellamont to be a caricature of Chapman. The play raises questions as to whether Chapman was talking about a tragedy of Byron as early as 1605. The relevant lines are those in which Bellamont tells the Captain 'I am now wryting the description of his death .... Imagine a great man were to be executed about the seuenth houre in a gloomy morning' (IV.i.66, 69–70).[19]

The third point which has been raised by those who support an earlier date is the reference in one of the Dobell letters to the 'thrice allowance of the Counsaile for the Presentment'.[20] The letter to the Master of the Revels (Sir George Buc), apparently by Chapman, points out that the Council's thrice-repeated permission for the presentation of the play should be an argument for Buc's allowing the play to be printed. However the letter does not specify whether permission had been given for three performances in a short span of time or for three over a period of two or three years.

Allardyce Nicoll and Elias Schwartz argue that Chapman was acquainted with Edward Grimeston who was his kinsman, and may well have seen Grimeston's manuscript before it was published.[21] Schwartz points out that Grimeston's *General Inventorie* was entered in the Stationers' Register in 1597, 1600 and 1605 before it was eventually published in 1607. Both Nicoll and Schwartz believe Chapman had begun writing the play before 1605 when he seems to have been talking about it, as *Northward Ho* suggests. Schwartz also believes that the 'thrice allowance' refers to performances on three occasions, possibly for three different years. However neither Nicoll nor Schwartz implies that the *Berowne* mentioned by Henslowe in 1602 was by Chapman.

Robert Ornstein argues that there is as good a case that Bellamont represents Drayton as that he does Chapman and hence dating the Byron plays on the basis of *Northward Ho* must be considered doubtful.[22] Clifford Leech, also writing about *Northward Ho*, is satisfied with the Chapman identification but claims the reference to Byron probably means only that Chapman was talking about the French court as if he were intimate with its members at that time.[23] J. B. Gabel argues that there was not time in 1605 for editions of Cayet and Matthieu (Grimeston's sources) to reach England, for Grimeston to translate them, for Chapman to write a play or plays about Byron, and for these to be mocked by the authors of *Northward Ho*.[24] He also states that the 'thrice allowance' can most simply be explained by a supposition that the Privy Council permitted *The Conspiracy and Tragedy of Byron* to be presented three times in the winter of 1607-8. The French ambassador, having heard of the presentations, was able to secure a prohibition against further performances, but a final performance was given in early March.

It appears that advocates of a date earlier than 1607 have not yet been able to prove their case. The 1602 play is almost certainly not Chapman's, and the evidence from *Northward Ho* is tantalising but inconclusive. The date suggested by Parrott and accepted by many others must, I think, be adhered to.

3. THEATRE AND ACTING COMPANY

The second Blackfriars playhouse was almost certainly the theatre of first performance as the title-page of the 1608 quarto indicates and the

Children of Blackfriars (earlier they had been the Children of the Queen's Revels) were the company to perform the play. Although *Bussy D'Ambois* was probably first performed by Paul's Boys, it was for the Children of Blackfriars that Chapman wrote his comedies in the early seventeenth century. Jonson and Marston also wrote for this company; Chapman's collaboration with them in *Eastward Ho* and the subsequent difficulties of the three authors are well known.

The evidence gathered by Richard Hosley about the second Blackfriars points clearly to a stage about half the size of those in the public theatres.[25] The fact that spectators were seated on either side of the stage probably in stage boxes, as well as in front and in three galleries, undoubtedly led to greater intimacy between actors and audience. The tiring-house façade, Hosley claims, consisted of three bays with a door in each, the middle one of which could be used for 'discoveries' when such were needed. In the gallery above these doors, there were boxes or rooms which served for action 'above' or which could accommodate spectators. One of these boxes at Blackfriars seems to have been a music-room with a curtain for concealing or revealing the musicians; the same room could be used for discoveries above. Hosley points out that the two Byron plays do not require action above and have no discoveries, although both were relatively common in Chapman's comedies. (There is one reference to music above in *The Tragedy of Byron*.) Like other plays written for the second Blackfriars, the Byron plays are divided into acts, suggesting the usual custom of inter-act music from the music-room. Other features of the Blackfriars stage such as suspension gear and a trap in the stage floor are not relevant to these plays.

The history of the Children of Blackfriars is well documented, partly because of disputes over the management of the company, and partly because of the number of occasions they found themselves in serious difficulties with the authorities.[26] *Philotas, Eastward Ho, The Isle of Gulls* and the Byron plays brought interrogations, warnings and sometimes spells in prison for players as well as authors, largely because of topical references to affairs at court or what were thought to be seditious parallels to actual events. Their repertoire during the eight years from 1600 is notable for its variety and experiments in form, dramatic technique and style: two of Jonson's satiric 'literary' comedies, Chapman's comedies of humours, several of Marston's major satiric comedies, one of the notable 'city comedies' of the age, *Eastward Ho*, the product of the collaboration of all three playwrights, and tragedies as diverse as Daniel's *Philotas*, Marston's *Sophonisba* and Chapman's *Conspiracy and Tragedy of Byron*. This repertoire suggests considerable versatility on the part of the actors, and since the playhouse was both 'notorious and profitable' (in Glynne Wickham's words), the actors were no doubt skilful as well. The names of two of them, Salomon Pavey and Nathaniel Field, have survived with no little fame.[27] There has been much discussion of their acting style, in particular their ability to cope with the demands of tragedy, but on this question there is little direct evidence beyond the actual texts of the plays they performed.[28]

What qualities, we might ask, has *The Conspiracy and Tragedy of Byron* in common with other tragedies written for the children's companies during this period which may be due to Chapman's awareness of his stage, his actors and his audience? Like *Philotas* and *Sophonisba*, *The Conspiracy and Tragedy of Byron* has an experimental form, owing little to the established kinds of tragedy in the public theatres. As we noted earlier, however, Chapman's 'experiment' may have as much to do with his knowledge of classical tragedy and his search for a new kind of tragedy, some ideal form of tragic poem set apart from the practicalities of theatrical performance.[29] R. A. Foakes in his consideration of the plays presented by the children's companies[30] observes that *Sophonisba* and *Bussy D'Ambois* have a marked epic quality, owing much to Marlowe, and this is even more pronounced in the Byron plays in their large-scale speeches, the eloquent expression of passionate feeling, and the expansion of metaphor and simile into extended epic similes. Though there is no chorus in the classical sense, characters involved in the action are often given a choral role to play. The emphasis throughout is on rhetoric rather than physical action: the central character is given his heroic stature through rhetorical description and reported action. In *Bussy D'Ambois*, for example, it is a messenger who reports the duel scene in which Bussy destroys his attackers; in *Byron*, the great deeds of the warrior are described in retrospect by Savoy and sometimes by Byron himself.

Rhetorical expansion and patterned speech seem to have been a mark of the heroic plays presented at Blackfriars to a comparatively well-educated and sophisticated audience. There was also a matching emphasis on formal ceremony and stylised movement. The ceremonial elements which Foakes has noted in *Sophonisba*, the processions, marches, dumb shows and masques, are perhaps not so marked in Chapman's double play, though there is one important masque in *The Tragedy*. Nevertheless Byron's temptation scenes in Brussels and at the French court, and the concluding scenes of the trial and execution have a theatrical emphasis on the great occasion and they resound

INTRODUCTION   9

with the rhetoric appropriate to such occasions. What appears to have been, in the original form of the play, a direct staging of the meeting between Byron and Queen Elizabeth must also have had splendid ceremonial as well as rhetorical display. In the critical discussion of the play, several of these aspects will be considered in greater detail.

4. CENSORSHIP AND THE TEXT

Any consideration of the text of *The Conspiracy and Tragedy of Byron* must begin with the question of censorship, the cuts and alterations apparent in the 1608 quarto even to the reader unacquainted with any external evidence. In his dedication of the plays to Sir Thomas Walsingham, Chapman speaks of 'these poor dismembered poems' and implies that Walsingham had attended a performance and would know the complete version: 'having heard your approbation of these in their presentment'.[31] Mention has already been made of the letter of the French ambassador, La Boderie, describing his strong complaint to the English authorities over a scene which does not appear in the 1608 quarto.[32] There is also a letter in the Dobell collection which seems to be addressed to the Master of the Revels and which is generally attributed to Chapman: this letter objects strenuously to the censorship of a play for publication after it has been allowed on the stage.[33]

In *The Conspiracy*, major alterations were made to the scene which describes Byron's embassy to Queen Elizabeth (Act IV, Scene i). It seems certain that the original version presented a formal meeting and exchange of speeches between the queen and Byron, with a subsequent interchange between Byron and the 'eminent councillor', rather than a lengthy report by Crequi of what was said. The speeches Crequi reports are mainly in direct discourse, and some of the transitions from reported to direct discourse are awkwardly made. Although Crequi is supposed to be telling the tale, at l. 156 he reports 'Then spake she to Crequi and Prince d'Auvergne'. The end of the scene is broken off with a half-line and no indication of an exit for Crequi and D'Aumont. It appears, therefore, that Buc objected to the presentation of Queen Elizabeth in her own person in this scene and that the alterations to the text were somewhat clumsily made (either in haste, or as a clue to the observant reader that the original was somewhat different). A portion of the scene may well be lost: at 223 lines, it is a remarkably short fourth act. However there is no indication of what other material it might have contained. The conjecture of Koeppel that the scene included the passage from Pierre Matthieu in which Elizabeth pointed to the heads of Essex and other traitors seems very unlikely in view of the tone of the surviving section.[34] The passage from Matthieu does not occur in Grimeston, Chapman's direct source.

In *The Tragedy of Byron*, it is the end of Act I and the beginning of Act II that seem to have been cut out. There is no act heading for the second act; instead a council scene appears to lead directly into the masque while the king remains on stage. Cupid, the presenter of the masque, speaks of it as an emblem of reconciliation between two fair Virtues whose 'emulation / Begat a jar' (II.i.18–19). When the masque ends, Henry declares himself well pleased with the show 'for that it figures/ The reconcilement of my queen and mistress' (II.i. 128–9). These references to a reconciliation would make more sense if the quarrel had been referred to or staged as dramatic action earlier in the play.

The well-known letter of the French ambassador, La Boderie (8 April 1608), makes clear the reasons for the censor's cuts in this part of the play.[35] La Boderie reports to the Marquis de Sillery, Secretary of State (or rather assistant to Villeroy, the actual Secretary of State, as Jacquot notes)[36] that he had complained strongly to Lord Salisbury about the 'comediens' who had dared to introduce the queen and Madame de Verneuil on the stage and to show the queen using angry words against the king's mistress and giving her a slap on the face ('un soufflet'). Not only had they disregarded the prohibition placed on the play but they had added things that had nothing to do with Marshal Byron and were totally false. La Boderie goes on to speak of the action taken against the company: three of the actors were imprisoned but the principal culprit, the author, escaped.

Another document of the time, a letter from Sir Thomas Lake to Lord Salisbury, confirms La Boderie's story, expressing King James's satisfaction at the action taken by Salisbury:

> His ma^{tie} was well pleased with that which your lo. advertiseth concerning the committing of the players y^t have offended in ye matters of France ....[37]

The intervention of an ambassador to secure the prohibition of a play and a penalty for both actors and playwright was a rare but not unknown event in Elizabethan and Jacobean England.[38] It is interesting to note similar official complaints in Paris: Sir Ralph Winwood, Elizabeth's ambassador, complained several times during 1602 to the French Chancellor, Monsieur de Villeroy, about 'certain base Comedians' and 'certaine Italian Comedians' who had dared to act plays concerned with contemporary English affairs, including the 'Tragedy of the late Queen of Scottes'. He tells Sir Robert Cecil with some pleasure of his success in obtaining an injunction against the presentation of these plays and the punishment of those responsible, even though 'some Standers by' objected that 'the Death of the Duke of Guise hath ben plaied at *London*' and 'by some others, that the *Massacre of St. Bartholomews* hath ben publickly acted, and this King represented upon the Stage'.[39]

The unsigned and undated letters from the White manuscript which Bertram Dobell published in *The Athenaeum* in 1901 (now Folger 420423) include two which may have been written by Chapman in connection with his difficulties over the Byron plays.[40] The first of these, addressed to Mr Crane, Secretary to the Duke of Lennox, speaks gratefully of the sanctuary given to the writer by the duke and asks why 'the forme of the cloud still hovers over me' and whether it may now be safe to leave 'when the matter is disperst'. There is a hint in these lines of how it came to be that 'the principal culprit, the author, escaped'. It is worth remembering, as we noted above, that Lennox was the brother of D'Aubigny who had been a friend and patron of Jonson and probably also of Chapman. The second letter, apparently addressed to the Master of the Revels, is directly relevant to the question of the text. The writer complains bitterly about 'what I suffer by your austeritie'. He declares that only two or three lines were 'crost' by the censor for the stage performance and that he did his utmost to suppress them but could not be held responsible for what the actors said: 'I see not myne owne Plaies; nor carrie the Actors tongues in my mouthe'. Further statements suggest that the Master of the Revels is attempting to prevent publication of the play: 'if the thrice allowance of the Counsaile for the Presentment gave not weight enoughe to drawe yours after for the presse, my Breath is a hopeles adition ...'. There has been some controversy over what this 'thrice allowance of the Counsaile for the Presentment' means, whether for three successive years, or for three occasions in a single season. Whatever the interpretation, it is clear that the Privy Council as well as the Master of the Revels was involved, and that the writer of the letter believed the Council's allowance should be sufficient for publication.

One other statement in the letter is of particular interest because it suggests the existence of two copies, of which the addressee has seen only one. We may, perhaps, infer a copy used in the playhouse and a copy prepared for the overview of the Master of the Revels and for the press:

> ... if you say (for your Reason) you know not if more then was spoken be now written no, no; nor can you know that, if you had bothe the Copies, not seeing the first at all: Or if you had seene it presented your Memorie could hardly confer with it so strictly in the Revisall to discerne the Adition; My short reason therefore can not sounde your severitie ....

After a long complaint against 'the bitter Informer before the French Ambassador', the writer begs the return of his 'Papers'.

In style, vocabulary and tone, the letters suggest Chapman's character and habitual way of writing. However, so long as doubt remains concerning the nature and provenance of the manuscript in which they appear, one cannot build a conclusive argument upon them.[41] If we accept the second letter as Chapman's and relate it to La Boderie's letter, we may infer that Sir George Buc asked for only a few lines to be cut out of the play for its original stage production, and that the Council gave allowance for the presentation of the play before La Boderie secured his first prohibition. We may infer also that after La Boderie obtained his injunction, the Children of Blackfriars took advantage of the court's absence from London not only to present the play again but to add material to it (how much is uncertain), which, La Boderie claimed, had nothing to do with Byron and was totally false. It was this production that spurred La Boderie to a second complaint to Salisbury and King James's angry reaction against the players and the author.

It is tempting to accept J. B. Gabel's argument that the added portions included the quarrel scene between queen and mistress.[42] Gabel argues that both the lost quarrel scene and the extant masque that pictures the reconciliation of queen and mistress were interpolations by an author or authors unknown. The difficulty with this argument is that Chapman, though complaining of the dismemberment of his play in the dedication to Walsingham, printed the masque as his own, as MacLure has pointed out.[43]

The letter to the Master of the Revels suggests that any additions made by the actors were small, presumably no more than brief improvisations. The letter goes on to say that if Buc had seen the play on the stage or had seen the first copy of the text, he would scarcely have been able to note the differences. After expressing his annoyance at the inordinate delay in granting a licence for printing the text, he asks for the return of his papers. The copy seems to have been returned to him eventually for publication, but with sufficiently large cuts marked on the text to make him complain in the dedication about 'these poor dismembered poems'. Whether these cuts involved only Elizabeth's meeting with Byron in *Consp.*, IV.i, or whether they also included the lost quarrel scene, we shall probably never know. Nevertheless, MacLure's and Ray's acceptance of the masque as a genuine part of the text is surely right.[44]

That fears concerning the play still existed at the time of printing is obvious from the well-known stop-press correction on sig. H2r from 'So long as idle and ridiculus King' to 'So long as such as he' (*Consp.*, V.ii.5).

5. THE TEXT

There is no doubt that the 1608 quarto should be the copy-text for any modern edition.

The 1625 quarto was apparently set up from a copy of the 1608 edition: the page structure is followed for a considerable part of the book and many of the same errors in spelling, lineation and verse printed as prose are repeated. There are, however, a number of corrections to the typography of the earlier edition – obviously wrong letters replaced, turned letters reversed – and a few corrections to speech headings and stage directions. It is possible that such corrections had been written by hand into the copy of the 1608 quarto which the 1625 printer used, or they may be the work of the 1625 compositor himself.

The 1625 quarto introduced a great many more errors than it corrected, some of them typographical, others reflecting a rapid and careless reading of the earlier quarto. Thus 'Franch County' (*Consp.*, I.i.41) in 1608 becomes 'French Bounty' in 1625; 'proiection' (*Consp.*, I.i.54) becomes 'protection' (meaningless in the context); 'I will not have my traine' (*Consp.*, I.i.112) becomes 'I will not have any traine'; and 'Semele' (*Consp.*, I.ii.37) becomes 'Semelo'. Words are omitted and sometimes a whole line is left out. Although certain speech headings and stage directions are corrected, new errors in these forms are introduced.

Some of the alterations attempt to clarify the sense of a metaphor or to use a more ordinary word rather than an unusual one. Thus 'joyne our streames' (*Consp.*, III.i.75) becomes 'joyne our forces' in 1625, and the orator's 'fairest similies' (*Consp.*, IV.i.87) becomes his 'fairest smiles'. These changes, like the corrections to speech headings and stage directions, may be the work of a corrector, or they may represent playhouse alterations written into a copy of the 1608 quarto used by the printer for the 1625 quarto. However, there are not enough such corrections to suggest that a manuscript prompt-book was used by the printer in addition to his copy of the earlier quarto.

Parrott believed the second quarto to be 'a genuine new edition, not a mere reprint of the first, but the changes which it shows are almost always for the worse and in many cases appear to be alterations by some proof-reader. Here and there, however, an alteration appears to be by the hand of the poet. In general, Q1 is much more correctly printed than Q2 ....'.[45] Of the examples Parrott cites of possible authorial correction in Q2, perhaps the most important occurs at II.i.70 in *The Conspiracy* which reads 'To thinke me an intelligencing Lord' in most copies of Q1; in Q2, 'instrument' is substituted for 'Lord', a reading which Parrott prefers and thinks must have been made by the author. However 'instrument' does occur in three copies of the 1608 quarto (the uncorrected sheet) and was presumably in the copy used for setting up the 1625 edition, a fact of which Parrott was unaware. As I argue in the notes, the proof-correction to 'Lord' in 1608 improves the scansion but substitutes a bland for a vigorous word and may well have been the work of an officious corrector whose touch can sometimes be suspected elsewhere.

Another alteration in the 1625 quarto which has aroused interest occurs on sig. O3r (*Trag.*, V.i.82) where 'sacred Iavelins' replaces Q1's 'feared Iavelins'. Parrott does not suggest authorial correction here but believes that '*feared* is more likely to be a misprint for *sacred* than *vice versa*'; he therefore prefers 'sacred'. However the substitution of 'sacred' in 1625 may well be due to a compositor's misreading of the 1608 'feared' in which the 'f' looked like a long 's' because of faint inking. There are a number of equally careless misreadings in the same sheet, as Q1's 'impartiall Iustice' becomes 'imperiall Iustice' in Q2, 'slacknesse' becomes 'slicknesse', and 'merry spirits' becomes 'many spirits', all meaningless alterations. There can be little doubt that 'feared' is the correct reading.

Parrott notes also a few changes in Q2, generally the addition of an emphatic word, which he thinks due to an actor's use of the script. Thus in *The Tragedy* at III.i.209, the line 'Not to be quencht, nor lessend' has an additional 'no' before 'nor' in Q2. Again, at V.ii.122 there seems to be a change for the sake of emphasis. When Harlay asks 'What will you say?', Byron replies 'I know it cannot be'. As Parrott points out, Q2 inserts 'then' before 'say' and drops 'I know'. But, as I have already indicated, there are no other signs, such as additional stage directions or mention of specific properties that would point to a prompt-book as copy for Q2.

It only remains to note a considerable number of small changes which in some cases indicate normal printing practice: thus the insertion of apostrophes where none existed in the earlier quarto, to indicate elided syllables. Other examples suggest a compositor's preferences, such as ''tis' for 'it is', 'untill' for 'till', and a curious and frequent substitution of 'noblenesse' for 'noblesse' where the metre suffers as a result of the change. In these instances, there is no reason to prefer the 1625 quarto to the 1608 since there is no evidence that it is authoritative in any way.

Several qualities of the 1608 quarto suggest that it was set up from a fair copy of Chapman's manuscript, perhaps a copy made by himself. The general clarity and good order of the text make it unlikely that it was derived from foul papers. A complicating factor might be the two copies spoken of in one of the Dobell letters, already mentioned above. If we take the letter as Chapman's, it can be postulated that one copy was used in the theatre and the second was prepared for publication and sent to Sir George Buc. One of these may well have been a fair copy in Chapman's own hand, the other a scribal transcript. There is no clear evidence, however, of scribal intervention in the 1608 text. The text has Chapman's characteristic punctuation, as noted by Nicholas Brooke, a heavy use of colons and semi-colons, often placed as emphatic markers for the ear and therefore the voice of the actor.[46] For example, the passage in the first scene of *The Conspiracy* in which Henry condemns La Fin for his profligate and litigious ways (I.i.154–62) uses semi-colons at the end of almost every phrase in Henry's catalogue of La Fin's vices. Similarly Chapman's frequent use of capital letters for generic nouns, personifications and other figures of speech is evident. Brooke suggests tentatively that they are being used for a purpose similar to that of the punctuation, for dramatic emphasis in the theatre, but this argument is difficult to prove.

That the original manuscript was the author's fair copy rather than the theatrical prompt-book is suggested by a number of factors. The stage directions are adequate and show familiarity with theatrical possibilities, but they are not particularly full. There are very few references to properties required on stage and, on one occasion, the entry of the painter with the portrait he is supposed to be painting is omitted altogether. Instead of entries at the beginning of some of the acts, there is merely a list of characters. Frequently at the end of a scene, the 'exit' or 'exeunt' is forgotten; the main character speaking at the close of the scene may be given an exit but the other characters are not (like La Brosse at the end of Act III in *The Conspiracy*).

Certain of the stage directions are explanatory, defining who particular characters are (*Enter the other Commissioners of Fraunce, Belieure, Brulart* .... B4v) or adding a phrase beyond the mere action that seems to betray the author's hand (*The King sodainely enters hauing determined what to doe.* N4r). Still others have a vagueness about them which suggests that the author is allowing the company to work out its own numbers for certain scenes (*others attending* N3r; *with two or three of the Guard* O1r; *cum aliis* O2v; *Enter Byron, a Bishop or two* Q4r). The 'Bishop or two' of this last direction becomes *Arch.* in the subsequent speech headings. There is a frequent use of single Latin words such as *manet, redit* and *solus*, but no consistent attempt to use Latin stage directions. One may also note such descriptive directions as *Sauoy, whispering with Laffin* (D2v), *Enter Varennes, whispering to Byron* (N4v) which seem to be typical of Chapman in other plays.

Other characteristics that point to the author's manuscript rather than to a 'tidied-up' prompt-book are the quite numerous variations in speech headings and the occasional appearance of redundant speech headings for a character already speaking, as *Hen.* on M2r, and of double entries for characters presumably already on stage, such as *Enter Soiss: Espe.*(Q1r). However there is little to suggest an author's foul papers and in general it seems most likely that the text from which the compositors worked was a fair copy, either Chapman's own manuscript or a scribal copy made from it.

The Conspiracy and Tragedy of Byron was printed by 'G. Eld for Thomas Thorppe'.[47] George Eld (or Elde) was a printer in London from 1604 to 1624. A large number of books appeared from his press, including Stow's *Annales* and Camden's *Remains*.[48] He printed many plays, including a number of editions of *Doctor Faustus* between 1609 and 1624, popular comedies, learned plays by William Alexander and Samuel Daniel and university plays. In a collection so varied, one would hesitate to say that Eld (or the booksellers, Thomas Thorpe and John Wright) specialised in one type of play rather than another, but it is noteworthy that he printed a number of plays presented by the children's companies, and in particular plays by Jonson, Chapman, Marston and Middleton.

On the whole, the 1608 quarto is a well-printed text from a print-shop well accustomed to doing plays. There are few examples of major corruptions of the text: perhaps five or six passages in the double play show evidence that something is wrong and no easy emendation is possible. Puzzling passages which may be corrupt are considered in the notes; for example *The Conspiracy*, III.iii.84, and *The Tragedy*,

INTRODUCTION 17

I.i.124 and V.iv.45. There are a number of typographical errors and other mistakes due to misreading of copy. Proof-reading seems to have been occasional and haphazard rather than a continuing process. Certain sheets show a number of important variants, whereas others have only a few small corrections of punctuation and spelling, leaving many obvious errors uncorrected. Most of the proof-reading was done on the later sheets of *The Conspiracy* and very little on *The Tragedy*. I have not noticed clear evidence of a change of compositor during the printing of the work, apart from a temporary shift from full stops to colons after speech headings which may be due merely to a shortage of type.

6. SOURCES

Emil Koeppel had shown in 1897 that Chapman's *Conspiracy and Tragedy of Byron* depended heavily upon the French historians of the reign of Henry IV, but it was F. S. Boas in 1903 who demonstrated conclusively that Chapman had used Edward Grimeston's *A General Inventorie of the History of France . . . translated out of French into English* (1607) as his major source.[49] Grimeston based his account on Jean de Serres's *Inventaire General* (1603), Pierre Matthieu's *Histoire de France durant Sept Années de Paix de Henri IV* (1605) and P. V. Cayet's *Chronologie Septenaire* (1605), but it cannot be shown that Chapman went to Grimeston's originals for episodes, characters or language.[50] Similar negative results apply to the *Histoire de la Vie et Mort du Comte d'Essex . . . La conspiration, prison, iugement, testament et mort du Duc de Biron* (1607) and to the English pamphlet on Byron's trial and death, *A True and perfect Discourse of the practises and Treasons of Marshall Biron* (1602) which show the popularity of the sensational story of Byron's fall and the contemporary awareness of the parallels between the fates of Essex and Byron.[51]

Chapman used Grimeston as Shakespeare used North's Plutarch, at times with great freedom, compressing scattered material into a single scene, omitting, shaping, enlarging; at times following his source closely, echoing the very language of the original. In general terms, he based *The Conspiracy* on widely separated passages from over two hundred pages of Grimeston's text, whereas for *The Tragedy* he used the detailed and dramatic account Grimeston gave of Byron's downfall, trial and execution in fifty pages of text.

There are a number of passages in the two plays which cannot be traced to Grimeston, or which are merely hinted at in Grimeston, and scholars have attempted to find other sources in Chapman's reading. The majority of these passages are speeches on particular themes rather than episodes affecting the action of the plays. Actual episodes in the plays whose source is doubtful or unknown can be listed fairly briefly since there are so few of them. The first and most important are the scenes of temptation in *The Conspiracy* as Savoy and La Fin draw Byron toward treachery. There are hints of such activity in Grimeston but the full development of action in relation to character and the overall ironic tone seem to be Chapman's work. The episode of the painter who is brought in to 'take' Byron's likeness is a part of this pattern of temptation, and no original has been found for this, although there are analogues in other plays, as the notes point out. Another episode in *The Conspiracy* provides more of a puzzle – Byron's embassy to Queen Elizabeth in the fourth act. The first long speech of the queen is drawn directly from Grimeston, but after l. 58, the interchanges between Byron and the queen and the interview with the eminent counsellor follow no known source, though as Parrott observes they sound like paraphrase.[52] If the speeches are not of Chapman's invention, they may have come from some lost pamphlet similar to the *Discours Grave et Eloquent de la Royne d'Angleterre au Mareschal de Biron l'an 1601* which was published in 1607 as part of the *Histoire de la Vie et Mort du Comte d'Essex* already mentioned.

In *The Tragedy* the lost scene of the altercation between the queen and Mme d'Entragues and the masque scene of reconciliation are the major episodes not accounted for by Grimeston, though Grimeston and other chroniclers of the time record festivities and masques as having taken place. Travellers' tales and gossip have usually been given as Chapman's most likely source for this material; his possible association with D'Aubigny and the Duke of Lennox and members of their households as mentioned above is relevant in this regard.

Most of the remaining additions to Grimeston are, as I have said, large-scale speeches on particular themes, sometimes closely integrated into the dramatic structure, sometimes more remote from character and action and taking on the quality of choral passages. Byron's speeches of aspiration in *The Conspiracy*, I.ii and II.i, clearly owe much to Marlowe's portrayal of Tamburlaine, the Guise and Mortimer. Picoté's speech of persuasion in I.ii on the unfashionableness of loyalty and the need to be true to one's self echoes popular Machiavellianism of the kind made theatrical by Marlowe's Barabas and the Guise. When La Fin describes his magical powers over the elements in II.i, he sounds like a petulant Owen Glendower but his speech is largely drawn from Seneca. Byron's megalomania when he tells Savoy that he will have a mountain carved in his image uses material drawn from Plutarch.[53] By far the largest number of allusions are made to classical texts and these have been closely studied by such scholars as F. L. Schoell, A. S. Ferguson, G. G. Loane, T. M. Parrott and J. Jacquot who have given us a sense of Chapman's reading and the nature of his commonplace books.[54] The indebtedness of the notes of this edition to these scholars will be obvious to any reader. Chapman used his classical sources much as he used Grimeston, sometimes merely paraphrasing in verse a prose passage that had impressed him, at other times using the source as a springboard for a much larger piece of sustained poetry.

Chapman's over-all management of his source material in the Byron plays has not always been highly regarded, the usual complaint being that he did not concentrate the material sufficiently to give the play a real drive toward tragedy. This complaint is not entirely justified if one regards *The Conspiracy* as the temptation and *The Tragedy* as the fall, a two-part structure of considerable intrinsic strength. In the first play, Chapman directs our attention to Byron and Henry as the great central figures of the drama and to Savoy and La Fin as tempters and provocateurs. The heroic past is described in narrative passages which nevertheless have an ironic context in terms of present action. Other events relevant to the action are telescoped in time (Byron's visit to Brussels and Savoy's arrival at the French court were a year apart but Chapman makes them contemporaneous) or mentioned briefly in passing (Henry's marriage to Marie de Medici and the subsequent birth of an heir to the throne).[55] The forty-day war between France and Savoy is omitted altogether, though there is a reference at the end of *The Conspiracy* to the possibility of a short sharp conflict. Chapman must have considered this war as too much of a diversion from his concentration upon the relationship between Henry and Byron, since he makes one of the results of the war, the capture of Bourg, a bone of contention between Henry and Byron before Savoy's departure, that is, before the war could have happened.[56] The atmosphere of *The Conspiracy* is serious but not tragic. There are comic elements in the way the conspirators manipulate the folly and vanity of Byron and even the vanity of the king. But there are also ominous tones which reveal Chapman's shaping of his material from the beginning: the use of such symbols as the Catiline carpet in the second scene, the careful placing of Byron's visit to the astrologer just after Savoy's apparent success, and the portrayal of Byron's ungoverned rage. The visit to

England and the queen's warning concerning ambitious subjects hints at the Essex rebellion and adds a further dimension of tragic irony as Byron refuses to see himself as either ambitious or a potential traitor.

In *The Tragedy*, Chapman used his source material much more directly because the chronicle account was already clearly focused upon the final stages of Byron's fall and needed little dramatic re-direction. Only in the trial scene did Chapman reduce the available material, particularly the long speeches of accusation and defence. The cuts he made here and the dramatic emphasis he gave to Byron's extraordinary range of passions in the last scenes add greatly to the tragic force of the play.

In writing his Byron plays, Chapman showed an awareness of the real dramatic power of the historical events. He made no attempt to add a fictional dimension by adding new characters, by complicating the basic plot or introducing subplots. He was not incapable of such additions and complications, as *Bussy D'Ambois* and the comedies illustrate, but the source on this occasion gave him everything he needed. There is a highly effective dramatic emphasis in *The Conspiracy* upon the three-way tension of Savoy, Byron and Henry; in *The Tragedy* the concentration is upon Byron and Henry, but finally upon Byron alone as he moves, raging and pleading, toward the scaffold.

7. THE PLAY

(a) Analogues and Influences

The Conspiracy and Tragedy of Byron is a two-part play which was planned as such rather than being a play with a sequel, added because of the popularity of the first part. The subject was a large one, and Chapman must have decided at an early point to give the play a spacious form. The influence of *Tamburlaine* was probably more important in this respect than that of I and II *Henry IV* since the central characters, Tamburlaine and Byron, dominate their respective plays in a way that Henry never does. However, all three double plays rise to a moment of reconciliation and triumph at the end of the first part and move toward darker tones in the second.[57]

Chapman's connection with Marlowe and the influence of Marlowe upon his poetry and drama have been commented upon before.[58] *The Blind Beggar of Alexandria* has been regarded as a parody or 'travesty' of the style of *Tamburlaine*, but if *The Blind Beggar* is set against *The Jew of Malta* and the Byron plays are compared with *Tamburlaine*, one can see more clearly the nature of Marlowe's influence. Chapman's play, like Marlowe's, is written throughout as a heroic poem, with large rhetorically organised speeches and passages of commentary that have a choral function. It makes few concessions to colloquialism of expression or realism of dialogue. In both plays, the aspiring spirit of the hero dominates the dramatic action. Yet the differences between the plays are more remarkable than the similarities. We see Byron first of all, as we see Tamburlaine, through the eyes of others who are critical if not contemptuous of his claims to greatness; when we are presented with the heroic character himself, his splendid flow of rhetoric seems to sweep all before it. The technique is also used by Shakespeare at the beginning of *Antony and Cleopatra*. However Byron's faults are underlined far more heavily from the beginning than are those of Antony and Tamburlaine. In the first scene, Savoy and his followers talk about Byron as proud and vain, as subject to flattery and as having an inflated idea of his own glory. When he appears in person in the following scene, his susceptibility to flattery is demonstrated at once so that the audience is bound to consider the other charges as possibly true. His magnificence, however, is by no means all hollow grandeur: his past deeds have been real ones and his conception of his own splendour has some basis in fact. His personal courage is no more in doubt than is that of Antony or Coriolanus. It is the ironic complexity of the portrait, the combination of great virtues with great faults that are in some way interdependent, that separate Byron from Marlowe's portrait of Tamburlaine and link him more directly with Shakespeare's characters.

Marlowe set *Tamburlaine* in a remote world of spectacular battles and pageantry where the heroic spirit had seemingly unlimited scope for its endeavours. In *The Conspiracy and Tragedy of Byron*, the great battles and triumphs belong to the past and the action is largely political. This difference may be due in part to the size and nature of the acting company compared with Marlowe's, the particular skills of the actors and the smaller scale of the Blackfriars theatre and stage, but is also very much a deliberate part of the design of the play. In the late sixteenth-century European court which is the focus of the action, the central heroic character finds himself without a function appropriate to his ideals. As Richard Ide points out, 'once the static, uncompromising hero is displaced from a heroic milieu that makes ambition virtue, his moral and social conflict with an antiheroic society is assured'.[59] It is therefore more useful to consider *The Conspiracy and Tragedy* in relation to other contemporary tragedies on historical themes which have important political and philosophical elements, in particular *Julius Caesar*, *Sejanus* and *Philotas*.

The plays I have mentioned, like *Catiline* and *Coriolanus* of somewhat later date and Chapman's own *Revenge of Bussy* and *Tragedy of Chabot*, can be compared with *The Conspiracy and Tragedy* because they are all plays about men involved in public affairs and are concerned with the authority of princes, the liberty and independence of the individual, the threat of actual or potential tyranny. The writers chose well-known characters and events from classical times or the recent past partly because the famous event or the notorious example of treachery in high places was important in gaining an audience – box-office considerations cannot be denied, although *Philotas* is no doubt an exception in this respect. But the choice may also have depended upon the fact that the well-known historical event allowed authors a measure of security against those in authority who looked for dangerous opinions. Dramatists who knew their craft were aware that drama by its very nature must inevitably present conflicting points of view, and were also aware of the potentialities for irony and ambiguity in the form. Yet they could at the same time disclaim any intent of reflecting upon contemporary events or persons in their own society. The fame of the historical happening and the strenuous disclaimer did not always prevent them from getting into trouble. They believed nevertheless that the issues of authority and tyranny were proper subjects for tragedy which a serious writer of the form could not escape. As Daniel said in his Apology, printed with *Philotas* in 1623 but probably written close to the first publication of the play in 1605:[60]

> And withall taking a subject that lay (as I thought) so farre from the time, and so remote a stranger from the climate of our present courses, I could not imagine that Enuy or ignorance could possibly haue made it, to take any particular acquaintance with vs, but as it hath a generall alliance to the frailty of greatnesse, and the vsuall workings of ambition, the perpetuall subiects of books and Tragedies.
>
> And for any resemblance, that thorough the ignorance of the History may be applied to the late Earle of Essex. It can hold in no proportion but only in his weaknesses, which I would wish all that loue his memory not to reuiue.[61]

Was Chapman taking a special risk in writing about contemporary French political upheavals rather than about classical events and personages? There could hardly be any suspicions of a hidden allegory when the representation was so directly historical, so close to the chronicles that many were reading. Perhaps Chapman counted on the relative stability of English affairs in 1607–8 and on the political orthodoxy of his interpretation of Byron's revolt to protect him from Privy Council interference. If he were at all worried about his treatment of the political and ethical issues, it is ironic that it was the gossip, the affair of the king's mistress, that got him and the players into trouble.[62]

When we consider the particular question of 'influence', it is difficult to show that Chapman drew any important lessons as to tragic form from these tragedies by his contemporaries, nor in his manner of dramatising historical sources: as always, he is independently minded. One well-known statement he made concerning historical truth in drama occurs in the epistle to *The Revenge of Bussy D'Ambois*: 'Poor envious souls they are that cavil at truth's want in these natural fictions; material instruction, elegant and sententious excitation to virtue, and deflection from her contrary, being the soul, limbs and limits of an autentical tragedy.'[63] This idea of truth differs from Jonson's 'truth of Argument', but there may have been a particular desire in this epistle to defend the lack of historical reference in *The Revenge* when he had so recently written a double play based upon well-attested historical materials. It is clear that he found in the historical account of Byron by Grimeston and the French chroniclers a sufficiently powerful and astonishing fable requiring little alteration and few additions for the sake of philosophical truth. In many respects he followed Jonson's practice in *Sejanus* (even though Jonson used a number of sources and Chapman only one), adapting and paraphrasing historical material very closely where it was suitable for his purpose, but devising whole scenes, altering the sequence of events and enlarging upon motivation from mere hints in the historians where the sources proved insufficient.

Like Jonson and Shakespeare also, he gave his audience some sense of the wider context of a conflict between powerful individuals: the conspiracy of Byron is set in a European world of diplomacy and war. But one would be rash to say that he learned how to do this from Jonson and Shakespeare since the material for this wider context was available to him in Grimeston. There is little feeling in the Byron plays of a whole society being affected by the conflict between Byron and Henry: one finds nothing comparable to the street riots, the surging crowds and the battles of *Julius Caesar*, or the fiercely competing factions, the sycophantic Senate and the struggling survivors of an older tradition in *Sejanus*. So far as France is concerned, Chapman limits the dramatic action to the nobility and the court.

The political and ethical issues of the play are clearly represented in the major characters, Byron and Henry, and to a lesser extent Savoy and La Fin. Action is as important as character in the delineation of these issues, so that the developing conflict between Henry and Byron becomes a paradigm of the opposition of different ideas about authority, the responsibilities of rulers and subjects, aspiration and ambition in a recently pacified society, and the integrity of self. But this is no abstract debate: the developing conflict becomes a tragic struggle for the hero between his own nature and view of himself and a world which grows increasingly hostile and eventually crushes him. The political and ethical problem play becomes a tragedy.

Chapman is probably closer to Shakespeare than to Jonson or Daniel in the way he introduces issues and ideas through large-scale characters whose motivation and qualities are of crucial importance in determining what happens. Daniel's severely classical figures show few of the characteristics of common humanity, and Jonson is more interested in presenting a powerfully satiric view of society, a generic portrait of tyranny and its victims. However there is nothing in Chapman's play to compare with Jonson's large gallery of representative figures, each with strongly marked characteristics seemingly asking for an actor's skill to interpret them on the stage.

In another respect, too, Chapman's work is like Shakespeare's in *Julius Caesar* and *Antony and Cleopatra*: his tragic hero has something of the aura of myth about him, an imaginative enlargement through imagery, allusion and choral comment which sets him apart from the other characters in the play. Chapman no doubt found hints for this kind of effect in the heroic characters of the Homeric poems as well as in Shakespeare. Nevertheless there is sometimes a disparity between the different elements associated with the hero, as MacLure has noted in an evocative passage which is concerned with all Chapman's tragic heroes:

> In these plays, then, the ethical argument, the political parable, and the autumnal, elegiac *mythos* of the hero are not always integrated, so that one can get a sense of discrete and separable layers of expression, something that it is tempting to call allegory. The hero is not all in the play, but has in the poet's imagination another life the shadow of which falls, often very undramatically, into the business of the action.[64]

Byron is not merely an ambitious noble seeking an outlet for his energy after the cessation of the civil wars; he is also a dreamer who would restore a lost heroic age to a corrupt world by a 'new creation', as he tells D'Auvergne and La Fin in the long opening speech of I.ii in *The Tragedy*. The shadow of 'another life' is again suggested in an allegorical passage at the beginning of III.i where Byron describes the subversion of virtue and divine purpose on earth, a speech which has only a distant connection with the political issues of the immediate conflict. The most deeply felt personal expression of an extra dimension occurs in Byron's speech in the final act of *The Tragedy* when he tells the Archbishop that the thwarted soul in an evil world must find its own way to heaven (V.iv.26–55), a passage which looks back to heightened moments of aspiration and striking images of the freedom of the individual will in both plays.

In formal terms, the pattern of the play resembles the general outline of Daniel's *Philotas*: the hint of a conspiracy against the ruler by a once-trusted supporter, informers pursuing their activities, accusation, trial and execution. There is far more about the process of temptation in Chapman's double play, but as in Daniel's play, the development of the plot is austere, stressing the essential conflict between major antagonists and dispensing with peripheral action and characters. The extravagant variety of so many Elizabethan plays is absent from both Daniel and Chapman. However Chapman follows no neo-classical model with respect to structure. The necessary qualities of tragedy, as he indicated in the epistle to *The Revenge of Bussy D'Ambois*, remain its general dignity of tone, loftiness of style and moral elevation.

There is one other influence that ought to be considered since it involves both political ideas and dramatic structure. In the way Chapman has organised his material, one may also see clear signs of the political morality stemming from Shakespeare's history plays and the Tudor moral histories behind them. Evidence of this tradition exists in the pattern of the hero's initial state of political innocence (though an innocence already somewhat bedazzled by worldly glory), a carefully planned temptation to treachery and a subsequent fall. The tempters, Picoté, Savoy and La Fin, are portrayed as subtle Machiavellians, clever with words and skilled in double-dealing. Set against them is the king, a wise and just ruler, who acts as good counsellor in the morality pattern. His severe warning to Byron at the end of *The Conspiracy* leads Byron to an admission of guilt and full repentance. In *The Tragedy*, this is followed by a relapse into treachery, persistence in the ways of error and a refusal to ask for mercy until it is too late.[65]

None of Chapman's other tragedies depends upon such a pattern of temptation, fall, accusation of guilt and the choice between mercy and final judgement, although there is a most interesting variation upon the pattern in *The Tragedy of Chabot*. Chabot has a proud sense of his own integrity and is as stubborn in declaring his innocence as Byron, though with far more reason. When Chabot is falsely accused and found guilty by the court, the king believes that he can now make the unbending man bend to ask for pardon, or at the very least to show gratitude for an act of mercy. After Chabot refuses to do so and is completely vindicated, the older dramatic pattern becomes paradoxical in the extreme as the king finds himself needing Chabot's forgiveness for having doubted him. Chabot's suffering at the end is undeserved except to the extent that he is the victim of spiritual pride in his own virtue which could not foresee nor allow doubt from any quarter.

In *The Conspiracy of Byron*, the king's apostrophe to innocence which brings Byron to his knees (a visual image of great importance in the play) stresses the thematic structure I have been describing:

> O Innocence, the sacred amulet
> 'Gainst all the poisons of infirmity,
> Of all misfortune, injury, and death,
> That makes a man in tune still in himself,
> Free from the hell to be his own accuser,
> Ever in quiet, endless joy enjoying ....   (*Consp.*, V.ii.85–90)

Byron's reply reflects the same moral pattern:

> 'Tis all acknowledged and, though all too late,
> Here the short madness of my anger ends.
> If ever I did good, I locked it safe
> In you, th'impregnable defence of goodness;
> If ill, I press it with my penitent knees
> To that unsounded depth whence nought returneth.
> *Henry.* 'Tis music to mine ears: rise then for ever
> Quit of what guilt soever till this hour,
> And nothing touched in honour or in spirit;
> Rise without flattery, rise by absolute merit.   (*Consp.*, V.ii.101–10)

We are reminded of the morality structure at several points in *The Tragedy* after Byron's 'trait'rous relapse'. Henry vows that he will pardon Byron, no matter how great his sin, should he ask for mercy:

> ... we will restrain
> With all forgiveness, if he will confess,
> His headlong course to ruin, and his taste
> From the sweet poison of his friendlike foes: (*Trag.*, I.iii.47–50)

And when Byron returns to court, there is a hint of a biblical parable in Henry's greeting:

> The faithful servant, right in Holy Writ,
> That said he would not come, and yet he came: (*Trag.*, III.ii.63–4)

As Parrott observes, the son who in *Matt.* xxi.28 would not go to the vineyard when his father commanded, but then repented, has become the faithful servant who would not come, but changed his mind.[66] Henry also refers to the familiar pattern of the prodigal son when he speaks of 'the kind father' and 'his riotous son' in the same scene.

Towards the end of *The Tragedy*, the emphasis upon the words 'pardon' and 'mercy' is striking. A good counsellor (in the morality tradition) urges Byron to 'humbly cast' all his former honours and merits 'at the king's mercy' (IV.i.39–41) but Byron refuses to admit any guilt or to seek for mercy until it is too late. This is not to say, of course, that Chapman's play is a moral history in the old style: he uses only such aspects of the structure and imagery of the political morality as suit his ironic and tragic pattern. Henry and Elizabeth as good counsellors are undoubtedly wise and virtuous, and even the eminent statesman at Elizabeth's court, though subtle in his temptation of Byron's loyalty, takes on the role of advisor to virtuous action. However Henry is a very human king: his vanity is sorely touched by Savoy in the first play, and he uses devious means to lure Byron into his power in the second. Nor is Byron portrayed simply as a sinner who repents, then relapses and is finally damned. Other aspects of his role will become clearer as we examine the structure and movement of the double play in more detail.

(b) Portrayal of Byron

Chapman's portrait of Byron is initially the character as presented by Grimeston, a complex portrait in itself since Grimeston depended upon more than one French chronicler and comments about Byron's qualities run through the whole history in which he is involved. Grimeston's summing up of Byron's character and career occurs after the execution; Chapman paraphrases much of this in Roncas's words to Savoy in the first scene of *The Conspiracy*. Byron's great valour is emphasised in Grimeston's account, his power of endurance, but also his vanity: he would often, instead of eating, 'feede his Fantasie with Glory and Vanity'.[67] The idea of excess is associated with Byron from an early point:

Nothing could make him vnhappy, but the excesse of his happines which depriued him of al gouernment & modesty. If he had bin lesse fortunate, he had bin more wise.[68]

The power of the passions affecting his nature and the lack of reason are noted time and again, both during the progress of the conspiracy and during the trial: 'The discours of Reason, or the iudgements of Truth preuaile not with a spirit transported with passions' is a typical comment.[69] Folly, vanity, an excessive sense of glory, the passions of choler and revenge – these are all noted along with his qualities of valour, energy and decision, but they do not mitigate or excuse the 'hellish treachery' which is properly punished by his death. 'The causes of his ruine are infinite,' says Grimeston, 'the contempt of piety is the chiefe: this ground taken away, all vices abound ....'[70]

The moral lesson which Byron's career enforces is stressed in Chapman's Prologue to the play: 'And see in his revolt how honour's flood / Ebbs into air when men are great, not good.' But this is not the whole of the story as Chapman tells it, and even in the Prologue the marvellous image of the rising of autumn's star and the phrase 'He touched heaven with his lance' suggest an attitude toward Byron that goes beyond a moralistic interpretation.[71]

Much of the interest of the double play lies in the way Chapman modifies and enlarges his central character from the portrait provided in his source. One of his techniques is a very extensive use of soliloquies and monologues in which Byron gives voice not only to his aspiration but also to a kind of supra-individualism, the free spirit of 'royal man'. These monologues are frequently undercut by the observations of others who have a greater grasp of the political realities and in some cases a greater understanding of moral wisdom.[72] The imagery of the play is also part of Chapman's technique of characterisation and once again it is the interplay between images of widely differing imaginative effect that is so striking. There are heroic images from classical epic and history – Hercules, Achilles, Curtius, Camillus – and images of unremitting struggle and powerful energy drawn from contemporary life; yet there are also satiric images, often with a comic cast to them, which reflect a vastly different view of Byron's behaviour. Roiseau's description of Byron's treatment at the archduke's court in Brussels and of Byron's response is of this kind:

Henry. Was he so courted?
Roiseau.   As a city dame
    Brought by her jealous husband to the court,
    Some elder courtiers entertaining him

> While others snatch a favour from his wife:
> One starts from this door, from that nook another,
> With gifts and junkets, and with printed phrase
> Steal her employment, shifting place by place
> Still as her husband comes: so Duke Byron
> Was wooed and worshipped in the archduke's court ....
>
> (*Consp.*, II.ii.1–9)

As with the monologues and soliloquies, the context in which such images appear is of vital dramatic interest. Most of the elaborate heroic images occur in Byron's own speeches at moments of decision or change of direction; when they occur elsewhere, in the mouths of La Fin or Savoy, the context is usually strongly ironic. The satiric images which point to the obsessive humours of Byron naturally occur in the mouths of those who are observing Byron with a critical eye.[73]

Chapman does not neglect the more conventional modes of characterisation: he pictures Byron acting upon and being acted upon by other men, sometimes in full awareness of the situation, sometimes almost totally ignorant of the role others have created for him. There are many small sketches of his character placed in the mouths of those around him, sympathetic, ironic and hostile. Chapman also makes use of the choral commentary by characters who step momentarily outside the action to comment upon it, a device particularly important towards the end of *The Tragedy*. Thus at the beginning of III.ii in *The Tragedy*, three courtiers speak in turn about Byron's situation and in general about fortune and honour:

> *Prâlin.* Come or be fetched, he quite hath lost his honour
> In giving these suspicions of revolt
> From his allegiance; that which he hath won
> With sundry wounds and peril of his life,
> With wonder of his wisdom and his valour,
> He loseth with a most enchanted glory,
> And admiration of his pride, and folly. (*Trag.*, III.ii.3–9)

There is a more fully developed example of this technique at V.iii.189–240, immediately after Byron has first heard the sentence of the court; five characters remain on stage to engage in a litany of lamentation for the fall of so great a man and wonder at his passionate fury.

(c) '*The Conspiracy*'

The Conspiracy opens in Paris with a debate among Savoy and his attendant lords on the advantages he may or may not gain from his visit to the French court. One of his purposes is to search out disaffected

French nobles who could be tempted to support the Savoyard cause and Byron is named as a possible candidate, by far the most promising. In a set piece which is, as I have said, drawn from Grimeston's concluding summary, Roncas describes Byron's nature:

> ... he is a man
> Of matchless valour, and was ever happy
> In all encounters ...
> He is past measure glorious; and that humour
> Is fit to feed his spirits, whom it possesseth
> With faith in any error, chiefly where
> Men blow it up with praise of his perfections;
>
> (*Consp.*, I.i.61–3; 71–4)

Byron makes his appearance in the second scene, set in Brussels where he is ambassador to the Archduke Albert for the signing of the Treaty of Vervins. Just before his entry, there are two brief speeches which are designed to affect the audience's view of him: Roisseau, one of Henry's servants, expresses his private fear that the attention being paid to Byron will 'taint his loyalty', and Picoté, a servant of the archduke, declares that the honours being done Byron are expressly for that purpose. Hence when Byron enters to 'loud music', his rhapsodic effusion on aspiration is ironically regarded, particularly when he notices the carpet spread before him but disregards the Catiline story woven into it. Nevertheless the force of his speech and the power of his images have some effect beyond the ironic qualification:

> 'Tis immortality to die aspiring,
> As if a man were taken quick to heaven;
> What will not hold perfection, let it burst ...
> ... Happiness
> Denies comparison of less or more,
> And not at most, is nothing ...
> ... like the shaft
> Shot at the sun by angry Hercules,
> And into shivers by the thunder broken,
> Will I be if I burst; and in my heart
> This shall be written: 'yet 'twas high and right'.
>
> (*Consp.*, I.ii.31–3; 38–40; 40–4)

As George Hibbard has noted, Byron's speeches of aspiration give no clear vision of a particular ambition; they seldom touch upon the trappings of royalty in spite of the way his tempters dangle such images before him.[74] His aspiration is rather an 'excessive desire for honour', as MacLure puts it,[75] and the images later in the play linking him with the Titans and with Hercules help to fill out this portrayal of an undefined, upward-reaching restlessness and desire.

When Picoté leads Byron to a place of private conference, the debate between them takes on a particular significance in relation to what happens later in the play. Picoté delivers what purports to be a philosophical justification of individual self-determination: nature has given the individual who has 'a habit of perfection' the absolute right to carve out his own 'highest dignities', to be his own 'rewarder'. Into his argument he insinuates the view that loyalty is old-fashioned, servile, a deprivation of the rights of the individual, what Ure calls 'pure Machiavellianism' of the popular Elizabethan kind.[76] Byron is not yet ready to accept such a point of view. His defence of loyalty is traditional, emphasising the bonds that hold men together in trust and freedom, and the dangerous ease with which such bonds can be shattered. If he is affected by Picoté's argument, he shows no signs of it.

It is not a conspiracy of Byron against the king that has been started but a conspiracy by Savoy and others against Byron to draw him into their toils by a clever policy of probing and using his weaknesses. The second and third acts of the play show the success of this conspiracy. The series of temptation scenes is nicely calculated by Savoy who is the playmaker, although Byron thinks he is the one who is calling the tune; their structure is ironic, as is much of the language. Byron declares that he will win La Fin and 'make him malleable as th'Ophir gold' although it is he himself that is being made malleable (II.i.148). La Fin who has been cast off by the king as a dangerous malcontent manages to arouse Byron's interest in his predicament and succeeds in leading Byron to Savoy when Byron believes that he is introducing La Fin to Savoy. Savoy overpraises Byron to the king to such an extent that Henry's sense of proportion is outraged and his personal vanity touched. His more moderate account of Byron's former exploits is quickly reported by Savoy to Byron in order to arouse the latter's anger. It is of great interest to note that Byron's military career is given a heroic narrative treatment in a strikingly ironic context, Savoy's hyperbolic account to Henry of Byron's legendary valour. All of this leads up to what Savoy and his followers had been hoping for, an angry clash between Byron and Henry which on the surface concerns Byron's choice of La Fin as a friend but which is more deeply related to Byron's hurt over Henry's dispraise of his achievements as saviour of France.

Chapman links the ironic action of these scenes closely to character. Savoy is himself a shrewd judge of character and rather proud of the fact, aware of Byron's self-image of grandeur and glory, but also of Henry's vanity, knowing just how far to go in rubbing the edge of that vanity without damaging his own cause. He is also a witty and amusing courtier, able to play a part to its limit and at the same time enjoy the irony of situation or language. Henry is no mere puppet in Savoy's hands, though Savoy disturbs his equanimity. He may be a little vain, occasionally pompous, but he is pictured also as a clear-sighted ruler, able to judge very accurately the discontents of a man like La Fin and the illusions by which Byron deceives himself. La Fin is given less individuality since he is of less importance to the plot: a malcontent, a spendthrift and wastrel in a time of peace, yet pleased with his talents as a deceiver of others, as an actor able to play a part successfully. He claims at one point to have magical powers, but nothing more is made of this until the end of *The Tragedy* where Byron defends himself before the judges by declaring that La Fin used powers of enchantment over him. It sounds like an excuse and the judges dismiss it as such.

However Chapman's main emphasis is directed upon Byron. In the indoctrination scenes, Byron is shown first of all as undertaking the new involvement with La Fin and Savoy almost in relief, as a substitute for the life of military action that has been denied him since the coming of peace:

> I am put off from this dull shore of ease
> Into industrious and high-going seas,
> Where, like Pelides in Scamander's flood,
> Up to the ears in surges I will fight
> And pluck French Ilion underneath the waves.   (*Consp.*, II.i.149-53)

It is a heroic image in tune with his character, but remarkably out of keeping with the task immediately in hand, the supposed winning over of La Fin.

Byron begins his persuasion of the already persuaded La Fin with one or two vivid images relating to 'the free-born powers of royal man' (III.i.31), but much of his argument echoes the specious opinions of Picoté concerning 'those mere politic terms / Of love, fame, loyalty':

> ... so all things here
> Have all their price set down from men's concepts,
> Which make all terms and actions good or bad ....   (*Consp.*, III.i.55-7)

'Policy' and 'politic' are almost always used by Chapman with a strongly pejorative connotation, suggesting the cunning wiles of a politician intent on his own advancement.[77] False oaths, double-dealing, the twisting of meanings in order to deceive are all part of the behaviour pattern of the politician. The great exemplars of these qualities in Chapman's plays are Monsieur in *Bussy D'Ambois*, Savoy and La Fin in the Byron plays, Baligny and Maillard in *The Revenge of Bussy D'Ambois* and Poyet, Lord Chancellor, in *The Tragedy of Chabot*. Very occasionally, 'policy' is used with a neutral or even a good connotation: Henry, for example, speaks of England as a place of health and temperance 'Where policies are not ruinous, but saving' (*Consp.*, II.ii.51). Byron himself is not a politician, or at least not a very successful one, being too passionate to be cunning; he is the victim of the wiles of Savoy and La Fin in *The Conspiracy* and the victim of Henry's wiles in *The Tragedy* when he is drawn back to court. Nevertheless at this point in *The Conspiracy* he is influenced sufficiently by Picoté and La Fin to take over something of the argument and the vocabulary of the Machiavellian sceptic. In describing 'love, fame, loyalty' as 'mere politic terms', Byron claims that such words are used by 'politicians' to keep man in a state of slavery, that the free-born individual ought to be able to rise above them. It is a notable perversion of Byron's doctrine of 'royal man'.

Byron's susceptibility to manipulation and his slight hold on rationality when passion begins to flow are made almost comically obvious as Savoy with his followers praises Byron in excessive terms and at the same time reports the somewhat disparaging remarks of the king about his military campaigns. Byron's explosion of wrath is exactly what Savoy had been aiming for and demonstrates his shrewd assessment of Byron's character. However, Chapman reveals another aspect of that character toward the end of the same long scene. The king enters and rebukes Byron for keeping such 'vermin' as La Fin close to his bosom (III.ii.215–16). One might have expected another outburst of rage, but on this occasion Byron curbs his tongue (as Savoy had urged him to do) and speaks with vigorous independence of the right of a man to choose his own friends, quite apart from the servile respect owed to the power of a prince. Byron's scorn of time-servers and insistence on freedom of choice appear as admirable qualities, even though the object of his concern is a worthless friend. The mixture of qualities that make up the man is clearly pointed to as Chapman juxtaposes them within a single scene.

A similar statement could be made about the scene in which Byron pays a visit to the astrologer, La Brosse (III.iii). Chapman's placing of this scene and his enlargement of its scope and meaning are most interesting, since Grimeston describes it very briefly in the summary of

Byron's career after the trial and execution and states that it had occurred when Byron first came to court. There are obvious dramatic reasons for placing the scene near the mid-point of *The Conspiracy*. Byron is at a cross-roads, wondering whether to follow the path of duty laid down for him by the king or to choose the more adventurous and dangerous road pointed out by the archduke and by Savoy. His visit to the astrologer gives him the opportunity to consider his future: his soliloquy before he meets La Brosse presents a sober and (for him) rational view of the dangers faced by a king's favourite or by anyone dependent for great place upon fortune. Another good dramatic reason for the scene lies in its ominous forecast of the future, not only in the actual prediction of Byron's death but also in its demonstration of Byron's ungoverned passions: in these respects it provides a clear link with the second play. The episode also reveals Byron's character in another aspect, his tendency to waver between a belief in fate or destiny (one should note his attitude to omens of disaster in *The Tragedy*) and a faith in his own freedom to determine his future. The tension between these two attitudes is unresolved until the very end of the play.

La Brosse makes two predictions during the scene. One concerns himself: 'This hour by all rules of astrology / Is dangerous to my person, if not deadly', and so it turns out to be. The fulfilment of the first makes the accuracy of the second prediction, the beheading of Byron for a deed recently done, seem all the more likely to the audience. La Brosse himself is a determinist: man can, through learning, discover what the stars will bring to pass but cannot prevent anything from happening. This is the substance of his lament that knowledge is the worthiest endeavour of mankind and yet is powerless to affect his destiny.

There is very little in La Brosse's soliloquy or in his conversation with Byron to suggest one of the most widely accepted doctrines of contemporary astrology, that the casting of a nativity revealed dispositions or inclinations, not an unavoidable fate. As Keith Thomas says, 'From Ptolemy to Partridge, it was a platitude of astrological writing to assert that the stars inclined, but did not compel.'[78] The first part of La Brosse's reading of Byron's horoscope comes closest to the astrologers' usual practice of identifying qualities in a client's nature as a result of astral influences:

> *La Brosse.* My son, I see that he whose end is cast
>   In this set figure is of noble parts,
>   And by his military valour raised
>   To princely honours; and may be a king,

> But that I see a *Caput Algol* here
> That hinders it, I fear. (*Consp.*, III.iii.48-53)

The reference to Caput Algol is in terms of 'hindering' rather than 'preventing', though this star was considered the most baleful of all.[79] His subsequent explication, after a series of threats and promises from Byron is, however, a definite prediction: 'the man hath lately done / An action that will make him lose his head'. Astrological predictions were, of course, frequently made in spite of the theoretical treatises by astrologers that warned against them.

After his initial outburst of fury and his physical violence against the wretched astrologer, Byron moves in the direction of a strong assertion of the freedom of the will, his freedom from any destiny announced by a reading of the stars. Though Byron's assertion is congruent with religious teaching about free will, Chapman does not give Byron a theological argument but rather a fundamental humanistic declaration that man with his gift of reason, his will and faculty of choice, is superior to the physical universe:

> I am a nobler substance than the stars
> And shall the baser overrule the better?
> Or are they better, since they are the bigger? (*Consp.*, III.iii.109-11)

At the end of the scene, Byron proclaims the independence of the free spirit in images which are among the most memorable of the play, giving a sense of splendid and heroic endeavour:

> ... be free, all worthy spirits,
> And stretch yourselves for greatness and for height;
> Untruss your slaveries, you have height enough
> Beneath this steep heaven to use all your reaches;
> 'Tis too far off to let you, or respect you.
> Give me a spirit that on this life's rough sea
> Loves t'have his sails filled with a lusty wind
> Even till his sail-yards tremble, his masts crack,
> And his rapt ship run on her side so low
> That she drinks water, and her keel ploughs air. (*Consp.*, III.iii.130-9)

And yet the audience must listen to this fine language with reservations growing out of its knowledge that Byron's 'will' and 'faculties of choice' and 'reason' have already been deceived, that his heroic ideal is not much more than passion and energy for an unworthy cause. The mere fact that he sought out an astrologer to learn his fate is a denial of the free choice of virtue and wisdom.[80] The beating up of the old man, a vivid stage image in its own right, reminds the audience of

Byron's tendency to ungoverned rage and again serves to qualify our view of Byron as a heroic individual.

Byron's embassy to Queen Elizabeth on Henry's behalf is the second mission abroad he has undertaken during the course of the play, and in many respects shows Byron at his most statesmanlike. Henry had decided to make Byron his ambassador as a possible curative measure for what Henry judged to be a dangerous imbalance of the humours in Byron's makeup:

> Duke Byron
> Flows with adust and melancholy choler,
> And melancholy spirits are venomous,
> Not to be touched but as they may be cured .... (*Consp.*, II.ii.42-5)

Henry's hope was that the temperate climate, the modest, free and just natures of the people, and the wise counsels of an exemplary court would restore Byron to a healthful state of mind. Byron, as Chapman portrays him, is much more than a 'humours' character, but the foundation given by his 'temperament', in the technical sense, is an important element in his makeup.

In the truncated fourth act of the play, the embassy to England is narrated rather than depicted on the stage: Crequi tells D'Aumont what happened and who said what to whom. It seems certain that Chapman originally placed both Queen Elizabeth and Byron on stage, recreating a memorable part of the Byron legend. The reported speeches are lengthy and formally organised: no doubt they reflect the character of the original scene, a public occasion demanding elaborate rhetoric rather than intimate conversation. It was probably an occasion also for pageantry and show in the stage production, though the hastily revised reported version gives little sense of this beyond Byron's admiring words about the state and majesty of the queen's rule and presence. One wonders if Byron and his attendants were all in black, as contemporary documents describe them. The 1602 play of 'burone' had required 'a blacke sewt of satten'. In a somewhat frantic letter to Lord Cobham, Raleigh mentions a night journey to London to secure 'a playne taffeta sute and a playne black saddell' to wear while he is attending the French delegation.[81] In contrast, the queen and her court were reported to have been resplendent. John Stow describes the scene as the queen met Byron during a hunt in 'Basen-parke':

> where the duke staied her comming, and did there see her in such royaltie and so attended on by the nobility, so costly furnished and mounted, as the like had seldome bin seene ....[82]

INTRODUCTION 37

Although Byron's elaborate compliments to the queen and to the English court, and Elizabeth's long complaint about Henry's failure to make the journey himself scarcely drive the drama forward, there are matters of interest in the speeches that have some relevance to the characters and action of the play. The scene presents Byron acting as Henry's loyal ambassador, as he scarcely had done in Brussels, and as a flattering orator in his address to the queen, paying tribute to a long-time supporter of Henry during the civil wars. The European scope of the action is broadened to include England. The reported speech of the queen also contains a strongly worded warning against the perils of ambition, a warning that points clearly to the fate of Essex, even though Elizabeth makes no mention of his name:

> But for a subject to affect a kingdom
> Is like the camel that of Jove begged horns,
> And such mad-hungry men as well may eat
> Hot coals of fire to feed their natural heat;
> For to aspire to competence with your king,
> What subject is so gross and giantly? (*Consp.*, IV.i.138–43)

This warning together with her discourse on the proper relation of subject to sovereign, by which each brings renown to the other, serves as the 'good counsel' which Byron so obviously needs. The eminent councillor's subtle testing of his loyalty and his sermon on faith and loyalty act in a similar way. In his courteous reply, as in his earlier response to the queen, Byron continues to present a public image of wisdom and loyalty, as if impressed by the temperate air and model rule of this kingdom. (The play offers parallels between Henry's rule and Elizabeth's but it is by no means clear that Byron sees the resemblance). This is the Byron that might have been, wise statesman and true servant of his king.

Once back in France, Byron pursues a violent change in direction, expressed in the restless image of the 'lusty courser'

> That hath been long time at his manger tied,
> High fed, alone, and when, his headstall broken,
> He runs his prison, like a trumpet neighs,
> Cuts air in high curvets, and shakes his head .... (*Consp.*, V.i.6–9)

Now that he has returned to 'faithful' rather than 'courtly' friends (the distinction he makes is ironic), the public image is quickly discarded. He is easily persuaded by La Fin to ask the king for the keeping of the citadel of Bourg. It is an unreasonable demand, as Savoy and La Fin well know, but Byron does not foresee Henry's refusal. Byron has been manipulated once more by his flattering friends. Henry reminds Byron of the great rewards he has given him for his military exploits over the years, but Byron in his anger is ready to discount them, given not 'For any love, but fear and force of shame' (*Consp.*, V.i.106). In his confidence of being worth more than any possible recompense, Byron is like Chabot when the king reminds Chabot of the great honours he has showered upon him (*Chabot*, II.iii.64ff.). The incident is the spark that ignites the explosion Savoy and La Fin have been hoping for. Byron is further provoked by Henry's laughter when Byron in his anger gives a highly coloured and exaggerated account of his great services to France, as if he alone were the saviour of his country. He is prevented from offering violence to the king only by D'Auvergne's forceful intervention. At this point occurs a sudden and remarkable change of heart in Byron as Henry describes the shallow creatures who have been poisoning his mind and apostrophises innocence as the virtue which alone can bring content and peace of mind. It is not entirely a credible change, occurring as it does so close to the heat of Byron's rage. Henry does not speak in a particularly intimate tone, suggesting the comradeship that once existed between them, but in elaborate figures of speech that concern justice and judgement. Byron appears to be affected by Henry's speech because he has not yet thought out the consequence of betrayal and is suddenly faced with the still powerful moral forces of loyalty and innocence. At any rate, he kneels for forgiveness, as the pattern of the morality play comes to the fore, and is welcomed by Henry back into his circle of trusted supporters. The first play ends with a light-hearted overhearing scene in which roles are reversed as Byron joins the king and his courtiers in their spying upon Savoy and the ladies.

(d) *The Tragedy*
At the beginning of *The Tragedy*, there is a speedy renewal of the conflicts of *The Conspiracy*, as the second part of *Henry IV* renews the conflicts of part I. In the first line, Henry speaks of 'Byron fallen in so trait'rous a relapse' as if it is already well known and goes on to talk about the honours he has showered upon him over the years. Janin, one of his ministers, points to possible dangers to the state because of suspected links between Byron, the Count Fuentes, Savoy and Spain. However Henry is not yet convinced that Byron has gone over to his enemies. In a speech which is a noble tribute to Byron's great qualities, he expresses his bewilderment that a man so honoured by his king, so

Henri IV engraved in 1846 by R. Graves after an earlier engraving by H. Goltzius (BBC Hulton Picture Library)

valiant in spirit, could be transformed into a traitor. But his doubts have been fuelled by information from La Fin who is spoken of in terms that suggest he may now be a double agent, Henry's spy as well as Savoy's:

> *Henry.* Yet do I long, methinks, to see La Fin
> Who hath his heart in keeping; since his state,
> Grown to decay and he to discontent,
> Comes near the ambitious plight of Duke Byron.
> ...
> In him, as in a crystal that is charmed,
> I shall discern by whom and what designs
> My rule is threatened .... (*Trag.*, I.i.87–90, 97–9)

The characterisation of Henry is strengthened as the young dauphin is brought in by a nurse to receive Henry's blessing and his prayer for a long and happy reign. The establishment of a secure and orderly succession after the turmoil of the civil wars has been one of Henry's great priorities: he makes much of the devastation France suffered from the wars so recently over. The sword which he places in his son's hand (with the nurse's help) is 'the religious sword of justice' and although the main emphasis of the speech is on the values of peace and order, the sword remains a dominant image throughout. It has three functions, to 'Cut from thy tree of rule all trait'rous branches / That strive to shadow and eclipse thy glories' (ll.113–14), to 'curb and end' any renewal of 'civil furies' in France and to defeat the external enemies of France, bringing back 'Just conquests, loaden with his enemies' spoils' (l.147). Henry hopes that his son will gain greater military honours than his father ever possessed. The appeals to peace and justice and the prayer to God give Henry's speech a sense of religious dedication, strengthening the case against Byron who is clearly one of these 'trait'rous branches'; yet it is not without references to royal absolutism, to the single glory the king feels he must possess and which rebels try to 'shadow and eclipse'. Chapman returns explicitly to this theme near the end of the play when Henry feels himself at last 'settled in my sun of height' (*Trag.*, V.i.138).

Immediately following this scene in which the demands of loyalty, peace and orderly succession are so eloquently presented, Byron appears discoursing just as eloquently to D'Auvergne and La Fin on the neglect he experiences now that the civil wars are over and on the disorder peace has brought to the land:

> The world is quite inverted, virtue thrown
> At vice's feet, and sensual peace confounds

Valour and cowardice, fame and infamy;
The rude and terrible age is turned again .... (*Trag.*, I.ii.14-17)

Byron's description of the state of affairs seems to be entirely his own and is given no validity by other characters or actions within the play. There could scarcely be a greater contrast in political terms than that between Henry's plea for the restorative qualities of peace[83] and Byron's Catiline-like desire to destroy the state in order to remake it:

We must reform and have a new creation
Of state and government, and on our chaos
Will I sit brooding up another world. (*Trag.*, I.ii.29-31)

The blasphemous image of the Holy Spirit[84] is followed by another vague reference to Byron's plans for the future greatness of France: he 'To the repairing of my country's ruins, / Will ruin it again to re-advance it' (ll.34-5). As Byron prepares to send La Fin to court to spy out the state of affairs, the fulsome flattery La Fin bestows upon him and the reckless confidence he shows in La Fin's loyalty augur dangerously for the future.

The council scene at court moves the play rapidly toward an open break between Henry and Byron. It is plain at once that Byron's secret intrigues have been revealed to the king, La Fin having made a full confession. With such a witness against him, his most trusted friend, Byron seems unlikely to be able to maintain his stance of outraged virtue whenever treachery is mentioned. However it is also apparent that 'politic' means are going to have to be used to lure Byron back to court to face his trial. The king finds himself forced to praise the civic virtues of an informer he had formerly characterised as 'fiend-like', the veritable dregs of society. He now decides to send off messengers to Byron asking him to return to court 'Without the slenderest intimation / Of any ill we know'. When the king turns to 'good La Fin' and bids him write to Byron to assure him that all is well at court, when he also asks La Fin to send these lying letters to Byron 'By some choice friend of his, or by his brother', the deviousness of his policy is made very evident. The king is not necessarily condemned but there is a slight shift in the balance of sympathy. Byron himself notes the king's 'mizzling breath of policy' when the series of messengers begins to arrive, but unfortunately for him, he does not delve deeply enough into the king's tactics.

The masque scene, which makes up a very brief Act II, has been criticised for having very little relevance, if any, to what is going on in the play. There has also been discussion about whether the act has been cut since it is so brief and lacks an act heading in the quarto, unlike all the other acts. As it stands, the masque is a celebration of the new concord between the queen and the king's mistress after some kind of dispute between them. The quarrel scene which the French ambassador described in his letter and which he strongly objected to has, of course, been cut out by the censor. An actual quarrel on stage, including the reported slap on the face, would have given much more dramatic point to this scene and to the king's pleasure in their reconciliation. Such a scene might have been placed at the beginning of Act II, as Parrott believed, or possibly a little earlier, between I.ii and I.iii, thus allowing La Fin dramatic time to travel from Byron's headquarters to the court. Chapman is generally careful about such matters.

Assuming some such original form, one might argue that not only would the serious action of the play receive a touch of lightness and festivity in the comedy of a trivial quarrel and the music and dancing of the masque; there would also be a contrapuntal voice to the general theme of discord and attempts at reconciliation in the kingdom. A somewhat different argument is advanced by Ure who says that the masque 'contains something in the nature of a reply to Byron's pose as the neglected peacetime soldier (ll.5–10), and the whole theme of the masque is an answer to his charge that sensual vice informs the kingdom ....'[85] One must admit, nevertheless, that the connection of the lyric celebration of virtue in the masque to the main action of the play is very tenuous, and that perhaps Chapman wanted to do no more than add variety to the spectacle, using the resources of a children's company and including the spice of gossip. The stage direction for the entrance of the masquers is '*Music and a song above*'. Singing as well as the accomplished speaking of lyrical or rhetorical verse had always been among the skills of the children's companies. Dance and further music are mentioned in a second stage direction after Cupid has begged for room to allow the measures to proceed. The bawdy riddle pronounced by Cupid, another courtly game of extensive tradition, is explicated in highly moral terms by Epernon. However, Epernon's misinterpretation, with its heavy stress on individual phrases, seems designed to raise laughter at every line. One must be inclined in the end, I think, to see the masque scene and whatever quarrel scene preceded it merely as light-hearted diversion from the growing intensity of the tragic design.

The play moves back and forth between Henry and Byron. In his provincial fortress, Byron is meditating upon statecraft and authority and sharing his thoughts with D'Auvergne who complains that he does not need such 'deep discourses' to enforce his loyalty to his friend. Byron condemns the kind of statecraft advocated by certain schools of thought in 'ingenious Italy' which is supposed to preserve a prince but leads to his destruction, and contrasts such policy with true authority which is derived from heaven. The whole speech seems at odds with the Catiline-like complaints and threats of Act I, Scene ii. It is curious that a powerful noble engaged in a conspiracy against his lawful sovereign should so attack Machiavellian doctrines and lament the appearance of the 'two abhorred twins', war and liberty, in contemporary society whereby 'the lamp of all authority goes out'. Yet Byron refuses always to acknowledge to himself that he may be acting traitorously or that he is undermining true authority. Here, as elsewhere in the play, he shows his fondness for moralising upon large questions of state from the point of view of a 'royal freedom', as if oblivious of his own obligations and responsibilities. He is also inclined to see himself as superior in his own proud manhood to lesser kings who can be condemned in such phrases as:

>   ... so are kings' revolts
> And playing both ways with religion
> Fore-runners of afflictions imminent.   (*Trag.*, III.i.45–7)

In his view, it is Henry who is forgetful of his obligations to his subjects, as the opening lines of the speech remind us: 'Dear friend, we must not be more true to kings / Than kings are to their subjects ...' (III.i.1–2), a statement which would sound as heretical at the court of James as it would at the court of Henry IV.[86] Whether there is an indirect and scornful reference to Henry's change of religion for the sake of supreme power in France in the phrase 'playing both ways with religion' must remain doubtful since it is not referred to anywhere else in the double play. Yet there are certainly indications in the speech of Byron's continuing criticism of princes who are interested only in power, in contrast with older ideals of the natural and God-given authority associated with heroic virtue. Such criticism is appropriate enough to Byron's role as self-declared saviour of the state. The emphasis on authority may not be altogether consonant with his rebellious individualistic temperament, but it does reflect his constant tendency to self-justification.

As the messengers from the king enter one after the other, Byron regards them with considerable suspicion. He will not be drawn to court by covert means: 'Blows, batteries, breaches, showers of steel and blood / Must be his downright messengers for me ...' (III.i.130–

1). Yet it is exactly the covert means, the 'mizzling breath of policy', which works upon him as he reads the letter from La Fin. His friends warn him of the danger of placing himself in the king's power and specifically warn him against too much trust in La Fin, but he wilfully pushes all such warnings aside in what can only be called blind folly and pride.

Byron returns to court at the very moment that Henry is declaring that he will not come. R. A. Foakes has complained that the confrontations between Byron and the king are static and that the play suffers as a result.[87] Yet the scene of Byron's return, like the later scene just before his arrest, is a major scene of confrontation, theatrically shaped, filled with powerful, shifting emotions, and highly ironic in the tragic sense since Byron knows nothing about La Fin's betrayal. Byron justifies the slowness of his return with staunch independence of mind and without flattery or pretence, maintaining that the king would never have been able to bring him in by force. When the king hints broadly that serious charges will be brought against him, he stubbornly declares his innocence, his freedom from all disloyal thoughts. The clash between them is postponed to another occasion as they go off to a game of tennis, but Henry warns Byron that much that is hidden will soon be brought to light.

Between this scene and Byron's arrest, Chapman draws a portrait of an old favourite out of favour. Though there is good reason for the king's frowning countenance, Byron and D'Auvergne comment on the crowd of time-servers surrounding the king and on the universal contempt with which they themselves are regarded:

> Now courtship goes a-ditching in their foreheads,
> And we are fallen into those dismal ditches;
> Why, even thus dreadfully would they be rapt
> If the king's buttered eggs were only spilt.   (*Trag.*, IV.i.86–9)

The satiric thrust of these speeches and the implied behaviour of the courtiers on stage is scarcely diluted by our knowledge of Byron's actual guilt. Chapman could rarely refrain from critical comments upon courtly society. In *Bussy D'Ambois* it is Bussy himself who provides the satiric commentary, particularly when the king urges him 'Speak home, Bussy!' (III.ii.1ff). In *The Revenge*, Baligny and Renel comment cynically upon the attitudes of courtiers in the opening scene and throughout the play; the somewhat more philosophical discourses of Clermont and the Guise add substance to the portrayal. In *Chabot* it is the Lord Chancellor and the Treasurer who display the nature of courtly 'policy' directed toward self-advancement at the expense of everyone else. The satiric element in *The Tragedy* is apparent but less pervasive than in others of Chapman's tragedies since Chapman is concerned to show that the king's insistence on justice remains valid. Nevertheless he has no hesitation in demonstrating less admirable qualities in the councillors around the king. They urge him to suppress his scruples, to act arbitrarily without the proper forms of justice, arguing that a king can perform such acts for the good of the state. As Ornstein points out, 'the political philosophy of his ministers is explicitly Machiavellian in theory and terminology'.[88]

Although there is some truth in Byron's observations about the subservience of courtiers to the whims and moods of a king, his total refusal to admit to any wrong-doing or to ask pardon suggests that he may really believe himself to be innocent. His belief in the greatness of his achievement as saviour of France and his absolute faith in his own powers of self-determination and judgement are the factors which give him such an astonishing confidence, a confidence which the audience increasingly regards as an overmastering delusion. Henry has not only much greater real power in the state, as D'Auvergne warns Byron; he is also politically and morally in the right. When Henry prays that he may act justly on the basis of the deepest consideration, and when he gives Byron what is clearly a last chance to confess his guilt, Chapman weights the balance firmly in Henry's favour. If ever there was a time when Byron should have bent his stubborn knee, this was the occasion, but Byron refuses to give way.

The whole scene of the card and chess games, of Byron's deliberately double-edged remarks to the queen about the ingratitude of kings, and of Henry's veiled comments in reply is developed with tragic suspense and irony of a high degree. Henry's final plea to his wilfully blind friend and his abrupt decision to act maintain the tension to the moment of the arrest. Henry confronts Byron once more after the arrest, outraged by Byron's continued adherence to the role of saviour of France and innocent victim, and this time he does not mince the severity of his words. Thereafter they do not meet again.

Henry's last appearance in the play (V.i) shows him with his councillors dealing with the continuing business of ruling the kingdom as he gives audience to the Spanish ambassador, asks his advisers about the effect abroad of Byron's arrest and enquires about the prisoners' reaction to their restraint. A graphic account of Byron's rage in prison brings only a moralising comment from Henry on what others should learn from his fate. He then concludes the scene with a brief statement celebrating the power he has achieved in his 'sun of height', beyond rivalry or envy. The passage effectively brings to an end the political movement of the play, from the threat of conspiracy and war in the kingdom to order finally secured, but the tone of the speech can only be described as one of smug satisfaction. Ornstein suggests that in his concentration on Byron's tragic fall, Chapman may simply have 'overlooked the need for a more positive political and moral affirmation at the end'. Nevertheless when this final statement is taken in combination with Henry's statement a few lines earlier on the peers who refuse to appear for the arraignment of Byron:

> I am resolved, and will no more endure
> To have my subjects make what I command
> The subject of their oppositions .... (*Trag.*, V.i.96–8)

one can sense, as Goldstein does, Chapman's deep-seated unease with royal absolutism.[89]

The trial itself is presented in a dramatically condensed fashion, when compared with the source: the major charges against Byron are read out and Byron makes a reasoned and comparatively brief defence against each of them. He is then, to his astonishment, confronted by La Fin who confirms the charges 'And so much more, as, had the prisoner lives / As many as his years, would make all forfeit' (V.ii.134–5). Enraged as well as astonished, Byron makes an impassioned, disordered speech, veering widely between denunciations of La Fin and declarations of his own valour and greatness which cannot be perceived by 'the owly eye / Of politic and thankless royalty' (ll.182–3). He proclaims the heroic ideal, whereby a single man can prop up a kingdom or subdue an empire, to a society and a king that he thinks have forgotten the nature of such an ideal. Yet clearly apparent in the speech, also, is Byron's inability to justify or account for the influence La Fin has had over him and his strong feeling that he has been trapped by placing himself in the hands of contemptible lesser men.

The trial is not rigged in advance, as Chabot's trial is: Byron's guilt is apparent in documents as well as in testimony. But it is obvious that the verdict has never been in doubt since the pre-trial discussions between the king and his councillors. After an implied promise to Byron that he will be heard again, the judges come quickly and unanimously to their decision.

There is a splendid theatricalism about the final scenes of the play, much of it derived from Grimeston's account where the extreme passions of the central actor in his last hours are vividly described. From the moment that Byron steps into the 'golden chamber' as a prisoner before scarlet-clad judges, contrasts between past honours and present humiliation are strikingly evident.[90] One can speculate about the staging. It seems likely that the tiring house would have been decorated with gold hangings, and no doubt chairs of state were brought in for the four splendidly attired judges. There would also be a bar where the prisoner was expected to stand. It is in this setting that Byron laments the change in his fortunes. During the trial and on the way to the scaffold, the battling emotions that afflict Byron are presented in vivid detail: his outrage against the judges and bitter reproaches to the chancellor, his scorn for the bishop, his sudden warmth of feeling when the old soldier speaks and his violent threats against the executioner.

But it is not with theatrical effect that Chapman is mainly concerned. In these final scenes, he is presenting a character stretched to the limit, racked by alternating moods of confidence and fear, as he finds himself struggling against forces that will not yield. It is the same character that Chapman has developed over nine acts, subject to outbursts of choler, stubbornly proud of his great military achievements, still a prey to self-delusion about his frequently proclaimed innocence. He continues to look upon himself as a martyr to the machinations of others, a victim of injustice and envy. His false optimism after the trial about the effect of his oratory upon the court (the audience already knows the verdict) is followed by sudden fears as he hears shouts and cries from without, and even to the last moment he looks for a reprieve. Yet gradually he is drawn to see his fate as inescapable, and slowly he comes to recognise his final dependence upon his own spiritual resources. He has nothing else left. As MacLure points out, 'the prolonged Herculean rage of a glorious spirit fastened to a dying animal, the furious wild boar at bay' is calmed as 'he is helped out of his frenzy by the last-minute tribute to his "better Angel" from a soldier standing by and rises finally out of himself to make the true Herculean discovery that he is one of the community of man'.[91] By such means Chapman shows this proud, rash, choleric man discovering a dignity that is greater than the pomp and honour of the earthly glory he had once enjoyed.

There is pride and self-assertion at the end: it has often been noted that Byron himself chooses the moment at which the executioner should strike. But there is also a strong sense of loss in his final statement, a lament for the human being who dies and does not return again to this earth, though the seasons pass and life is renewed. The elements are mixed in the final tragic effect of the play, just as they have been in the portrait of Byron throughout.

Chapman has given his hero a kind of apotheosis at the end of the play, transforming the rebellious and ambitious noble of the political morality, as Ure says, 'to an archetype of the dying tragic hero'.[92] Yet the question remains: does the structure of the play shift markedly toward tragedy in these final scenes? I would argue that although the double play is strikingly political in its issues and conflicts, as much so as *Sejanus* or *Coriolanus*, a tragic structure is evident from an early point in *The Conspiracy*. This structure grows out of one of the well-established patterns of Elizabethan tragedy: ambition, pride and wilful blindness in the central figure in conflict with harsh circumstances imposed by fate or destiny so that an ironic tension is created which can only be released by a tragic catastrophe. Woven into this structure is the moralistic interpretation of events which sees the breaking of moral laws concerned with truth, loyalty and allegiance as inevitably followed by retribution. The fact that the two structures co-exist does not imply confusion: they represent different possible ways of interpreting the same experience. Renaissance tragedy often seems to find its characteristic tensions in the conflict between a view of the world as a place where moral laws operate with great severity and a view of the world as a place where aspiring, wilful, strong-minded individuals suffer defeat because of their very aspiration or defiance.

The tragic pattern of blind pride and fall is pointed to in choral passages, like those spoken by Prâlin, Vitry and Epernon as they wait to hear whether Byron will return to court to face the charges against him (*Trag.*, III.ii.3–30). The captain of Byron's guard who brings him warnings of danger after he has returned to court comments in even stronger terms:

> Yet doth that senseless apoplexy dull you?
> The devil or your wicked angel blinds you,
> Bereaving all your reason of a man,
> And leaves you but the spirit of a horse
> In your brute nostrils: only power to dare.   (*Trag.*, IV.i.106–10)

During the trial, Byron himself recognises, at least in part, this fault or failure within his own aspiring, questing nature:

> What man is he
> That is so high but he would higher be?
> So roundly sighted but he may be found
> To have a blind side, which by craft pursued,

> Confederacy, and simply trusted treason,
> May wrest him past his angel and his reason? (*Trag.*, V.ii.168–73)

However, the tragic pattern is broadened and deepened in the final scenes of the play through the poetic intensity Chapman gives to the language and the imaginative power of his images. Byron's bitter complaints against the world that frustrates his aspirations and hinders his dreams of self-realisation are given greater emotional force as Byron is increasingly isolated and stripped of his worldly rewards. The moral pattern is never lost sight of, particularly in the stress Chapman gives to Henry's inner conflict over the action he must take, his obvious concern that justice should be done, and the prayer he utters before the moment of decision. Byron is undoubtedly guilty of the charges brought against him and wrong in his stubborn pride, but the play allows some worth to his dreams of greatness and some validity to his sense of betrayal. As Hibbard writes:

> Not only is Chapman intensely aware in this play of the conflict that can arise between the moral law and the need of the individual for self-determination, but he also shares with the Marlowe who wrote *Doctor Faustus* a sense of the tragic position of Renaissance man in a universe that he was coming to know better than it had been known before, but which he could not influence .... [93]

One of the clearest pointers to the tragic irony of the play lies in the choral passage spoken by Epernon after Byron has received notice of sentence of death. It should be read in the context of the other choral speeches of the same scene, but its emphatic position as the first of the comments, from a character who is generally shown to be sympathetic to Byron, though loyal to Henry, gives it a special significance:

> O of what contraries consists a man!
> Of what impossible mixtures! Vice and virtue,
> Corruption and eternesse, at one time,
> And in one subject, let together loose.
> We have not any strength but weakens us,
> No greatness but doth crush us into air.
> Our knowledges do light us but to err,
> Our ornaments are burthens, our delights
> Are our tormentors, fiends that raised in fears
> At parting shake our roofs about our ears. (*Trag.*, V.iii.189–98)

It is 'corruption and eternesse', that 'impossible mixture', that Byron learns to cope with before he dies. The tragic formulation which this speech expresses is not an afterthought in the play but the development of a pattern that is apparent from the beginning and gives the double play its toughness and its emotional force as tragedy.

In attempting to reach a balanced view of the play, critics have not been slow to point out its obvious dramatic faults.[94] It is too long and becomes tedious at times because of its repetitious quality: more than one critic has wished that Chapman had concentrated the material into a single play.[95] It is also lacking in action and there is too little variety in the kinds of action it presents, though one should note that reported action (rather than staged action), ceremony and ritual, and the rhetorical expansion of dialogue were characteristic of tragedy at the private theatres where the skills of the boy actors were exploited in these directions. More important, perhaps, is the claim that because of repetition and irrelevancies, it lacks the compulsive drive that tragedy demands. As for characterisation, one is struck by the absence of subordinate characters with any sense of life about them: they are observers of the drama, sometimes actors in the main events, but seldom have a function beyond that of attendance upon the primary figures. Occasionally one or two of them act as chorus, commenting upon the meaning of the action and the nature of Byron's character and ambition. The major characters have a greater depth but they are rarely shown to us in any intimate moments. There is more 'inwardness' in the portrait of Henry than there is in the portrait of Byron. Byron usually addresses his friend, D'Auvergne, as if he were a public seminar meeting, and his soliloquies and monologues have a rhetorical organisation that suggests the epic or the older neo-Senecan drama. Yet when all these faults have been admitted, Chapman's achievement in developing an appropriate tragic form for his thoughtful and often profound exploration of human experience, political and spiritual, remains a remarkable one.

(e) Verse and imagery
The quality of the dialogue and the nature of the verse and imagery demand a little more attention at this point. Much of the dialogue of the play consists of long speeches, often elaborately shaped. *Bussy D'Ambois* and other tragedies of Chapman have such speeches too, but there is often more of the give and take of conversation in these plays than in *Byron*. There is a considerable rhetorical interest in speeches of persuasion like Picoté's, or the king's long speech at the end of *The Conspiracy*; the heroic narratives of great battles of the past, in Savoy's description to Henry of Byron's achievements, have

an epic scope to them. Rhetorical elaboration, however, is not Chapman's only reason for the large-scale speeches of the play. It seems clear that he wished to lift the action and the characters from the realistic contemporary moment (though this is never lost sight of) to a larger and more permanent context: it is his method of universalising the story. There are times when a modern audience would like greater intimacy in the forms of address, more individuality in the speaking voices of different characters. Chapman was certainly capable of this sort of thing, but no doubt it seemed contrary to his sense of the artistic integrity of the whole.

There is much variety in the verse of the play in spite of the epic qualities we have been noting. Byron's first speech at the archduke's court (a soliloquy) is a rapturous expression of his dreams of aspiration, crowded with images from the classics. The flow of verse has something of Marlowe's freedom of rhythm and cumulative power.[96] The speeches of persuasion and temptation are closely reasoned in compact groups of lines:

> The habit of a servile loyalty
> Is reckoned now amongst privations,
> With blindness, dumbness, deafness, silence, death,
> All which are neither natures by themselves
> Nor substances but mere decays of form
> And absolute decessions of nature;
> And so, 'tis nothing, what shall you then lose? (*Consp.*, I.ii.89–95)

Passages of philosophical reflection have the serious dignity that we associate with the best of Chapman's non-dramatic verse:

> O the strange difference 'twixt us and the stars:
> They work with inclinations strong and fatal
> And nothing know, and we know all their working
> And nought can do, or nothing can prevent!
> Rude ignorance is beastly, knowledge wretched;
> The heavenly powers envy what they enjoin .... (*Consp.*, III.iii.5–10)

Sometimes, such reflective passages echo or transpose lines from his poems: thus much of Epernon's choral comment on Byron at the time of his fall, 'O of what contraries consists a man' (*Trag.*, V.iii.189–98) is found also in *The Teares of Peace* (ll.676–83) which was published in 1609 but may have been written earlier.[97] Noteworthy also is Chapman's ironic control, in a dramatic sense, over the hyperbolic passages he puts into Byron's mouth, as over the narratives of Savoy, so that every exaggeration is nicely calculated for its effect.[98] There is perhaps less dramatic control over epic similes which illustrate the philosophical observations and the deductions he draws from these, or which enlarge upon emotion or touch upon the basic themes of the play. Chapman sometimes seems carried away by the potentiality for enlargement lying within a particular image.

A notable example occurs in the confrontation between Henry and Byron in Act III, Scene ii, of *The Conspiracy*. Henry condemns Byron for choosing such a friend as La Fin whom he describes in a series of dark and violent images, concluding with 'La Fiend and not La Fin he should be called'. Byron's reply makes use of equally strong images, contrasting men 'in themselves entire' who 'march safe with naked feet on coals of fire' with the servility of those who worship the power of princes:

> The stallion, power, hath such a besom tail
> That it sweeps all from justice .... (*Consp.*, III.ii.236–7)

Henry's lengthy response warns Byron against treason, but at this point, in order to describe the evil effects of flattery, Henry launches into an elaborate simile about the poet who is praised to the skies by those he has begged to supply 'heralds' for his book:

> And as a glorious poem fronted well
> With many a goodly herald of his praise,
> So far from hate of praises to his face
> That he prays men to praise him, and they ride
> Before, with trumpets in their mouths, proclaiming
> Life to the holy fury of his lines – (*Consp.*, III.ii.247–52)

and so on, for ten more lines. It is all very interesting in terms of Chapman's attitude to publishing practices of the time, the gathering together of literary friends to vouch for one's artistic genius, but it moves in a rather startling fashion away from the substance of the quarrel between Henry and Byron.

Yet there are many more images which are part of the close texture of plot, character and idea and which seem emotionally appropriate to dramatic situation. Some of these, as we have noted already, are expansions of the major themes of the play, touching them with the kind of imaginative intensity that properly belongs to poetic drama. The language of the play is constantly figurative, not in the compressed, elliptical form of Shakespeare's late plays but in the expansive, large-scale fashion associated with epic poetry.

The verse itself is marked by rather more rhyme than one might

INTRODUCTION 53

expect in blank verse of the period. Speeches commonly end with rhyming couplets or with two pairs of couplets; there are also rhyming couplets within speeches. Chapman has a fondness, too, for alliteration to stress certain words or to shape patterns of sound within the line:

> If they bring me out, they shall see I'll hatch
> Like to the blackthorn that puts forth his leaf,
> Not with the golden fawnings of the sun,
> But sharpest showers of hail and blackest frosts:
> Blows, batteries, breaches, showers of steel and blood
> Must be his downright messengers for me,
> And not the mizzling breath of policy ....   (*Trag.*, III.i.126–32)

As the same passage indicates, stress and rhythm are frequently varied to suit the meaning. Since the speeches tend to be long, the verse paragraph is an important element of structure, and may vary from two or three lines to ten or fifteen. Rhythm, syntax and meaning work admirably together in these paragraphs: when there is an outpouring of emotion – rising aspiration, anger, contempt, bitterness – the vigorous movement of the verse matches the emotion. Though rhetorical organisation and the large-scale elaboration of similes may suggest epic, the verse of the play is primarily dramatic.

8. STAGE HISTORY

Mention has already been made of the early performances of *The Conspiracy and Tragedy of Byron* by the Children of Blackfriars in 1608 and the subsequent difficulties which led to the arrest of several members of the company.[99] There is no specific record of further performances; however, the imprint of the 1625 quarto adds to the original 1608 title-page 'Acted lately in two Playes, at the Blacke-friers' the new phrase 'and other publique Stages'. The re-issue of the play during Chapman's lifetime, the only one of his plays to have been so re-issued, may possibly indicate renewed interest after a revival.

There is no evidence of later productions apart from a mention of the title, *Byrons Conspiracy*, in a list of plays 'allowed to the Duke's Company' at the theatre in Lincolns Inn Fields, dated August 1668.[100]

It is remarkable how little direct information there is about the acting skills of the child actors. Jonson's tribute to Salomon Pavey for his great ability in acting the parts of old men is well known, and the parts written for women, especially in tragedy, by playwrights like

Shakespeare and Webster who were closely associated with the theatre may suggest exceptional talent in boy actors with the adult companies. It is clear that the children's companies were popular and attracted much attention in the first decade of the seventeenth century, though whether this was because of the topicality of their plays, the novelty of the city comedies, their involvement in controversy and scandal, or whether it had anything to do with high standards of acting and production we have few means of judging. The variety of the plays they acted and some of the skills they must have had in being able to present such plays successfully have been discussed by a number of scholars.[101] On the evidence of the plays, M. Shapiro has postulated different acting styles for different plays, or even for parts of plays: a naturalistic style for city comedy, a formal declamatory style for tragedy which deliberately sets a greater distance between spectator and action, and another variety of the formal style which Shapiro calls parodic, though it is difficult to imagine any acting company of the time, children's or adult, making such clear-cut distinctions.[102] Each play makes its own demands, and no doubt stage tradition would also play a part: these are likely to have been the major factors. Reavley Gair, on the other hand, sees a development in the repertoire and hence acting styles of Paul's boys in the first eight years of the seventeenth century, from Marston's Antonio plays and the War of the Theatres plays to a less sensational and more distinctly moral kind of drama, due in part to the changing management of the company and to the increasing puritan attacks on the theatre.[103] He also documents the growing older of the boy actors during the period so that they were often referred to as 'youths'; as well as changing in size and voice, the senior boy-actors gained in experience as actors. Such a consideration must give us pause when we think of the first presentation of *Bussy D'Ambois*, for example, in the later period of the company.[104] The Children of Blackfriars, the main rivals of the Children of Paul's, may well have gone through a similar development between 1600 and 1608.

In tragedy, it seems likely that the boy or young-men actors made good use of their school training in rhetoric[105] and turned what might have been considered disadvantages (size, voice, personal presence, etc.) to positive virtues by emphasising poise, vocal modulation and gesture.[106] Writers like Chapman, Jonson and Marston (in *Sophonisba*) wrote tragedies for them which gave their particular gifts for rhetoric and poetry full scope, while avoiding colloquial speech and action which might have encouraged mimicry in the actors and amusement in the audience. Decorum was obviously important in a play like *The Conspiracy and Tragedy*, as Shapiro again notes, which presented monarchs and great nobles on the stage.[107]

A Note on Spelling and Punctuation
In general, the punctuation of the 1608 quarto has been followed since it seems to be related not only to syntax but also to rhetorical patterns and the requirements of actors' delivery. However there is much lightening of the punctuation in order to make the text readable and useful: the very numerous semi-colons are often reduced to commas, or altered to full stops where sense demands, and brackets are for the most part altered to commas. Similarly the constant use of capital letters in the quarto has been considerably reduced. In his edition of *Bussy D'Ambois*, Nicholas Brooke suggested tentatively that Chapman's use of capital letters may indicate a kind of emphasis, but one cannot be sure enough about this to make it an essential part of the text. Capital letters have been retained for personifications where these seemed to have a special figurative importance.

Elisions have been avoided, in line with the practice of the Revels editions, except where metre demands them. The quarto is carefully printed in this respect, particularly where the second person singular of the verb is to be sounded or elided.

This edition has followed Parrott in the spelling of names of characters. In the quarto, 'La Fin' sometimes appears as 'Laffin' but the former has been chosen for the sake of consistency. 'Soissons' is also variable, often appearing as 'Soisson'. The quarto consistently spells 'Epernon' as 'Espernon', but since this latter form appears only once in the dialogue, it seemed unnecessary to alter the generally accepted modern form.

Collation
I have collated fifteen copies of the 1608 quarto, chiefly from xerox copies, from the following university and other libraries: Bodleian, Boston Public Library, British Library (two copies, C.12.g.5 and C.30.e.2), California (Clark Library), Chapin Library (Williams College), Folger, Harvard, Huntington, Pennsylvania, Texas (one of four copies), Victoria and Albert Museum (Dyce), Worcester College (two copies, one *Consp.* only). Ray has collated seven additional copies, though one is mutilated. I have also collated with the V. & A. 1608 quarto two copies of the 1625 quarto from the British Library and Cambridge.

NOTES TO INTRODUCTION

1. MacLure, p. 132.
2. See Brooke, pp. xix–xxvi; also MacLure and Jacquot.
3. MacLure, p. 16.
4. Epistle to *Seaven Bookes of the Iliads*, 1598.
5. Jacquot, p. 48.
6. MacLure, p. 21; R. Ornstein, 'The Dates of Chapman's Tragedies Once More', *M.P.*, LIX (1961), 61; C. Leech, 'Three Times *Ho* and a Brace of Widows: some Plays for the Private Theatre', *Elizabethan Theatre*, III, ed. David Galloway (1973), 27; A. Nicoll, 'The Dramatic Portrait of George Chapman', *P.Q.*, XLI (1962), 222ff.
7. Jacquot, p. 4.
8. F. S. Boas, 'Edward Grimeston, Translator and Sergeant-at-arms', *M.P.*, III (1906), 397. See also G. N. Clark, *Eng. Hist. Rev.*, XLIII (1928), 585–98.
9. Boas, pp. 395–7; Jacquot, p. 13; MacLure, p. 7.
10. Herford and Simpson, II, 4, 6.
11. *Ibid.*, I, 31.
12. *Ibid.*, I, 198; B. Dobell, *Athenaeum* (30 March 1901), p. 403.
13. Herford and Simpson, I, 198.
14. B. Dobell, *Athenaeum* (6 April 1901), p. 433.
15. 'Ludovick Stuart', *D.N.B.* Lennox appears to have kept in touch with his relatives and to have helped them when he could. During his visit to Paris in February, 1604/5, he obtained Henry's remission of a severe sentence upon M. D'Entragues, D'Auvergne, and 'the lady Marquise' who had been implicated in a breach-of-promise suit against the king: see *Salisbury Papers*, XVII (1938), 53.
16. See p. 10.
17. Parrott, p. 591.
18. R. A. Foakes and R. T. Rickert, *Henslowe's Diary* (Cambridge, 1961), pp. 216, 217.
19. Dekker and Webster, *Northward Ho*, *The Dramatic Works of Thomas Dekker*, ed. F. Bowers, II, 449.
20. Dobell, *Athenaeum* (6 April 1901), p. 433. See pp. 11, 12 below and Appendix II.
21. Nicoll, 'The Dramatic Portrait of George Chapman', p. 224; E. Schwartz, 'The Date of Chapman's Byron Plays', *M.P.*, LVIII (1961), 201–2.
22. Ornstein, 'The Dates of Chapman's Tragedies Once More', *M.P.*, LIX (1961), 61–4.
23. Leech, 'Three Times *Ho*', p. 27.
24. J. B. Gabel, 'The Date of Chapman's *Conspiracy and Tragedy*', *M.P.*, LXVI (1968–9), 331.
25. R. Hosley, 'The Playhouses', *The Revels History of Drama in English*, III (London, 1975), 228–9.

26 H. N. Hillebrand, *The Child Actors: A Chapter in Elizabethan Stage History* (Urbana, 1926), pp. 192–201; Glynne Wickham, *Early English Stages*, vol. II, pt. II, pp. 129–36.
27 Ben Jonson's 'Epitaph on S.P. a Child of Q. El. Chappel' is a warm and graceful tribute to one such actor; Nathaniel (or Nathan) Field gained a reputation as a child actor, later as an adult actor with the King's Men and a playwright. He acted the part of Bussy D'Ambois in 1607, and Chapman addressed verses to 'his loved son, Nat Field, and his Weathercock Woman' when Field's play, *A Woman is a Weathercock*, was printed in 1612. See Wickham, *Early English Stages*, vol. II, pt. II, p. 136.
28 G. K. Hunter, *Antonio and Mellida The First Part* (London, 1965), p. xvi. See also introductions to Revels Plays editions of *Antonio's Revenge* (R. Gair, 1978), *Eastward Ho* (R. Van Fossen, 1979), *The Malcontent* (G. K. Hunter, 1975); also R. Gair, *The Children of Paul's: The Story of a Theatre Company 1553–1608* (Cambridge, 1982). Note further discussion on pp. 53–5.
29 See p. 1 above.
30 R. A. Foakes, 'Tragedy at the Children's Theatres after 1600: A Challenge to the Adult Stage', *Elizabethan Theatre*, II, ed. David Galloway (1970), 55.
31 See p. 67.
32 See pp. 4, 10.
33 See p. 11.
34 Parrott (p. 607) notes the observations of Fleay and Koeppel.
35 See Appendix II for a translation of La Boderie's letter.
36 Jacquot, p. 41.
37 E. K. Chambers, *The Elizabethan Stage*, III, 53–4.
38 The best known intervention is that of the Spanish ambassador, Gondomar, who had been caricatured on the stage along with his master in Thomas Middleton's *A Game at Chess* in 1624.
39 Sir Ralph Winwood, *Memorials of the Affairs of State in the Reigns of Queen Elizabeth and King James I* (London, 1725), I, 398, 425.
40 The letters which Dobell believed to be Chapman's were published in the *Athenaeum* on 30 March 1901, p. 403, and 6 April 1901, p. 433. See Appendix II.
41 Jacquot refers to the opinion of Mr Giles Dawson of the Folger Library that the letters had been collected together as models of letters of various kinds (p. 12, n. 33).
42 J. B. Gabel, 'The Original Version of Chapman's Tragedy of Byron', *J.E.G.P.*, LXIII (1964), 433–40.
43 MacLure, p. 20n.
44 *Ibid.*, p. 20n.; Ray, pp. 384–5.
45 Parrott, p. 623.
46 Brooke, pp. lxxv–lxxvi.
47 The title-page reads: 'The Conspiracie, and Tragedie of Charles Duke of

Byron, Marshall of France. Acted lately in two playes, at the Black-Friers. Written by George Chapman. Printed by G. Eld for Thomas Thorppe ... 1608'. The title-page of the second quarto is: 'The Conspiracie, and Tragoedy of Charles Duke of Byron, Marshall of France. Acted lately in two Playes, at the Black-Friers, and other publique Stages. Written by George Chapman. London. Printed by N.O. for Thomas Thorp. 1625.' The double play was entered in the Stationers Register on 5 June 1608: 'Ent. T. Thorp: lic. G. Buck: a booke called The Conspiracy and Tragedie of Charles Duke of Byronn, by Georg Chapman, single fee.'

48 R. B. McKerrow (ed.), *A Dictionary of Printers and Booksellers in England, Scotland and Ireland ... 1557-1640* (London, 1910).

49 F. S. Boas, 'The Source of Chapman's *The Conspiracie and Tragedie of Charles, Duke of Byron* and *The Revenge of Bussy D'Ambois*', *Athenaeum* (10 Jan. 1903), pp. 51-2. Cf. Parrott, p. 594.

50 E. Schwartz, 'The Date of Chapman's Byron Plays', *M.P.*, LVIII (1961), p. 201.

51 See Appendix III for a discussion of the Essex parallels.

52 Parrott, p. 607.

53 *Consp.*, II.i.107ff.n. and *Consp.*, III.ii.142n.

54 Schoell, *Études* and 'Commonplace Book'; Ferguson; Loane, 'Notes ...'; and 'More Notes ...'; Parrott, 'The Text'; Jacquot.

55 See *Consp.*, I.i.85-90 and 198-203. For the birth of the dauphin, see *Consp.*, IV.i.144.

56 See *Consp.*, V.i.20ff.

57 A. Leggatt, 'Tone and Structure in Chapman's *Byron*', *S.E.L.*, XXIV (Spring 1984), 307-26.

58 Brooke, p. xxii; MacLure, pp. 6off.; E. Rees, 'Chapman's *Blind Beggar* and the Marlovian Hero', *J.E.G.P.*, LVII (1958), 60-3.

59 R. S. Ide, *Possessed with Greatness, the Heroic Tragedies of Chapman and Shakespeare* (London, 1980) p. 15.

60 Chambers in *Eliz. Stage*, III, 276, states that The Apology is fixed by its own data to the autumn of 1604, and he lists it with the first edition of the play in 1605. There has been much disagreement about whether it was added to some copies of the 1605 quarto, since none with this addition seem to exist today. The Apology was printed with the *Whole Works* in 1623. L. Michel in his edition of the play (*The Tragedy of Philotas by Samuel Daniel*, New Haven, 1949) believes it was written in 1605, the year Daniel was called before the Council: pp. 39-42.

61 Michel, *op. cit.*, pp. 156, 157. Cf. Spenser's 'Letter to Raleigh' concerning possible misconstructions of *The Faerie Queene*. Annabel Patterson in a recent book, *Censorship and Interpretation* (Madison, 1984), has shown how writers from the middle of the sixteenth century had, as a result of censorship, developed 'a system of communication in which ambiguity becomes a creative and necessary instrument ...' (p. 11). In a chapter concerned with Jonson's strategies in *Sejanus*, she writes; 'Censorship

INTRODUCTION 59

encouraged the use of historical or other uninvented texts, such as translations from the classics, which both allowed an author to limit his authorial responsibility for the text ... and, paradoxically, provided an interpretive mechanism' (p. 57).

62 Chapman's complaint to Sir George Buc (if the Dobell letters are genuine) is revealing: 'Whosoever it were that first plaied the bitter Informer before the French Ambassador for a matter so far from offence; And of so much honor for his maister ...'. See Appendix II.

63 Parrott, p. 77.

64 MacLure, p. 112. Cf. Jacquot, p. 150.

65 In a generally Marxist interpretation of Chapman's tragedies, Leonard Goldstein observes of *Byron*: 'We watch not so much a political play as a morality play concerning the corruption and fall of a man who has lost his virtue' (*George Chapman: Aspects of Decadence in Early Seventeenth Century Drama* (Salzburg, 1975), p. 360).

66 Parrott, p. 614.

67 Grimeston, p. 992.

68 *Ibid.*, p. 816.

69 *Ibid.*, p. 966.

70 *Ibid.*, p. 993.

71 The argument of Ennis Rees that Chapman has made 'Byron completely in the wrong', that he is 'the living embodiment of that chaotic and destructive nature which is opposed to the divine and rational world which Chapman reverenced' (pp. 52-3) is a moralistic interpretation that many critics have found simplistic (E. Rees, *The Tragedies of George Chapman: Renaissance Ethics in Action*, Cambridge, 1954). MacLure (pp. 9, 110ff.) and Ide (*Possessed with Greatness*, p. 11) are among those who have criticised his view of the play, as of Chapman's tragedies generally. His argument has found some support from E. Schwartz in 'Chapman's Renaissance Man: Byron Reconsidered' (*J.E.G.P.*, LVIII (1959), 613-26) and from D. Crawley in *Character in Relation to Action in the Tragedies of George Chapman* (Salzburg, 1974).

72 Ure, pp. 124-7.

73 Cf. *Consp.*, III.ii.9-21.

74 G. Hibbard, 'Goodness and Greatness: an Essay on the Tragedies of Ben Jonson and George Chapman', *Renaissance and Modern Studies*, XI (1967), 43.

75 MacLure, p. 135.

76 Ure, p. 132.

77 Robert Ornstein notes that Chapman uses the word 'policy' to indicate a failure of past moral values in the present age, some kind of decay of social order (*The Moral Vision of Jacobean Tragedy*, Madison, 1960, 50-1).

78 K. Thomas, *Religion and the Decline of Magic* (New York, 1971), p. 330.

79 J. Parr, 'The Duke of Byron's Malignant *Caput Algol*', *S.P.*, XLIII (1946), p. 198.

80 Ure, p. 135.
81 E. Edwards, *The Life of Sir Walter Raleigh* (London, 1868), pp. 234–5.
82 John Stow, *The Annales of England* (London, 1605), p. 1411.
83 Ide argues that Byron is trying to usurp the very role the king is playing in bringing order to the state (*Possessed with Greatness*, p. 151). It is one of the epic hero's traditional functions to found, cleanse or restore the state.
84 See note on *Trag.*, I.ii.30–1.
85 Ure, p. 138.
86 Jacquot, p. 149.
87 Foakes, 'Tragedy at the Children's Theatres', p. 58.
88 Ornstein, *The Moral Vision of Jacobean Tragedy*, p. 69. There was clearly debate in England at the time over the prerogative of the king in relation to the administration of justice (J. W. Allen, *English Political Thought 1603–1660*, London, 1938). James was sure of his power to act, and Bacon in his writings appears to support the power of the monarch in this respect (Allen, p. 52).
89 Ornstein, p. 68; Goldstein, *George Chapman*, p. 361.
90 As Parrott observes, Byron's speech about the Golden Chamber in the Palace of Justice is drawn largely from Grimeston, but there, as in Pierre Matthieu, the passage is a comment by the author on the remarkable change in Byron's fortunes rather than an exclamatory speech by the prisoner himself.
91 MacLure, pp. 142–3.
92 Ure, p. 142. Schwartz, however, calls it an 'illusory apotheosis' which permits 'no doubt as to where Chapman finally stands. He unequivocally rejects the heroic ideal represented by Bussy' ('Chapman's Renaissance Man: Byron Reconsidered', *J.E.G.P.*, LVIII (1959), 626). Allen Bergson, likewise, sees in the final scene 'the irony of Byron's final, self-deceiving assumption of martyrdom and physical transcendence' ('The Ironic Tragedies of Marston and Chapman: Notes on Jacobean Tragic Form', *J.E.G.P.*, LXIX (1970), 627).
93 Hibbard, 'Goodness and Greatness', p. 45.
94 MacLure calls the double play 'a fine dramatic poem' and a 'secular oratorio' which must be understood on its own terms (p. 132). Ide justifies many aspects of the play as stemming from a different kind of dramaturgy: 'Characters such as Bussy and Byron appear to represent intellectual concepts; they are more like walking ideograms than mimetic, naturalistic representations of life .... Plot seems manipulated to advance a thesis' (*Possessed with Greatness*, pp. 13–14).
95 Hibbard, p. 47.
96 Cf. *Consp.*, I.ii.22ff.
97 Parrott, pp. 620–1.
98 Cf. *Consp.*, II.ii.65ff.; also *Consp.*, III.iii.106–16.
99 See above pp. 10–11.
100 W. Van Lennep (ed.), *The London Stage 1660–1800*, I, 140.

101 Hillebrand, *The Child Actors*; M. Shapiro, *Children of the Revels* (New York, 1977); Gair, *The Children of Paul's*. See also pp. 7–8 above and nn. 28 and 30.
102 Shapiro, pp. 115–16.
103 Gair, pp. 154–6.
104 *Ibid.*, p. 159.
105 Andrew Gurr, *The Shakespearean Stage 1574–1642* (Cambridge, 1980), p. 95.
106 Shapiro, p. 116.
107 *Ibid.*, p. 117.

THE CONSPIRACY
OF CHARLES DUKE OF BYRON

Duc de Biron as warrior in Henry IV's battles to end the civil wars and unify France (Archives Photographiques Larousse)

THE CONSPIRACY OF CHARLES DUKE OF BYRON

[DRAMATIS PERSONAE

HENRY IV, *King of France.*
DUKE OF SAVOY.
DUKE OF BYRON.
D'AUVERGNE, *Charles de Valois, a natural son of Charles IX, and friend of Byron.*
ALBERT, *Archduke of Austria and ruler of the Spanish Netherlands.*
EPERNON,
SOISSONS,
NEMOURS, } *French noblemen.*
D'AUMONT,
CREQUI,
LA FIN, *a discontented French nobleman.*
RONCAS, *the ambassador of Savoy at the French court.*
ROCHETTE, } *nobles attending the Duke of Savoy.*
BRETON,
BELLIÈVRE, } *French Commissioners in Brussels.*
BRULART,
ROISEAU, *a French gentleman with Byron's embassy to Brussels.*
PICOTÉ, *a French gentleman in the service of Albert.*
D'AUMALE, *a French nobleman in exile at Brussels.*
ORANGE, *son of William the Silent, in the service of Albert.*
MANSFIELD, *a German soldier at Albert's court.*
VITRY, *captain of the guard at the French court.*
JANIN, *a French minister of state.*
LA BROSSE, an astrologer.
Three Ladies *at the French court.*
A Painter.
Attendants, Servants.

SCENE: *Paris and Brussels.*]

DRAMATIS PERSONAE] Phelps.

The Conspiracy of Charles Duke of Byron
The Epistle

To my honourable and constant friend, Sir Thomas Walsingham, Knight: and to my much loved from his birth, the right toward and worthy gentleman his son, Thomas Walsingham, Esquire.

Sir, though I know you ever stood little affected to these unprofitable rites of dedication (which disposition in you hath made me hitherto dispense with your right in my other impressions), yet, lest the world may repute it a neglect in me of so ancient and worthy a friend (having heard your approbation of these in their presentment), I could not but prescribe them with your name; and that my affection may extend to your posterity, I have entitled to it, herein, your hope and comfort in your generous son, whom I doubt not that most reverenced mother of manly sciences, to whose instruction your virtuous care commits him, will so profitably initiate in her learned labours that they will

---

1. *constant*] faithful, steadfast.
Sir Thomas Walsingham] Walsingham (1568–1630) was a country gentleman less concerned with the court and public affairs than his cousin, Sir Francis Walsingham. He was the patron and friend of Marlowe, according to the publisher, Edward Blunt, who dedicated Marlowe's *Hero and Leander* to him in 1598; Chapman dedicated his continuation of the poem to Lady Walsingham.
2. *toward*] promising, precocious.
3. *Thomas Walsingham*] Sir Thomas's son, born in 1600, was clearly the object of his parents' care with respect to education and upbringing. He was knighted in 1613 and later became a member of Parliament.
6. *impressions*] printed works.
8. *these*] these plays.
9. *their presentment*] their presentation on stage.
prescribe] inscribe at the front of: a latinism.
11. *entitled*] added the dedication, inscribed.
generous] Chapman is thinking of Latin 'generosus': of high birth, of noble nature or magnanimous spirit.
12. *mother . . . sciences*] Probably Cambridge University: a Thomas Walsingham matriculated as a fellow-commoner of King's College in 1606. *Alumni Cantabrigienses* notes that he was doubtless the son and heir of Sir Thomas. There is no record of a degree.

make him flourish in his riper life, over the idle lives of our 15
ignorant gentlemen, and enable him to supply the honourable
places of your name, extending your years and his right noble
mother's (in the true comforts of his virtues) to the sight of
much and most happy progeny; which most affectionately
wishing, and dividing these poor dismembered poems betwixt 20
you, I desire to live still in your graceful loves, and ever

The most assured at your commandments,

George Chapman.

16. *supply ... places*] fill the positions of rank and honour belonging to Sir Thomas's family; no doubt also the 'place' of Sir Thomas as an accomplished patron of the arts.

17. *right noble mother*] Lady Walsingham, keeper of the queen's wardrobe after James's accession, is said to have danced in masques and taken part in court festivities (*D.N.B.*).

20. *these ... poems*] Chapman probably refers to the text of the plays he is publishing, incomplete because of the cuts imposed by the censor.

21. *graceful*] friendly, bestowing favour.

22. *assured ... commandments*] pledged to your service or wishes.

Prologus

When the uncivil, civil wars of France
Had poured upon the country's beaten breast
Her battered cities, pressed her under hills
Of slaughtered carcasses, set her in the mouths
Of murderous breaches, and made pale despair⸺5
Leave her to ruin, through them all, Byron
Stepped to her rescue, took her by the hand,
Plucked her from under her unnatural press
And set her shining in the height of peace.
And now new cleansed, from dust, from sweat and blood,⸺10
And dignified with title of a duke,
As when in wealthy autumn, his bright star,
Washed in the lofty ocean, thence ariseth,
Illustrates heaven and all his other fires
Outshines and darkens, so admired Byron⸺15

1. *the uncivil, civil wars of France*] Chapman refers to the religious wars in France between the Huguenots and the Catholic League, and the continuing struggles between royal authority, great nobles and foreign interventionists from 1562 until 1594 when Henry of Navarre finally established his authority in France as Henry IV. He had succeeded to the throne after the assassination of Henry III in August 1589, but it took several more years before the Catholic Leaguers and their Spanish allies were overcome. Byron's father, the old Marshal Byron, had supported Henry III before 1589 but accepted the new king on his accession and helped to establish his power. The younger Byron took an active part in Henry's expeditions against Spanish forces in Burgundy and the Low Countries after 1594 until peace was made with Spain and Savoy at Vervins in 1598.

5. *breaches*] gaps in fortifications made by artillery, murderous because large numbers of soldiers were killed in assault and defence of such breaches.

8. *unnatural press*] the weight of carcasses (l. 4) of her own people, hence 'unnatural'. 'Press' is also an instrument of torture and execution.

12. *his bright star*] Sirius, whose rising marked the beginning of the harvest season. Parrott notes that the simile is from Homer, which Chapman translates (referring to Diomede inspired by Pallas): 'Like rich Autumnus' golden lampe, whose brightnesse men admire / Past all the other host of starres when with his chearefull face / Fresh washt in loftie Ocean waves he doth the skies enchase' (*Iliads*, v, 6–8).

14. *Illustrates*] makes lustrous or bright.

All France exempted from comparison.
He touched heaven with his lance, nor yet was touched
With hellish treachery; his country's love
He yet thirsts, not the fair shades of himself,
Of which empoisoned spring when policy drinks   20
He bursts in growing great, and rising, sinks:
Which now behold in our conspirator,
And see in his revolt how honour's flood
Ebbs into air when men are great, not good.

15–16. *Byron ... comparison*] Byron removed all of France from comparison, had no rivals in France.

17. *He touched ... lance*] Chapman may be thinking of the boast of Lysimachus in Plutarch's *De Alexandri magni fortuna aut virtute* (338B): 'The Byzantines now come to me when I am touching Heaven with my spear' (Babbitt, p. 447).

19. *thirsts*] desires vehemently, longs for.

the fair shades] beautiful but unsubstantial images of himself as perceived in a mirror or pond. Ferguson suggests a reference to Narcissus in the images 'thirsts', 'fair shades' and 'empoisoned spring' (p. 223).

20–1.] Policy is personified to give the sense of a 'politician', one skilled in the arts of government who, when he gives way to self-love, drinks from a poisoned spring and swelling up with self-love brings about his own destruction.

23. *flood*] the full tide, which 'ebbs into air'.

23–4.] There are numerous examples of play on the words 'great' and 'good' in Chapman's tragedies. Cf. *Caesar and Pompey*: 'O, my Cornelia, let us still be good, / And we shall still be great; and greater far / In every solid grace than when the tumour / And bile of rotten observation swell'd us.' (V.i.181–4).

Act I

ACT I SCENE i

[*Enter*] SAVOY, RONCAS, ROCHETTE, BRETON.

Savoy. I would not for half Savoy but have bound
    France to some favour by my personal presence
    More than yourself, my lord ambassador,
    Could have obtained; for all ambassadors,
    You know, have chiefly these instructions: 5
    To note the state and chief sway of the court
    To which they are employed, to penetrate
    The heart and marrow of the king's designs,
    And to observe the countenances and spirits
    Of such as are impatient of rest,   10
    And wring beneath some private discontent.
    But past all these there are a number more
    Of these state criticisms, that our personal view
    May profitably make, which cannot fall
    Within the powers of our instruction   15
    To make you comprehend. I will do more

ACT I SCENE i] ACTUS I. SCENA I. *Q1*.

1–23.] The signing of the Treaty of Vervins took place in Paris and Brussels in May 1598, Marshal Byron being sent as Henry's special ambassador to Brussels to witness the archduke's signature and taking of the oath. Savoy did not come to Paris until December 1599, but Chapman brings the two events together. He follows his source closely in describing Savoy's reasons for his visit.

2. *favour*] special goodwill.
6. *state*] nobles, great men of the realm (*O.E.D.*, 26a).
chief sway] controlling power or influence.
8. *heart and marrow*] innermost, secret parts. 'Heart' suggests also the vital or essential centre, and 'marrow' the inner strength of the king's designs.
9. *countenances*] outward appearance or bearing.
spirits] inner natures, including also the idea of mettle or vital energy.
10. *rest*] inactivity.
11. *wring*] writhe, perhaps with a suggestion of facial grimace.
13. *state criticisms*] observations of political affairs.
personal view] first-hand observation.

> With my mere shadow than you with your persons.
> All you can say against my coming here
> Is that, which I confess, may for the time
> Breed strange affections in my brother Spain; 20
> But when I shall have time to make my cannons
> The long-tongued heralds of my hidden drifts,
> Our reconcilement will be made with triumphs.
>
> *Roncas.* If not, your highness hath small cause to care,
> Having such worthy reason to complain 25
> Of Spain's cold friendship and his lingering succours,
> Who only entertains your griefs with hope
> To make your med'cine desperate.
>
> *Rochette.* My lord knows
> The Spanish gloss too well, his form, stuff, lasting,
> And the most dangerous conditions 30
> He lays on them with whom he is in league.
> The injustice in the most unequal dower
> Given with the infanta, whom my lord espoused,

17. *mere shadow*] reflected image, insubstantial when compared with the physical presence of the other lords, yet more effective. He may refer also to the 'shadow' cast by the sun-like ruler.

20. *strange affections*] estranged or unfriendly feelings.

my brother Spain] Philip III of Spain. Savoy had married Philip's half-sister, Catherine.

21. *have time*] see the right moment.

22. *long-tongued heralds*] Flames of the cannons are like tongues from the cannon mouths; and as cannons are said to 'speak', so they will act like heralds, announcing his hidden plans.

drifts] schemes, plots.

23. *triumphs*] public spectacles or pageants.

26. *lingering succours*] long-delayed help.

27. *entertains ... hope*] answers your grievances promisingly.

28. *To ... desperate*] to make in the end your remedy or cure utterly hopeless.

29. *gloss ... form, stuff, lasting*] words used of cloth or fabrics, 'gloss' being the surface lustre, 'form' the shape given to the material, 'stuff' the material itself, and 'lasting' its enduring quality, perhaps with a reference to the cloth known as 'everlasting', a hard-wearing material used for the suits of sergeants and bailiffs. 'Gloss' was often used figuratively to suggest deceptive appearance (*O.E.D.*, 1b). See *Consp.*, I.ii.35–7, III.i.49–51 and *Trag.*, V.ii.178–83 for such figurative uses.

30. *conditions*] provisos, stipulations.

32. *unequal*] inadequate or unfair.

33. *infanta*] a daughter of the king of Spain or Portugal, not necessarily the eldest daughter.

                Compared with that her elder sister had,
                May tell him how much Spain's love weighs to him,   35
                When of so many globes and sceptres held
                By the great king, he only would bestow
                A portion but of six score thousand crowns
                In yearly pension with his highness' wife,
                When the infanta wedded by the archduke   40
                Had the Franch County and Low Provinces.
Breton. We should not set these passages of spleen
                'Twixt Spain and Savoy. To the weaker part,
                More good by sufferance grows than deeds of heart;
                The nearer princes are, the further off   45
                In rites of friendship. My advice had never
                Consented to this voyage of my lord
                In which he doth endanger Spain's whole loss
                For hope of some poor fragment here in France.
Savoy. My hope in France you know not, though my counsel;   50

41. Franch County] *Q1;* Franche-Comté *Parrott.*

---

34. *her elder sister*] Isabella, who married Archduke Albert of Austria. There had been talk of a marriage between Savoy and Isabella, but Philip II reserved her for the archduke, and Savoy had to be content with her younger sister.

35. *weighs*] The literal sense is that of counting out money or gold by weight as part of the 'unequal dower'; figuratively, 'is worth in value'.

36. *globes*] orbs, representing sovereignty (with sceptres).

38. *portion*] marriage portion.

39. *pension*] a sum paid regularly as a subsidy, in this case in lieu of a fixed dowry.

41. *the Franch County*] the Franche-Comté, lying between France and Switzerland north of Geneva, held as a Spanish dependency. It had been invaded by Henry IV but not conquered. With Savoy, it provided a route for Spanish forces from Italy to the Low Countries.

Low Provinces] Belgium and the Netherlands.

42. *passages of spleen*] hot-tempered altercations or disputes.

44. *sufferance*] patient endurance.

deeds of heart] deeds of defiant courage, related to the hot temper implied by spleen.

45. *nearer*] geographically closer, but closer also in terms of affection. Breton points out that princes who are closely bound in these ways tend to neglect displays of friendship. Note Elizabeth's words to Byron in *Consp.*, IV.i.25ff.

47. *voyage*] enterprise, expedition.

48. *endanger*] risk.

50. *though my counsel*] although my counsellor (*O.E.D.*, 11b); or possibly, 'although (you know) my general purposes'.

And for my loss of Spain, it is agreed
That I should slight it. Oft-times princes' rules
Are like the chymical philosophers';
Leave me then to mine own projection
In this our thrifty alchemy of state;   55
Yet help me thus far, you that have been here
Our lord ambassador, and in short inform me
What spirits here are fit for our designs.
Roncas. The new-created Duke Byron is fit,
Were there no other reason for your presence   60
To make it worthy; for he is a man
Of matchless valour and was ever happy
In all encounters, which were still made good
With an unwearied sense of any toil,
Having continued fourteen days together   65

---

62. valour] *Parrott;* valure *Q1.*

52. *slight*] disregard as of no consequence.
rules] principles of procedure to be followed in the pursuit of an art or science (*O.E.D.*, II, 7).
53. *chymical philosophers'*] those learned in alchemy. The meaning seems to be that the strategies of princes are often as mysterious as the principles by which the alchemists work and are known only to themselves. Alchemists were supposed to create wealth out of base metals. Savoy implies that his stratagems will win advantages for his country out of what is apparently a loss, the loss of Spain's favour and support.
54. *projection*] in alchemy, the casting of the powder of the philosophers' stone upon a metal in fusion to transmute it into gold or silver (*O.E.D.*).
55. *thrifty ... state*] Everything is used, even small quantities of base materials (hence 'thrifty') in this political alchemy or statecraft.
58. *spirits*] persons of specific character or disposition (*O.E.D.*, 9).
59–82.] The passage in Grimeston from which these lines are taken occurs after the account of Byron's execution and forms a summing-up of his character and reputation (p. 992). It comes originally from Cayet, as Koeppel points out.
61. *worthy*] worthwhile.
62. *valour*] Q1's 'valure' is not quite the equivalent of 'valour' since it can mean 'physical strength, power, or might' (*O.E.D.*, 1b) as well as 'courage' and 'worthiness'. Chapman may have had physical strength in mind, though the following phrase, 'happy / In all encounters' suggests military engagements where courage was a prime asset.
happy] successful, with additional sense of fortunate (*O.E.D.*, 3, 5).
63. *still*] always.
made good] carried out, fulfilled.
64.] without any sense of weariness after physical exertion.

Upon his horse; his blood is not voluptuous
Nor much inclined to women; his desires
Are higher than his state and his deserts
Not much short of the most he can desire,
If they be weighed with what France feels by them.   70
He is past measure glorious; and that humour
Is fit to feed his spirits, whom it possesseth,
With faith in any error, chiefly where
Men blow it up with praise of his perfections;
The taste whereof in him so soothes his palate   75
And takes up all his appetite that oft-times
He will refuse his meat and company
To feast alone with their most strong conceit;
Ambition also cheek by cheek doth march
With that excess of glory, both sustained   80
With an unlimited fancy that the king,
Nor France itself, without him can subsist.
Savoy. He is the man, my lord, I come to win;
And that supreme intention of my presence
Saw never light till now, which yet I fear   85
The politic king, suspecting, is the cause
That he hath sent him so far from my reach
And made him chief in the commission
Of his ambassage to my brother archduke,
With whom he is now; and, as I am told,   90

---

66. *his . . . voluptuous*] his temper or disposition is not given to sensual pleasure.

68. *state*] estate.

68–70. *his deserts . . . them*] What he deserves is close to the utmost he can desire if it be measured against what France gains as a result of his achievements.

71. *glorious*] eager for glory; also some hint of the older meaning: ostentatious, boastful, proud (*O.E.D.*, 1).

72. *whom it possesseth*] 'It' is the 'humour' of glory which possesses Byron's spirit to such an extent that he will have faith in any error which feeds it.

74. *blow it up*] inflate or puff it up.

75. *soothes*] pleases, satisfies, with a secondary sense of flatters, gratifies with blandishments.

78. *with . . . conceit*] with the very idea of them (i.e., his perfections).

86. *politic*] shrewd.

88. *commission*] the body of commissioners assigned to the embassy to Brussels.

89. *ambassage*] embassy. See ll. 1–23n. above.

SC I] THE CONSPIRACY OF CHARLES DUKE OF BYRON 75

  So entertained and fitted in his humour
  That ere I part I hope he will return
  Prepared, and made the more fit for the physic
  That I intend to minister.
Roncas.   My lord,
  There is another discontented spirit   95
  Now here in court, that for his brain and aptness
  To any course that may recover him
  In his declinèd and litigious state,
  Will serve Byron as he were made for him
  In giving vent to his ambitious vein,   100
  And that is de La Fin.
Savoy.   You tell me true,
  And him I think you have prepared for me.
Roncas. I have, my lord, and doubt not he will prove
  Of the yet taintless fortress of Byron
  A quick expugner, and a strong abider.   105
Savoy. Perhaps the battery will be brought before him
  In this ambassage, for I am assured
  They set high price of him and are informed
  Of all the passages and means for mines
  That may be thought on to his taking in.   110

---

101. de La Fin] *Parrott;* De Laffin *Q1.*

---

 91. *fitted*] catered to, probably with a pun on the idea of being neatly and suitably clothed by his hosts.
 93. *fit*] ready, being already 'fitted in his humour'.
 physic] medicine, perhaps in the special sense of a purge.
 94. *minister*] supply, serve.
 97. *recover*] restore.
 98. *litigious*] involved in litigation.
 100. *vein*] that quality or inclination toward ambition described at l. 91 as a humour. La Fin will be valuable to Byron (and to Savoy and his party) by providing an outlet or vent for Byron's ambitious humour.
 102. *prepared for me*] made approaches to him on my behalf, perhaps implying the offer of bribes.
 105. *expugner*] one who takes by storm.
 abider] one who continues staunchly, who will not give up.
 106. *battery*] artillery.
 before him] i.e., to attack the fortress of Byron's integrity.
 108. *They ... him*] They, the archduke and his court, value him highly.
 109. *passages ... mines*] terms continuing the metaphor of an assault upon a fortress, referring to narrow means of access and suitable places for planting explosives.
 110. *his taking in*] his capture, as of a fortress.

76 THE CONSPIRACY OF CHARLES DUKE OF BYRON [ACT I

     Enter HENRY *and* LA FIN.

  The king comes and La Fin, the king's aspect
  Folded in clouds.
Henry.   I will not have my train
  Made a retreat for bankrupts nor my court
  A hive for drones: proud beggars and true thieves,
  That with a forcèd truth they swear to me   115
  Rob my poor subjects, shall give up their arts
  And henceforth learn to live by their deserts.
  Though I am grown by right of birth and arms
  Into a greater kingdom, I will spread
  With no more shade than may admit that kingdom   120
  Her proper, natural and wonted fruits;
  Navarre shall be Navarre and France still France:
  If one may be the better for the other
  By mutual rites, so, neither shall be worse.
  Thou art in law, in quarrels and in debt   125
  Which thou wouldst quit with count'nance; borrowing
  With thee is purchase, and thou seekst by me,
  In my supportance, now our old wars cease

---

 112. *Folded in clouds*] using the sun image for the king, whose face is clouded with a frown.
 113. *retreat*] a place of seclusion or privacy.
 114–17.] Proud bankrupts and veritable thieves, who by virtue of their pretended or affected oath sworn to me rob my subjects (i.e., who exploit their privileged position in my train), shall give up their deceits and contrivances and learn to live by what they deserve.
 118–22.] Henry's 'growth' from the kingdom of Navarre to the whole realm of France was well known; audiences and readers would link this with King James's move from Scotland to England. Using the image of a tree to describe the expansion of his power, Henry declares that its protective shade will not hinder the growth of the kingdom's natural fruits and that both Navarre and France will maintain their traditional well-being. (Cf. *Consp.*, I.i.176ff. and note also *Basilicon Doron* where James insists that a good king must ensure the prosperity and welfare of his subjects: *S.T.S.*, 1944, p. 55.)
 121. *wonted*] accustomed.
 124. *mutual rites*] mutual ties, treaties.
 125. *law*] law-suits.
 126. *quit*] pay off, settle.
 count'nance] bearing, suggesting boldness or effrontery.
 127. *purchase*] booty, as by an act of pillage (*O.E.D.*, 1, 8).
 128. *supportance*] assistance or backing. La Fin is going to continue his pillage in peacetime to an even worse degree.

SC I]   THE CONSPIRACY OF CHARLES DUKE OF BYRON   77

  To wage worse battles with the arms of peace.
La Fin. Peace must not make men cowards, nor keep calm 130
  Her pursy regiment with men's smothered breaths;
  I must confess my fortunes are declined,
  But neither my deservings nor my mind.
  I seek but to sustain the right I found
  When I was rich, in keeping what is left 135
  And making good my honour as at best,
  Though it be hard. Man's right to everything
  Wanes with his wealth, wealth is his surest king;
  Yet justice should be still indifferent.
  The overplus of kings in all their might 140
  Is but to piece out the defects of right:
  And this I sue for, nor shall frowns and taunts,
  The common scarecrows of all poor men's suits,
  Nor misconstruction that doth colour still

---

130. cowards,͏ *Q2, Parrott;* cowherds *Q1.*

---

 130. *cowards*] The correction in Q2 to 'cowards' is supported by Parrott; Waith (*Ideas of Greatness*, p. 124) points to a phrase in Chapman's *Odysseys*, 'cow-herd soul', where Chapman also seems to intend the pun. In *Eastward Ho*, Quicksilver accuses Golding of being a cowherd's son, incapable of bearing arms; Golding retorts that Quicksilver is a rakehell and a coward (I.i.172ff.).

 131. *pursy regiment*] corpulent or short-winded rule, with no doubt a pun on 'pursy' suggesting the rule of the purse. Cf. *Hamlet*, 'in the fatness of these pursy times', III.iv.153.

 smothered breaths] suppressed or stifled speech.

 133. *mind*] temper or spirit (*O.E.D.*, 15) as well as mental faculties.

 136. *as at best*] as it was when my fortunes were at their best.

 138. *wealth . . . king*] Cf. *The Jew of Malta*, 'who is honour'd now but for his wealth' (I.i.115), and the opening scene of *Volpone*. The king as a source of patronage and honour could not be as effective as wealth.

 139. *indifferent*] neutral, unbiased.

 140. *The overplus of kings*] the additional or surplus powers of kings. La Fin would limit such powers to a mere making-up of defects in the rights and honours of his subjects, granting or restoring what is their due. The king would thus be severely limited in his powers of patronage, a limitation unlikely to appeal to Henry IV, or to James I. The speech is a curious amalgam of the attitudes of the malcontent and those of the free subject speaking boldly to his king, but Chapman has included one or two 'machiavellian' phrases that make the audience suspicious of La Fin's bold assumption of injured virtue.

 141. *piece out*] complete, make up for.

 defects] shortcomings, whatever is lacking.

 144. *misconstruction*] the act of misconstruing, mistaking the meaning of something.

 colour] stain, misrepresent, disguise.

>   Licentiate justice, punishing good for ill,   145
>   Keep my free throat from knocking at the sky,
>   If thunder chid me, for my equity.
> *Henry.* Thy equity is to be ever banished
>   From court, and all society of noblesse,
>   Amongst whom thou throwst balls of all dissension;   150
>   Thou art at peace with nothing but with war,
>   Hast no heart but to hurt, and eatst thy heart
>   If it but think of doing any good.
>   Thou witchest with thy smiles, suckst blood with praises,
>   Mockst all humanity, society poisonst,   155
>   Cozenst with virtue, with religion
>   Betrayst and massacrest; so vile thyself
>   That thou suspectst perfection in others.
>   A man must think of all the villanies
>   He knows in all men to decipher thee,   160
>   That art the centre to impiety.
>   Away and tempt me not.

145. Licentiate] *Q1, Parrott;* Licentiary *Q2, Pearson, Shepherd.*

---

145. *Licentiate justice*] sanctioned justice as practised by licensed men of law, but 'licentiate' could also mean unrestrained, freed from rules (*O.E.D.*, 2) and no doubt La Fin intends the ambiguity.

146–7.] Nothing can prevent me as a free man from complaining to the gods for justice, even if Jove's thunder should warn me against doing so. Cf. *The Spanish Tragedy*, III.vii.1–18.

148. *equity*] legal right.

149. *noblesse*] nobility, persons of noble rank; also those possessing nobility of mind.

150. *balls ... dissension*] a reference to the golden apple thrown among the gods by Eris (Strife) at the wedding of Peleus and Thetis, now become cannon balls in keeping with the imagery of war. In *Basilicon Doron*, James I wrote about 'courtiers and servants the prince might have about him' and observed: 'Thinke a quarrellous man a pest in your companie' (p. 119).

152. *heart ... heart*] The first 'heart' is used in the sense of courage, the second refers to the vital feelings; to 'eat one's heart' was to suffer or die from vexation (*O.E.D.*, 47).

154. *Thou witchest*] You bewitch.

suckst ... praises] draw blood out of the victim (like a parasite) while praising him.

156. *Cozenst virtue*] cheat with all the appearance of being virtuous.

156–7.] betray and massacre under the name of religion.

158. *suspectst*] are suspicious of.

160. *decipher*] detect, discover the true meaning of.

161. *centre*] the 'centre attractive' or focus where all forms of impiety meet.

La Fin.   But you tempt me
   To what, thou sun, be judge and make him see.   *Exit.*
Savoy. Now by my dearest marquisate of Saluces,
   Your majesty hath with the greatest life   165
   Described a wicked man, or rather thrust
   Your arm down through him to his very feet
   And plucked his inside out, that ever yet
   Mine ears did witness, or turned ears to eyes;
   And those strange characters writ in his face,   170
   Which at first sight were hard for me to read,
   The doctrine of your speech hath made so plain
   That I run through them like my natural language.
   Nor do I like that man's aspect, methinks,
   Of all looks where the beams of stars have carved   175
   Their powerful influences. And, O rare,
   What an heroic, more than royal spirit
   Bewrayed you in your first speech, that defies
   Protection of vile drones that eat the honey

   164.] The marquisate of Saluces or Saluzzo, on the Italian side of the Alps, was a sore point between France and Savoy for a number of years. Originally seized from France by Savoy during the reign of Henry III, its fate was supposed to be decided by papal arbitration after the Treaty of Vervins. The pope renounced this task and Savoy's visit to the French court accomplished little, though the issue was constantly on his mind (and tongue, Chapman suggests). A brief war between France and Savoy in 1601 led to a settlement by which France ceded Saluzzo to Savoy but obtained much more in return, rounding off her territories in the south-east. In the play, Henry gives Savoy assurances of settlement at the end of his visit to France (*Consp.*, V.ii.196–8).
   165. *with ... life*] in the most lifelike fashion.
   169. *turned ... eyes*] created a vivid image for the eyes out of words which the ears have heard.
   170. *characters*] significant marks or symbols engraved on an object. 'Characters' were sometimes used to indicate astrological aspects such as conjunctions and oppositions (see 'aspect', l. 174) but here the reference is to marks or signs left on his face by astrological influences and denoting to the initiated the inner nature of the man.
   172. *doctrine*] explanation, instruction.
   173. *natural*] native.
   174. *aspect*] appearance, countenance, but implies also the astrological sense of the relative positions of the planets and hence their influence upon the earth and upon this man's appearance. The aspect of the planets has affected the aspect of the man, as the following lines indicate.
   178. *Bewrayed*] revealed.
   defies] rejects, disdains (*O.E.D.*, 5)
   179–80.] Schoell quotes a passage from Erasmus's *Parabolae sive Similia*

80 THE CONSPIRACY OF CHARLES DUKE OF BYRON [ACT I

    Sweat from laborious virtue, and denies 180
    To give those of Navarre, though bred with you,
    The benefits and dignities of France.
    When little rivers by their greedy currents,
    Far far extended from their mother springs,
    Drink up the foreign brooks still as they run 185
    And force their greatness when they come to sea
    And justle with the ocean for a room,
    O how he roars and takes them in his mouth
    Digesting them so to his proper streams
    That they are no more seen, he nothing raised 190
    Above his usual bounds, yet they devoured
    That of themselves were pleasant, goodly floods.
Henry. I would do best for both, yet shall not be secure
    Till in some absolute heirs my crown be settled;
    There is so little now betwixt aspirers 195
    And their great object in my only self

which may well have suggested the metaphor in these lines ('Chapman's "Commonplace Book"', *M.P.*, XVII (1919–20), 214).
    181. *those ... you*] The reference to James and the Scottish nobles and gentlemen who followed him to England seems inescapable. Cf. l. 118n. above.
    183ff.] Savoy is obviously flattering Henry by laying much stress on Henry's declaration that he will be just in his dealings with Navarre and France. The little rivers with their 'greedy currents' are no doubt the courtiers from Navarre (Scotland) who devour many benefits in the new, foreign land to which they have migrated, but are themselves devoured by the king when they dare to compete for the highest place and honour. Parrott notes other uses of this extended simile in Chapman's poems, *De Guiana*, ll. 56–62, *Of Friendship*, ll. 6–10; it appears with a different interpretation in *Chabot*, I.i.196–202. James I had used a similar image in his first 'Speech in Parliament' in 1603. After describing how England and France had grown out of 'divers Dutchies' to their present unified states, he continued: 'For even as little brookes lose their names by their running and fall into great Rivers, and the very name and memorie of the great Rivers swallowed up in the Ocean: so by the conjunction of divers little Kingdomes in one, are all these private differences and questions swallowed up.' (*The Workes*, London, 1616, p. 489).
    185. *still*] ever.
    186. *force*] urge.
    187. *for a room*] for sufficient space; also for a place or office at court.
    189. *his ... streams*] his own currents.
    192. *floods*] rivers.
    193. *secure*] free from care, untroubled (Lat. *securus*).
    194. *absolute*] undoubted.
    196. *their ... object*] the crown or supreme power; 'my only self' refers to

SC II] THE CONSPIRACY OF CHARLES DUKE OF BYRON 81

  That all the strength they gather under me
  Tempts combat with mine own. I therefore make
  Means for some issue by my marriage,
  Which with the great duke's niece is now concluded, 200
  And she is coming; I have trust in heaven
  I am not yet so old but I may spring,
  And then I hope all trait'rous hopes will fade.
Savoy. Else may their whole estates fly, rooted up
  To ignominy and oblivion; 205
  And, being your neighbour, servant and poor kinsman,
  I wish your mighty race might multiply
  Even to the period of all empery.
Henry. Thanks to my princely cousin: this your love
  And honour shown me in your personal presence 210
  I wish to welcome to your full content;
  The peace I now make with your brother archduke,
  By Duke Byron, our lord ambassador,
  I wish may happily extend to you
  And that at his return we may conclude it. 215
Savoy. It shall be to my heart the happiest day
  Of all my life, and that life all employed
  To celebrate the honour of that day.   *Exeunt.*

    [ACT I SCENE ii]
    [*Enter*] ROISEAU.

Roiseau. The wondrous honour done our Duke Byron
  In his ambassage here, in the archduke's court,

---

203. trait'rous] *Q1, Parrott*; traytors *Q2, Pearson*; traitors' *Shepherd.* 212.
I now make] *Q1 (corr.), Q2*; now made *Q1 (uncorr.), Parrott.*

---

the fact that he alone holds the crown and without undisputed succession it could go to any great 'aspirer'.
 198. *mine own*] my own strength.
 198–9. *make Means*] take steps.
 199. *issue*] offspring.
 200. *great duke's niece*] Marie de Medici, whom Henry married in 1600.
 202. *spring*] produce, bring forth, often used of a tree or seed (*O.E.D.*, 14b). Cf. *Bussy D'Ambois*, I.i.120.
 204. *fly*] disappear.
 208. *the . . . empery*] the end of the world when royal authority and all earthly kingdoms will vanish.
 211. *content*] satisfaction.
 212. *the peace*] the Treaty of Vervins, 1598.

82   THE CONSPIRACY OF CHARLES DUKE OF BYRON   [ACT I

  I fear will taint his loyalty to our king.
  I will observe how they observe his humour
  And glorify his valour, and how he   5
  Accepts and stands attractive to their ends,
  That so I may not seem an idle spot
  In train of this ambassage, but return
  Able to give our king some note of all
  Worth my attendance; and see, here's the man   10
  Who, though a Frenchman and in Orleans born,
  Serving the archduke, I do most suspect
  Is set to be the tempter of our duke.
  I'll go where I may see, although not hear.

    Enter PICOTÉ, *with two other[s] spreading a carpet.*

Picoté. Spread here this history of Catiline   15
  That earth may seem to bring forth Roman spirits
  Even to his genial feet, and her dark breast
  Be made the clear glass of his shining graces;
  We'll make his feet so tender they shall gall
  In all paths but to empire, and therein   20
  I'll make the sweet steps of his state begin.
        Exit [PICOTÉ *with Servants.*]

21.1. PICOTÉ *with Servants*] *Parrott.*

 4.] I will take note of how they watch his disposition in order to take advantage of it (*O.E.D.*, 'observe', 6, 7).
 6. *stands attractive*] holds himself ready to absorb or draw in (their purposes).
 7. *spot*] blemish; or a spot on a peacock's tail, since the tail could be compared with the splendid train of an ambassador's entourage. Loane notes 'as spots in his train', *The Widow's Tears*, I.ii.20.
 14.] Roiseau's statement suggests the upper stage level where he can watch the action and remain visible to the audience.
 15. *history of Catiline*] Catiline was a 'Roman spirit' of a particularly destructive kind, and a failed conspirator. There is undoubted irony in the use of this legend on a carpet spread before Byron's feet as a part of his temptation.
 17. *genial*] pertaining to generation, as if Byron were a god of generation inspiring the earth to bring forth the spirits of ancient Romans.
 18. *glass*] mirror.
 19. *gall*] chafe.
 21. *the sweet . . . state*] Picoté hopes that Byron is starting out on the 'path to empire' where he promises to make each step delightful to his appetite for rank and splendour. The rare carpet and the music that greet Byron's entrance are devices to this end. 'State' is both high rank and the pomp and ceremony that goes with it.

Loud music, and enter BYRON.

Byron. What place is this? What air? What region?
    In which a man may hear the harmony
    Of all things moving? Hymen marries here
    Their ends and uses and makes me his temple.   25
    Hath any man been blessèd, and yet lived?
    The blood turns in my veins; I stand on change,
    And shall dissolve in changing; 'tis so full
    Of pleasure not to be contained in flesh;
    To fear a violent good abuseth goodness,   30
    'Tis immortality to die aspiring,
    As if a man were taken quick to heaven.
    What will not hold perfection let it burst;
    What force hath any cannon, not being charged,
    Or being not discharged? To have stuff and form   35
    And to lie idle, fearful, and unused,

22.] 'The first line is an unmistakable recollection of Seneca's *Hercules*, waking from the mad fury in which he has killed his wife and children: Quis hic locus, quae regio, quae mundi plaga?' (Waith, *Ideas of Greatness*, pp. 133–4).

23–4. *the harmony ... moving*] the music of the spheres.

24. *Hymen*] god of marriage, associated with wedding songs. In his state of rapture, Byron feels himself become the temple of Hymen where the movement of all heavenly bodies and their 'ends and uses' are reconciled in music. The phrase might seem blasphemous to a 17th-century audience, aware of the Biblical injunction that the body is the temple of the Holy Ghost (1 Cor. iii.16); Byron's use of 'blessèd' in l. 26 carries on the religious imagery.

26. *blessèd*] enjoying supreme felicity, often used of the saints in paradise.

27. *The blood ... veins*] The blood changes direction in his blood-vessels, presumably meaning that he is dizzy with excitement. I have not been able to find an analogue.

I stand on change] a paradoxical expression indicating that he remains firmly in a state of alteration or mutation. Cf. 1 *Tamb.*, II.vii.24–5: 'Still climbing after knowledge infinite / And always moving as the restless spheres'.

28. *And shall ... changing*] The phrase implies the dissolution of the body or the separation of soul and body in the process of metamorphosis (*O.E.D.*, 'dissolve', 6).

'tis so full] The antecedent of 'it' is obscure but may well be the total experience.

30. *violent*] intense, very powerful.

32. *quick*] alive.

33. *hold*] contain; possibly also the sense of 'maintain'.

35. *stuff and form*] 'Stuff' is the material that can be worked upon; 'form' the shaping power or determining principle that operates upon the basic material. Cf. *Consp.*, I.i.29.

Nor form nor stuff shows; happy Semele
That died compressed with glory! Happiness
Denies comparison of less or more,
And not at most, is nothing: like the shaft 40
Shot at the sun by angry Hercules
And into shivers by the thunder broken
Will I be if I burst; and in my heart
This shall be written: yet 'twas high and right.
                                        Music again.
Here too? They follow all my steps with music 45
As if my feet were numerous and trod sounds
Out of the centre, with Apollo's virtue
That out of every thing his each part touched
Struck musical accents; wheresoe'er I go
They hide the earth from me with coverings rich 50
To make me think that I am here in heaven.

                Enter PICOTÉ *in haste.*

Picoté. This way, your highness.
Byron.   Come they?
Picoté.   Ay, my Lord.
                                          Exeunt.

    37. *Semele*] a daughter of Cadmus, mother of Bacchus by Zeus; her aspiration to see her lover in his glory brought about her death.
    38. *compressed*] sexually embraced (by Zeus). Note Preface to *The Iliads of Homer* (ed. R. Hooper, London, 1898, p. xcii) '... and a virgin of that isle compressed by that Genius, who being quick with child ...', a passage quoted by *O.E.D.*
    39. *denies comparison*] rejects any comparative degree.
    40-2.] See *The Shadow of Night*, ll. 255-61 and gloss: 'Here he alludes to the fiction of *Hercules*, that in his labor at *Tartessus* fetching away the oxen, being (more then he liked) heat with the beames of the Sunne, he bent his bow against him, &c. *Vt ait Pherecides in 3. lib. Historiarum.* (P. B. Bartlett, *Poems*). Cf. *Chabot*, II.ii.84-5 which repeats the phrase, 'yet 'twas high and right'.
    46. *numerous*] rhythmical, measured.
    47. *Out of the centre*] from the centre of the earth, or simply from the earth itself (as central to the universe).
    virtue] the power or influence inherent in a supernatural being.
    49. *accents*] notes. Accents were marks set over words or syllables to indicate the musical notes to which they were to be sung (*O.E.D.*, 7).
    50. *coverings rich*] He apparently does not take in the message of the carpet.

Enter the other Commissioners of France, BELLIÈVRE,
BRULART [*with*] D'AUMALE, ORANGE.

Bellièvre. My Lord d'Aumale, I am exceeding sorry
   That your own obstinacy to hold out
   Your mortal enmity against the king, 55
   When Duke du Maine and all the faction yielded
   Should force his wrath to use the rites of treason
   Upon the members of your senseless statue,
   Your name and house, when he had lost your person,
   Your love and duty.
Brulart.   That which men enforce 60
   By their own wilfulness, they must endure
   With willing patience and without complaint.
D'Aumale. I use not much impatience nor complaint,
   Though it offends me much to have my name
   So blotted with addition of a traitor, 65
   And my whole memory with such despite
   Marked and begun to be so rooted out.
Brulart. It was despite that held you out so long
   Whose penance in the king was needful justice.
Bellièvre. Come, let us seek our duke and take our leaves 70
   Of th'archduke's grace.
                                       Exeunt.

52.3. *with*] Parrott.

53ff.] D'Aumale refused to accept Henry IV as rightful king of France even after Mayenne (du Maine), head of the League which had resisted Henry's claim, had finally submitted to Herny in 1596. D'Aumale was therefore an exile in Brussels.
   55. *mortal*] deadly, aiming at his death.
   56. *faction*] party (in opposition to the central authority of the king, i.e., the Catholic League).
   57. *rites of treason*] formal procedures of trial and execution used against traitors.
   58. *members*] limbs.
   senseless] without physical sensation.
   60. *enforce*] compel.
   63. *use*] display or show habitually.
   65. *addition*] title, something added to a person's name.
   66. *despite*] contempt.
   68. *despite*] 'contemptuous behaviour' may be part of the meaning, linking it with the use of 'despite' in l. 66. However Brulart seems to give the word a stronger sense, that of spiteful or malicious anger (*O.E.D.*, 4).
   69. *penance*] punishment (*O.E.D.*, 5).

Enter BYRON *and* PICOTÉ.

Byron. Here may we safely breathe?
Picoté. No doubt, my lord, no stranger knows this way;
Only the archduke and your friend, Count Mansfield,
Perhaps may make their general scapes to you
To utter some part of their private loves 75
Ere your departure.
Byron. Then I well perceive
To what th'intention of his highness tends;
For whose and others here, most worthy lords,
I will become, with all my worth, their servant
In any office but disloyalty; 80
But that hath ever showed so foul a monster
To all my ancestors, and my former life,
That now to entertain it, I must wholly
Give up my habit in his contrary,
And strive to grow out of privation. 85
Picoté. My lord, to wear your loyal habit still
When it is out of fashion, and hath done
Service enough, were rustic misery:
The habit of a servile loyalty
Is reckoned now amongst privations, 90
With blindness, dumbness, deafness, silence, death,
All which are neither natures by themselves

71.2. Enter *BYRON* and *PICOTÉ*] Parrott's addition 'above' to the s.d. seems to me clearly wrong because of the entries and exits of other characters to Byron later in the scene, particularly Mansfield's entry 'at another door'. Nor would the upper level be appropriate in theatrical terms for so long a dialogue between Byron and Picoté.

71. *breathe*] draw breath; perhaps also 'whisper'.

74. *general scapes*] common or collective escapes.

79. *worth*] merit, attainments.

81. *showed*] appeared.

84. *habit*] customary behaviour; also costume (see following lines).
his contrary] its contrary, i.e., loyalty.

85. *privation*] deprivation, losing my former life entirely.

88. *rustic misery*] rural wretchedness, poverty.

89. *habit*] costume or outward demeanour (as above) but also linked with 'privations' so that it refers to the logical distinction between having or possessing (*habitus*) and privation, the deprivation of qualities or things (*privatio*). Ferguson notes Chapman's use of Aristotle's definitions, p. 224.

92. *natures*] particular qualities or characteristics considered as entities (*O.E.D.*, 3).

Nor substances, but mere decays of form
And absolute decessions of nature;
And so, 'tis nothing, what shall you then lose?   95
Your highness hath a habit in perfection
And in desert of highest dignities,
Which carve yourself, and be your own rewarder.
No true power doth admit privation
Adverse to him, or suffers any fellow   100
Joined in his subject; you superiors,
It is the nature of things absolute
One to destroy another; be your highness
Like those steep hills that will admit no clouds,
No dews, nor least fumes bound about their brows,   105
Because their tops pierce into purest air,
Expert of humour; or like air itself
That quickly changeth, and receives the sun
Soon as he riseth, everywhere dispersing
His royal splendour, girds it in his beams   110

93. *substances*] actual things, materials of which bodies are formed and by which they may possess certain properties (*O.E.D.*, 6).
mere] entire.
94. *absolute decessions*] total running down or diminution.
nature] the creative, regulative physical power operating in the material world (*O.E.D.*, IV, 11).
96. *a habit in perfection*] possession of extreme excellence or flawlessness, yet continuing also the metaphor of dress and outward demeanour from l. 89.
97. *desert*] worthiness.
98. *carve yourself*] serve, apportion for yourself, be your own carver (*O.E.D.*, 9a, b).
99ff.] Both Schoell and Ferguson refer to passages from Plutarch's *De primo frigido* from which Chapman drew (Schoell, Appendices to *Études*, p. 208; Ferguson, pp. 223–5). Ferguson notes that Plutarch's argument is entirely physical but Chapman transfers it to the moral question. 'Power' is force, vigour, energy; 'him' and 'his' in ll. 100 and 101 refer back to 'power', and 'subject' is the possessor of the power, or perhaps in more abstract terms the substance in which the power inheres.
101. *you superiors*] you superior beings (such as Byron).
102. *things absolute*] objects in nature independent of restraining forces. Picoté suggests that those who are superior in rank and merit are independent free agents likely to destroy one another.
104–15.] The image comes from Plutarch, *De primo frigido* (951B) (Schoell, p. 208).
107. *Expert of humour*] devoid of mists and vapour (Lat. *expers*, having no part in, devoid of).
110. *girds it*] clothes it.

And makes itself the body of the light.
Hot, shining, swift, light and aspiring things
Are of immortal and celestial nature;
Cold, dark, dull, heavy of infernal fortunes
And never aim at any happiness.   115
Your excellency knows that simple loyalty,
Faith, love, sincerity, are but words, no things,
Merely devised for form; and as the legate,
Sent from his holiness to frame a peace
'Twixt Spain and Savoy, laboured fervently,   120
For common ends, not for the duke's particular,
To have him sign it; he again endeavours,
Not for the legate's pains, but his own pleasure,
To gratify him; and being at last encountered
Where the flood Tessin enters into Po,   125
They made a kind contention which of them
Should enter th'other's boat; one thrust the other,
One leg was over, and another in,
And with a fiery courtesy, at last
Savoy leaps out into the legate's arms,   130
And here ends all his love and th'other's labour;
So shall these terms and impositions,
Expressed before, hold nothing in themselves
Really good, but flourishes of form;
And further than they make to private ends   135
None wise or free their proper use intends.

---

134. form] *Q1* (*corr.*); fame *Q1* (*uncorr.*), *Q2*.

---

   111. *the body of the light*] the physical substance that manifests the light.
   114. *infernal*] belonging to the underworld, the realm of the dead.
   118. *form*] conventional behaviour, outward ceremony.
   118ff.] Cardinal Aldobrandino, nephew of the Pope, sent to negotiate a peace between France and Savoy (not Spain and Savoy as stated in l. 120), had much difficulty in persuading the Duke of Savoy to sign the treaty accepted by his ambassadors until this episode of the boat on the Po. The event is still two years in the future but Chapman uses history very often in an illustrative fashion. (See Grimeston, p. 939.)
   123. *Not . . . pains*] not for the trouble the legate had taken.
   125. *Tessin*] Ticino River.
   132. *impositions*] ascription of names.
   134. *flourishes of form*] ostentatious embellishments of ceremony.
   135. *make*] contribute (*O.E.D.*, 79).
   136. *proper*] characteristic, particular.

Byron. O 'tis a dangerous and a dreadful thing
 To steal prey from a lion, or to hide
 A head distrustful in his opened jaws;
 To trust our blood in others' veins, and hang   140
 'Twixt heaven and earth in vapours of their breaths;
 To leave a sure pace on continuate earth
 And force a gait in jumps from tower to tower,
 As they do that aspire from height to height.
 The bounds of loyalty are made of glass,   145
 Soon broke, but can in no date be repaired;
 And as the Duke d'Aumale, now here in court,
 Flying his country, had his statue torn
 Piece-meal with horses, all his goods confiscate,
 His arms of honour kicked about the streets,   150
 His goodly house at Annet razed to th'earth,
 And, for a strange reproach of his foul treason,
 His trees about it cut off by their waists;
 So, when men fly the natural clime of truth
 And turn themselves loose out of all the bounds   155
 Of justice and the straight way to their ends,
 Forsaking all the sure force in themselves
 To seek without them that which is not theirs,
 The forms of all their comforts are distracted,
 The riches of their freedoms forfeited,   160
 Their human noblesse shamed, the mansions
 Of their cold spirits eaten down with cares,

---

142. pace] *Q1 (corr.);* place *Q1 (uncorr.), Q2.*   continuate] *Q1 (corr.);* continuall *Q1 (uncorr.), Q2.*   143. gait] *This ed.;* gate *Q1, Parrott.*

140–1.] The emphasis on trusting blood and breath suggests the utter dependence of one's life upon someone else where treachery is involved. The image becomes ironic retrospectively since Byron later on places his life in La Fin's hands and is betrayed.

142. *sure pace*] secure step.
 continuate] continuous in space.

143. *force a gait*] take a course or path by violent effort. (See 'gate', *O.E.D.*, sb.²: usually 'gait' was spelled 'gate' until the 18th century. Note also l. 194 below and n.)

157. *force*] vigour, strength.
158. *without*] outside.
159.] The natural shapes of all their comforts are disordered, torn apart.
161. *mansions*] dwelling-places.
162. *eaten down*] consumed, devoured.

                    And all their ornaments of wit and valour,
                    Learning and judgement, cut from all their fruits.

                        [*Enter the* ARCHDUKE ALBERT.]

Albert. O, here were now the richest prize in Europe,   165
       Were he but taken in affection.
       Would we might grow together and be twins
       Of either's fortune, or that, still embraced,
       I were but ring to such a precious stone.
Byron. Your highness' honours and high bounty shown me   170
       Have won from me my voluntary power,
       And I must now move by your eminent will;
       To what particular objects, if I know
       By this man's intercession, he shall bring
       My uttermost answer and perform betwixt us   175
       Reciprocal and full intelligence.
Albert. Even for your own deservèd royal good,
       'Tis joyfully accepted; use the loves
       And worthy admirations of your friends,
       That beget vows of all things you can wish,   180
       And be what I wish: danger says, no more.   *Exit.*

                    Enter MANSFIELD *at another door.*

                                                    Exit PICOTÉ.
Mansfield. Your highness makes the light of this court stoop
       With your so near departure; I was forced

164.1.] *Parrott.*

    164. *their fruits*] whatever they produce or achieve.
    165–6.] The notion of a prize being taken is that of a valuable ship or wealthy city being captured. The method of capture is 'affection' or good will.
    171. *my voluntary power*] my power to act according to my own free will.
    174. *this man's*] Picoté's.
    intercession] The Latin sense of 'going between' is dominant.
    175. *uttermost*] most complete, final.
    181.1. Enter *MANSFIELD*] Count Mansfield was a German soldier of great fame who had fought in the wars of Charles V and Philip II and who was now involved in the administration of the Low Countries. Parrott notes that he was more than eighty years of age at this time.
    182. *stoop*] bend downward (in regret), as of the light of a star or other heavenly body (*O.E.D.*, 3b).

             To tender to your excellence, in brief,
             This private wish, in taking of my leave,   185
             That in some army royal, old Count Mansfield
             Might be commanded by your matchless valour
             To the supremest point of victory;
             Who vows for that renown all prayer and service:
             No more, lest I may wrong you.   *Exit* MANSFIELD.
Byron.   Thank your lordship.   190

             Enter D'AUMALE *and* ORANGE.

D'Aumale. All majesty be added to your highness,
             Of which I would not wish your breast to bear
             More modest apprehension than may tread
             The high gate of your spirit, and be known
             To be a fit bound for your boundless valour.   195
Orange. So Orange wisheth, and to the deserts
             Of your great actions their most royal crown.

                        Enter PICOTÉ.

Picoté. Away, my lord, the lords enquire for you.
                              Exit BYRON [*and* PICOTÉ.]
                    Orange, D'Aumale, Roiseau [*remain.*]
Orange. Would we might win his valour to our part.
D'Aumale. 'Tis well prepared in his entreaty here,   200
             With all state's highest observations;
             And to their form and words are added gifts:
             He was presented with two goodly horses,
             One of which two was the brave beast Pastrana,
             With plate of gold, and a much prizèd jewel,   205

198.1. *and* PICOTÉ] *Parrott.*   198.2. *remain*] *This ed.; Manet Q1.*

   194. *gate*] road or path (*O.E.D.*, sb.²). D'Aumale's elaborate compliment wishes royal majesty upon Byron and bids him not to apprehend this idea of majesty modestly but as appropriate to the high path of his noble spirit and the suitable realm for his courage which knows no limits.
   195. *bound*] boundary or limit but also the territory enclosed by a boundary. Cf. *1H4*, V.iv.89–90: 'When that this body did contain a spirit, / A kingdom for it was too small a bound'.
   200. *entreaty*] reception.
   201. *observations*] regards, honours. (*O.E.D.*'s earliest example is 1644.)
   205. *plate of gold*] vessels or utensils made of gold.

   Girdle and hangers set with wealthy stones,
   All which were valued at ten thousand crowns;
   The other lords had suits of tapestry
   And chains of gold, and every gentleman
   A pair of Spanish gloves, and rapier blades.   210
   And here ends their entreaty, which I hope
   Is the beginning of more good to us
   Than twenty thousand times their gifts to them.

   Enter ALBERT, BYRON, BELLIÈVRE, MANSFIELD *with others.*

Albert. My lord, I grieve that all the setting forth
   Of our best welcome made you more retired;   215
   Your chamber hath been more loved than our honours,
   And therefore we are glad your time of parting
   Is come to set you in the air you love.
   Commend my service to his majesty,
   And tell him that this day of peace with him   220
   I'll hold as holy. All your pains, my lords,
   I shall be always glad to gratify
   With any love and honour your own hearts
   Shall do me grace to wish expressed to you.
        [*Exeunt all except Roiseau.*]
Roiseau. Here hath been strange demeanour, which shall fly 225
   To the great author of this embassy.   [*Exit.*]

213.1. MANSFIELD *with others*] *Parrott;* MANSFIELD, ROISEAU *with others Q1.*
224.1. *Exeunt ... Roiseau*] *This ed.*   226. *Exit*] *Parrott.*   226. FINIS
Actus I *follows l. 226 in Q1.*

---

 206. *Girdle and hangers*] belt and loop (from which the sword is hung), usually ornamented.
 208. *suits of tapestry*] sets of tapestry ('suit', 'suite' *O.E.D.*, 18), probably in the form of hangings. The list of gifts is accurately reproduced from Grimeston, p. 816.
 215. *more retired*] more withdrawn into seclusion.
 225–6.] Roiseau seems to be a self-designated spy rather than an agent appointed to the special embassy by Henry. Nevertheless his actions suggest the watchfulness and undercover means a king in Henry's position must use.

Act II

ACT II SCENE i

[*Enter*] SAVOY, LA FIN, RONCAS, ROCHETTE, BRETON.

Savoy. Admit no entry, I will speak with none.
    Good signior de La Fin, your worth shall find
    That I will make a jewel for my cabinet
    Of that the king, in surfeit of his store,
    Hath cast out as the sweepings of his hall;   5
    I told him, having threatened you away,
    That I did wonder this small time of peace
    Could make him cast his armour so securely
    In such as you, and, as 'twere, set the head
    Of one so great in counsels on his foot,   10
    And pitch him from him with such guardlike strength.
La Fin. He may perhaps find he hath pitched away
    The axletree that kept him on his wheels.
Savoy. I told him so, I swear, in other terms
    And not with too much note of our close loves,   15

ACT II SCENE i] ACTUS 2. SCENA I. *Q1*.   11. guardlike] *Q1, Q2;* guardless *Parrott.*

   1.] Savoy's first line is obviously spoken to an attendant who is either offstage or who enters with them and immediately goes off again. There is no indication of a servant's entry in the s.d.

   3. *cabinet*] safe repository for jewels etc., used figuratively of his treasury of friends.

   4. *in surfeit ... store*] in the excess of his abundant supply.

   6. *having ... away*] when he ordered you with threats to depart from court.

   8. *cast ... securely*] throw off his armour so confidently (*Lat. securus*, untroubled, hence negligent).

   10. *on his foot*] Ferguson suggests a reference to the game of football in 'on his foot' and 'pitch him from him'; he quotes *C. of E.*, II.i.82–3: 'Am I so round with you, as you with me, / That like a football you do spurn me thus?' (p. 226).

   11. *guardlike*] Parrott's emendation to 'guardless' is tempting, particularly after 'securely' which is used in the sense of 'without care'. However the image of vigorous movement in 'pitch' and physical power in 'strength' may perhaps justify the retention of 'guardlike', i.e., like a powerful guard.

   15. *close*] secret.

94   THE CONSPIRACY OF CHARLES DUKE OF BYRON [ACT II

        Lest so he might have smoked our practices.
La Fin. To choose his time and spit his poison on me
        Through th'ears and eyes of strangers!
Savoy.   So I told him,
        And more than that, which now I will not tell you.
        It rests now then, noble and worthy friend,   20
        That to our friendship we draw Duke Byron,
        To whose attraction there is no such chain
        As you can forge and shake out of your brain.
La Fin. I have devised the fashion and the weight;
        To valours hard to draw, we use retreats;   25
        And to pull shafts home, with a good bow-arm,
        We thrust hard from us: since he came from Flanders
        He heard how I was threatened with the king,
        And hath been much inquisitive to know
        The truth of all, and seeks to speak with me;   30
        The means he used, I answered doubtfully,
        And with an intimation that I shunned him,
        Which will, I know, put more spur to his charge;
        And if his haughty stomach be prepared
        With will to any act for the aspiring   35
        Of his ambitious aims, I make no doubt
        But I shall work him to your highness' wish.
Savoy. But undertake it and I rest assured.
        You are reported to have skill in magic
        And the events of things at which they reach   40

---

   16. *smoked our practices*] smelled out our plots.
   24. *the ... weight*] i.e., of the chain, l. 22.
   25. *valours*] those of great worthiness.
   draw] attract, entice.
   retreats] withdrawals.
   26. *shafts*] arrows.
  with a good bow arm] The left arm holding the bow is thrust forward while the right hand holds the shaft and string.
   28. *threatened with the king*] charged with menaces by the king.
   31. *means*] the method Byron used to draw him out.
   35. *aspiring*] reaching, attaining (*O.E.D.*, 8).
   39. *skill in magic*] Parrott notes that the only hint in Grimeston as to La Fin's skill in the magic arts occurs during the trial when Biron claims that La Fin bewitched him. The large claims La Fin makes later in this scene (ll. 107ff.) are drawn from Seneca's *Hercules Oetaeus*, ll. 454–71, not from Seneca's *Medea* as Parrott suggests.
   40. *events*] outcomes.

SC I] THE CONSPIRACY OF CHARLES DUKE OF BYRON 95

  That are in nature apt to overreach,
  Whom the whole circle of the present time
  In present pleasures, fortunes, knowledges,
  Cannot contain; those men, as broken loose
  From human limits, in all violent ends   45
  Would fain aspire the faculties of fiends;
  And in such air breathe his unbounded spirits,
  Which therefore well will fit such conjurations:
  Attempt him then by flying; close with him
  And bring him home to us, and take my dukedom. 50
La Fin. My best in that and all things vows your service.
Savoy. Thanks to my dear friend and the French Ulysses.
     Exit SAVOY [*and* Lords *except La Fin.*]

     Enter BYRON.

Byron. Here is the man. My honoured friend, La Fin!
  Alone and heavy countenanced? On what terms
  Stood th'insultation of the king upon you?   55
La Fin. Why do you ask?
Byron.   Since I would know the truth.
La Fin. And when you know it, what?

51. service] *Q1;* servant *Parrott.*   52.1. *Exit* SAVOY *and* Lords *except* LA FIN] *Ray; Exit* SAVOY *Q1; Exit* SAVOY *cum suis Parrott.*

---

  41. *in nature*] in their own character.
  apt to overreach] inclined to reach beyond set limits. *Cf.* Harry Levin, *The Overreacher* (Harvard, 1952).
  45. *violent ends*] forceful or very intense purposes.
  46. *aspire*] aim at. There is more than a hint of *Doctor Faustus* in Savoy's speech: in the idea of an individual that cannot be contained within human limits in the particular combination of 'pleasures, fortunes, knowledges', and in the references to 'fiends' and 'conjurations'. The speech is also an ironic comment on Byron's own speech of aspiration in the preceding scene.
  49. *flying*] attacking as with a hawk. The hawking metaphor is continued in 'close with him' (grapple with him) and 'bring him home'. There may also be a pun on 'fly' as familiar spirit or devil. 'Flying' would thus refer to La Fin's use of a familiar spirit to tempt the aspirer, Byron.
  close with him] like a hawk closing with its prey, but also in the sense of coming to an agreement.
  51. *vows your service*] Although Parrott finds the phrase unintelligible, I read 'my best' as subject of 'vows' and 'service' as object.
  52. *Ulysses*] Traditionally, Ulysses (Odysseus) was considered the wisest of the Greek leaders during the siege of Troy.
  55. *insultation*] insult, contemptuous speech.

Byron.   I'll judge betwixt you,
    And, as I may, make even th'excess of either.
La Fin. Alas my lord, not all your loyalty,
    Which is in you more than hereditary,   60
    Nor all your valour, which is more than human,
    Can do the service you may hope on me
    In sounding my displeased integrity;
    Stand for the king as much in policy
    As you have stirred for him in deeds of arms   65
    And make yourself his glory and your country's,
    Till you be sucked as dry and wrought as lean
    As my flayed carcass: you shall never close
    With me as you imagine.
Byron.   You much wrong me
    To think me an intelligencing instrument.   70
La Fin. I know not how your so affected zeal
    To be reputed a true-hearted subject
    May stretch or turn you. I am desperate.

---

70. instrument] *Q1 (uncorr.), Q2, Pearson, Shepherd, Parrott;* Lord *Q1 (corr.), Ray.*

---

    58. *make even . . . either*] balance out the immoderate feelings of each.
    63. *sounding*] searching out, taking the depth of.
    64. *policy*] statecraft or diplomacy: a comparatively neutral use of the term.
    65. *stirred*] been active.
    68. *close*] come to grips.
    70. *intelligencing instrument*] agent for collecting information, spy. Parrott thought that Chapman himself had changed 'lord' to 'instrument' in Q2 (assuming that Chapman had overseen the reprinting), but he did not realise that Q2 had derived the word from an uncorrected sheet in Q1. Ray restores 'lord' from the corrected sheet. But the question remains whether the proof-corrector was attempting to correct the scansion on his own by substituting the one-syllable 'lord' for the more vigorous 'instrument'. There are other corrections which might possibly suggest a 'busybody' proof-reader: thus 'She much more' is corrected to 'She much the more' (*Consp.*, IV.i.183); 'Not grant me this suit?' to 'Not grant me that?' (*Consp.*, V.i.68); and 'The blue sphere of the air' to 'The blue space of the air' (*Consp.*, V.ii.74). There is not enough evidence to argue that the corrector has frequently interfered with the text, but in this case I have assumed he has done so, and I have retained 'instrument' as the stronger word.
    71. *affected*] cherished. But the sense 'artificially displayed as a kind of affectation' was common in the early 17th century, and La Fin may intend the irony.
    73. *stretch . . . you*] strain or alter (your natural qualities).

    If I offend you, I am in your power;
    I care not how I tempt your conquering fury,   75
    I am predestined to too base an end
    To have the honour of your wrath destroy me,
    And be a worthy object for your sword.
    I lay my hand, and head too, at your feet
    As I have ever, here I hold it still: 80
    End me directly, do not go about.
Byron. How strange is this! the shame of his disgrace
    Hath made him lunatic.
La Fin.   Since the king hath wronged me
    He thinks I'll hurt myself. No, no, my lord,
    I know that all the kings in Christendom,   85
    If they should join in my revenge, would prove
    Weak foes to him, still having you to friend;
    If you were gone (I care not if you tell him)
    I might be tempted then to right myself.   *Exit.*
Byron. He has a will to me and dares not show it;   90
    His state decayed, and he disgraced, distracts him.

                 LA FIN [*returns.*]

La Fin. Change not my words, my lord; I only said
    I might be tempted then to right myself;
    Temptation to treason is no treason;
    And that word 'tempted' was conditional too,   95
    If you were gone; I pray inform the truth.   [*Going.*]
Byron. Stay, injured man, and know I am your friend,
    Far from these base and mercenary reaches,
    I am, I swear to you.
La Fin.   You may be so;
    And yet you'll give me leave to be La Fin,   100
    A poor and expuate humour of the court;

91.1. *returns*] *This ed.; Redit Q1.*   96. *Going*] *This ed.; Exitur. Q1.*

---

  81. *go about*] lit. move round in a circle, hence, be indirect.
  90. *a will to me*] an inclination toward me.
  91. *distracts*] confuses, bewilders.
  96. *inform*] report.
  98. *reaches*] devices, contrivances.
  101. *expuate*] spat out as from the mouth.
    humour] bodily fluid such as bile or phlegm, carried on in the phrase 'good blood', since blood was also one of the bodily fluids.

But what good blood came out with me, what veins
And sinews of the triumphs now it makes,
I list not vaunt; yet will I now confess,
And dare assume it, I have power to add 105
To all his greatness and make yet more fixed
His bold security. Tell him this, my lord,
And this, if all the spirits of earth and air
Be able to enforce, I can make good;
If knowledge of the sure events of things, 110
Even from the rise of subjects into kings
And falls of kings to subjects hold a power
Of strength to work it, I can make it good;
And tell him this too: if in midst of winter
To make black groves grow green, to still the thunder, 115
And cast out able flashes from mine eyes
To beat the lightning back into the skies
Prove power to do it, I can make it good;
And tell him this too: if to lift the sea
Up to the stars when all the winds are still, 120
And keep it calm when they are most enraged;
To make earth's driest plains sweat humorous springs,
To make fixed rocks walk, and loose shadows stand,
To make the dead speak, midnight see the sun,
Midday turn midnight, to dissolve all laws 125
Of nature and of order, argue power

122. plains] *Parrott;* palms *Q1, Q2,* Ray.

---

102. *what good . . . me*] La Fin may refer to noble companions who have left the court with him.

102–3.] Blood, veins and sinews are the vital elements of health and strength in an organism; the metaphor refers to the court. The 'triumphs' may be the celebrations the court is now 'making' for the visit of the Duke of Savoy.

104. *list not vaunt*] do not wish to boast.

107ff.] See l. 39 above and n.

110. *sure events*] certain outcomes.

113. *to work it*] to bring it about.

116. *able*] powerful (*O.E.D.*, 5)

122. *earth's driest plains*] Chapman's source for this passage, Seneca's *Hercules Oetaeus,* ll. 454–71, supports Parrott's emendation, though the Q1 reading, 'palms', may still convince some readers of its genuineness, particularly because of the association of the humours with dry or sweating hands.

humorous] throwing up mists or vapours.

123. *loose*] unattached, wandering.

stand] stop, stay still.

	Able to work all, I can make all good:	
	And all this tell the king.	
Byron.	'Tis more than strange	
	To see you stand thus at the rapier's point	
	With one so kind and sure a friend as I.	130

La Fin. Who cannot friend himself is foe to any,
    And to be feared of all, and that is it
    Makes me so scorned; but make me what you can,
    Never so wicked and so full of fiends,
    I never yet was traitor to my friends: 135
    The laws of friendship I have ever held
    As my religion; and for other laws,
    He is a fool that keeps them with more care
    Than they keep him safe, rich, and popular;
    For riches and for popular respects   140
    Take them amongst ye, minions, but for safety
    You shall not find the least flaw in mine arms
    To pierce or taint me. What will great men be
    To please the king and bear authority!   *Exit.*
Byron. How fit a fort were this to handsel fortune! 145
    And I will win it though I lose myself;
    Though he prove harder than Egyptian marble

---

133. scorned; ... can,] *Parrott;* scorned, ... can; *Q1*.   145. fort] *Q1 (?);* sort *Q2, Parrott.*

135.] This line echoes strongly in *The Tragedy* when Byron finds it impossible to believe that his friend, La Fin, has betrayed him.

138–9.] La Fin joins Picoté as an exponent of the moral relativism associated with popular Machiavellianism.

140. *For riches*] as for riches.

popular respects] deference, attentive courtesies from the people.

141. *minions*] courtiers, in a pejorative sense. La Fin allows courtiers their goals of wealth and popularity and claims that only security (for his friends) is important to him.

145. *fort*] A damaged letter makes it uncertain whether the word is 'fort' or 'sort' (in the sense of 'lot' or a cast of dice). Parrott, like the earlier editors, preferred 'sort' though admitting that 'fort' went well with 'win' in the following line. I read 'fort' because of the way the image is carried on and because of Chapman's fondness for fortress imagery throughout the play, even if the alliteration is a little excessive here.

handsel] offer a token or gift on a special day or when inaugurating a new enterprise. To 'handsel fortune' is to make fortune propitious.

147. *Egyptian marble*] Marble from foreign sources was thought to be harder than local varieties.

I'll make him malleable as th'Ophir gold.
I am put off from this dull shore of ease
Into industrious and high-going seas, 150
Where, like Pelides in Scamander's flood,
Up to the ears in surges I will fight
And pluck French Ilion underneath the waves.
If to be highest still, be to be best,
All works to that end are the worthiest; 155
Truth is a golden ball cast in our way
To make us stripped by falsehood: and as Spain,
When the hot scuffles of barbarian arms
Smothered the life of Don Sebastian,
To gild the leaden rumour of his death 160
Gave for a slaughtered body, held for his,
A hundred thousand crowns, caused all the state
Of superstitious Portugal to mourn
And celebrate his solemn funerals;
The Moors to conquest thankful feasts prefer, 165

149. ease] *Parrott;* East *Q1.*

148. *Ophir gold*] Ophir was the legendary biblical home of the finest gold.
150. *industrious*] busy or active. The adjectives 'industrious' and 'high-going' suggest the world of new activity he is about to enter.
151. *Pelides ... flood*] Achilles (Pelides) fought the river-god, Xanthus, when the Scamander threatened to flood and destroy the Greek forces (*Iliad*, XXII).
152. *surges*] violent waves.
153.] Byron now thinks of himself as destroyer of the state rather than its saviour, like Achilles intent on the destruction of Troy (Ilion).
156. *Truth ... ball*] a reference to the legend of Atalanta who was outstripped ('stripped') in a race because she could not refrain from picking up the golden apples cast in her way by her suitor, Hippomenes. 'Stripped' may also mean 'denuded', 'fleeced by trickery'. 'Falsehood' refers to those who play false, as Hippomenes did. The sense is obscure, but Byron seems to be saying that compared with achievement (i.e., winning a race) what is called 'truth' is an illusion designed to deceive people's minds, like the royal coffin containing the body of the Switzer.
159. *Don Sebastian*] King of Portugal, killed at the battle of Alcazar in 1578 when aiding a claimant to the Moorish throne (see Peele's *Battle of Alcazar*). Grimeston mentions the large ransom paid by Spain for the supposed body of the king and then describes in vivid detail the history of the man who claimed to be Sebastian twenty years later (p. 952).
161. *held for his*] supposed to be his.
163. *superstitious*] credulous.
165. *prefer*] promote, put forward. The Moors are putting on feasts of gratitude for their conquest.

SC II]   THE CONSPIRACY OF CHARLES DUKE OF BYRON   101

  And all made with the carcass of a Switzer;
  So in the giantlike and politic wars
  Of barbarous greatness, raging still in peace,
  Shows to aspire just objects are laid on
  With cost, with labour, and with form enough,   170
  Which only makes our best acts brook the light,
  And their ends had, we think we have their right;
  So worst works are made good with good success
  And so for kings, pay subjects carcasses.   *Exit.*

      [ACT II   SCENE ii]
     Enter HENRY, ROISEAU.

Henry. Was he so courted?
Roiseau.   As a city dame
  Brought by her jealous husband to the court,
  Some elder courtiers entertaining him
  While others snatch a favour from his wife:
  One starts from this door, from that nook another,   5
  With gifts and junkets, and with printed phrase
  Steal her employment, shifting place by place
  Still as her husband comes: so Duke Byron
  Was wooed and worshipped in the archduke's court,
  And as th'assistants that your majesty   10

  166. *Switzer*] Swiss mercenary.
  167. *politic*] political, relating to a state.
  168. *barbarous greatness*] foreign, outlandish power; 'barbarous' suggests also 'savage, cruel' (Lat. *barbarus*).
  169. *shows*] public displays or spectacles.
aspire] attain, reach toward.
just objects] appropriate goals.
  170. *form*] orderly arrangement, proper shape.
  171. *brook*] endure, tolerate. It is the shapeliness of the spectacle alone that makes our best deeds endure the light of such public displays.
  172–3.] Our best acts, having achieved their ends or goals, we think we have a title to the real thing, the ideal. The extended simile is tortuous and ambiguous, but it is clear that it is concerned with ends and means, as l. 173 makes plain.
  174.] And so render to subjects carcasses instead of kings.

  6. *junkets*] sweetmeats, delicacies.
printed phrase] phrase good enough to print, a choice phrase.
  7. *Steal her employment*] secretly take up her time and employ her on their 'business'.

        Joined in commission with him or myself,
        Or any other doubted eye appeared,
        He ever vanished; and as such a dame
        As we compared with him before, being won
        To break faith to her husband, lose her fame,   15
        Stain both their progenies, and coming fresh
        From underneath the burthen of her shame,
        Visits her husband with as chaste a brow,
        As temperate and confirmed behaviour,
        As she came quitted from confession: 20
        So from his scapes would he present a presence,
        The practice of his state adultery
        And guilt that should a graceful bosom strike
        Drowned in the set lake of a hopeless cheek.
Henry. It may be he dissembled; or suppose   25
        He be a little tainted: men whom virtue
        Forms with the stuff of fortune, great and gracious,
        Must needs partake with fortune in her humour
        Of instability, and are like to shafts
        Grown crook'd with standing, which to rectify   30
        Must twice as much be bowed another way.
        He that hath borne wounds for his worthy parts
        Must for his worst be borne with; we must fit
        Our government to men, as men to it:

    12. *doubted eye*] watchful person he didn't trust.
    16. *both their progenies*] the parentage or lineage of both (*O.E.D.*, 5).
    19. *confirmed*] settled.
    20. *quitted*] absolved.
    21. *scapes*] transgressions, wanderings astray.
    presence] nobility of bearing.
    23. *graceful*] virtuous, possessed of graces of character.
    24. *set lake*] calm, unchanging lake. 'Set' is used of a rigid or unchanging facial expression; Chapman has combined the image of a lake where guilt is drowned without troubling its surface and the image of a face that shows no blush of shame on its cheek.
    hopeless] that gives no hope of better things.
    26–7.] Virtue is the shaping power that forms the basic material (stuff) provided by fortune, and although virtue may make them great, possessing also graces of character, they will continue to have the typical instability of fortune within them.
    28. *humour*] disposition.
    29. *shafts*] of arrows or lances.
    30. *standing*] stacked and unused, left idle.

SC II] THE CONSPIRACY OF CHARLES DUKE OF BYRON 103

> In old time, they that hunted savage beasts 35
> Are said to clothe themselves in savage skins;
> They that were fowlers when they went on fowling
> Wore garments made with wings resembling fowls;
> To bulls, we must not show ourselves in red,
> Nor to the warlike elephant in white. 40
> In all things governed, their infirmities
> Must not be stirred nor wrought on; Duke Byron
> Flows with adust and melancholy choler,
> And melancholy spirits are venomous,
> Not to be touched but as they may be cured: 45
> I therefore mean to make him change the air
> And send him further from those Spanish vapours
> That still bear fighting sulphur in their breasts,
> To breathe awhile in temperate English air
> Where lips are spiced with free and loyal counsels, 50
> Where policies are not ruinous, but saving,
> Wisdom is simple, valour righteous,
> Humane, and hating facts of brutish forces;
> And whose grave natures scorn the scoffs of France,
> The empty compliments of Italy, 55
> The any-way encroaching pride of Spain,
> And love men modest, hearty, just and plain.

35ff.] The passage is translated from Erasmus's *Parabolae* (quoted by Schoell, 'Chapman's "Commonplace Book"', *M.P.*, XVII, 204).

37. *fowling*] hunting or snaring wild fowl.

42. *stirred*] roused, set in motion.
wrought on] worked on.

43. *adust*] dry, parched; a medical term used in relation to the humours and applied to a body that was dry, hot, sallow, etc. (*O.E.D.*, 3).
melancholy choler] a combination of the two humours, one causing sullenness, the other rash anger.

47. *vapours*] fogs, exhalations, sometimes used of the humours within the body.

48. *fighting sulphur*] discharge of gunpowder. Henry claims that Byron has been breathing too long the 'strong, unsavoury smoke' (*O.E.D.* quotes Chapman, *Iliad*, XIV, 346) of his warmongering Spanish (Savoyard) companions.

50. *spiced with*] seasoned, flavoured with.

53. *facts*] evil deeds, crimes.

54. *scoffs*] derisive jests.

55. *compliments*] ceremonious words and actions or gestures.

56. *any-way encroaching*] encroaching in any and every direction.

104 THE CONSPIRACY OF CHARLES DUKE OF BYRON [ACT II

[*Enter*] SAVOY, *whispering with* LA FIN.

Savoy. [*Aside*] I'll sound him for Byron; and what I find
    In the king's depth, I'll draw up and inform
    In excitations to the duke's revolt   60
    When next I meet with him.
La Fin. [*Aside*]   It must be done
    With praising of the duke, from whom the king
    Will take to give himself; which, told the duke,
    Will take his heart up into all ambition.
Savoy. [*Aside*] I know it, politic friend, and 'tis my purpose.   65
                                            Exit LA FIN.
[*To Henry*] Your majesty hath missed a royal sight,
The Duke Byron on his brave beast Pastrana
Who sits him like a full-sailed argosy
Danced with a lofty billow, and as snug
Plies to his bearer, both their motions mixed;   70
And being considered in their site together,
They do the best present the state of man
In his first royalty ruling, and of beasts
In their first loyalty serving – one commanding
And no way being moved, the other serving   75

    58. *sound*] The metaphor of using a line and lead to sound for depth is carried on in 'the king's depth'.
    62–3. *from whom ... himself*] The king will detract from Byron's praise in order to give himself some credit.
    67–81.] Byron on Pastrana has many analogues in the literature of the time. One might note Sidney's portrait of Dorus on horseback in *The Arcadia*: 'But he (as if Centaurlike he had bene one peece with the horse) was no more moved, than one is with the going of his owne legges: and in effect so did he command him, as his owne limmes, for though he had both spurres and wande, they seemed rather markes of soveraintie, then instruments of punishment ...' (*Complete Works*, ed. A. Feuillerat, I, 178–9). Another example is Claudius' praise of a Norman horseman to Laertes in *Hamlet*, IV.vii.83–8. The image also suggests one of the many contemporary equestrian statues.
    68. *argosy*] a merchant vessel of the largest size, originally thought of as from Ragusa or Venice.
    69. *danced*] tossed as in a dance.
    70. *plies*] bends.
    71. *site*] attitude, situation.
    73. *In ... ruling*] in the Garden of Eden.
    75. *moved*] aroused, affected by emotion. In the four-term rhetorical figure 'commanding ... moved ... serving ... compelled', 'moved' is parallel and opposite to 'compelled' and therefore suggests in its negative context 'unmoved by any feeling of pride or heated emotion'.

                    And no way being compelled – of all the sights
                    That ever my eyes witnessed; and they make
                    A doctrinal and witty hieroglyphic
                    Of a blest kingdom, to express and teach
                    Kings to command as they could serve, and subjects   80
                    To serve as if they had power to command.
Henry. You are a good old horseman, I perceive,
                    And still out all the use of that good part;
                    Your wit is of the true Pierian spring
                    That can make anything of anything.   85
Savoy. So brave a subject as the duke, no king
                    Seated on earth can vaunt of but your highness,
                    So valiant, loyal, and so great in service.
Henry. No question he sets valour in his height
                    And hath done service to an equal pitch,   90
                    Fortune attending him with fit events
                    To all his vent'rous and well-laid attempts.
Savoy. Fortune to him was Juno to Alcides,
                    For when or where did she but open way
                    To any act of his? What stone took he   95
                    With her help, or without his own lost blood?
                    What fort won he by her, or was not forced?
                    What victory but 'gainst odds? On what commander,

    78. *doctrinal*] instructive.
witty] clever, ingenious.
hieroglyphic] emblem.
    80. *as*] as though.
    82. *a good old horseman*] Henry makes a jocular remark about Savoy's ability to ride any horse (or topic) for all its worth.
    83. *still out*] distill out.
    part] function, almost in the sense of an actor's 'part' as horseman.
    84. *the true Pierian spring*] a spring sacred to the Muses in Pieria, a region of Thessaly supposed to be the home of the Muses. Pope's lines in the *Essay on Criticism* are well known: 'A little learning is a dangerous thing; / Drink deep, or taste not the Pierian spring . . .' (ll. 215–16).
    86. *brave*] stout-hearted, also showy in his splendour.
    87. *Seated*] enthroned.
    89. *in his height*] on the loftiest eminence.
    90. *pitch*] summit, height.
    91. *fit events*] appropriate outcomes.
    92. *vent'rous*] venturous, daring.
    93. *Juno to Alcides*] as hostile to him as Juno was to Hercules; ll. 94–101 are drawn from Plutarch's *De Alexandri magni* II, 9 (340E, F).
    95. *stone*] the stone of a city or citadel (synecdoche).
    97. *forced*] overcome by force.

Sleepy or negligent, did he ever charge?
What summer ever made she fair to him? 100
What winter not of one continued storm?
Fortune is so far from his creditress
That she owes him much, for in him her looks
Are lovely, modest and magnanimous,
Constant, victorious; and in his achievements 105
Her cheeks are drawn out with a virtuous redness
Out of his eager spirit to victory
And chaste contention to convince with honour;
And, I have heard, his spirits have flowed so high
In all his conflicts against any odds 110
That, in his charge, his lips have bled with fervour.
How served he at your famous siege of Dreux?
Where the enemy, assured of victory,
Drew out a body of four thousand horse
And twice six thousand foot, and like a crescent 115
Stood for the signal; you, that showed yourself
A sound old soldier, thinking it not fit
To give your enemy the odds and honour
Of the first stroke, commanded de la Guiche
To let fly all his cannons, that did pierce 120
The adverse thickest squadrons and had shot
Nine volleys ere the foe had once given fire.
Your troop was charged, and when your duke's old father
Met with th'assailants, and their grove of reiters

106. *drawn out*] delineated as in a portrait.
108. *chaste contention*] virtuous endeavour.
convince] conquer, overcome.
111. *in his charge*] as he led a charge of cavalry.
112. *siege of Dreux*] Chapman follows closely Grimeston's account of the battle of Ivry which took place when Mayenne tried to raise the siege of Dreux. Parrott notes that Grimeston uses the marginal note 'Siege of Dreux' on p. 748 when describing the battle of Ivry.
113. *assured*] confident (rather than 'certain' in a modern sense).
118. *odds*] advantage.
119. *de la Guiche*] Henry's Master of Artillery on the field.
123. *father*] Armand de Gontaut, Baron de Biron, a soldier of considerable fame who gave his support to Henry when he succeeded to the throne; he was killed at the siege of Epernay in 1592.
124. *grove*] The troop of cavalry with their lances is being compared to a thick wood; Grimeston uses the phrase 'groue of Reistres' (p. 749).
reiters] German cavalry.

SC II]   THE CONSPIRACY OF CHARLES DUKE OF BYRON   107

    Repulsed so fiercely, made them turn their beards   125
    And rally up themselves behind their troops,
    Fresh forces seeing your troops a little severed
    From that part first assaulted gave it charge,
    Which then this duke made good, seconds his father,
    Beats through and through the enemy's greatest strength,   130
    And breaks the rest like billows 'gainst a rock,
    And there the heart of that huge battle broke.
Henry. The heart but now came on, in that strong body
    Of twice two thousand horse, led by du Maine,
    Which, if I would be glorious, I could say   135
    I first encountered.
Savoy.   How did he take in
    Beaune in view of that invincible army
    Led by the Lord Great Constable of Castile!
    Autun and Nuits, in Burgundy chased away
    Viscount Tavannes' troops before Dijon,   140
    And puts himself in, and there that was won.
Henry. If you would only give me leave, my lord,
    I would do right to him, yet must not give –
Savoy. A league from Fountaine François, when you sent him
    To make discovery of the Castile army,   145
    When he discerned 'twas it, with wondrous wisdom
    Joined to his spirit, he seemed to make retreat,
    But when they pressed him, and the Baron of Lux

    128. *gave it charge*] made an impetuous attack upon it.
    134. *du Maine*] more commonly Mayenne, brother of Henry Duke of Guise. After the murder of his brother, he commanded the League against Henry IV but was defeated several times and eventually submitted in 1596. Cf. *Consp.*, I.ii.56.
    135. *if ... glorious*] Grimeston's narrative at this point proceeds to a vivid account of Henry's valour in meeting Mayenne's attack (p. 749). 'Glorious' is 'boastful'.
    138. *Lord Great Constable*] Ferdinando de Velasco, commander of the Spanish army supporting the League in 1595. Henry's victories at Beaune, Autun and Nuits led to his conquest of the whole of Burgundy.
    144. *Fountaine François*] Fontaine Française, some 30 km. north-east of Dijon, where Henry gained one of his major victories against the League in 1595. De Serres and Grimeston give most of the credit to Henry, but Chapman has made Savoy choose those events during the battle which serve to glorify Byron (pp. 781–2).
    147. *spirit*] ardour, courage.
    148. *Baron of Lux*] Grimeston reports that the Baron of Lux was sent out

        Set on their charge so hotly that his horse
        Was slain and he most dangerously engaged,   150
        Then turned your brave duke head, and with such ease
        As doth an echo beat back violent sounds
        With their own forces, he, as if a wall
        Start suddenly before them, pashed them all
        Flat as the earth, and there was that field won.   155
Henry. Y'are all the field wide.
Savoy.   O, I ask you pardon.
        The strength of that field yet lay in his back,
        Upon the foe's part; and what is to come
        Of this your marshal, now your worthy duke,
        Is much beyond the rest: for now he sees   160
        A sort of horse troops issue from the woods
        In number near twelve hundred; and retiring
        To tell you that the entire army followed,
        Before he could relate it, he was forced
        To turn head and receive the main assault   165
        Of five horse troops, only with twenty horse.
        The first he met he tumbled to the earth
        And broke through all, not daunted with two wounds,
        One on his head, another on his breast,
        The blood of which drowned all the field in doubt.   170
        Your majesty himself was then engaged,
        Your power not yet arrived, and up you brought

with Byron to discover whether the enemy's full army were approaching and describes the incident in which Byron saved the life of Lux. Parrott notes that Lux was a close friend of Byron's (p. 603).

    151. *turned ... head*] turned to face the enemy.

    152-3.] Schoell quotes from Erasmus's *Parabolae*: 'Sicut echo non sonat nisi cum reddit acceptam vocem' ('Commonplace Book', p. 213). Chapman quite typically makes the image far more vigorous and changes the observed natural phenomenon to a conflict.

    154. *start*] spring up, leap.

    pashed] crushed.

    157. *in his back*] to the rear.

    161. *sort*] group or company (*O.E.D.*, II, 17). Shakespeare's usage, 'Sent from a sort of tinkers to the King' (*2H6*, III.ii.277) and Chapman's 'as a sort of beasts, Kept by their Guardians' (*Iliads*, To the Reader, ll. 145-6) suggest a crowd or herd without much order.

    167. *tumbled*] cast down.

    170. *drowned ... doubt*] The blood from Byron's wounds filled all the army with concern about the outcome of the battle.

                The little strength you had, a cloud of foes
                Ready to burst in storms about your ears;
                Three squadrons rushed against you, and the first   175
                You took so fiercely that you beat their thoughts
                Out of their bosoms from the urgèd fight;
                The second all amazed you overthrew,
                The third dispersed, with five and twenty horse
                Left of the four score that pursued the chase.   180
                And this brave conquest now your marshal seconds
                Against two squadrons, but with fifty horse;
                One after other he defeats them both
                And made them run, like men whose heels were tripped,
                And pitch their heads in their great general's lap;   185
                And him he sets on, as he had been shot
                Out of a cannon; beats him into rout,
                And as a little brook being overrun
                With a black torrent, that bears all things down
                His fury overtakes, his foamy back   190
                Loaded with cattle and with stacks of corn
                And makes the miserable plowman mourn;
                So was du Maine surcharged, and so Byron
                Flowed over all his forces, every drop
                Of his lost blood bought with a worthy man;   195
                And only with a hundred gentlemen
                He won the place, from fifteen hundred horse.
Henry. He won the place?
Savoy.   On my word, so 'tis said.
Henry. Fie, you have been extremely misinformed.
Savoy. I only tell your highness what I heard: 200
                I was not there; and though I have been rude
                With wonder of his valour, and presumed
                To keep his merit in his full career,

   177. *urgèd fight*] the fight to which they had been exhorted and for which their 'thoughts' (l. 176) had been prepared.
   182. *but with*] with only.
   185. *great general*] Mayenne.
   186. *sets on*] attacks.
   193. *surcharged*] overwhelmed (maintaining the figure of the flood).
   201. *rude*] unskilful, also unmannerly.
   202. *presumed*] dared, took the liberty of.
   203.] To praise his merit at the full, in its full gallop. 'Full career' refers to the charging gallop of a horseman.

110 THE CONSPIRACY OF CHARLES DUKE OF BYRON [ACT II

> Not hearing you when yours made such a thunder,
> Pardon my fault since 'twas t'extol your servant.   205
> But is it not most true that 'twixt ye both
> So few achieved the conquest of so many?
>
> *Henry.* It is a truth must make me ever thankful,
> But not performed by him: was not I there?
> Commanded him, and in the main assault   210
> Made him but second?
> *Savoy.*   He's the capital soldier
> That lives this day in holy Christendom,
> Except your highness – always except Plato.
> *Henry.* We must not give to one, to take from many:
> For, not to praise our countrymen, here served   215
> The general My Lor' Norris, sent from England,
> As great a captain as the world affords,
> One fit to lead and fight for Christendom;
> Of more experience, and of stronger brain,

---

216. My Lor'] *Q1*; My Lord *Q2*; Mylor' *Parrott*.

204.] Savoy's statement sounds more than a trifle sarcastic, though he tries to make amends in the following apology. 'Not hearing' can refer to the fact that he has paid too little attention to Henry's interjections, or to his previous statement that he 'was not there' and reports only what he 'heard'. 'Yours' is ambiguous in its reference, suggesting both Henry's 'merit' as a soldier and his 'career' in the battle charges, and 'thunder' is the thunder of hooves and of fame.

211. *capital*] chief.

213. *always except Plato*] 'It goes without saying that the greatest is excluded from comparisons.' I have not been able to trace this as a proverbial expression, but it is clear that Savoy's tone is impertinent. Chapman shows Savoy playing upon Henry's vanity with great cleverness and apparent delight in ironic remarks that can be taken in more than one sense.

216. *My Lor' Norris*] Sir John Norris and Sir Roger Williams (l. 224) were celebrated Elizabethan soldiers who had fought with Leicester in the Low Countries. Norris commanded an expedition to Brittany in May 1591 to aid Henry IV against the Catholic Leaguers and their Spanish allies, and Williams led a detachment of this force at Dieppe where Essex joined him in August with reinforcements. The siege of Rouen which Henry mounted with their assistance was a failure on this occasion. However Norris met with considerable success on a later expedition to aid Henry's forces in Brittany in 1593–4. He died in 1597.

217–18.] Note Essex's description of Henry IV in his *Apologie* (pr. 1603): 'a King, who, for his admirable valure, and often fighting with his owne hands, was not onely the most famous, but the most renowed Captaine of Christendome ...' (sig. B1).

SC II]   THE CONSPIRACY OF CHARLES DUKE OF BYRON   111

As valiant for abiding; in command   220
On any sudden, upon any ground,
And in the form of all occasions
As ready and as profitably dauntless;
And here was then another, Colonel Williams,
A worthy captain, and more like the duke   225
Because he was less temperate than the general;
And being familiar with the man you praise,
Because he knew him haughty and incapable
Of all comparison, would compare with him,
And hold his swelling valour to the mark   230
Justice had set in him, and not his will;
And as in open vessels filled with water
And on men's shoulders borne, they put treen cups
To keep the wild and slippery element
From washing over, follow all his sways   235
And tickle aptness to exceed his bounds
And at the brim contain him, so this knight
Swum in Byron, and held him but to right.

220. *abiding*] enduring, holding out.
221. *sudden*] immediate need or emergency.
ground] reason, solid basis.
222.] And in the manner proper to all occasions.
224. *Colonel Williams*] Sir Roger Williams, a Welsh soldier with wide experience in expeditions against Spanish forces, was mentioned by Essex in his *Apologie* as having accompanied him to Portugal: 'But though I had no charge, I made my brother Generall of the horse, my faithful friend Sir *Roger Williams* Colonel of the infantery ...' (sig. A4v). Chapman may have recollected this passage in using the term 'Colonel' since he no doubt was an avid reader of the *Apologie* in 1603. Camden tells us in his *Annales* that Essex attended the funeral of Williams at 'Pauls Church' in 1595 along with 'as many military men as were in the City'. Camden's account of his character is like Henry's observation of both Williams and Byron: 'he might have been equalled with the famousest Captaines of our age, if with more wary wisedome he could have tempered the heat of his warlike minde' (3rd ed. 1635, trans. R. Norton, p. 451).
229. *compare*] vie.
230. *mark*] limit, boundary. Any just appraisal would set limits to his valour though his 'will' (desire) would acknowledge no such limits.
233. *treen cups*] cups made of wood.
236. *tickle*] unsteady (adj.). 'His' and 'him' in ll. 235–7 refer to the water but help to keep Byron's nature in mind in the analogy with water.
238. *Swum*] floated, like the treen cups, in Bryon's unstable disposition.

> But leave these hot comparisons, he's mine own,
> And, than what I possess, I'll more be known. 240

Savoy. [*Aside*] All this shall to the duke: I fished for this.

Exeunt.

241.1.] FINIS. *Actus Secundi. follows l. 241.1 in Q1.*

239. *hot*] sharp, heated.
240.] I'll be known to be greater than my possessions.

Act III

ACT III SCENE i

Enter LA FIN, BYRON *following unseen.*

La Fin. [*Aside*] A feignèd passion in his hearing now,
Which he thinks I perceive not, making conscience
Of the revolt that he hath urged to me,
Which now he means to prosecute, would sound
How deep he stands affected with that scruple.   5
[*Aloud*] As when the moon hath comforted the night
And set the world in silver of her light,
The planets, asterisms and whole state of heaven
In beams of gold descending; all the winds
Bound up in caves, charged not to drive abroad   10
Their cloudy heads; an universal peace
Proclaimed in silence of the quiet earth;
Soon as her hot and dry fumes are let loose,
Storms and clouds mixing, suddenly put out
The eyes of all those glories, the creation   15
Turned into chaos, and we then desire,
For all our joy of life, the death of sleep;
So when the glories of our lives, men's loves,

ACT III SCENE i] ACTUS 3. SCENA I. *Q1*.   6. *Aloud*] This ed.

2. *conscience*] scruple, tenderness of conscience.
5. *that scruple*] La Fin wishes to take a 'sounding' as to the depth of Byron's conscience in the matter of revolt, a scruple he is now going to pretend to possess.
8. *asterisms*] constellations.
10. *Bound ... caves*] In Roman mythology, the winds were kept chained in deep caves by Aeolus, god of the winds, except when he chose to release them.
13. *her ... and dry fumes*] 'Her' is presumably the earth's. In the medieval classification of the elements, hot and dry are associated with fire, but earth (cold and dry) might exhale such vapours or fumes into the atmosphere and disturb the balance of the elements, as La Fin describes.
15. *those glories*] moon and stars.
16. *chaos*] the confused, unformed state of the universe before the elements were brought into a state of order by God's second act of creation. Cf. Byron's graphic description of a return to chaos, *Trag.*, I.ii.17ff.

   Clear consciences, our fames, and loyalties,
   That did us worthy comfort, are eclipsed,   20
   Grief and disgrace invade us; and for all
   Our night of life besides, our misery craves
   Dark earth would ope and hide us in our graves.
Byron. How strange is this!
La Fin.   What! Did your highness hear?
Byron. Both heard and wondered that your wit and spirit,   25
   And profit in experience of the slaveries
   Imposed on us, in those mere politic terms
   Of love, fame, loyalty, can be carried up
   To such a height of ignorant conscience,
   Of cowardice, and dissolution,   30
   In all the free-born powers of royal man.
   You that have made way through all the guards
   Of jealous state, and seen on both your sides
   The pikes' points charging heaven to let you pass,
   Will you, in flying with a scrupulous wing   35
   Above those pikes to heavenward, fall on them?
   This is like men that, spirited with wine,
   Pass dangerous places safe, and die for fear
   With only thought of them, being simply sober.
   We must, in passing to our wishèd ends   40
   Through things called good and bad, be like the air
   That evenly interposed betwixt the seas
   And the opposèd element of fire,
   At either toucheth, but partakes with neither,
   Is neither hot nor cold, but with a slight   45

27. *mere politic terms*] Byron deliberately belittles love, fame and loyalty as merely expedient terms which help to enslave the free man.
 30. *dissolution*] enfeeblement, or more strongly, disintegration.
 31. *royal man*] Chapman's classic exposition of these 'free-born powers' is in *Bussy D'Ambois*, II.i.194–9.
 33. *jealous state*] watchful or suspicious power.
 34. *charging heaven*] warning or threatening heaven. The image is that of one seeking glory in battle or a struggle for power.
 35. *flying ... wing*] flying guided by conscience or principle (rather than by a desire for glory).
 36. *fall on them*] become the victim of power.
 43. *opposed element*] Fire is opposed to water in the pattern of the four elements. This passage is from Plutarch, *De primo frigido*, 951D (Schoell, p. 209).
 45. *slight*] light, insubstantial.

And harmless temper mixed of both th'extremes.
La Fin. 'Tis shrewd.
Byron.   There is no truth of any good
    To be discerned on earth, and by conversion
    Nought therefore simply bad; but as the stuff
    Prepared for arras pictures is no picture   50
    Till it be formed, and man hath cast the beams
    Of his imaginous fancy through it,
    In forming ancient kings and conquerors
    As he conceives they looked and were attired,
    Though they were nothing so: so all things here   55
    Have all their price set down from men's concepts,
    Which make all terms and actions good or bad
    And are but pliant and well-coloured threads
    Put into feignèd images of truth;
    To which to yield and kneel, as truth-pure kings,   60
    That pulled us down with clear truths of their gospel,
    Were superstition to be hissed to hell.
La Fin. Believe it, this is reason.
Byron.   'Tis the faith
    Of reason and of wisdom.
La Fin.   You persuade
    As if you could create: what man can shun   65
    The searches and compressions of your graces?

56. concepts] *Q1;* conceits *Shepherd, Parrott.*   66. your graces] *Q1;* your Grace's *Parrott.*

---

46. *temper*] disposition.
49. *simply*] wholly.
stuff] woven material.
50. *arras pictures*] pictures woven into the tapestry fabric.
52. *imaginous*] image-making.
55–7.] Loane notes *Caesar and Pompey*, III.i.39, 'Who cares for up or down, when all's but thought?', and *Hamlet*, II.ii.248–50, 'for there is nothing either good or bad, but thinking makes it so'.
56. *price*] value.
concepts] conceits or opinions.
60. *truth-pure kings*] kings whose words are sure truths.
61. *pulled us down*] forced us to kneel. The image of kings and conquerors woven into a tapestry is carried on in these lines: we should no more submit and kneel to general opinions about what is good and bad than we should to ancient kings in tapestry pictures.
63. *reason*] well-supported argument, agreeable to the reason.
63–4. *the faith ... wisdom*] the belief required by reason and wisdom.
66. *searches and compressions*] the searching out and succinct expression (of

Byron. We must have these lures when we hawk for friends,
    And wind about them like a subtle river
    That, seeming only to run on his course,
    Doth search yet as he runs, and still finds out   70
    The easiest parts of entry on the shore;
    Gliding so slyly by, as scarce it touched,
    Yet still eats something in it: so must those
    That have large fields and currents to dispose.
    Come, let us join our streams, we must run far   75
    And have but little time: the Duke of Savoy
    Is shortly to be gone, and I must needs
    Make you well known to him.
La Fin.   But hath your highness
    Some enterprise of value joined with him?
Byron. With him and greater persons.
La Fin.   I will creep   80
    Upon my bosom in your princely service;
    Vouchsafe to make me known. I hear there lives not
    So kind, so bountiful and wise a prince,
    But in your own excepted excellence.
Byron. He shall both know and love you: are you mine?   85
La Fin. I take the honour of it, on my knee,
    And hope to quite it with your majesty.   [*Exeunt.*]

---

87. *Exeunt*] Phelps; *Exit Q1*.

truths). One might have expected 'comprehensions' rather than 'compressions' in this context. Perhaps Chapman conflated the Latin verbs 'comprimo, compressus' (press or squeeze together) and 'comprehendo, comprehensus' (grasp, take hold of, apprehend) in this single word, suggesting both meanings.

   your graces] your exceptional qualities or virtues. *O.E.D.* notes *Macbeth*, 'the King-becoming Graces' (IV.iii.91). Parrott's correction to 'your Grace's' seems unnecessary.

   67. *lures*] artificial quarries constructed of feathers with a long cord attached, used by the falconer to recall a falcon or hawk.

   71. *easiest ... shore*] the soft parts of the bank which the river eats away as it follows its course ('eats something in it'). 'Subtle river' suggests not only the crafty insinuating stream that glides slily by, but also the Latin sense of 'subtilis', thin, slender, not a headlong torrent.

   74. *dispose*] manage, direct.

   78. *your highness*] La Fin moves rapidly from 'highness' to 'princely' to 'your majesty' in the following lines.

   84. *excepted*] excluded.

   87. *quite it*] requite it.

[ACT III Scene ii]

Enter SAVOY, RONCAS, ROCHETTE, BRETON, [Servant].

Savoy. La Fin is in the right and will obtain;
    He draweth with his weight, and like a plummet
    That sways a door, with falling off pulls after.
Roncas. Thus will La Fin be brought a stranger to you
    By him he leads; he conquers that is conquered,   5
    That's sought as hard to win, that sues to be won.
Savoy. But is my painter warned to take his picture,
    When he shall see me and present La Fin?
Rochette. He is, my lord, and as your highness willed,
    All we will press about him and admire   10
    The royal promise of his rare aspect,
    As if he heard not.
Savoy.   'Twill inflame him.
    Such tricks the archduke used t'extol his greatness,
    Which compliments, though plain men hold absurd,
    And a mere remedy for desire of greatness,   15
    Yet great men use them as their state potatoes,
    High cullises, and potions to excite
    The lust of their ambition; and this duke
    You know is noted in his natural garb
    Extremely glorious, who will therefore bring   20
    An appetite expecting such a bait.

0.1. Servant] *This ed.*   16. their state] *Q1 (corr.);* they eate *Q1 (uncorr.).*

0.1. *Servant*] A servant or attendant is needed at l. 22 to fetch the painter. There is no entry marked for the painter but he must come in with his materials well before l. 117.
    1. *in the right*] following the proper course.
    obtain] succeed, gain what he is after.
    2. *plummet*] ball or lump of lead, here used to pull a door to.
    7. *take his picture*] sketch or paint his likeness.
    8. *present*] bring forward, introduce.
    11. *rare aspect*] remarkably fine appearance.
    15. *mere*] complete.
    16. *state*] concerned with political ends.
    potatoes] sweet potatoes, 'supposed to have aphrodisiac qualities, to which there are frequent references' (*O.E.D.*). Cf. *Wiv.*, V.v.17.
    17. *high cullises*] rich broths.
    19. *garb*] behaviour.
    20. *glorious*] eager for glory: cf. *Consp.*, I.i.71.
    21. *expecting*] awaiting, ready for.

He comes: go instantly and fetch the painter.
                                            [*Exit* Servant.]

                  Enter BYRON, LA FIN.

Byron. All honour to your highness –
Savoy.   'Tis most true. [*Embracing him.*]
    All honours flow to me, in you their ocean;
    As welcome, worthiest duke, as if my marquisate   25
    Were circled with you in these amorous arms.
Byron. I sorrow, sir, I could not bring it with me
    That I might so supply the fruitless compliment
    Of only visiting your excellence,
    With which the king now sends me t'entertain you;   30
    Which notwithstanding doth confer this good,
    That it hath given me some small time to show
    My gratitude for the many secret bounties
    I have, by this your lord ambassador,
    Felt from your highness; and in short, t'assure you   35
    That all my most deserts are at your service.

                  [*Enter* Painter.]

Savoy. Had the king sent me by you half his kingdom,
    It were not half so welcome.
Byron.   For defect
    Of whatsoever in myself, my lord,
    I here commend to your most princely service   40
    This honoured friend of mine.
Savoy.   Your name, I pray you sir?
La Fin. La Fin, my lord.
Savoy.   La Fin? [*To Roncas*] Is this the man
    That you so recommended to my love?

22.1. *Exit* Servant] *This ed.*   23.1. *Embracing him*] *Parrott.*   36.1.
Enter Painter] *This ed.*   42. *To Roncas*] *Parrott.*

---

    25. *my marquisate*] of Saluces. Savoy takes every opportunity of stressing the warmth of his attachment to this marquisate which was the chief subject of negotiation with Henry during his visit to the French court.
    28. *supply*] add to.
    36. *most deserts*] best qualities, greatest merits.
    36.1.] Where the painter should enter is at the prompter's or stage director's discretion since there is no indication in the quarto.

Roncas. The same, my lord.
Savoy.   Y'are next my lord the duke
　The most desired of all men. [*To Byron*] O my lord,   45
　The king and I have had a mighty conflict
　About your conflicts and your matchless worth
　In military virtues, which I put
　In balance with the continent of France,
　In all the peace and safety it enjoys,   50
　And made even weight with all he could put in
　Of all men's else, and of his own deserts.
Byron. Of all men's else? Would he weigh other men's
　With my deservings?
Savoy.   Ay, upon my life,
　The English general, the My Lor' Norris,   55
　That served amongst you here, he paralleled
　With you at all parts, and in some preferred him;
　And Colonel Williams, a Welsh colonel,
　He made a man that at your most contained you,
　Which the Welsh herald of their praise, the cuckoo,   60
　Would scarce have put in his monology –
　In jest, and said with reverence to his merits.
Byron. With reverence? Reverence scorns him! By the spoil
　Of all her merits in me, he shall rue it.

45. *To Byron*] Parrott.　52. his] *Q1* (*corr.*); their *Q1* (*uncorr.*).

---

49. *continent*] whole continuous area.
52. *all men's else*] all other men's.
57. *at all parts*] in all points.
59. *that . . . you*] at your very height of merit comprehended you within his greater merit. There may be some sense also of 'contained' as 'checked' or 'restrained'.
60.] The cuckoo as 'Welsh herald' is imagined as monotonously singing the praises of the Welsh: perhaps a proverbial expression (Tilley, A233). Cf. Middleton, *A Trick to Catch the Old One*, IV.v.206–8: 'Why, thou rogue of universality, do not I know thee? Thy sound is like the cuckoo, the Welsh ambassador.' In Dekker's play, *The Welsh Embassador* (*c.* 1621–3), Eldred tells how the cuckoo was so named along the Welsh borders because when the first cuckoo came in spring, the Welsh raiders made their appearance: 'and so fright the ymen that they to still theire wrawlinge bastards cry out, husht the welsh embassador comes' (IV.ii.67–80, *Dramatic Works*, IV, 361, ed. F. Bowers).
61. *monology*] monologue.
63. *spoil*] damaging, pillaging. 'Her merits' are the qualities of reverence in Byron which ought to receive reward instead of being pillaged.

120　THE CONSPIRACY OF CHARLES DUKE OF BYRON [ACT III

  Did ever Curtian Gulf play such a part?　　　　　　　65
  Had Curtius been so used if he had brooked
  That ravenous whirlpool, poured his solid spirits
  Through earth dissolvèd sinews, stopped her veins,
  And rose with savèd Rome upon his back,
  As I swum pools of fire and gulfs of brass　　　　　　70
  To save my country, thrust this venturous arm
  Beneath her ruins, took her on my neck
  And set her safe on her appeasèd shore?
  And opes the king a fouler bog than this
  In his so rotten bosom, to devour　　　　　　　　　　75
  Him that devoured what else had swallowed him,
  In a detraction so with spite embrued,
  And drown such good in such ingratitude?
  My spirit as yet but stooping to his rest
  Shines hotly in him, as the sun in clouds,　　　　　　 80
  Purpled and made proud with a peaceful even;
  But when I throughly set to him, his cheeks
  Will, like those clouds, forgo their colour quite
  And his whole blaze smoke into endless night.

  65. *Curtian Gulf*] Chapman may have drawn the story of Curtius from a number of sources (Parrott suggests Livy, and Schoell Plutarch). When a great gulf opened in the Roman forum, disaster threatened until Curtius, a noble Roman youth, having heard the oracle rode his horse into the gulf which then closed over his head. Byron asks whether Curtius would have been treated as he has been, had Curtius survived the ordeal.
  66. *brooked*] endured.
  68. *earth dissolvèd sinews*] probably 'earth's dissolved sinews', a suppressed genitive.
  70. *gulfs of brass*] gulfs of molten metal, suggestive of the interior of the earth and of hell (cf. Othello's vision of hell: 'roast me in sulphur, / Wash me in steep-down gulfs of liquid fire!' *Oth*., V.ii.282–3). The 'pools' and 'gulfs' Byron swam through to save his country are the battle encounters of his career, 'fire' and 'brass' referring to the flame and smoke of the firing of cannons which were often constructed with bores of brass.
  71. *venturous*] daring.
  73. *appeasèd*] pacified.
  77. *detraction*] disparagement.
  embrued] steeped, saturated (*O.E.D.*, 5)
  79–84.] The setting sun, suggested by 'stooping' and 'set', is Byron's fiery spirit in relation to the king. The sun is usually an image of royalty, as in *Richard II*, but Byron makes the king's glory merely the reflection on clouds of the setting sun, a glory which will disappear in night as soon as Byron's sun has gone elsewhere.

Savoy. Nay nay, we must have no such gall, my lord,   85
    O'erflow our friendly livers; my relation
    Only delivers my inflamèd zeal
    To your religious merits, which methinks
    Should make your highness canonised a saint.
Byron. What had his arms been without my arm   90
    That with his motion made the whole field move?
    And this held up, we still had victory.
    When overcharged with number, his few friends
    Retired amazed, I set them on assured,
    And what rude ruin seized on I confirmed;   95
    When I left leading, all his army reeled,
    One fell on other foul, and as the Cyclop
    That, having lost his eye, struck every way,
    His blows directed to no certain scope;
    Or as the soul departed from the body,   100
    The body wants coherence in his parts,
    Cannot consist, but sever and dissolve;
    So, I removed once, all his armies shook,
    Panted and fainted and were ever flying,
    Like wandering pulses spersed through bodies dying.   105
Savoy. It cannot be denied, 'tis all so true

   86. *friendly livers*] The liver was thought to be the seat of the passions, in particular of love, hence 'friendly'. A liver overflowing with gall or bile would produce the bitter passion of Byron's previous speech.
   88. *religious*] sacred, holy, to be venerated (Lat. *religiosus*).
   91. *his*] its.
   92. *this*] this arm (doubtless his sword arm).
   94. *amazed*] overcome with fear.
   assured] made confident or secure.
   95. *rude ruin*] violent destruction.
   confirmed] established firmly.
   97. *foul*] shamefully (*O.E.D.*, adv., C3).
   Cyclop] singular form, used occasionally instead of 'Cyclops'. The comparison of a leaderless army to the Cyclops blinded by Ulysses (*Odyssey*, IX) and the further comparison to a body losing its soul are derived from Plutarch's *De Alexandri magni*, (336F, 337A), as Parrott points out. In certain phrases, Chapman keeps remarkably close to Xylander's Latin version of Plutarch.
   99. *scope*] mark aimed at.
   101. *wants*] lacks.
   102. *consist*] hold together.
   sever] separate.
   dissolve] disintegrate.
   105. *spersed*] dispersed.

122　THE CONSPIRACY OF CHARLES DUKE OF BYRON [ACT III

   That what seems arrogance is desert in you.
Byron. What monstrous humours feed a prince's blood,
   Being bad to good men, and to bad men good!
Savoy. Well, let these contradictions pass, my lord,   110
   Till they be reconciled, or put in form
   By power given to your will, and you present
   The fashion of a perfect government;
   In mean space but a word, we have small time
   To spend in private, which I wish may be   115
   With all advantage taken: Lord La Fin –
            [*They converse apart.*]
Roncas. Is't not a face of excellent presentment?
   Though not so amorous with pure white and red,
   Yet is the whole proportion singular.
Rochette. That ever I beheld!
Breton.   It hath good lines   120
   And tracts drawn through it; the purfle rare.
Roncas. I heard the famous and right learned Earl
   And Archbishop of Lyons, Pierce Pinac,

---

113. perfect] *Shepherd;* prefect *Q1, Q2.* 121. purfle] *Q1;* profile *Parrott.*
123. Pierce] *Q2;* Pierse *Q1;* Pierre *Parrott.*

---

 107. *desert*] a quality worthy of reward.
 111. *in form*] in orderly arrangement.
 114. *in mean space*] in the meantime.
 117. *presentment*] delineation, representation. The lords are clustered about the painter, admiring his work as previously arranged.
 118. *pure . . . red*] colours associated with lovers' complexions.
 121. *tracts*] lineaments, features (*O.E.D.*, 7).
 purfle] contour or outline, the outline of the face as drawn by the artist: sometimes = profile (*O.E.D.*, 3), but more often at this period refers to the border or outline of anything.
 123. *Pierce Pinac*] Grimeston interpolates a brief history of 'Peter de Pinac, Primate of France, Archbishop of Lyons' who rose high in the king's favour and then suffered disgrace (p. 849). He continues: 'The Duke of *Biron* did see him in his sicknesse and assisted at his funerall. No man lyuing did better iudge of the nature of men by the consideration of their visages: hee did diuine the Marshall *Birons* fortune by his countenance, and the proportion of his visage, for hauing considered it some-what curiously, hee sayd vnto his Sister after his departure. *Hee hath the worst Phisiognomie that euer I obserued in my life, as of a man that would perish miserably.*' (p. 851). Parrott notes the incongruity in Roncas's speech but considers it as an introduction to a more favourable judgement. Perhaps a few lines should be spoken *sotto voce* as an ironic counterpoint to the extravagant flattery Byron is meant to overhear.

SC II] THE CONSPIRACY OF CHARLES DUKE OF BYRON 123

<blockquote>

Who was reported to have wondrous judgement
In men's events and natures by their looks,   125
Upon his deathbed, visited by this duke,
He told his sister, when his grace was gone,
That he had never yet observed a face
Of worse presage than this; and I will swear
That, something seen in physiognomy,   130
I do not find in all the rules it gives
One slenderest blemish tending to mishap,
But, on the opposite part, as we may see
On trees late blossomed, when all frosts are past,
How they are taken and what will be fruit: 135
So on this tree of sceptres I discern
How it is loaden with appearances,
Rules answering rules, and glances crowned with glances.

Byron. What! Does he take my picture?
                        He snatches away the picture.
Savoy.   Ay, my lord.
Byron. Your highness will excuse me; I will give you   140
My likeness put in statue, not in picture,
And by a statuary of mine own
</blockquote>

139.1. S.D.] *follows l. 138 in Q1.*

---

125. *events*] fates or destinies.
130. *something seen*] somewhat versed.
physiognomy] the art of foretelling the destiny as well as the character of a person from the lines on his face.
  131. *rules*] principles of the art of physiognomy.
  133. *the opposite part*] the other hand.
  135. *how ... taken*] how the fruit has 'taken' and begun to grow.
  136. *tree of sceptres*] The tree with promising fruit is compared to a tree laden with royal insignia suggesting the future of Byron and his descendants, a royal 'family tree'.
  137. *appearances*] clear manifestations.
  138.] The rules or principles of physiognomy are all in agreement and flashes of light as from royal sceptres complete the picture. The complimentary rhetoric of Roncas may seem at this point to have more sound than meaning. Cf. the Painter scenes in *Timon of Athens* (c. 1605–8), I.i.30ff. and V.i.1–113.
  139. *take my picture*] paint my portrait (cf. l. 7 above).
  139.1.] I have placed the stage direction after Byron's exclamation since the quarto's placing of it at the end of Roncas's speech suggests that Roncas snatches the picture. Parrott notes the ambiguity.
  142. *statuary*] sculptor. Chapman draws much of this speech from Plutarch's *De Alexandri magni*, as Parrott and Schoell (p. 211) have noted. Plutarch

124 THE CONSPIRACY OF CHARLES DUKE OF BYRON [ACT III

> That can in brass express the wit of man
> And in his form make all men see his virtues;
> Others that with much strictness imitate 145
> The something-stooping carriage of my neck,
> The voluble and mild radiance of mine eyes,
> Never observe my masculine aspect
> And lion-like instinct it shadoweth,
> Which envy cannot say is flattery. 150
> And I will have my image promised you
> Cut in such matter as shall ever last,
> Where it shall stand, fixed with eternal roots,
> And with a most unmovèd gravity;
> For I will have the famous mountain Oros, 155
> That looks out of the duchy where I govern
> Into your highness' dukedom, first made yours,
> And then with such inimitable art
> Expressed and handled, chiefly from the place
> Where most conspicuously he shows his face, 160
> That though it keep the true form of that hill
> In all his longitudes and latitudes,
> His height, his distances and full proportion,
> Yet shall it clearly bear my counterfeit,

describes the excellence of Alexander's sculptor, Lysippus, and speaks of another sculptor, Stasicrates, who proposed carving a likeness of Alexander into Mount Athos (*Oratio*, II, 2; 335A-E).

143. *wit*] mental faculty.
144. *form*] outward shape of the statue.
146. *something-stooping*] somewhat inclining, with a suggestion of leaning forward in friendly acknowledgement.
147. *voluble*] often turning, or expressive: there may be a hint of both meanings with respect to eyes. The descriptive phrases in ll. 146-9 derive from Plutarch on Alexander, not from Grimeston on Byron.
148. *aspect*] appearance.
149. *shadoweth*] prefigures, symbolises.
150. *envy*] ill will, malice.
154. *gravity*] dignity; also a punning allusion to weight (Lat. *gravitas*).
155. *the famous ... Oros*] an imaginary mountain, supposedly in Burgundy overlooking Savoy. The name may derive, as Parrott suggests, from the Greek ὄρος (mountain), with perhaps a reference to δράω (I look), frequent in Homer, as 'looks out' in l. 156 suggests.
159. *expressed*] formed into an image.
handled] treated artistically.
164. *counterfeit*] likeness.

SC II]   THE CONSPIRACY OF CHARLES DUKE OF BYRON   125

>   Both in my face and all my lineaments; 165
>   And every man shall say, this is Byron.
>   Within my left hand I will hold a city,
>   Which is the city Amiens, at whose siege
>   I served so memorably; from my right
>   I'll pour an endless flood into a sea 170
>   Raging beneath me, which shall intimate
>   My ceaseless service drunk up by the king,
>   As the ocean drinks up rivers and makes all
>   Bear his proud title. Ivory, brass and gold
>   That thieves may purchase, and be bought and sold, 175
>   Shall not be used about me; lasting worth
>   Shall only set the Duke of Byron forth.
>
> *Savoy.* O that your statuary could express you
>   With any nearness to your own instructions!
>   That statue would I prize past all the jewels 180
>   Within my cabinet of Beatrice,
>   The memory of my grandame Portugal.
>   Most royal duke, we cannot long endure
>   To be thus private; let us then conclude
>   With this great resolution: that your wisdom 185
>   Will not forget to cast a pleasing veil
>   Over your anger, that may hide each glance
>   Of any notice taken of your wrong,
>   And show yourself the more obsequious.
>   'Tis but the virtue of a little patience; 190
>   There are so oft attempts made 'gainst his person

168. *Amiens*] Byron moves this city from Picardy, where he and Henry besieged it in 1597, to the slopes of his imaginary mountain in Burgundy, but he may be thinking of a representation on the mountain of one of his greatest successes. Both city and river are part of Plutarch's description of the Mount Athos project.
   174. *Bear . . . title*] accept his rule.
   175. *purchase*] get possession of.
   179. *instructions*] directions given.
   181. *cabinet of Beatrice*] the jewel case of Queen Beatrice of Portugal, Savoy's grandmother.
   182. *memory*] memorial.
   183. *endure*] continue.
   189. *obsequious*] compliant, obedient.
   191–4.] In describing an attempt on Henry's life in 1600, Grimeston writes: 'It is miraculous what hath past in diuers conspiracies against the King, and

That sometimes they may speed, for they are plants
That spring the more for cutting, and at last
Will cast their wishèd shadow; mark ere long –

Enter NEMOURS, SOISSONS.

See who comes here, my lord; as now no more, 195
Now must we turn our stream another way.
My lord, I humbly thank his majesty
That he would grace my idle time spent here
With entertainment of your princely person,
Which, worthily, he keeps for his own bosom. 200
My lord, the Duke Nemours? and Count Soissons?
Your honours have been bountifully done me
In often visitation; let me pray you
To see some jewels now, and help my choice
In making up a present for the king. 205
Nemours. Your highness shall much grace us.
Savoy.   I am doubtful
That I have much incensed the Duke Byron
With praising the king's worthiness in arms
So much past all men.
Soissons.   He deserves it highly.
Exit [SAVOY *with the* Lords], *Byron, La Fin* [*remain*].
Byron. What wrongs are these, laid on me by the king, 210
To equal others' worths in war with mine!
Endure this, and be turned into his mule
To bear his sumptures; honoured friend be true,
And we will turn these torrents. Hence, the king!
                                    Exit LA FIN.

209.1. SAVOY *with the* Lords] *Parrott.*   remain] *This ed.*; manet Byr: Laffin. *Q1.*   212. mule] *This ed.*; moile *Q1*; moil *Parrott.*   214. Hence, the king!] *Parrott*; hence. The King. *Q1*; En. The King, *Q2.*

---

how Diuinly God hath deliuered him. It was one of the causes which made the Duke of *Sauoye* seems so resolute to hold the accord which hee had made with the King at *Paris*, for the Marquisate of Saluces, hauing vnderstood that the King had beene so often threatned by the attempts of such Murtherers, presuming that it was not possible but some one would hit ...' (p. 914).

192. *sometimes*] at some time.
speed] succeed.
195. *as now*] as of now.
211. *To equal*] to make equal, compare.
213. *sumptures*] sumpters, packs or saddlebags.
214. *Hence, the king*] Q1 prints 'The King' in italics as part of the s.d. *Exit*

Enter HENRY, EPERNON, VITRY, JANIN.

Henry. Why suffer you that ill-aboding vermin 215
  To breed so near your bosom? Be assured
  His haunts are ominous; not the throats of ravens
  Spent on infected houses, howls of dogs
  When no sound stirs at midnight, apparitions
  And strokes of spirits, clad in black men's shapes 220
  Or ugly women's, the adverse decrees
  Of constellations, nor security
  In vicious peace are surer fatal ushers
  Of feral mischiefs and mortalities
  Than this prodigious fiend is, where he fawns: 225
  La Fiend, and not La Fin, he should be called.
Byron. Be what he will, men in themselves entire
  March safe with naked feet on coals of fire:
  I build not outward, nor depend on props,
  Nor choose my consort by the common ear, 230
  Nor by the moonshine in the grace of kings;

---

224. *feral*] Parrott; femall *Q1, Q2*.

Laffi. Parrott is surely right in restoring this phrase to the end of Byron's speech since there is an entry for Henry immediately below.
  215. *ill-aboding*] ill-boding, ominous.
  218. *spent*] expended. The phrase 'to spend the tongue or mouth' was used of hounds that had scented their prey (*O.E.D.*, 9b).
  infected houses] households affected by disease, especially the plague.
  220. *strokes*] sudden attacks or afflictions.
  222–3. *security ... peace*] a false sense of safety in a depraved time of peace.
  224. *feral*] deadly, fatal: Parrott's conjecture, from Bradley (p. 625). 'Female' in the sense of 'effeminate' is surely too weak a word for this context.
  225. *prodigious*] ominous, also monstrous or unnatural.
  227. *entire*] complete, with all their powers undiminished.
  228.] Cf. Chapman's *Hymnus in Cynthiam*: 'As at thy altars, in thy Persicke Empire, / Thy holy women walkt with naked soles / Harmlesse, and confident, on burning coles' (ll. 129–31). Bartlett notes: 'The description of the Persian women and the reference to Strabo in Chapman's gloss both come from Comes, *Myth.*, III, 18, "De Diana"' (p. 426).
  229. *I ... outward*] I do not build beyond the boundaries or foundations of my own house; fig., I do not count on what is external to myself. Cf. *Consp.*, IV.i.195–8.
  230. *consort*] companion. There may also be a hint of 'consort' as a company of musicians playing or singing together, because of the reference to 'ear'.
  231. *moonshine*] deceptive appearance. 'Moonshine in the water' was a proverbial expression for appearance without substance: cf. *L.L.L.*, V.ii.208.

So rare are true deservers loved or known
That men loved vulgarly are ever none,
Nor men graced servilely for being spots
In princes' trains, though borne even with their crowns;   235
The stallion, power, hath such a besom tail
That it sweeps all from justice, and such filth
He bears out in it that men mere exempt
Are merely clearest; men will shortly buy
Friends from the prison or the pillory   240
Rather than honour's markets. I fear none
But foul ingratitude and detraction
In all the brood of villany.

Henry.   No? not treason?
Be circumspect, for to a credulous eye
He comes invisible, veiled with flattery,   245
And flatterers look like friends, as wolves like dogs.
And as a glorious poem fronted well
With many a goodly herald of his praise,
So far from hate of praises to his face
That he prays men to praise him, and they ride   250
Before, with trumpets in their mouths, proclaiming
Life to the holy fury of his lines:
All drawn, as if with one eye he had leered
On his loved hand and led it by a rule;

---

233. *vulgarly*] in a common or ordinary fashion.
none] i.e., deservers.
234. *spots*] Cf. *Consp.*, I.ii.7.
236. *besom*] broom-like.
238–9. *men ... clearest*] Only men free (from any taint of power) are altogether clear from blame.
247. *fronted*] prefaced. Many Elizabethan books were introduced by poems written in praise of the author by his friends. There may also be a reference to the splendid illustrated title-pages of such books: note 'drawn' in l. 253 and many other references to visual elements.
252. *holy fury*] an ironic reference to a doctrine that Chapman took very seriously, the 'diuine Fury' he attributes to Homer in the Dedication to the *Odysseys*. Bartlett notes Chapman's source as Ficino's *In Platonis Ionem, vel de furore poetico* (p. 486).
253. *leered*] glanced sideways.
254. *led it by a rule*] 'And as the foolish poet that still writ / All his most self-lov'd verse in paper royal, / Or parchment rul'd with lead ...' (*Revenge of Bussy*, II.i.184–6). This passage is derived, as Parrott notes, from Catullus, carm. xxii.

That his plumes only imp the Muses' wings,   255
He sleeps with them, his head is napped with bays,
His lips break out with nectar, his tuned feet
Are of the great last the perpetual motion;
And he puffed with their empty breath believes
Full merit eased those passions of wind,   260
Which yet serve but to praise and cannot merit,
And so his fury in their air expires:
So de La Fin and such corrupted heralds,
Hired to encourage and to glorify,
May force what breath they will into their cheeks   265
Fitter to blow up bladders than full men;
Yet may puff men too, with persuasions
That they are gods in worth and may rise kings
With treading on their noises; yet the worthiest
From only his own worth receives his spirit,   270
And right is worthy bound to any merit;
Which right shall you have ever: leave him, then,
He follows none but marked and wretched men.
And now for England you shall go, my lord,

255.] That his plumes alone strengthen the Muses' wings: an image from falconry, to 'imp' being to engraft the bird's wings with feathers to improve its flight (*O.E.D.*, 4).

256. *napped with bays*] a deliberately ironic phrase, since 'bays' could be the laurel wreath of a poet's crown, or woollen cloths from East Anglia, of which the commonest sort woven in Colchester was known as crown bay. 'Napped' refers to the process of raising and trimming the 'nap' or pile of the cloth; hence its use with 'bays' undercuts the poet's dream of a laurel crown (suggested Sue Margeson).

257. *nectar*] the drink of the gods, suggesting eloquence or honeyed verse.

his tuned feet] his musical feet (cf. 'As if my feet were numerous and trod sounds', *Consp.*, I.ii.45–6) with a pun on 'feet' as poetic measures.

258. *the great last*] the last sphere, the primum mobile; hence his poetic feet are tuned to the perpetual motion of the last sphere (Ferguson). There is probably a pun on 'last' as the shoemaker's wooden model for the foot.

259. *puffed*] inflated, puffed up.

260. *eased*] set free.

261. *merit*] become worthy of esteem.

262. *his fury*] the 'holy fury' of l. 252, an inspired madness.

269. *their noises*] the clamour of the flattery they make.

271.] That claim for justice is deserving that is tied to merit.

273. *marked*] fated, destined.

                Our lord ambassador to that matchless queen;   275
                You never had a voyage of such pleasure,
                Honour and worthy objects; there's a queen
                Where nature keeps her state, and state her court,
                Wisdom her study, continence her fort;
                Where magnanimity, humanity,   280
                Firmness in counsel and integrity,
                Grace to her poorest subjects, majesty
                To awe the greatest, have respects divine,
                And in her each part all the virtues shine.
                        Exit HENRY [*and* Lords], *Byron* [*remains*].
Byron. Enjoy your will awhile, I may have mine.   285
                Wherefore, before I part to this ambassage,
                I'll be resolved by a magician
                That dwells hereby, to whom I'll go disguised
                And show him my birth's figure, set before
                By one of his profession, of the which   290
                I'll crave his judgement, feigning I am sent
                From some great personage, whose nativity
                He wisheth should be censured by his skill.
                But on go my plots, be it good or ill.   *Exit.*

                        [ACT III   SCENE iii]
                            Enter LA BROSSE.

La Brosse. This hour by all rules of astrology
                Is dangerous to my person, if not deadly.
                How hapless is our knowledge to foretell

284.1. *Exit* HENRY *and* Lords] *Ray; Exit Hen. & Sav. Q1, Q2; Exit* Henry *cum suis Parrott.   Byron remains*] *This ed.; manet Byron Q1.*   291. feigning] *Q1 (fayning); saying Q2.*   1. *La Brosse] Shepherd; not in Q1, Q2.*

---

   275. *that matchless queen*] Elizabeth. A similar passage of elaborate praise for Elizabeth by a French king occurs in *Bussy D'Ambois*, I.ii.16ff.
   277. *objects*] aims.
   278.] Where nature holds her proper position of greatness and magnificence has her court.
   279. *continence*] chastity.
   283. *respects divine*] religious regard.
   289. *my birth's figure*] my horoscope.
   set before] drawn up previously.
   293. *censured*] judged.

And not be able to prevent a mischief;
O the strange difference 'twixt us and the stars: 5
They work with inclinations strong and fatal
And nothing know, and we know all their working
And nought can do, or nothing can prevent!
Rude ignorance is beastly, knowledge wretched;
The heavenly powers envy what they enjoin;   10
We are commanded t'imitate their natures
In making all our ends eternity,
And in that imitation we are plagued,
And worse than they esteemed that have no souls
But in their nostrils, and like beasts expire;   15
As they do that are ignorant of arts,
By drowning their eternal parts in sense
And sensual affectations: while we live
Our good parts take away, the more they give.

[Enter] BYRON *solus disguised like a Carrier of letters.*

Byron. *[Aside]* The forts that favourites hold in princes' hearts,   20
In common subjects' loves, and their own strengths
Are not so sure and unexpugnable
But that the more they are presumed upon,
The more they fail; daily and hourly proof
Tells us prosperity is at highest degree   25

6. *inclinations*] an astronomical term referring to 'the position of the plane of a planet's orbit' (*O.E.D.*) but also used in the more general sense of 'influences'.
10. *envy*] begrudge, perhaps with some sense of malicious intent. The accent is on the second syllable, parallel with 'enjoin'.
15. *their nostrils*] The breath of life was associated with nostrils (see Gen. vii.22) but the rational soul was more than this.
like ... expire] die like beasts, not breathing out souls but only the breath of life. 'Expire' carries both senses, 'die' and 'breathe out' (Lat. *exspirare*).
17. *their ... parts*] their intellectual and spiritual natures.
18. *affectations*] pursuits.
19.] The line is obscure unless regarded as a summary of all that La Broose has been saying: 'they', presumably the heavenly powers, give to men the ability to gain knowledge, arts and skills, but the more they give the more they seem to take away of our good or eternal parts.
19.1.] Grimeston has Byron thus disguised. For Chapman's source for this scene, see Appendix 1.
25–8.] These lines are based on two passages from Plutarch's *De fortuna* (100A, 97F) as Schoell notes (p. 211).

        The fount and handle of calamity:
        Like dust before a whirlwind those men fly
        That prostrate on the grounds of Fortune lie;
        And being great, like trees that broadest sprout,
        Their own top-heavy state grubs up their root.   30
        These apprehensions startle all my powers
        And arm them with suspicion 'gainst themselves,
        In my late projects; I have cast myself
        Into the arms of others, and will see
        If they will let me fall, or toss me up   35
        Into th'affected compass of a throne.
        [*To La Brosse*] God save you, sir!
La Brosse.   Y'are welcome, friend: what would you?
Byron. I would entreat you, for some crowns I bring,
        To give your judgement of this figure cast,
        To know, by his nativity there seen,   40
        What sort of end the person shall endure
        Who sent me to you and whose birth it is.
La Brosse. I'll herein do my best in your desire.
        The man is raised out of a good descent
        And nothing older than yourself, I think.   45
        Is it not you?
Byron.   I will not tell you that;
        But tell me on what end he shall arrive.
La Brosse. My son, I see that he whose end is cast
        In this set figure is of noble parts,
        And by his military valour raised   50
        To princely honours; and may be a king,
        But that I see a *Caput Algol* here

    26. *handle*] occasion.
    31. *apprehensions*] perceptions; also anticipations of an unknown, perhaps dreaded future.
    36. *affected*] sought after.
    compass] circle.
    39. *this figure cast*] this horoscope set out or calculated; this table showing the disposition of the heavenly bodies at the time of birth (see ll. 48–9).
    52. *Caput Algol*] properly Caput Medusae, Medusa's head, a group of stars in the constellation Perseus, one of which is Algol. Johnstone Parr quotes Ptolemy from a Renaissance text: 'Under the xxii degree of Taurus ryseth a sterre fixed of the first magnitude that Astronomers call Perseus sone of Jupiter that smote the heed of Meduse ... Ptholomaeus and other Astronomyers say that when Mars is conjoined with this sterre they that ben borne under the

That hinders it, I fear.
Byron. A *Caput Algol*?
What's that, I pray?
La Brosse. Forbear to ask me, son;
You bid me speak what fear bids me conceal. 55
Byron. You have no cause to fear, and therefore speak.
La Brosse. You'll rather wish you had been ignorant
Than be instructed in a thing so ill.
Byron. Ignorance is an idle salve for ill,
And therefore do not urge me to enforce 60
What I would freely know: for by the skill
Shown in thy aged hairs, I'll lay thy brain
Here scattered at my feet and seek in that
What safely thou must utter with thy tongue,
If thou deny it. 65
La Brosse. Will you not allow me
To hold my peace? What less can I desire?
If not, be pleased with my constrainèd speech.
Byron. Was ever man yet punished for expressing
What he was charged? Be free and speak the worst.
La Brosse. Then briefly this: the man hath lately done 70
An action that will make him lose his head.
Byron. Cursed be thy throat and soul, raven, screech-owl, hag!
[*Beating La Brosse.*]
La Brosse. O hold, for heaven's sake, hold!
Byron. Hold on I will.
Vault and contractor of all horrid sounds,
Trumpet of all the miseries in hell, 75

---

64. must] *Q1;* may'st *Shepherd.* 72.1. *Beating La Brosse*] *Parrott.*

constellacyon shall have theyr heedes smyten of if God shape not remedy' ('The Duke of Byron's Malignant *Caput Algol*', *S.P.*, XLIII (1946), 198). Chapman draws the term 'Caput Algol' from Grimeston.

54–69.] The passage is based on a tense and ironic dialogue in Seneca's *Oedipus* (ll. 511–29) between Oedipus and Creon when Creon returns from necromancy, as noted by J. W. Cunliffe in *The Influence of Seneca on Elizabethan Tragedy*, and by Parrott. Byron threatens La Brosse with violence if he refuses to talk.

72. *hag*] witch.
73. *Hold on*] continue, go on (as opposed to 'hold' as 'stop').
74.] Like a cavern you draw together all repulsive sounds.

> Of my confusions, of the shameful end
> Of all my services; witch, fiend, accursed
> For ever be the poison of thy tongue,
> And let the black fume of thy venomed breath
> Infect the air, shrink heaven, put out the stars, 80
> And rain so fell and blue a plague on earth
> That all the world may falter with my fall.

La Brosse. Pity my age, my lord.
Byron.   Out, prodigy,
> Remedy of pity, mine of flint,
> Whence with my nails and feet I'll dig enough 85
> Horror and savage cruelty to build
> Temples to massacre: dam of devils take thee!
> Had'st thou no better end to crown my parts?
> The bulls of Colchis, nor his triple neck
> That howls out earthquakes; the most mortal vapours 90
> That ever stifled and struck dead the fowls
> That flew at never such a sightly pitch,
> Could not have burnt my blood so.

La Brosse.   I told truth
> And could have flattered you.

Byron.   O that thou had'st!
> Would I had given thee twenty thousand crowns 95
> That thou had'st flattered me; there's no joy on earth,

---

76. *confusions*] discomfitures.
81. *fell*] dire.
   blue] pale, suggesting the plague-stricken. *O.E.D.* gives no use of blue as the colour associated with plagues before 1742 but suggests that blue had evil connotations in relation to candle flames when ghosts were near and the colour of burning brimstone.
84. *Remedy of pity*] cure for pity (?). Parrott thinks the phrase meaningless and believes there may be a corruption since the line lacks a syllable. He notes P. A. Daniel's suggestion '[Thou] remedy of pity'; i.e., Thou reason for discarding all pity (p. 625).
88. *parts*] qualities.
89. *bulls of Colchis*] two wild bulls in Colchis with hooves of bronze and breath of flame, which Jason had to harness to win the Golden Fleece.
   triple neck] of Cerberus, Pluto's triple-headed dog, mentioned in l. 101.
90. *mortal vapours*] the deadly fumes supposed to rise from Lake Avernus in Campania, one of the entrances to Hades.
92. *sightly pitch*] conspicuous height; 'pitch' is 'the height to which a falcon or other bird of prey soars before swooping down on its prey' (*O.E.D.*).
96–100.] No joy on earth, no matter how rational or holy it seems, is any-

> Never so rational, so pure and holy,
> But is a jester, parasite, a whore,
> In the most worthy parts, with which they please,
> A drunkenness of soul and a disease. 100
>
> La Brosse. I knew you not.
> Byron.   Peace, dog of Pluto, peace!
> Thou knewest my end to come, not me here present:
> Pox of your halting human knowledges!
> O death, how far off hast thou killed! How soon
> A man may know too much, though never nothing! 105
> Spite of the stars and all astrology,
> I will not lose my head, or if I do,
> A hundred thousand heads shall off before.
> I am a nobler substance than the stars
> And shall the baser overrule the better? 110
> Or are they better, since they are the bigger?
> I have a will and faculties of choice,
> To do or not to do, and reason why
> I do or not do this; the stars have none,
> They know not why they shine, more than this taper, 115
> Nor how they work, nor what. I'll change my course,
> I'll piece-meal pull the frame of all my thoughts
> And cast my will into another mould:
> And where are all your *Caput Algols* then?
> Your planets all, being underneath the earth 120
> At my nativity, what can they do?

thing but a mocking delusion (jester, parasite, whore), and even in their worthiest qualities with which they please us, these joys are no more than drunkenness or a fever of the soul. (Parrott reads it somewhat differently: 'there is no earthly joy so pure but that it becomes a parasite etc. when it begins to flatter a soul intoxicated with pride', p. 607).

101. *I knew you not*] Byron may have removed part of his disguise, though his speeches have made clear who he is.

106ff.] In his wrath, Byron approaches the scornful contempt toward the stars that Edmund expresses in *King Lear* ('This is the excellent foppery of the world . . .', I.ii.112ff), though without Edmund's sardonic humour. Byron remains in two minds about stars, omens, fortune and destiny throughout the double play.

120–1.] A planet's position underneath the earth was regarded as being in an unfavourable aspect (Parr, *op. cit.*, pp. 197–8). However Byron declares that a planet beneath the earth at his nativity could have no influence upon him, perhaps following the widely accepted doctrine that a planet in the ascendant or directly overhead exerted the greatest power.

Malignant in aspects? in bloody houses?
Wild fire consume them! One poor cup of wine,
More than I use, that my weak brain will bear,
Shall make them drunk and reel out of their spheres   125
For any certain act they can enforce.
O that mine arms were wings, that I might fly
And pluck out of their hearts my destiny!
I'll wear those golden spurs upon my heels
And kick at fate; be free, all worthy spirits,   130
And stretch yourselves for greatness and for height;
Untruss your slaveries, you have height enough
Beneath this steep heaven to use all your reaches;
'Tis too far off to let you, or respect you.
Give me a spirit that on this life's rough sea   135
Loves t'have his sails filled with a lusty wind
Even till his sail-yards tremble, his masts crack,
And his rapt ship run on her side so low
That she drinks water, and her keel ploughs air.
There is no danger to a man that knows   140
What life and death is; there's not any law
Exceeds his knowledge, neither is it lawful

---

124. that] *Q1*; than *Parrott*.

122. *Malignant in aspects*] 'Aspects' refers to the relative positions of the planets and the way they look upon one another; 'malignant' to their evil or fatal influence in certain positions.

bloody houses] Certain planets in certain signs of the zodiac (houses) could portend a violent death, hence 'bloody'. The heavens were divided into twelve equal parts or 'houses' by great circles from north to south, but 'houses' were also the twelve signs of the zodiac, each 'considered as the seat of the greatest influence of a particular planet' (*O.E.D.*).

126. *For*] So far as.

129. *those golden spurs*] Loane notes: 'The star-shaped rowel of the spur is referred to. Cf. *Ovid's Banquet*, st. 86, where the stars are called heaven's "spurry tapers"; *Iliads*, XIX, 368, "And like a star it cast a spurry ray"' (p. 251).

132. *Untruss your slaveries*] Undo the bonds that make you into slaves.

133. *steep*] lofty.

reaches] acts involving reaching out after some desire.

134. *let*] hinder.

respect] pay attention to.

138. *rapt*] carried off (by the winds).

140–5.] from Plutarch's *De fato* (574A) as Schoell points out (p. 212). Cf. *Bussy*, II.i.198ff.

SC I]   THE CONSPIRACY OF CHARLES DUKE OF BYRON   139

> To such affectionate profit as we wish,
> Being so much set on fire with his deserts
> That they consume us, not to be restored
> By your presentment of him, but his person;
> And we had not thought that he whose virtues fly   25
> So beyond wonder and the reach of thought
> Should check at eight hours' sail, and his high spirit
> That stoops to fear, less than the poles of heaven,
> Should doubt an under billow of the sea,
> And, being a sea, be sparing of his streams;   30
> And I must blame all you that may advise him,
> That, having helped him through all martial dangers,
> You let him stick at the kind rites of peace,
> Considering all the forces I have sent
> To set his martial seas up in firm walls   35
> On both his sides for him to pass at pleasure,
> Did plainly open him a guarded way
> And led in nature to this friendly shore.
> But here is nothing worth his personal sight,
> Here are no wallèd cities; for that crystal   40

25. not] *Parrott; not in Q1.*

---

23. *restored*] renewed.
24. *presentment of*] representing.
  but] but only by.
25. *not*] not in Q; the sense requires a 'not' in the line, as Parrott notes. The source in Grimeston (p. 945) supports the correction.
27. *check at*] recoil from: a hawking image, linked with 'fly' and 'stoops'.
28. *poles of heaven*] the two points in the celestial sphere, north and south, about which the fixed stars appear to revolve.
29. *doubt*] fear.
30. *being a sea*] the monarch compared to an ocean, a favourite metaphor of Chapman's. Cf. *Consp.*, I.i.186–92.
  sparing] frugal, niggardly.
  his streams] the currents of his power, generosity, gratitude, etc.
35–6.] The 'martial seas' that threatened to overcome Henry in France have been confined behind 'firm walls' so that he can move at pleasure through his kingdom. The image suggests the safe passage of the Israelites through the Red Sea (Exod. xiv) and leads to the idea of a safe crossing of the English Channel in ll. 37–8.
38. *in nature*] naturally.
40. *that crystal*] the crystalline sphere in the heavens, the outermost sphere of all, and hence heaven itself. Bartlett notes several references in Chapman's poetry to the hardness of the crystalline sphere (p. 468). However Ferguson

>   Sheds with his light his hardness and his height
>   About our thankful person and our realm,
>   Whose only aid we ever yet desired.
>   And now I see the help we sent to him,
>   Which should have swum to him in our own blood   45
>   Had it been needful, our affections
>   Being more given to his good than he himself,
>   Ends in the actual right it did his state,
>   And ours is slighted; all our worth is made
>   The common stock and bank, from whence are served   50
>   All men's occasions; yet, thanks to heaven,
>   Their gratitudes are drawn dry, not our bounties.
>   And you shall tell your king that he neglects
>   Old friends for new, and sets his soothèd ease
>   Above his honour; marshals policy   55
>   In rank before his justice, and his profit
>   Before his royalty; his humanity gone,
>   To make me no repayment of mine own.
> D'Aumont. What answerèd the duke?
> Crequi.   In this sort:
>   Your highness' sweet speech hath no sharper end   60
>   Than he would wish his life, if he neglected
>   The least grace you have named; but to his wish
>   Much power is wanting: the green roots of war
>   Not yet so close cut up but he may dash
>   Against their relics to his utter ruin,   65
>   Without more near eyes, fixed upon his feet,

rejects the connection between crystal, heaven and providential care, and suggests instead that the crystalline sphere is a sphere of water (following Roger Bacon and Milton), hence like the sea that encircles and protects England (pp. 232–3). But the phrase 'Whose only aid' in l. 43 seems to me a clear argument for the idea of providence.

46. *affections*] good will.
48. *the actual right*] the real justice.
49. *ours*] our right, i.e., what is due to us.
51. *occasions*] needs, requirements.
54. *his soothèd ease*] the ease he has been flattered or cajoled into.
55. *policy*] political expediency.
57. *humanity*] courtesy.
62. *grace*] favour.
64. *close cut up*] cut up finely or closely.
65. *relics*] remnants.
66. *near*] careful, narrowly focused.

Than those that look out of his country's soil;
And this may well excuse his personal presence,
Which yet he oft hath longed to set by yours,
That he might imitate the majesty 70
Which so long peace hath practised and made full
In your admired appearance, to illustrate
And rectify his habit in rude war.
And his will to be here must needs be great,
Since heaven hath throned so true a royalty here 75
That he thinks no king absolutely crowned
Whose temples have not stood beneath this sky,
And whose height is not hardened with these stars,
Whose influences for this altitude,
Distilled and wrought in with this temperate air 80
And this division of the element,
Have with your reign brought forth more worthy spirits
For counsel, valour, height of wit and art,
Than any other region of the earth,
Or were brought forth to all your ancestors. 85
And as a cunning orator reserves
His finest similes, best-adorning figures,
Chief matter and most moving arguments
For his conclusion; and doth then supply

    72. *illustrate*] shed lustre upon, adorn.
    73. *rectify his habit*] correct his bearing. The idea is that Henry, long engaged in rough warfare, would like to imitate the bearing and demeanour of majesty Elizabeth has developed in her many years of peace.
    77. *temples*] places of worship, where a king may seek the blessing of God. An argument might be made for 'forehead', following 'crowned'.
    78. *height*] exalted position.
    hardened] made firm, as the stars are fixed in their sphere. Cf. Chapman's 'De Guiana': 'Guiana, whose rich feet are mines of golde, / Whose forehead knockes against the roofe of Starres' (ll. 18–19).
    79. *influences*] flowing in of an ethereal fluid from the stars that act upon the characters or destinies of men.
    altitude] high point.
    80. *Distilled*] imparted.
    wrought in] worked in, incorporated.
    81.] this distribution or sharing of the element of temperate air. In the heightened language of his courtly compliments, Byron's images are characteristically vague.
    89. *supply*] fill up, complete.

His ground-streams laid before, glides over them, 90
Makes his full depth seen through, and so takes up
His audience in applauses past the clouds:
So in your government, conclusive Nature,
Willing to end her excellence in earth
When your foot shall be set upon the stars, 95
Shows all her sovereign beauties, ornaments,
Virtues and raptures; overtakes her works
In former empires, makes them but your foils;
Swells to her full sea, and again doth drown
The world in admiration of your crown. 100
D'Aumont. He did her, at all parts, confessèd right.
Crequi. She took it yet but as a part of courtship,
And said he was the subtle orator
To whom he did too gloriously resemble
Nature in her and in her government. 105
He said he was no orator but a soldier,
More than this air in which you breathe hath made me,
My studious love of your rare government,
And simple truth, which is most eloquent;
Your empire is so amply absolute 110
That even your theatres show more comely rule,
True noblesse, royalty and happiness
Than others' courts; you make all state before
Utterly obsolete, all to come twice sod.

---

112. noblesse] *Q1;* noblenesse *Q2.*   113. others] *Q1;* other *Q2.*

---

90. *ground-streams*] deepest currents (of his thought). The stream metaphor is carried on in 'glides over' and 'full depth'.
93. *conclusive*] reaching a conclusion (in her demonstration of sovereign beauties).
97. *raptures*] ecstasies or exaltations of mind.
overtakes] goes beyond.
101. *at all parts*] in all respects.
confessèd] manifest.
102. *a part of courtship*] an aspect of courtly behaviour, with perhaps also a suggestion of 'part' as 'role'.
104. *too gloriously*] too splendidly, in a spirit of exaggeration.
resemble] compare.
107.] The change to direct discourse in this line again demonstrates the probable alteration of the whole scene.
110. *absolute*] free from all imperfection.
114. *twice sod*] stale, unpalatable. 'Sod' means boiled, hence 'twice sod' refers to something stale (*O.E.D.*).

>   And therefore doth my royal sovereign wish 115
>   Your years may prove as vital as your virtues,
>   That, standing on his turrets this way turned,
>   Ordering and fixing his affairs by yours,
>   He may at last, on firm grounds, pass your seas
>   And see that maiden-sea of majesty 120
>   In whose chaste arms so many kingdoms lie.
> D'Aumont. When came she to her touch of his ambition?
> Crequi. In this speech following, which I thus remember:
>   If I hold any merit worth his presence,
>   Or any part of that your courtship gives me, 125
>   My subjects have bestowed it; some in counsel,
>   In action some, and in obedience all;
>   For none knows with such proof as you, my lord,
>   How much a subject may renown his prince,
>   And how much princes of their subjects hold. 130
>   In all the services that ever subject
>   Did for his sovereign, he that best deserved
>   Must, in comparison, except Byron;
>   And to win this prize clear, without the maims
>   Commonly given men by ambition, 135
>   When all their parts lie open to his view,
>   Shows continence past their other excellence.
>   But for a subject to affect a kingdom
>   Is like the camel that of Jove begged horns,
>   And such mad-hungry men as well may eat 140
>   Hot coals of fire to feed their natural heat;
>   For to aspire to competence with your king,

---

116. *vital*] life-giving.

119. *on firm grounds*] on firm foundations, suggesting both safe ships (bottoms) and sound reasons.

120. *maiden-sea of majesty*] majesty as ample as the sea and as yet pure and untouched.

122. *touch of*] reference to, hint of.

129. *renown*] give renown to.

130.] A subject would normally hold or possess something of value from his prince but Elizabeth notes how much a prince may possess from her subjects.

132. *except Byron*] consider Byron an exception.

136. *parts*] qualities, abilities.

137. *continence*] self-restraint.

139.] A fable of Aesop tells how the camel lost its ears as a result of Jove's anger. For another version, see *Revenge of Bussy*, II.i.176ff.

142. *competence*] rivalry, the act of competing.

What subject is so gross and giantly?
He having now a dauphin born to him,
Whose birth, ten days before, was dreadfully 145
Ushered with earthquakes in most parts of Europe,
And that gives all men cause enough to fear
All thought of competition with him.
Commend us, good my lord, and tell our brother
How much we joy in that his royal issue, 150
And in what prayers we raise our heart to heaven,
That in more terror to his foes and wonder
He may drink earthquakes and devour the thunder;
So we admire your valour and your virtues,
And ever will contend to win their honour. 155
Then spake she to Crequi and Prince d'Auvergne,
And gave all gracious farewells; when Byron
Was thus encountered by a councillor
Of great and eminent name, and matchless merit:
I think, my lord, your princely dauphin bears 160
Arion on his cradle through your kingdom
In the sweet music joy strikes from his birth.
He answered: And good right; the cause commands it.
But, said the other, had we a fifth Henry
To claim his old right, and one man to friend 165
Whom you well know, my lord, that for his friendship
Were promised the vice-royalty of France,

---

151. heart] *Q1*; hearts *Parrott*.   165. claim] *Q1*; proclaime *Q2*.

144.] Grimeston recounts the birth of the dauphin in 1601 as having been preceded by earthquakes (p. 946). Henry's son was later Louis XIII.

156. *to Crequi*] Since Crequi is reporting these speeches, this line is a further indication of hasty and incomplete revision.

158. *a councillor*] There seems little doubt that Robert Cecil, Earl of Salisbury, is meant (note ll. 220–3 below which echo lines from Chapman's sonnet to Cecil). If he was presented on the stage along with Queen Elizabeth in the original version of this scene, he could not have been named since he was still very much alive in 1608. It was to Salisbury that the French ambassador complained about this play.

160. *dauphin*] spelt Daulphin in Q1, as often in the 17th century, hence the reference to Arion whose music attracted the dolphin that saved his life. There were many Renaissance paintings and sculptures of Arion riding the dolphin's back.

165. *his old right*] Henry V's claim to the throne of France which Shakespeare exploited in an early scene of *H5*.

SC I]   THE CONSPIRACY OF CHARLES DUKE OF BYRON   145

> We would not doubt of conquest, in despite
> Of all those windy earthquakes. He replied:
> Treason was never guide to English conquests,   170
> And therefore that doubt shall not fright our dauphin;
> Nor would I be the friend to such a foe
> For all the royalties in Christendom.
> Fix there your foot, said he, I only give
> False fire, and would be loth to shoot you off.   175
> He that wins empire with the loss of faith
> Out-buys it, and will bankrupt; you have laid
> A brave foundation by the hand of virtue;
> Put not the roof to fortune. Foolish statuaries
> That under little saints suppose great bases   180
> Make less, to sense, the saints; and so where fortune
> Advanceth vile minds to states great and noble,
> She much the more exposeth them to shame,
> Not able to make good and fill their bases
> With a conformèd structure. I have found,   185
> Thanks to the blesser of my search, that counsels
> Held to the line of justice still produce
> The surest states, and greatest being sure;
> Without which fit assurance in the greatest,
> As you may see a mighty promontory   190
> More digged and under-eaten than may warrant
> A safe supportance to his hanging brows,

---

175. off] *Q2*; of *Q1*.   183. much the more] *Q1 (corr.);* much more *Q1 (uncorr.)*.

---

175. *false fire*] a blank discharge of firearms (*O.E.D.*).
shoot you off] provoke you to any outburst. Byron is compared to a firearm or cannon.
177. *Out-buys*] buys at a price beyond the value.
bankrupt] become bankrupt.
179–85.] Chapman's source for this simile, as Parrott and Schoell (p. 212) have noted, is Plutarch's *De Alexandri magni* (337C).
179. *statuaries*] sculptors, makers of statues.
180. *suppose*] place, as for support. Chapman has the Latin meaning of 'suppono' (place under) in mind.
bases] pedestals; perhaps also a punning reference to 'bases' as fundamental principles, the special holy qualities of sainthood.
181. *to sense*] to perception.
185. *a conformèd structure*] a structure shaped according to the right model.
188. *states*] positions of power or high rank.

All passengers avoid him, shun all ground
That lies within his shadow, and bear still
A flying eye upon him; so great men,   195
Corrupted in their grounds and building out
Too swelling fronts for their foundations,
When most they should be propped are most forsaken;
And men will rather thrust into the storms
Of better grounded states than take a shelter   200
Beneath their ruinous and fearful weight;
Yet they so oversee their faulty bases
That they remain securer in conceit,
And that security doth worse presage
Their near destructions than their eaten grounds.   205
And therefore heaven itself is made to us
A perfect hieroglyphic to express
The idleness of such security
And the grave labour of a wise distrust
In both sorts of the all-inclining stars,   210
Where all men note this difference in their shining,
As plain as they distinguish either hand:
The fixed stars waver, and the erring stand.
D'Aumont. How took he this so worthy admonition?

---

210. all-inclining] *Q2, Parrott;* all-enclying *Q1.*   213. waver] *Q2;* maver *Q1.*

---

   193. *passengers*] travellers on foot.
   195. *flying eye*] swiftly moving, unsettled eye.
   196. *corrupted ... grounds*] unsound in their foundations. A Latin pun from 'corruptum' (ruined or wasted) is possible.
   197. *too ... fronts*] a reference to the Elizabethan practice of building out overhanging upper storeys above the ground level. Taking shelter under the 'penthouse' of such an overhanging building is part of the same image in ll. 199–201.
   202. *oversee*] look over the top of; the sense of 'overlook, neglect' is probably also present (*O.E.D.*, 6).
   203. *securer*] safer; also with the sense of Latin 'securus', carefree, free from anxiety.
   in conceit] in personal judgement.
   205. *their eaten grounds*] their undermined foundations.
   209. *grave labour*] serious mental toil.
   210. *all-inclining*] slanting with respect to the horizon in their ascents and descents.
   213.] 'The fixed stars twinkle, whereas the planets, or *erring*, i.e., wandering, stars, shine steadily' (Parrott, p. 608).

SC I]   THE CONSPIRACY OF CHARLES DUKE OF BYRON   147

Crequi. Gravely applied, said he, and like the man   215
    Whom all the world says overrules the stars;
    Which are divine books to us, and are read
    By understanders only, the true objects
    And chief companions of the truest men;
    And, though I need it not, I thank your counsel,   220
    That never yet was idle, but sphere-like
    Still moves about and is the continent
    To this blest isle.   [*Exeunt.*]

---

223. *Exeunt*] Ray; not in *Q1*, *Q2*.

  216. *overrules*] prevails against.
  218. *objects*] objects of observation.
  220–3.] As Ferguson notes, there is a similar image in Chapman's sonnet to Cecil at the end of the *Iliads*: 'Wherein as th'Ocean walks not, with such waues, / The Round of this Realme, as your Wisedomes seas; / Nor, with his great eye, sees; his Marble, saues / Our State, like your Vlyssian policies: / So, none like HOMER hath the World enspher'd; / Earth, Seas, & heauen, fixt in his verse, and mouing;' (ll. 5–10; Bartlett, p. 397).
  221. *sphere-like*] like a heavenly sphere.
  222. *continent*] solid orb or sphere, the all-containing foundation (*O.E.D.*, 3c).
  223.] Crequi's speech ends abruptly with an incomplete line, and although the sense is complete, there is no hint of forward-moving action, nothing to lead up to the exits of the two speakers. The scene has been cut and one can only guess at the way the original scene was concluded.

Act V

ACT V SCENE i
Enter BYRON, D'AUVERGNE, LA FIN.

Byron. The circle of this embassy is closed,
   For which I long have longed for mine own ends,
   To see my faithful, and leave courtly friends,
   To whom I came, methought, with such a spirit
   As you have seen a lusty courser show   5
   That hath been long time at his manger tied,
   High fed, alone, and when, his headstall broken,
   He runs his prison, like a trumpet neighs,
   Cuts air in high curvets, and shakes his head,
   With wanton stoopings 'twixt his forelegs, mocking   10
   The heavy centre, spreads his flying crest

ACT V SCENE i] ACTUS 5. SCENA I. *Q1*.   10. stoopings] *This ed.;* stopings *Q1;* stoppings *Parrott.*

4–14.] an epic simile from Homer, as Loane has pointed out. The passage describes Paris going into battle: 'And as a faire Steed, proud / With ful-given mangers, long tied up and now (his head-stall broke) / He breakes from stable, runnes the field and with an ample stroke / Measures the center, neighs and lifts aloft his wanton head, / About his shoulders shakes his Crest, and where he hath bene fed / Or in some calme floud washt or (stung with his high plight) he flies / Amongst his femals, strength puts forth, his beautie beautifies, / And like Life's mirror beares his gate – so Paris from the towre / Of loftie Pergamus came forth ...' (*Iliads*, VI, 543–51). Cf. also *Venus and Adonis*, ll. 259ff.
   7. *headstall*] the part of a bridle or halter that fits round the head (*O.E.D.*).
   8. *runs*] flees.
   9. *curvets*] leaps of a horse 'in which the fore-legs are raised together and equally advanced and the hind-legs raised with a spring before the fore-legs reach the ground' (*O.E.D.*).
   10. *stoopings*] The quarto 'stopings' has been read as 'stoppings' by other editors but could well be the compositor's misreading of 'stoopings'. Q1's punctuation supports the latter interpretation: 'shakes his head: / (With wanton stopings, twixt his forelegs) mocking / The heauy center;'. The second phrase within the parenthesis makes little sense in relation to 'stoppings', but with 'stoopings' it suggests observation of a horse's behaviour.
   11. *The heavy centre*] the earth, heavy centre of the universe.
   11–12. *spreads ... ensign*] The flying mane of the horse resembles the ensign carried by a horseman in a cavalry charge.

SC I]   THE CONSPIRACY OF CHARLES DUKE OF BYRON   149

        Like to an ensign, hedge and ditches leaping,
        Till in the fresh mead, at his natural food,
        He sees free fellows and hath met them free.
        And now, good friend, I would be fain informed   15
        What our right princely lord, the Duke of Savoy,
        Hath thought on to employ my coming home.
La Fin. To try the king's trust in you, and withal
        How hot he trails on our conspiracy,
        He first would have you beg the government   20
        Of the important citadel of Bourg,
        Or to place in it any you shall name;
        Which will be wondrous fit to march before
        His other purposes, and is a fort
        He rates in love above his patrimony;   25
        To make which fortress worthy of your suit,
        He vows, if you obtain it, to bestow
        His third fair daughter on your excellence,
        And hopes the king will not deny it you.
Byron. Deny it me? Deny me such a suit?   30
        Who will he grant, if he deny it me?
La Fin. He'll find some politic shift to do't, I fear.
Byron. What shift, or what evasion can he find?
        What one patch is there in all policy's shop,
        That botcher-up of kingdoms, that can mend   35

---

13. mead] *conj. Brereton;* meate *Q1;* meat *Parrott.*

    13. *fresh mead*] Brereton's conjecture, reported by Parrott, is probably correct; the compositor may have been influenced by 'food' to print 'meat'. 'Meat' can be defended as a variation on 'green meat', a phrase used of grass and herbs (see *O.E.D.* 'green', 4).
    19. *trails on*] follows the track of: a metaphor from hunting.
    21. *important*] having great import or significance.
    Bourg] a town in south-eastern France, close to the border with Savoy, and still at this time under Savoy's rule. It was one of the counters in the bargaining between Savoy and Henry over the marquisate of Saluces (Grimeston, p. 903). During the short war between Savoy and France in 1600, Byron conquered the town of Bourg but not the citadel. He was angered by the king's refusal to promise him the keeping of the citadel when it should be captured or surrendered, but there is no hint in Grimeston that Savoy put him up to this request. Chapman makes of the incident a central turning point in the relationship between Henry and Byron.
    34. *policy's shop*] Policy is envisaged as a tailor in his shop, a mender of old garments.
    35. *botcher-up*] patcher-up. A botcher was a tailor who did repairs.

The brack betwixt us, any way denying?
D'Auvergne. That's at your peril.
Byron. Come, he dares not do't.
D'Auvergne. Dares not? Presume not so; you know, good
  duke,
That all things he thinks fit to do, he dares.
Byron. By heaven, I wonder at you; I will ask it   40
  As sternly and secure of all repulse
  As th'ancient Persians did when they implored
  Their idol, fire, to grant them any boon,
  With which they would descend into a flood
  And threaten there to quench it, if they failed   45
  Of that they asked it.
La Fin. Said like your king's king;
  Cold hath no act in depth, nor are suits wrought,
  Of any high price, that are coldly sought.
  I'll haste, and with your courage comfort Savoy.
                                              Exit LA FIN.
D'Auvergne. I am your friend, my lord, and will deserve   50
  That name with following any course you take;
  Yet, for your own sake, I could wish your spirit
  Would let you spare all broad terms of the king,
  Or, on my life, you will at last repent it.

36. *brack*] breach, rupture.
any way denying] if he denies me in any way.
42. *As th'ancient Persians*] The comparison is drawn from Plutarch's *De primo frigido* (950E) as Parrott and Schoell (p. 213) have noted.
47. *act*] action.
in depth] at great depths; again from the *De primo frigido* (949D).
50. *friend*] D'Auvergne's loyalty to Byron is set in contrast in both plays with La Fin's elaborate protestations of friendship.
53. *broad terms*] outspoken language. Grimeston notes this characteristic of Byron at a point a little closer to his downfall: 'He let scape many other Words, which his Maiesties presence and the Lawe of Duty should haue restrayned.' (p. 967). The phrase also links Byron with Essex whose friends warned him against 'his proud neglect of duty and observance' toward the queen (Camden, *Annals*, 1635, p. 552). In his *Apologie* (1604), Bacon describes how he had often warned Essex 'that the onely course to be held with the Queene, was by obsequiousnesse and obseruance ... My Lord on the other side had a setled opinion, that the Queene could be brought to nothing, but by a kind of necessitie and authority; and I well remember, when by violent courses at any time he had got his will, he wold aske me: Now Sir: *whose principles be true?*' (pp. 15–16).

SC I]   THE CONSPIRACY OF CHARLES DUKE OF BYRON   151

Byron. What can he do?
D'Auvergne.   All that you cannot fear.   55
Byron. You fear too much; be by when next I see him,
    And see how I will urge him in this suit.
    He comes: mark you, that think he will not grant it.

            Enter HENRY, EPERNON, SOISSONS, JANIN.

    I am become a suitor to your highness.
Henry. For what, my lord, 'tis like you shall obtain.   60
Byron. I do not much doubt that; my services,
    I hope, have more strength in your good conceit
    Than to receive repulse in such requests.
Henry.   What is it?
Byron. That you would bestow on one whom I shall name
    The keeping of the citadel of Bourg.   65
Henry. Excuse me sir, I must not grant you that.
Byron. Not grant me that?
Henry.   It is not fit I should:
    You are my governor in Burgundy,
    And province governors that command in chief
    Ought not to have the charge of fortresses;   70
    Besides, it is the chief key of my kingdom
    That opens towards Italy, and must therefore
    Be given to one that hath immediately
    Dependence on us.
Byron.   These are wondrous reasons.
    Is not a man depending on his merits   75
    As fit to have the charge of such a key
    As one that merely hangs upon your humours?
Henry. Do not enforce your merits so yourself;
    It takes away their lustre and reward.
Byron. But you will grant my suit?

---

58. he will not grant it] *Parrott; separate line in Q1.*   67. that] *Q1 (corr.);*
this sute *Q1 (uncorr.).*   78. enforce] *Q1 (corr.);* inferre *Q1 (uncorr.).*

67–70.] Henry displays a shrewd political sense in insisting that the governors of provinces and the captains of important citadels or fortresses should not be the same persons. The move toward royal absolutism in the age is reflected in the efforts of monarchs to make officials and military commanders directly dependent on them.

Henry.   I swear I cannot,   80
    Keeping the credit of my brain and place.
Byron. Will you deny me then?
Henry.   I am enforced:
    I have no power, more than yourself, in things
    That are beyond my reason.
Byron.   Than myself?
    That's a strange slight in your comparison;   85
    Am I become th'example of such men
    As have least power? Such a diminutive?
    I was comparative in the better sort,
    And such a king as you would say, I cannot
    Do such or such a thing, were I as great   90
    In power as he; even that indefinite 'he'
    Expressed me full: this moon is strangely changed.
Henry. How can I help it? Would you have a king
    That hath a white beard, have so green a brain?
Byron. A plague of brain! What doth this touch your brain?   95
    You must give me more reason, or I swear –
Henry. Swear, what do you swear?
Byron.   I swear you wrong me,
    And deal not like a king, to jest and slight
    A man that you should curiously reward;
    Tell me of your gray beard? It is not gray   100
    With care to recompense me, who eased your care.
Henry. You have been recompensed from head to foot.
Byron. With a distrusted dukedom. Take your dukedom

    83. *more than yourself*] any more than you have.
    85. *slight*] trifle, small matter: the meaning is carried on in 'least' and 'diminutive' (l. 87). 'Slight' as 'insult, display of contempt' has no *O.E.D.* entry before 1701, but 'to slight' with the sense 'to treat with indifference or disrespect' was in use in the 16th century. Chapman seems to have intended both meanings.
    87. *diminutive*] miniature; probably also the grammatical term expressing a very small version of something, in keeping with the following terms 'comparative' and 'that indefinite he'.
    88. *comparative*] made the object of comparison.
    sort] category.
    99. *curiously*] attentively, with great care.
    101. *recompense*] reward. Chapman may also have thought (as in 'recompensed', l. 102) of the Latin 're-compensare', to equalise one thing with another by weighing.

	Bestowed on me, again; it was not given	
	For any love, but fear and force of shame.	105
Henry.	Yet 'twas your honour; which, if you respect not,	
	Why seek you this addition?	
Byron.	Since this honour	
	Would show you loved me, too, in trusting me,	
	Without which love and trust, honour is shame,	
	A very pageant and a property;	110
	Honour with all his adjuncts I deserve,	
	And you quit my deserts with your gray beard.	
Henry.	Since you expostulate the matter so,	
	I tell you plain, another reason is	
	Why I am moved to make you this denial	115
	That I suspect you to have had intelligence	
	With my vowed enemies.	
Byron.	Misery of virtue,	
	Ill is made good with worse! This reason pours	
	Poison for balm into the wound you made;	
	You make me mad, and rob me of my soul	120
	To take away my tried love and my truth.	
	Which of my labours, which of all my wounds,	
	Which overthrow, which battle won for you,	
	Breeds this suspicion? Can the blood of faith,	
	Lost in all these to find it proof and strength,	125
	Beget disloyalty? All my rain is fall'n	
	Into the horse-fair, springing pools and mire,	
	And not in thankful grounds or fields of fruit;	
	Fall then before us, O thou flaming crystal,	

110. *pageant*] empty show.
property] an object used in a show, with no real substance.
112. *quit*] requite, reward.
113. *expostulate*] argue as an aggrieved person.
125. *to find it*] to find for it (i.e., faith).
proof] a trial successfully accomplished.
127. *horse-fair*] gathering of sellers and buyers of horses, suggesting with the following words a field trampled into mud.
springing] welling out of the ground.
128. *thankful grounds*] grateful lands, grateful for the rain and therefore fertile.
129. *flaming crystal*] empyrean or highest heaven, the sphere of the pure element of fire; 'uncorrupted register' in l. 130 suggests heaven where all men's deeds are recorded. Byron's vaunt in these lines is excessive, as it was in his earlier outburst to Savoy, and is immediately undercut by Henry's laughter.

That art the uncorrupted register 130
Of all men's merits, and remonstrate here
The fights, the dangers, the affrights and horrors
Whence I have rescued this unthankful king;
And show, commixed with them, the joys, the glories
Of his state then, then his kind thoughts of me, 135
Then my deservings, now my infamy.
But I will be mine own king: I will see
That all your chronicles be filled with me,
That none but I and my renownèd sire
Be said to win the memorable fields 140
Of Arques and Dieppe, and none but we of all
Kept you from dying there in an hospital;
None but myself that won the day at Dreux,
A day of holy name, and needs no night;
Nor none but I at Fountaine François burst 145
The heart-strings of the leaguers; I alone
Took Amiens in these arms and held her fast,
In spite of all the pitchy fires she cast,
And clouds of bullets poured upon my breast,
Till she showed yours and took her natural form; 150
Only myself, married to victory,
Did people Artois, Douai, Picardy,

---

130. *register*] registrar, keeper of a register.
131. *remonstrate*] show plainly.
135. *state*] greatness, power.
139. *my renowned sire*] See *Consp.*, II.ii.123n.
141. *Arques and Dieppe*] campaigns in Normandy in which Henry defeated the League soon after he became king, with the help of the old Marshal Byron and his son.
143. *Dreux*] the battle of Ivry: see *Consp.*, II.ii.112n.
144. *needs no night*] does not need the darkness and forgetfulness of night.
145. *Fountaine François*] See *Consp.*, II.ii.144ff.
147. *Amiens*] the siege of Amiens in 1597: see *Consp.*, III.ii.168–9. Loane notes the implied image of Menelaus struggling with Proteus through many transformations until the sea-god resumed his natural shape, in *Odyssey*, IV.
148. *pitchy fires*] fires giving off black smoke.
cast] shot forth.
150. *showed yours*] showed herself yours.
152–3.] The list comes from Grimeston, p. 790: Artois and Picardy are provinces in northern France, Saint-Paul a 'county', Douai, Bethune, Bapaume and Courcelles the towns that Byron conquered on Henry's behalf during the campaign of 1596–7.

SC II] THE CONSPIRACY OF CHARLES DUKE OF BYRON   155

    Bethune and Saint-Paul, Bapaume, and Courcelles,
    With her triumphant issue.
Henry.   Ha, ha, ha.
                           Exit [*with the* Lords].
              Byron drawing and is held by D'Auvergne.
D'Auvergne. O hold, my lord; for my sake, mighty spirit!   155
              Exit [BYRON *followed by* D'AUVERGNE.]

[ACT V   SCENE ii]
Enter BYRON, D'AUVERGNE *following unseen.*

Byron. Respect revenge, slaughter, repay for laughter!
    What's grave in earth, what awful, what abhorred
    If my rage be ridiculous? I will make it
    The law and rule of all things serious.
    So long as idle and ridiculous kings   5

---

154. *with the* Lords] *Ray.*   155.1. BYRON *followed by* D'AUVERGNE]
Parrott.   5. idle and ridiculous kings] *Q1* (idle and ridiculus King)
(*uncorr.*), *Q2*; such as he *Q1* (*corr.*).   kings] *Shepherd*; King *Q1* (*uncorr.*),
Q2.

---

   154. *her*] victory's.
   154.1.] This episode, Byron's subsequent tirade against the king and his
desire for revenge were suggested by a brief passage in Grimeston, as Parrott
and Ray note: 'This deniall did so transport the Duke of *Biron*, and thrust him
into such strange and diuilish resolutions, as one morning being in his bed at
Chaumont, he made an enterprise vpon the Kings person … but it was not
executed.' (p. 961). Chapman's contemporaries no doubt would think also of
how Essex laid his hand upon his sword when Queen Elizabeth gave him a
'cuffe on the ear' for turning his back to her, and how he had to be forcibly
restrained (see Appendix III).

   1.] Think revenge, slaughter, repayment for laughter! Q1 has a faint comma
after 'Respect' but 'respect' as a noun has little meaning in this context. As a
verb it was commonly used for 'regard', 'consider' or 'heed' (*O.E.D.*, 2).
'Repay' may be a noun, or a verb parallel to 'respect'.
   2. *grave*] serious, weighty.
   5.] Most surviving copies of Q1 (15 out of 22, according to Ray's count, I,
372) have 'So long as such as he', a line which because of its innocuous character and lack of enough syllables suggests a stop-press substitution. Greg (*A
Bibliography*, I, 408), Parrott (*M.L.R.*, Oct. 1908, p. 51) and Gabel (*P.B.S.A.*,
LVIII (1964), 467) believe this to be an example of censorship while printing
was in progress or the correction of a nervous proof-reader. Editors note also

Are suffered, soothed, and wrest all right to safety,
So long is mischief gathering massacres
For their cursed kingdoms, which I will prevent.
Laughter? I'll fright it from him, far as he
Hath cast irrevocable shame, which ever 10
Being found is lost, and lost returneth never.
Should kings cast off their bounties with their dangers?
He that can warm at fires where virtue burns,
Hunt pleasure through her torments; nothing feel
Of all his subjects suffer, but long hid 15
In wants and miseries, and having passed
Through all the gravest shapes of worth and honour,
For all heroic fashions to be learned
By those hard lessons, show an antic vizard,
Who would not wish him rather hewed to nothing 20
Than left so monstrous? Slight my services?
Drown the dead noises of my sword in laughter?
My blows as but the passages of shadows

that the sheets with this 'correction' contain a new error not in the uncorrected sheets ('gae' instead of 'age' at l. 155 below) and the addition of an unnecessary 'the' (l. 135) on the same page (sig. H4r). Gabel believes that there may have been some disarrangement of type when 'the' was added to this page. There are too few corrections on the inner forme of H to show clearly the direction of the changes, in contrast with the outer forme of H where the corrections are numerous and decisive.

 6. *suffered*] endured, tolerated.
soothed] humoured.
wrest] twist, pervert.
safety] freedom from danger, security.
 8. *prevent*] baffle, frustrate. It is not at all clear what Byron would want to frustrate, unless it is the ridiculous kings being suffered and soothed in this way.
 9–11. *far as he ... never*] Compression makes the meaning very obscure; perhaps, 'the king has cast away shame as far as possible, which even if found is lost again and never returns'; or, 'shame, if found and acknowledged, is lost in the sense of becoming something else, but if lost completely, never returns'.
 12. *bounties*] liberality.
 13–19.] In his excitement, Byron turns from an image of the king as one who warms himself at a fire where Virtue is being burned to death ('hunt pleasure through her torments') to a different series of images in which the king passes through the hardships of his campaigns to the outward semblance of worth and honour without learning the demeanour appropriate to heroes; instead he can put on only the grotesque mask ('antic vizard') of the fool, as when he laughs at Byron.
 22. *dead*] deadly.

            Over the highest and most barren hills,
            And use me like no man, but as he took me   25
            Into a desert, gashed with all my wounds
            Sustained for him, and buried me in flies?
            Forth vengeance, then, and open wounds in him
            Shall let in Spain and Savoy.
                    Offers to draw and D'Auvergne again holds him.
D'Auvergne.   O my lord,
            This is too large a licence given your fury;   30
            Give time to it; what reason suddenly
            Cannot extend, respite doth oft supply.
Byron. While respite holds revenge, the wrong redoubles,
            And so the shame of sufferance; it torments me
            To think what I endure at his shrunk hands,   35
            That scorns the gift of one poor fort to me,
            That have subdued for him, O injury,
            Forts, cities, countries, ay, and yet my fury – [*Going.*]

                            [*Enter* HENRY.]

Henry. Byron?
D'Auvergne.   My lord, the king calls.
Henry.   Turn, I pray.
            How now? From whence flow these distracted faces?   40
            From what attempt return they, as disclaiming
            Their late heroic bearer? What, a pistol?
            Why, good my lord, can mirth make you so wrathful?
Byron. Mirth? 'Twas mockery, a contempt, a scandal
            To my renown for ever; a repulse   45
            As miserably cold as Stygian water

---

38. *Going*] This ed.; *Exieunt Q1; Exeunt Q2; Exiturus Parrott.*   38.1. *Enter* HENRY] *Parrott.*

31–2.] These lines are translated from Seneca's *Agamemnon* (ll. 129–30), as Parrott notes, quoting Cunliffe, p. 97.
   32. *extend*] offer, grant.
   34. *sufferance*] patient endurance.
   35. *shrunk*] not open or generous.
   40. *distracted*] deranged, as of a madman.
   41. *attempt*] enterprise.
   46. *Stygian water*] water from the river Styx, thought to well up from the earth in a few places. Parrott quotes Pliny's *Natural History* (XXX, 53) and Plutarch's *Alexander* where the cold and poisonous nature of the water is

>   That from sincere earth issues, and doth break
>   The strongest vessels, not to be contained
>   But in the tough hoof of a patient ass.
> *Henry.* My lord, your judgement is not competent 50
>   In this dissension; I may say of you,
>   As fame says of the ancient Eleans
>   That in th'Olympian contentions
>   They ever were the justest arbitrators,
>   If none of them contended, nor were parties; 55
>   Those that will moderate disputations well
>   Must not themselves affect the coronet;
>   For as the air contained within our ears,
>   If it be not in quiet, nor refrains
>   Troubling our hearing with offensive sounds, 60
>   But our affected instrument of hearing
>   Replete with noise and singings in itself,
>   It faithfully receives no other voices;
>   So of all judgements, if within themselves
>   They suffer spleen and are tumultuous, 65
>   They cannot equal differences without them.
>   And this wind, that doth sing so in your ears,

---

60. sounds] *Q1 (corr.);* sound *Q1 (uncorr.).*

---

stressed and the legend of the ass's hoof as the only possible container. Chapman's odd phrase 'sincere earth' shows that he probably used Plutarch's *De primo frigido* (954C) as Schoell (p. 213) points out ('e sincera terra errumpunt').

    47. *sincere earth*] clean or uncorrupted ground.

    52–66.] The ancient Eleans and the discussion of air within the ears occur together in Plutarch's *Platonicae Quaestiones* (1000A, B). See Schoell, p. 214.

    52. *Eleans*] The city-state of Elis controlled the Olympiads at Olympia for a long period and appointed the judges for each contest. Strict rules were enforced to ensure impartiality.

    57. *affect*] aim at.

coronet] the victor's wreath, but the word glances at Byron's aspirations.

    58–63.] Henry describes the effect of tinnitus, a ringing in the ears.

    59. *refrains*] desists.

    61. *affected*] afflicted.

    63. *faithfully*] accurately.

    64. *judgements*] faculties for comparison and judgement belong to individuals. Cf. l. 50.

    65. *spleen*] ill-temper, fit of passion.

tumultuous] turbulent, disorderly; perhaps 'causing tumults'.

    66.] They cannot judge impartially differences or disagreements beyond themselves.

I know is no disease bred in yourself
But whispered in by others; who in swelling
Your veins with empty hope of much, yet able 70
To perform nothing, are like shallow streams
That make themselves so many heavens to sight,
Since you may see in them the moon and stars,
The blue space of the air, as far from us,
To our weak senses, in those shallow streams 75
As if they were as deep as heaven is high;
Yet with your middle finger only, sound them,
And you shall pierce them to the very earth.
And therefore leave them and be true to me,
Or you'll be left by all; or be like one 80
That in cold nights will needs have all the fire,
And there is held by others and embraced
Only to burn him: your fire will be inward
Which not another deluge can put out.
            Byron kneels while the King goes on.
O Innocence, the sacred amulet 85
'Gainst all the poisons of infirmity,
Of all misfortune, injury, and death,
That makes a man in tune still in himself,
Free from the hell to be his own accuser,
Ever in quiet, endless joy enjoying, 90
No strife nor no sedition in his powers,
No motion in his will against his reason,
No thought 'gainst thought, nor, as 'twere in the confines
Of wishing and repenting, doth possess
Only a wayward and tumultuous peace, 95

---

74. space] *Q1 (corr.);* sphare *Q1 (uncorr.).*

72. *heavens to sight*] To the sight, the heavens appear reflected in the shallow streams.
77. *sound*] measure the depth.
85–98.] Schoell notes (p. 215) that this passage is drawn from Plutarch's *Moralia: Maxime cum principibus viris philosophe esse disputandum* (777C). Henry's speech is a good example of Chapman's adaptation of a passage from a philosopher to give moral substance to his tragic pattern. Though appropriate to Henry's character as a wise king and having some bearing on the dramatic action, it also has a choral function as an expression of moral truth.
94. *doth possess*] he doth possess.

> But, all parts in him friendly and secure,
> Fruitful of all best things in all worst seasons,
> He can with every wish be in their plenty;
> When the infectious guilt of one foul crime
> Destroys the free content of all our time. 100

Byron. 'Tis all acknowledged and, though all too late,
> Here the short madness of my anger ends.
> If ever I did good, I locked it safe
> In you, th'impregnable defence of goodness;
> If ill, I press it with my penitent knees 105
> To that unsounded depth whence nought returneth.

Henry. 'Tis music to mine ears: rise then for ever
> Quit of what guilt soever till this hour,
> And nothing touched in honour or in spirit;
> Rise without flattery, rise by absolute merit. 110

Enter EPERNON *to the King, Byron, etc.*

Epernon. Sir, if it please you to be taught any courtship, take you to your stand: Savoy is at it with three mistresses at once; he loves each of them best, yet all differently.

Henry. For the time he hath been here, he hath talked a volume greater than the Turk's Alcoran; stand up close; his lips go 115 still. [*Retiring with* BYRON *and the* Lords.]

Enter SAVOY *with three* Ladies.

Savoy. Excuse me, excuse me; the king has ye all.
1st Lady. True, sir, in honourable subjection.

---

116. *Retiring ... Lords*] *Parrott.*   116.1. *Enter* SAVOY *with three* Ladies] *Parrott; follows l. 110.1 in Q1.*

96–8.] All his qualities or capacities being harmonious, they bring forth abundance of good in even the worst conditions so that he can be in all his desires in the midst of good. Chapman's emphasis on innocence and conscience gives the speech a Christian colouring it does not possess in Plutarch.

102.] Parrott notes that this line repeats a commonplace that goes back to Horace: 'Ira furor brevis est' from *Epistles*, I, ii. 62.

112. *stand*] a place where the king and the other lords may overhear Savoy and the ladies while remaining unobserved.

115. *stand up close*] stand concealed.

115–16. *his lips go still*] he never stops talking.

117. *has ye all*] possesses all of you sexually.

SC II] THE CONSPIRACY OF CHARLES DUKE OF BYRON 161

2nd Lady. To the which we are bound by our loyalty.
Savoy. Nay your excuse, your excuse. Intend me for affection? 120
You are all bearers of his favours, and deny him not your
opposition by night.
3rd Lady. You say rightly in that, for therein we oppose us to
his command.
1st Lady. In the which he never yet pressed us. 125
2nd Lady. Such is the benediction of our peace.
Savoy. You take me still in flat misconstruction, and conceive
not by me.
1st Lady. Therein we are strong in our own purposes; for it
were something scandalous for us to conceive by you. 130
2nd Lady. Though there might be question made of your fruitfulness, yet dry weather in harvest does no harm.
Henry. [*Aside*] They will talk him into Savoy; he begins to hunt
down.
Savoy. As the king is, and hath been, a most admired and the 135
most unmatchable soldier, so hath he been, and is, a sole
excellent and unparalleled courtier.
Henry. [*Aside*] Pauvre ami, merci.
1st Lady. Your highness does the king but right, sir.
2nd Lady. And heaven shall bless you for that justice with 140
plentiful store of want in ladies' affections.
Savoy. You are cruel, and will not vouchsafe me audience to
any conclusion.
1st Lady. Beseech your grace conclude, that we may present

135–6. and the most] *Q1 (corr.)*; and most *Q1 (uncorr.)*.

120. *your excuse*] your pretext.
120. *Intend ... affection?*] Design me for love?
122. *opposition*] encounter (often used of physical combat: see *O.E.D.*, 5b).
125. *pressed*] constrained, forced; also pressed beneath his body.
127–8. *conceive not by me*] do not understand me.
129. *strong*] steadfast.
131. *fruitfulness*] potency.
133–4. *he ... down*] 'To hunt down' is to bring a quarry to bay or to run it to earth; however the *O.E.D.*'s first example is from 1719. The difficulty about the phrase is that Savoy seems to be getting nowhere in his hunting of the ladies; rather the hunter has become the hunted and as Henry says, 'They will talk him into Savoy.' Parrott interprets 'to weaken, to flag' and is probably right.
136. *sole*] unique.
142. *vouchsafe me audience*] grant me hearing.

162   THE CONSPIRACY OF CHARLES DUKE OF BYRON [ACT V

>   our curtsies to you and give you the adieu.   145
> *Savoy.* It is said the king will bring an army into Savoy.
> *2nd Lady.* Truly we are not of his council of war.
> *Savoy.* Nay, but vouchsafe me–
> *3rd Lady.* Vouchsafe him, vouchsafe him, else there's no play
>   in't.   150
> *1st Lady.* Well, I vouchsafe your grace.
> *Savoy.* Let the king bring an army into Savoy, and I'll find him
>   sport for forty years.
> *Henry.* [*Aside*] Would I were sure of that, I should then have a
>   long age and a merry.   155
> *1st Lady.* I think your grace would play with his army at bal-
>   loon.
> *2nd Lady.* My faith, and that's a martial recreation.
> *3rd Lady.* It is next to impious counting.
> *Savoy.* I am not he that can set my squadrons overnight, by   160
>   midnight leap my horse, curry seven miles, and by three
>   leap my mistress; return to mine army again, and direct as

155. age] *Q1 (uncorr.);* gae *Q1 (corr.).*

---

148. *vouchsafe me*] allow me.
151. *play*] jest, sport.
153. *forty years*] an oblique reference to the forty-day war between France and Savoy which took place subsequent to this visit and in which Henry was notably successful. Chapman does not include any direct mention of the war in the play: see *Intro.*, p. 19.
156. *balloon*] a game played with 'a large inflated ball of strong double leather struck to and fro by the arm defended by a bracer of wood' (*O.E.D.*).
159. *impious counting*] This may be a reference to the impious numbering of the people of Israel and Judah ordered by David, contrary to the will of God, and undertaken unwillingly by Joab and the captains of the army. It was a diversion from their usual martial activities. David was given a choice of three punishments for his impiety: see 2 Sam. xxiv. (Suggested by A. K. Jenkins.)
160–4.] Henry's prowess as a lover was part of his legend; his mistresses, Gabrielle D'Estrées and Henriette de Balzac (Mlle D'Entragues of *The Tragedy*), seem to have been well known in England. Apparently Queen Elizabeth took delight in the gossip of the French court as recounted by Sir Ralph Winwood in his despatches (Winwood, *Memorials of the Affairs of State in the Reigns of Queen Elizabeth and King James I*, London, 1725, I, 426). Parrott notes that Sully mentions in his *Memoirs* an occasion when Henry disguised himself as a peasant to cross enemy lines in order to visit his mistress (p. 610).
160. *set my squadrons*] arrange my detachments of soldiers in battle order. *overnight*] the night before.
161. *curry*] ride with speed. *O.E.D.* quotes this example and suggests it may derive from 'currier' or 'courier'.

I were infatigable; I am no such tough soldier.
1st Lady. Your disparity is believed, sir.
2nd Lady. And 'tis a piece of virtue to tell true.
3rd Lady. God's me, the king!
Savoy. Well, I have said nothing that may offend.
1st Lady. 'Tis hoped so.
2nd Lady. If there be any mercy in laughter.
Savoy. I'll take my leave.
 (*To Henry*) After the tedious stay my love hath made,
 Most worthy to command our earthly zeal,
 I come for pardon, and to take my leave;
 Affirming, though I reap no other good
 By this my voyage, but t'have seen a prince
 Of greatness, in all grace so past report,
 I nothing should repent me; and to show
 Some token of my gratitude, I have sent
 Into your treasury the greatest jewels
 In all my cabinet of Beatrice,
 And of my late-deceasèd wife, th'Infanta,
 Which are two basins and their ewers of crystal,
 Never yet valued for their workmanship
 Nor the exceeding riches of their matter;
 And to your stable, worthy Duke of Byron,
 I have sent in two of my fairest horses.
Byron. Sent me your horses? Upon what desert?
 I entertain no presents but for merits,

179. treasury] *Q1 (corr.);* treasure *Q1 (uncorr.), Q2.*

---

163. *infatigable*] indefatigable.
171. *love*] Savoy is referring to the love and respect he owes to his host, but 'tedious stay' and the whole episode of the three ladies were suggested by a passage in Grimeston (after several pages on the disputes between the two rulers): 'Foreseeing they would soone giue him leaue to be gone, for already they sayd in iest, in the Antichamber, *That they must send him away by an Edict.* He had therefore found a fauourable pretext for his stay. He was (or made shewe to be) in loue with one of the rarest beauties in the Court, and seemed not to care for all other affayres in respect of her.' (p. 903).
176. *grace*] virtue, excellence.
180. *cabinet of Beatrice*] See *Consp.*, III.ii.181n.
181. *my late-deceasèd wife*] Parrott notes that Savoy's wife, the Infanta Catherine, had died in 1597.
183. *valued*] matched in value.
184. *matter*] the substance of which the basins and ewers were made.
188. *entertain*] receive, admit.

        Which I am far from at your highness' hands,
        As being of all men to you the most stranger;   190
        There is as ample bounty in refusing
        As in bestowing, and with this I quit you.
Savoy. Then have I lost nought but my poor goodwill.
Henry. Well, cousin, I with all thanks welcome that,
        And the rich arguments with which you prove it,   195
        Wishing I could, to your wish, welcome you.
        Draw for your marquisate the articles
        Agreed on in our composition,
        And it is yours; but where you have proposed
        In your advices my design for Milan,   200
        I will have no war with the King of Spain,
        Unless his hopes prove weary of our peace;
        And, princely cousin, it is far from me
        To think your wisdom needful of my counsel,
        Yet love, oft-times, must offer things unneedful;   205
        And therefore I would counsel you to hold
        All good terms with his Majesty of Spain:
        If any troubles should be stirred betwixt you,
        I would not stir therein but to appease them;
        I have too much care of my royal word   210
        To break a peace so just and consequent,
        Without force of precedent injury;
        Endless desires are worthless of just princes
        And only proper to the swinge of tyrants.
Savoy. At all parts spoke like the Most Christian King.   215
        I take my humblest leave, and pray your highness
        To hold me as your servant and poor kinsman,

---

199. *proposed*] *Q2; porpos'd Q1 (corr.); purposed Q1 (uncorr.).*

---

   190. *the most stranger*] the least acquainted.
   198. *composition*] agreement.
   199. *proposed*] contemplated as a possibility, imagined.
   200. *advices*] communications.
   Milan] At this time, Milan was under Spain's control and Count Fuentes was in command of the Spanish forces.
   206–7. *to hold . . . terms*] to keep on good terms.
   211. *consequent*] important, of consequence.
   213. *worthless*] unworthy.
   214. *swinge*] oppressive rule.

SC II]   THE CONSPIRACY OF CHARLES DUKE OF BYRON   165

> Who wisheth no supremer happiness
> Than to be yours. To you, right worthy princes,
> I wish for all your favours poured on me   220
> The love of all these ladies mutually;
> And, so they please their lords, that they may please
> Themselves by all means. And be you assured,
> Most lovely princesses, as of your lives,
> You cannot be true women if true wives.   *Exit.*   225

Henry. Is this, he, Epernon, that you would needs persuade us courted so absurdly?

Epernon. This is even he, sir, howsoever he hath studied his parting courtship.

Henry. In what one point seemed he so ridiculous as you would   230
present him?

Epernon. Behold me, sir, I beseech you behold me; I appear to you as the great Duke of Savoy with these three ladies.
                            [*Epernon mimics Savoy.*]

Henry. Well, sir, we grant your resemblance.

Epernon. He stole a carriage, sir, from Count d'Auvergne here.   235

D'Auvergne. From me, sir?

Epernon. Excuse me, sir, from you, I assure you: here, sir, he lies at the Lady Antoinette, just thus, for the world, in the true posture of Count d'Auvergne.

D'Auvergne. Y'are exceeding delightsome.   240

Henry. Why is not that well? It came in with the organ hose.

Epernon. Organ hose? A pox on't! Let it pipe itself into contempt; he hath stolen it most feloniously, and it graces him like a disease.

Henry. I think he stole it from D'Auvergne indeed.   245

233.1. *Epernon mimics Savoy*] This ed.   238. Antoinette] *Shepherd;* Antoniette *Q1.*

---

235. *carrriage*] bearing, posture.
238. *lies at*] importunes, courts (*O.E.D.*, 6a).
241–2. *organ hose*] 'the padded trunk-hose which came into fashion in France during the latter part of the sixteenth century' (Parrott). There are many satirical references to the fashion: 'he bought his doublet in Italy, his round hose in France' (*Mer. V.*, I.ii.66–7); 'his long sawsedge-hose' (*Tale of a Tub*, I.iv.10–13).
242–3.] Epernon picks up the reference to 'organ' as a wind instrument which can 'pipe itself (the fashion) into contempt'. Cf. *Ham.*, III.ii.361, where the recorder is called a 'little organ'.

Epernon. Well, would he had robbed him of all his other diseases! He were then the soundest lord in France.
D'Auvergne. As I am, sir, I shall stand all weathers with you.
Epernon. But, sir, he has praised you above the invention of rhymers. 250
Henry. Wherein? or how?
Epernon. He took upon him to describe your victories in war, and where he should have said you were the most absolute soldier in Christendom (no ass could have missed it), he delivered you for as pretty a fellow of your hands as any 255 was in France.
Henry. Marry, God dild him!
Epernon. A pox on him!
Henry. Well, to be serious, you know him well
To be a gallant courtier: his great wit 260
Can turn him into any form he lists,
More fit to be avoided than deluded.
For my Lord Duke of Byron here well knows
That it infecteth where it doth affect;
And where it seems to counsel, it conspires. 265
With him go all our faults, and from us fly
With all his counsel, all conspiracy. [*Exeunt.*]

267.] *Finis Actus Quinti, & vltimi.* follows l. 267 in *Q1*.

247. *soundest*] healthiest (with particular reference to being clear of syphilis, spoken of at the time as the French disease).
253. *absolute*] complete.
255. *as pretty a fellow*] as gallant a man.
of your hands] with respect to your valour in action (but carrying an innuendo of Henry's prowess as a lover).
257. *dild*] reward, requite (from 'yield').
260. *wit*] cleverness.
262. *deluded*] beguiled, deceived (i.e., no one can hope to deceive him).
264.] That it (his great wit) taints like a disease where it touches anyone.

THE TRAGEDY
OF CHARLES DUKE OF BYRON

THE TRAGEDY OF CHARLES DUKE OF BYRON

[DRAMATIS PERSONAE

HENRY IV, *King of France.*
DUKE OF BYRON.
D'AUVERGNE, *a friend of Byron.*
LA FIN.
EPERNON,
SOISSONS,
D'ESCURES, } *French noblemen.*
MONTIGNY,
VIDAME *of Chartres, La Fin's nephew.*
JANIN, *a French minister.*
CHANCELLOR (*Bellièvre*).
ARCHBISHOP.
HARLAY,
POTIER, } *judges.*
FLEURY,
Spanish Ambassador.
VITRY,
PRÂLIN, } *captains of the guard.*
LA BRUNEL, *captain of Byron's guard.*
VARENNES, *lieutenant of Byron's guard.*
Brother, *La Force, Byron's brother-in-law.*
QUEEN, *Marie de Medici, second wife of Henry IV.*
D'ENTRAGUES, *Henriette de Balzac, mistress of Henry IV.*
CUPID, *presenter of the masque.*
Four Ladies *in the masque.*
Sister, *Byron's sister.*
DAUPHIN, *the infant child of Henry and Marie.*
Messenger.
Hangman.
Boy.
Soldier.
Nurse, Attendants, Soldiers, Guards, Torchbearers, Officers of state.

SCENE: *Paris and Dijon.*]

---

facing The execution of the marechal de Biron in the courtyard of the Bastille, 31 July 1602 (Archives Photographiques Larousse)

The Tragedy of Charles Duke of Byron

Act I

ACT I SCENE i
[*Enter*] HENRY, VIDAME, D'ESCURES, EPERNON, JANIN.

Henry. Byron fallen in so trait'rous a relapse
    Alleged for our ingratitude! What offices,
    Titles of honour, and what admiration
    Could France afford him that it poured not on?
    When he was scarce arrived at forty years,   5
    He ran through all chief dignities of France.
    At fourteen years of age he was made Colonel
    To all the Suisses serving then in Flanders;
    Soon after he was Marshal of the camp,
    And shortly after, Marshal General;   10
    He was received High Admiral of France
    In that our parliament we held at Tours,
    Marshal of France in that we held at Paris.
    And at the siege of Amiens he acknowledged
    None his superior but ourself, the King;   15
    Though I had there the princes of the blood,
    I made him my Lieutenant-General,
    Declared him jointly the prime peer of France,
    And raised his barony into a duchy.
Janin. And yet, my lord, all this could not allay   20
    The fatal thirst of his ambition;
    For some have heard him say he would not die
    Till on the wings of valour he had reached
    One degree higher, and had seen his head

ACT I SCENE i] ACTUS I. SCENA I. *Q1*.

  2ff.] A similar list of honours granted is recounted by the king to Chabot, also with an expectation of gratitude (*Chabot*, II.iii.64ff.).
  8. *Suisses*] Swiss mercenaries.
  9. *camp*] army on campaign.

Set on the royal quarter of a crown; 25
Yea, at so unbelieved a pitch he aimed
That he hath said his heart would still complain
Till he aspired the style of sovereign.
And from what ground, my lord, rise all the levies
Now made in Italy? From whence should spring 30
The warlike humour of the Count Fuentes,
The restless stirrings of the Duke of Savoy,
The discontent the Spaniard entertained
With such a threatening fury, when he heard
The prejudicial conditions 35
Proposed him in the treaty held at Vervins,
And many other braveries this way aiming,
But from some hope of inward aid from hence?
And that all this directly aims at you
Your highness hath by one intelligence 40
Good cause to think; which is your late advice
That the sea army now prepared at Naples
Hath an intended enterprise on Provence,
Although the cunning Spaniard gives it out
That all is for Algier.
Henry. I must believe 45
That, without treason bred in our own breasts,
Spain's affairs are not in so good estate

---

37. braveries] *Q2;* beaueries *Q1.*

---

25. *royal quarter*] 'Quarters' usually refer in heraldry to the divisions of a shield. Janin may be referring to the royal device on the chief quarter of a shield, or (more likely) to the sovereign's head engraved on a gold coin (crown). French gold coins after 1384 had on the obverse side a shield surmounted by a crown (*O.E.D.*, 'crown').

26. *pitch*] the height to which a falcon soars before swooping down on its prey (*O.E.D.*, 18). Cf. 'wings of valour', l. 23.

28. *aspired the style*] attained the ceremonial dignities and titles.

29. *ground*] motive, reason.

31. *humour*] temper.

Count Fuentes] commander of a Spanish army in Italy, supposed not to be a threat to France after the Treaty of Vervins, but whom the Duke of Savoy hoped to draw to his support if the intrigue with Byron bore fruit.

33. *Spaniard*] Philip III, King of Spain.

37. *braveries*] acts of bravado.

38. *inward aid*] internal help, subversion.

40. *intelligence*] communication as from a spy.

47. *estate*] condition.

To aim at any action against France;
And if Byron should be their instrument,
His altered disposition could not grow 50
So far wide in an instant, nor resign
His valour to these lawless resolutions
Upon the sudden, nor without some charms
Of foreign hopes and flatteries sung to him.
But far it flies my thoughts that such a spirit, 55
So active, valiant and vigilant,
Can see itself transformed with such wild furies;
And like a dream it shows to my conceits
That he who by himself hath won such honour,
And he to whom his father left so much, 60
He that still daily reaps so much from me
And knows he may increase it to more proof
From me than any other foreign king,
Should quite against the stream of all religion,
Honour and reason, take a course so foul, 65
And neither keep his oath, nor save his soul.
Can the poor keeping of a citadel,
Which I denied to be at his disposure,
Make him forgo the whole strength of his honours?
It is impossible, though the violence 70
Of his hot spirit made him make attempt
Upon our person for denying him;
Yet well I found his loyal judgement served
To keep it from effect; besides, being offered
Two hundred thousand crowns in yearly pension, 75
And to be general of all the forces
The Spaniards had in France, they found him still
As an unmatched Achilles in the wars,
So a most wise Ulysses to their words,

51. *wide*] astray, mistaken.
57. *wild furies*] unbridled passions, perhaps with hint of the Latin Furiae, thought to inflame men.
58. *conceits*] thoughts.
62. *more proof*] greater fulfilment.
68. *disposure*] disposal.
79–80.] Chapman follows Grimeston (p. 959) in this reference to Ulysses blocking his ears to avoid hearing the Sirens; however in *Odyssey*, XII, Odysseus blocks the ears of his crew and has himself tied to the mast as they pass by the island of the Sirens.

SC I]   THE TRAGEDY OF CHARLES DUKE OF BYRON   173

  Stopping his ears at their enchanted sounds; 80
  And plain he told them that although his blood,
  Being moved, by nature were a very fire
  And boiled in apprehension of a wrong,
  Yet should his mind hold such a sceptre there
  As would contain it from all act and thought 85
  Of treachery or ingratitude to his prince.
  Yet do I long, methinks, to see La Fin
  Who hath his heart in keeping; since his state,
  Grown to decay and he to discontent,
  Comes near the ambitious plight of Duke Byron. 90
  My Lord Vidame, when does your lordship think
  Your uncle of La Fin will be arrived?
Vidame. I think, my lord, he now is near arriving,
  For his particular journey and devotion
  Vowed to the holy Lady of Loretto 95
  Was long since past, and he upon return.
Henry. In him, as in a crystal that is charmed,
  I shall discern by whom and what designs
  My rule is threatened; and that sacred power
  That hath enabled this defensive arm, 100
  When I enjoyed but an unequal nook
  Of that I now possess, to front a king
  Far my superior, and from twelve set battles
  March home a victor, ten of them obtained

---

101. but an] *Q2;* but in an *Q1.*

---

 81. *blood*] temper, passion.
 85. *contain*] restrain.
 90. *plight*] condition.
 94. *particular*] private.
 95. *the holy ... Loretto*] the Virgin Mary whose shrine at Loretto in Ancona on the Adriatic coast of Italy was a great centre of pilgrimage from the 15th century onward. There is no hint as yet that La Fin's journey was a pretended pilgrimage: its true nature is revealed in the next scene. (See Grimeston, p. 963.)
 97. *crystal*] crystal ball.
 101. *unequal nook*] Navarre, not equal in extent to the kingdom of France.
 102. *front*] confront.
 a king] Henry III of France. The reference is to the wars initiated by the Guise against Henry of Navarre during the last years of Henry III's reign. Henry was assassinated in 1589.
 104–5.] It is puzzling why Chapman should put into Henry's mouth a denial

Without my personal service, will not see 105
A trait'rous subject foil me, and so end
What his hand hath with such success begun.

Enter a Lady *and a* Nurse *bringing the* Dauphin.

Epernon. See the young Dauphin brought to cheer your
    highness.
Henry. My royal blessing and the King of Heaven
    Make thee an aged and a happy king. 110
    Help, nurse, to put my sword into his hand.
    Hold, boy, by this; and with it may thy arm
    Cut from thy tree of rule all trait'rous branches
    That strive to shadow and eclipse thy glories.
    Have thy old father's angel for thy guide, 115
    Redoubled be his spirit in thy breast,
    Who when this state ran like a turbulent sea
    In civil hates and bloody enmity,
    Their wraths and envies, like so many winds,
    Settled and burst; and like the halcyon's birth 120
    Be thine to bring a calm upon the shore,
    In which the eyes of war may ever sleep
    As overmatched with former massacres,

---

123. overmatched] *Q2;* ouermacht *Q1;* overwatch'd *Shepherd.*

---

of his personal involvement in most of the great battles of his career when Henry elsewhere in the play affirms his part in them. Ray argues that Henry wished to emphasise the divine protection afforded his kingdom whether he took part in a battle or not. The text may be corrupt here, e.g., the compositor reading 'ten' for 'none' or 'non'. Cf. l. 148 below.

111.] The incident of placing a sword in the infant's hand and the blessing is mentioned briefly in Grimeston (p. 946, misnumbered 964).

115.] Henry prays that his guardian angel may also be his son's guide. The belief in personal angels or attendant spirits remained widespread; cf. Milton's *Comus.*

115–22.] These lines, including the reference to the halcyon, are based on Plutarch's *De fortuna Romanorum,* 321C (Schoell, p. 215).

120. *Settled and burst*] quieted with a blow and rent apart (their wraths and envies). For 'settled' in this sense, see *O.E.D.*, 'settle', v. 21.

halcyon's birth] 'The ancients fabled that it bred about the time of the winter solstice in a nest floating on the sea, and that it charmed the wind and waves so that the sea was specially calm during the period.' (*O.E.D.*).

123. *overmatched*] overcome.

SC I] THE TRAGEDY OF CHARLES DUKE OF BYRON 175

When guilt made noblesse feed on noblesse,
All the sweet plenty of the realm exhausted, 125
When the nak'd merchant was pursued for spoil,
When the poor peasants frighted neediest thieves
With their pale leanness, nothing left on them
But meagre carcasses sustained with air,
Wand'ring like ghosts affrighted from their graves, 130
When with the often and incessant sounds
The very beasts knew the alarum bell,
And, hearing it, ran bellowing to their home:
From which unchristian broils and homicides
Let the religious sword of justice free 135
Thee and thy kingdoms governed after me.
O heaven! Or if th'unsettled blood of France
With ease and wealth renew her civil furies,
Let all my powers be emptied in my son
To curb and end them all, as I have done. 140
Let him by virtue quite cut off from Fortune

---

124. guilt made] *Ray*; gultie, made *Q1*; guilty, made *Q2*; guilty mad *Shepherd*; guilty lust made *Parrott*.   141. cut off] *Shepherd*; out of *Q1, Q2*.

---

124. *guilt made*] Q1's 'gultie, made' has given rise to a number of conjectures. The compositor may have misread copy, which was perhaps 'gulte' (guilt), although this would leave the line a syllable short. I have accepted this, though without much conviction. Parrott thinks a word may have dropped out, in part because Chapman always preferred to accent 'noblesse' on the first syllable; he keeps 'guilty' and tentatively adds 'lust'. The comma between 'gultie' and 'made' in Q1 suggests another possibility, that Chapman intended 'guilty' with a pause following, so that it takes on the sense of 'the guilty' or 'guiltiness'.

125–33.] This graphic description of the effects of war is reminiscent of Burgundy's speech at the end of Shakespeare's *Henry V* although the stress here is on the hunger and extreme poverty of the people rather than on untilled fields and unpruned vineyards.

137. *unsettled blood*] disturbed temper, with a suggestion of a loss of balance among the humours; perhaps also 'blood' as 'hot head' as in 'young bloods'. In a time of wealth and ease, the bloods might well become restless.

141. *Fortune*] Henry's reference to Fortune is like Pompey's in *Caesar and Pompey* (II.iv.129–44). Both passages derive from Plutarch's *De fortuna Romanorum* (317E, F, 318), as Parrott notes, where Fortune voluntarily deserts former empires and divests herself of wings, sandals and 'unstable globe' to remain permanently with Rome. However Henry prays that his son by his 'virtue' will compel Fortune to lose her wings and abandon her 'turning stone'; he thus sets up a tension between virtue and fortune that also exists in Plutarch's *De Alexandri magni fortuna aut virtute* and which Peter Ure believes is the true

Her feathered shoulders and her wingèd shoes,
And thrust from her light feet her turning stone,
That she may ever tarry by his throne.
And of his worth let after ages say, 145
He fighting for the land and bringing home
Just conquests, loaden with his enemies' spoils,
His father passed all France in martial deeds,
But he his father twenty times exceeds. [*Exeunt.*]

[ACT I   SCENE ii]

Enter the DUKE OF BYRON, D'AUVERGNE *and* LA FIN.

Byron. My dear friends, D'Auvergne and La Fin,
We need no conjurations to conceal
Our close intendments to advance our states
Even with our merits, which are now neglected;
Since Bretagne is reduced, and breathless war 5
Hath sheathed his sword and wrapped his ensigns up,
The king hath now no more use of my valour,
And therefore I shall now no more enjoy
The credit that my service held with him:
My service that hath driven through all extremes, 10
Through tempests, droughts, and through the deepest floods,
Winters of shot, and over rocks so high
That birds could scarce aspire their ridgy tops.

---

147. loaden] *Q1;* laden *Shepherd.*   5. Bretagne] *Shepherd;* Britaine *Q1.*

---

dynamic of the play in relation to Byron ('The Main Outline of Chapman's Byron').
    145–9.] As Loane notes, Henry echoes Hector's prayer for his son in *Iliads,* VI, 516–18.
    148. *passed*] surpassed.

  2. *conjurations*] swearing together of oaths.
  3. *close intendments*] secret projects.
  5. *Bretagne*] Brittany.
   reduced] conquered.
  10–13.] Schoell (pp. 215–16) cites Plutarch's *De Alexandri magni* (327C). The 'birdless rock' of the Greek is enlarged in Xylander's Latin to 'altitudines saxorum ad quae evolare aues nequeant'.
  12. *Winters of shot*] winters filled with projectiles or bullets (of hail, snow etc.). *O.E.D.* quotes Holland, *Pliny* (1601): 'Arrows, quarrels, stones, bullets and such like shot'.

SC II]   THE TRAGEDY OF CHARLES DUKE OF BYRON   177

> The world is quite inverted, virtue thrown
> At vice's feet, and sensual peace confounds   15
> Valour and cowardice, fame and infamy;
> The rude and terrible age is turned again,
> When the thick air hid heaven, and all the stars
> Were drowned in humour, tough and hard to pierce,
> When the red sun held not his fixèd place,   20
> Kept not his certain course, his rise and set
> Nor yet distinguished with his definite bounds,
> Nor in his firm conversions were discerned
> The fruitful distances of time and place
> In the well-varied seasons of the year;   25
> When th'incomposed incursions of floods
> Wasted and eat the earth, and all things showed
> Wild and disordered: nought was worse than now.
> We must reform and have a new creation
> Of state and government, and on our chaos   30

15. *sensual peace*] Byron's contempt for 'sensual peace' or for 'the most base fruits of a settled peace' at *Trag.*, IV.i.1 is in accord with his character as a great warrior who finds it difficult to adjust to a time of peace or to find an outlet for his energies. His condemnation of peace is linked with his Catiline-like aspiration to destroy the state in order to remake it. Peace is associated with the gratification of the senses, as opposed to the hard disciplines of war.

confounds] confuses.

17–28.] Chapman's source is Plutarch, *De esu carnium* (993D, E) as Schoell notes, p. 216. 'Rude' suggests savage, uncivilised: the passage in Plutarch describes a savage period of early life when the eating of meat became a necessity. As elsewhere, Chapman's paraphrase frequently adopts the English words closest to the Latin without much apparent concern for idiomatic usage.

17. *turned*] returned (*O.E.D.*, 21). The word also suggests a great cycle of turn and return.

19. *humour*] vapour.

tough] viscous, thick and cohesive.

22. *distinguished*] separated (governs 'rise and set').

23. *conversions*] returns of the sun after reaching its most southerly position; solstices (*O.E.D.*, 3). The Latin 'conversio' in Chapman's source may be interpreted as the periodical return of the seasons caused by the revolution of the heavenly bodies.

24. *distances*] differences, diversities (*O.E.D.*, 2).

26. *incomposed*] disordered: again the Latin word 'incompositus' is dominant.

27. *eat*] devoured, ravaged (past tense, pronounced 'et').

30–1.] The somewhat blasphemous comparison Byron makes between himself and the Holy Spirit, surely an example of *hubris*, refers to Gen. i.2 as Loane has noted. Cf. also Milton, *P.L.*, I, 19–22.

30. *chaos*] unformed, disordered matter.

           Will I sit brooding up another world.
           I, who through all the dangers that can siege
           The life of man have forced my glorious way
           To the repairing of my country's ruins,
           Will ruin it again to readvance it;   35
           Roman Camillus saved the state of Rome
           With far less merit than Byron hath France;
           And how short of this is my recompense.
           The king shall know I will have better price
           Set on my services, in spite of whom   40
           I will proclaim and ring my discontents
           Into the farthest ear of all the world.
La Fin. How great a spirit he breathes! How learn'd, how
           wise!
           But, worthy prince, you must give temperate air
           To your unmatched and more than human wind,   45
           Else will our plots be frost-bit in the flower.
D'Auvergne. Betwixt ourselves we may give liberal vent
           To all our fiery and displeased impressions,
           Which nature could not entertain with life
           Without some exhalation; a wronged thought   50
           Will break a rib of steel.
Byron.   My princely friend,
           Enough of these eruptions; our grave counsellor

   31. *brooding up*] hatching out.
   32. *siege*] besiege.
   35.] This line suggests Catiline's ambitions. The link between Byron and Catiline was made in *Consp.*, I.ii.15.
   36. *Camillus*] Camillus saved Rome from the invasion of the Gauls in 387 B.C. Grimeston calls Byron 'an other Camillus' (p. 993) but Chapman may also be drawing upon Plutarch's *Life of Camillus*: cf. *Bussy*, I.i.68.
   39. *price*] value.
   45. *wind*] breath, but also with some sense of the force of a winter gale in the metaphor of ll. 44–6. 'Vent' (l. 47) suggests the Latin 'ventus' (wind), and the image is maintained in 'exhalation' (l. 50), the giving off of vapour, sometimes a fiery vapour or meteor.
   48. *impressions*] strong effects produced on the mind and feelings (*O.E.D.*, 6b).
   49. *entertain*] accommodate.
   50. *exhalation*] breathing out; see l. 45n.
wronged] dishonoured, treated unjustly.
   52. *eruptions*] outbursts.

Well knows that great affairs will not be forged	
But upon anvils that are lined with wool;	
We must ascend to our intention's top	55
Like clouds that be not seen till they be up.	

La Fin. O, you do too much ravish, and my soul
    Offer to music in your numerous breath,
    Sententious, and so high it wakens death.
    It is for these parts that the Spanish king   60
    Hath sworn to win them to his side
    At any price or peril; that great Savoy
    Offers his princely daughter, and a dowry
    Amounting to five hundred thousand crowns,
    With full transport of all the sovereign rights   65
    Belonging to the State of Burgundy;
    Which marriage will be made the only cement
    T'effect and strengthen all our secret treaties.
    Instruct me therefore, my assurèd prince,
    Now I am going to resolve the king   70
    Of his suspicions, how I shall behave me.

Byron. Go, my most trusted friend, with happy feet;
    Make me a sound man with him; go to court
    But with a little train, and be prepared
    To hear, at first, terms of contempt and choler,   75
    Which you may easily calm and turn to grace,
    If you beseech his highness to believe
    That your whole drift and course for Italy,
    Where he hath heard you were, was only made
    Out of your long well-known devotion   80
    To our right holy Lady of Loretto,
    As you have told some of your friends in court;

---

82. your] *Q1;* my *Q2.*

52–4.] Parrott notes a similar image in *The Duchess of Malfi,* III.ii.328–30.
58. *numerous*] rhythmical or harmonious (cf. *Consp.,* I.ii.46).
59. *Sententious*] full of wisdom.
so high . . . death] so lofty it would call even the dead to attention.
60. *parts*] qualities.
63–8.] Chapman draws these details from Grimeston (p. 961) in almost identical language.
65. *transport*] transference.
81. *Lady of Loretto*] See *Trag.,* I.i.95n.

And that in passing Milan and Turin
They charged you to propound my marriage
With the third daughter of the Duke of Savoy;   85
Which you have done, and I rejected it,
Resolved to build upon his royal care
For my bestowing, which he lately vowed.
La Fin. O, you direct as if the god of light
　　Sat in each nook of you, and pointed out   90
　　The path of empire, charming all the dangers,
　　On both sides armed, with his harmonious finger.
Byron. Besides, let me entreat you to dismiss
　　All that have made the voyage with your lordship,
　　But specially the curate, and to lock   95
　　Your papers in some place of doubtless safety,
　　Or sacrifice them to the god of fire,
　　Considering worthily that in your hands
　　I put my fortunes, honour, and my life.
La Fin. Therein the bounty that your grace hath shown me,   100
　　I prize past life and all things that are mine,
　　And will undoubtedly preserve and tender
　　The merit of it, as my hope of heaven.
Byron. I make no question; farewell, worthy friend.
　　　　　　　　　　　　　　　Exit [BYRON *and others*].

[ACT I　SCENE iii]

[*Enter*] HENRY, CHANCELLOR, LA FIN, D'ESCURES, JANIN;
　　Henry having many papers in his hand.

Henry. Are these proofs of that purely Catholic zeal
　　That made him wish no other glorious title
　　Than to be called the scourge of Huguenots?

104.1. BYRON *and others*] *Parrott.*

---

89. *god of light*] Apollo, the sun god, also god of prophecy ('pointed out the path of empire'), and of music ('harmonious finger').

95. *curate*] Mention is made in Grimeston (p. 963) of a curate who had travelled with La Fin to Italy and whom Byron had urged La Fin to dismiss. However Chapman makes nothing of the curate in the later disclosure of treason to Henry. The papers Byron refers to in l. 96 were not burned but reached the king, as the next scene reveals.

3. *scourge of Huguenots*] Cf. *Trag.*, V.i.78–9. However Byron's reputation as scourge of the Protestants is given little weight in the play.

SC III] THE TRAGEDY OF CHARLES DUKE OF BYRON 181

Chancellor. No question, sir, he was of no religion;
    But, upon false grounds by some courtiers laid,   5
    Hath oft been heard to mock and jest at all.
Henry. Are not his treasons heinous?
All.   Most abhorred.
Chancellor. All is confirmed that you have heard before
    And amplified with many horrors more.
Henry. Good de La Fin, you were our golden plummet   10
    To sound this gulf of all ingratitude;
    In which you have with excellent desert
    Of loyalty and policy expressed
    Your name in action; and with such appearance
    Have proved the parts of his ingrateful treasons,   15
    That I must credit more than I desired.
La Fin. I must confess, my lord, my voyages
    Made to the Duke of Savoy and to Milan
    Were with endeavour that the wars returned
    Might breed some trouble to your majesty,   20
    And profit those by whom they were procured;
    But since in their designs your sacred person
    Was not excepted, which I since have seen,

---

    4. *he was of no religion*] Byron's irreligion is mentioned in Grimeston's summary of his character as the chief reason for his downfall. In spite of careful instruction in religion during his youth, 'upon false principles which he did learne of some Courtiars, he did often mocke at all Religion' (p. 993). In the same passage Grimeston reports 'He was oftentimes seen to iest at the Masse, & to laugh at them of the Reformed Religion, with whom he had bin bred vp from his infancy.' None of this mockery is evident in the play, though Byron clearly adopts a relativistic morality from Picoté and La Fin. At the end of *The Tragedy* there are suggestions of a personal spirituality that has little time for the orthodox comforts offered by the Church.
    10–14.] Henry's praise of La Fin is in striking contrast with his denunciation of him in *The Conspiracy*. The use of an informer as one of the necessary instruments of state and the fulsome praise given to such an informer are developed much further by Jonson in *Catiline* when Cicero exalts Fulvia as saviour of Rome, though expressing his revulsion in private.
    10. *golden plummet*] a plummet of surpassing value (usually of lead for sounding depth).
    13. *policy*] political wisdom.
    14. *Your . . . action*] Henry suggests that La Fin has brought the conspiracy to an end by revealing it, hence the pun on *La Fin*, the end.
    appearance] clear manifestation.
    17–28.] La Fin's motive for betraying Byron and confessing to the king is drawn from Grimeston (p. 963).

It so abhorred me that I was resolved
To give you full intelligence thereof, 25
And rather choosed to fail in promises
Made to the servant than infringe my fealty
Sworn to my royal sovereign and master.
Henry. I am extremely discontent to see
This most unnatural conspiracy, 30
And would not have the Marshal of Byron
The first example of my forcèd justice;
Nor that his death should be the worthy cause
That my calm reign, which hitherto hath held
A clear and cheerful sky above the heads 35
Of my dear subjects, should so suddenly
Be overcast with clouds of fire and thunder;
Yet on submission, I vow still his pardon.
Janin. And still our humble counsels, for his service,
Would so resolve you, if he will employ 40
His honoured valour as effectually
To fortify the state against your foes
As he hath practised bad intendments with them.
Henry. That vow shall stand; and we will now address
Some messengers to call him home to court, 45
Without the slend'rest intimation
Of any ill we know; we will restrain,
With all forgiveness if he will confess,
His headlong course to ruin, and his taste
From the sweet poison of his friendlike foes: 50
Treason hath blistered heels; dishonest things
Have bitter rivers, though delicious springs.
D'Escures, haste you unto him and inform,
That having heard by sure intelligence
Of the great levies made in Italy 55

48. With all] *Parrott;* Withal *Q1.*   51–2.] *Italic in Q1.*

---

32. *forcèd*] enforced.
33. *worthy*] sufficiently weighty.
39. *service*] benefit.
40. *resolve*] assure.
43. *intendments*] intentions.
51–2.] The couplet is printed in italics in Q1, no doubt to mark it as a *sententia*, as Parrott suggests. Treason may be spoken of as having blistered heels through always running a 'headlong course to ruin' (l. 49). 'Bitter rivers' and 'delicious springs' look back to 'sweet poison' (l. 50).

SC III]   THE TRAGEDY OF CHARLES DUKE OF BYRON   183

  Of arms and soldiers, I am resolute
  Upon my frontiers to maintain an army,
  The charge whereof I will impose on him;
  And to that end expressly have commanded
  De Vic, our Lord Ambassador in Suisse,   60
  To demand levy of six thousand men,
  Appointing them to march where Duke Byron
  Shall have directions; wherein I have followed
  The counsel of my Constable, his gossip,
  Whose liked advice I made him know by letters,   65
  Wishing to hear his own, from his own mouth;
  And by all means conjure his speediest presence.
  Do this with utmost haste.
D'Escures.   I will, my lord
            Exit D'ESCURES.
Henry. My good Lord Chancellor, of many pieces
  More than is here of his conspiracies   70
  Presented to us by our friend La Fin,
  You only shall reserve these seven and twenty,
  Which are not those that most conclude against him
  But mention only him, since I am loth
  To have the rest of the conspirators known.   75
Chancellor. My lord, my purpose is to guard all these
  So safely from the sight of any other
  That in my doublet I will have them sewed,
  Without discovering them to mine own eyes
  Till need or opportunity requires.   80
Henry. You shall do well, my lord, they are of weight;
  But I am doubtful that his conscience

---

73. most] *Shepherd;* must *Q1, Q2.*

 64. *Constable*] the commander-in-chief of the army in the king's absence and chief military judge.
 gossip] close friend.
 66. *his own*] i.e., advice.
 67. *conjure*] implore.
 69. *pieces*] Cf. Grimeston, p. 963: 'Of many papers which La Fin presented vnto the King, they made choise of 27. peeces, which were not those which concluded most against the Duke of *Biron*, but which made mention onely of him . . . .'
 73. *most*] Parrott notes the passage in Grimeston (quoted above) which supports his emendation from the Q 'must'.
 82. *doubtful that*] uncertain whether.

        Will make him so suspicious of the worst
        That he will hardly be induced to come.
Janin. I much should doubt that too, but that I hope   85
        The strength of his conspiracy as yet
        Is not so ready that he dare presume
        By his refusal to make known so much
        Of his disloyalty.
Henry.   I yet conceive
        His practices are turned to no bad end;   90
        And good La Fin, I pray you write to him
        To hasten his repair, and make him sure
        That you have satisfied me to the full
        For all his actions, and have uttered nought
        But what might serve to banish bad impressions.   95
La Fin. I will not fail, my lord.
Henry.   Convey your letters
        By some choice friend of his, or by his brother;
        And for a third excitement to his presence,
        Janin, yourself shall go, and with the power
        That both the rest employ to make him come,   100
        Use you the strength of your persuasions.
Janin. I will, my lord, and hope I shall present him.
                         Exit JANIN, [*and* LA FIN].

102.1. *and* LA FIN] *This ed.*

---

    89. *conceive*] am of the opinion that.
    91–7.] Henry's political expediency is made clear at this point, not only through his use of an informer but also by asking that a 'choice friend' or 'brother' should carry the deceptive letters to draw Byron within reach of his power.
    92. *repair*] return.
    98. *excitement*] inducement.
    102.1.] The assumption by Parrott that the end of Act I is missing is based on the fact that only Janin is given an exit. There are other examples of acts concluding without an exeunt (*Consp.*, I, III, IV – perhaps also incomplete –, V; *Trag.*, IV, V). However it seems unlikely that a minor character like Janin would be given a specific exit and not Henry at the end of an act. An exit for Henry at this point and his entry immediately after in the next scene is also unlikely, even if music was played between the acts. It appears that there was an intervening scene, probably the first scene of Act II, since this is the only occasion in *The Conspiracy* or *The Tragedy* where the Latin heading for an act has been omitted. As the text stands, however, it seems reasonable to leave Henry on the stage with the chancellor at the end of the scene to receive the courtiers who enter in II.i with news of the masque.

Act II

[ACT II SCENE i]

Enter EPERNON, SOISSONS, VITRY, PRÂLIN, *etc.* [*to Henry*].

Epernon. Will't please your majesty to take your place?
  The masque is coming.
Henry.   Room, my lords, stand close.

  Music and a song above, and Cupid *enters with a table written, hung about his neck; after him two torch-bearers; after them* MARIE, D'ENTRAGUES, *and 4 ladies more with their torchbearers, etc. Cupid speaks.*
Cupid. My lord, these nymphs, part of the scattered train
  Of friendless virtue, living in the woods
  Of shady Arden, and of late not hearing   5
  The dreadful sounds of war, but that sweet Peace
  Was by your valour lifted from her grave,
  Set on your royal right hand, and all Virtues
  Summoned with honour and with rich rewards
  To be her handmaids: these I say, the Virtues   10
  Have put their heads out of their caves and coverts
  To be her true attendants in your court:
  In which desire I must relate a tale

0.1. *to Henry*] *This ed.; to the King* Parrott.   12. her] *Q1;* your *Shepherd, Parrott.*

2.] Masques at court in the winter of 1601–2 are described by Grimeston immediately after a passage in which the king asks the Vidame when his uncle, La Fin, would arrive: 'This Winter, the Court was full of Iolity and Sports, the Queene hauing made a very Rich and Sumptuous Maske, calling fifteene Princesses and Ladies of the Court vnto her, which represented sixteene Vertues, whereof the Queene made the first. The Duke of *Vendosme* beeing attired like *Cupid*, marched before the Queene . . .' (p. 958).
  2.1. a song above] an indication of the use of a gallery above the stage for music in the Blackfriars theatre.
  2.2. table] tablet.
  2.3. *MARIE*] Henry's queen, Marie de Medici.
  D'ENTRAGUES] Henriette de Balzac, the king's mistress.
  5. Arden] the traditional location for pastorals or romances.

185

Of kind and worthy emulation
'Twixt these two Virtues, leaders of the train.   15
This on the right hand is Sophrosyne,
Or Chastity, this other Dapsyle
Or Liberality; their emulation
Begat a jar, which thus was reconciled.
I, having left my goddess mother's lap   20
To hawk and shoot at birds in Arden groves,
Beheld this princely nymph with much affection.
Left killing birds, and turned into a bird,
Like which I flew betwixt her ivory breasts,
As if I had been driven by some hawk,   25
To sue to her for safety of my life;
She smiled at first, and sweetly shadowed me
With soft protection of her silver hand;
Sometimes she tied my legs in her rich hair
And made me, past my nature, liberty,   30
Proud of my fetters. As I pertly sat
On the white pillows of her naked breasts,
I sung for joy; she answered note for note,
Relish for relish, with such ease and art
In her divine division that my tunes   35
Showed like the god of shepherds' to the Sun's,

16–18.] a tactful disposition of opposite virtues between the two. Sophrosyne is from the Greek word for temperance or chastity; Dapsyle from the Greek adjective for bountiful or liberal. In *Hero and Leander*, IV, 237, Chapman describes one of the doves of Venus as 'bountie-louing *Dapsilis*'.

19. *jar*] dispute.

20ff.] The iconography of Cupid in the sonnets and lyrics of the age is an elaborate set of variations on a few images: eyes and blindness, wings, bow, arrows, torches, kisses, games etc., so that one cannot begin to trace descent or influence. Parrott has shown that Cupid's game of penny-prick with Sophrosyne is a recollection of Lyly's famous song, 'Cupid and my Campaspe', but the links between the image of Cupid sporting on the lady's breasts and Lodge's songs, 'Rosalind's Madrigal' and 'Rosalind's Description', are attractive parallels and no more. One might also cite Marlowe's *Hero and Leander*, I, 39–44, where Cupid mistakes Hero for Venus and flies to lay his head on her breast.

21. *hawk*] hunt by flying.

34. *relish*] ornament in music, grace-note (*O.E.D.*, sb., 2).

35. *division*] the dividing of notes in a rapid passage of melody.

36.] The contest between Pan and Apollo, between the shepherd's pipes and the lyre, is suggested. The jury, which included the Muses, gave the victory to

Compared with hers; ashamed of which disgrace,
I took my true shape, bow, and all my shafts
And lighted all my torches at her eyes,
Which set about her in a golden ring, 40
I followed birds again from tree to tree,
Killed and presented, and she kindly took.
But when she handled my triumphant bow
And saw the beauty of my golden shafts,
She begged them of me; I, poor boy, replied 45
I had no other riches, yet was pleased
To hazard all and stake them 'gainst a kiss
At an old game I used, called penny-prick.
She, privy to her own skill in the play,
Answered my challenge; so I lost my arms, 50
And now my shafts are headed with her looks,
One of which shafts she put into my bow
And shot at this fair nymph, with whom before
I told your majesty she had some jar.
The nymph did instantly repent all parts 55
She played in urging that effeminate war,
Loved and submitted; which submission
This took so well, that now they both are one;

Apollo. Marsyas, the satyr, is sometimes represented as Apollo's opponent in this contest.
 the Sun's] i.e., the Sun's god, Apollo.
 40. *set*] having set.
 48. *penny-prick*] 'It appears to have consisted in aiming at a penny, perhaps placed originally as the Prick or mark for shooting at' (*O.E.D.*).
 53. *this fair nymph*] Henriette d'Entragues.
 54. *some jar*] some debate or dispute: see l. 19 above.
 56. *that effeminate war*] Letters from 'Mr. Winwood to Mr. Secretary Cecyll' in April and May 1602 describe discords at the French court because of the presence there of the king's mistress, 'which the Queen did take with so much Impatience, that during her aboad there, she kept her self retyred in her Chamber ... spending the whole Day in her Bed, in Tears and Lamentations ... being invited by the King to the *Comedy*, whether he did conduct the *Marquise* she refused to goe her selfe ...' (Sir Ralph Winwood, *Memorials of the Affairs of State*, 1725, I, 406–7). There are also suggestions of a reconciliation of sorts between queen and mistres in May 1602 and again in June after Byron's arrest (p. 421). Chapman may have heard such gossip from D'Aubigny, as suggested in the Introduction (p. 4) or from other sources.
 58. *This*] the queen.
 they both are one] In the reconciliation of Sophrosyne and Dapsyle, Chapman

And as for your dear love their discords grew,
So for your love they did their loves renew. 60
And now to prove them capable of your court,
In skill of such conceits and qualities
As here are practised, they will first submit
Their grace in dancing to your highness' doom,
And pray the press to give their measures room. 65

    Music, Dance, etc. which done Cupid speaks.
If this suffice for one court compliment,
To make them gracious and entertained,
Behold another parcel of their courtship
Which is a rare dexterity in riddles,
Shown in one instance, which is here inscribed. 70
Here is a riddle, which if any knight
At first sight can resolve, he shall enjoy
This jewel here annexed; which though it show
To vulgar eyes no richer than a pebble,
And that no lapidary nor great man 75
Will give a sou for it, 'tis worth a kingdom;
For 'tis an artificial stone composed
By their great mistress, Virtue, and will make
Him that shall wear it live with any little
Sufficed, and more content than any king. 80
If he that undertakes cannot resolve it,
And that these nymphs can have no harbour here,
It being considered that so many Virtues
Can never live in court, he shall resolve
To leave the court and live with them in Arden. 85

is probably glancing at the union of Chastity and Love, of Diana and Venus, which Renaissance Platonists postulated upon a single line in Virgil's *Aeneid* (I, 315) and certain other sources. See Edgar Wind, *Pagan Mysteries of the Renaissance*, pp. 74, 166.

    62. *conceits*] fanciful, ingenious expressions or actions.
    65. *press*] crowd thronging to see the masque.
    measures] dances.
    67. *gracious*] in grace or favour.
    68. *parcel*] small portion.
    70. *here inscribed*] on the table hung about his neck.
    73. *jewel*] an allusion perhaps to the jewel of chastity.
    77. *artificial*] contrived by artifice or skill.
    82. *harbour*] shelter, sojourn.

Epernon. Pronounce the riddle: I will undertake it.
Cupid. 'Tis this, sir.
> What's that a fair lady most of all likes,
> Yet ever makes show she least of all seeks:
> That's ever embraced and affected by her, 90
> Yet never is seen to please or come nigh her:
> Most served in her night-weeds, does her good in a corner,
> But a poor man's thing, yet doth richly adorn her:
> Most cheap, and most dear, above all worldly pelf,
> That is hard to get in, but comes out of itself? 95

Epernon. Let me peruse it, Cupid.
Cupid. Here it is.
Epernon. Your riddle is good fame.
Cupid. Good fame? How make you that good?
Epernon. Good fame is that a good lady most likes, I am sure.
Cupid. That's granted. 100
Epernon. 'Yet ever makes show she least of all seeks': for she likes it only for the virtue, which is not glorious.
Henry. That holds well.
Epernon. 'Tis 'ever embraced and affected by her', for she must persevere in virtue or fame vanishes; 'yet never is 105 seen to please or come nigh her', for fame is invisible.
Cupid. Exceeding right.
Epernon. 'Most served in her night-weeds', for ladies that most wear their night-weeds come least abroad, and they that come least abroad serve fame most, according to this: *Non* 110

---

102. the virtue] *Q1*; virtue *Q2, Shepherd, Parrott.*

88ff.] Literary riddles with a double sense were popular at the time, as Parrott notes, particularly in Italian collections by Straparola, Stigliani and others. The *Piacevoli Notti* of Straparola was translated into French by Pierre Larivey and published in numerous editions from 1576 onwards. The *Notti* combines songs, dances and narratives concluded by riddles which the assembled company tried to solve. The riddles were frequently obscene, but had innocent solutions which the ladies who told the stories pretended to accept (Michele De Filippis, 'The Literary Riddle in Italy to the end of the sixteenth century', *Univ. of Cal. Publ. in Mod. Phil.* XXXIV (1948), 14, 38–9). No direct source for Cupid's riddle has been found, though it is similar in tone to several of Straparola's. An equally bawdy one occurs in *Bussy*, III.ii.249–54, when Monsieur is interviewing the merry waiting-women.

102. *glorious*] boastful or ostentatious.

forma sed fama in publicum exire debet.
Henry. 'Tis very substantial.
Epernon. 'Does her good in a corner': that is, in her most retreat from the world, comforts her; 'but a poor man's thing':
 for every poor man may purchase it, yet 'doth richly adorn' 115
 a lady.
Cupid. That all must grant.
Epernon. 'Most cheap' for it costs nothing, and 'most dear' for
 gold cannot buy it; 'above all worldly pelf', for that's transi-
 tory, and fame eternal. It is 'hard to get in': that is, hard to 120
 get; 'but comes out of itself', for when it is virtuously de-
 served with the most inward retreat from the world, it
 comes out in spite of it; and so, Cupid, your jewel is mine.
Cupid. It is: and be the virtue of it yours.
 We'll now turn to our dance, and then attend 125
 Your highness' will as touching our resort,
 If Virtue may be entertained in court.
Henry. This show hath pleased me well, for that it figures
 The reconcilement of my queen and mistress:
 Come, let us in and thank them, and prepare 130
 To entertain our trusty friend Byron. *Exeunt.*

131.] *Finis Actus Secundi follows l. 131 in Q1.*

 111.] 'It is not outward form but fame that ought to go out in public.' Schoell
(p. 72) notes a source in Plutarch's *Mulierum virtutes* (242E).
 112. *substantial*] of substance, probable.
 124. *virtue*] special efficacy or power.
 126. *resort*] access.
 128. *figures*] represents through images.

Act III

ACT III   SCENE i
Enter BYRON, D'AUVERGNE.

Byron. Dear friend, we must not be more true to kings
　Than kings are to their subjects; there are schools
　Now broken ope in all parts of the world,
　First founded in ingenious Italy,
　Where some conclusions of estate are held   5
　That for a day preserve a prince, and ever
　Destroy him after; from thence men are taught
　To glide into degrees of height by craft
　And then lock in themselves by villany.
　But God, who knows kings are not made by art   10
　But right of nature, nor by treachery propped
　But simple virtue, once let fall from heaven
　A branch of that green tree, whose root is yet
　Fast fixed above the stars; which sacred branch

ACT III SCENE i] ACTUS 3. SCENA I. *Q1*.

　0.1.] Grimeston notes that Byron was at Dijon when the king's messengers attempted to draw him to court.
　2. *schools*] schools of thought, as of groups of disciples following the principles and ideas of particular scholars. In the following lines, it is clear that the doctrines of Machiavelli, or their popular misrepresentation, are being referred to.
　4. *ingenious*] clever, talented.
　5. *conclusions of estate*] propositions regarding government.
　10. *art*] cunning skill, artfulness.
　11. *by ... nature*] by the just title given by nature, God's regulative agency operating in the physical world. Byron says nothing at this point about the inheritance of kingship, so that 'right of nature' could have radical implications in line with his opinions elsewhere in the play. However the emphasis on the 'sacred branch' that fell from heaven gives a general sense of orthodoxy to the whole speech.
　13–14. *A branch ... stars*] The 'green tree' may be the tree of life which grew in the Garden of Eden and which is 'in the midst of the paradise of God' in Rev. ii.7 and xxii.1–2. Whether Chapman had any awareness of the world tree reaching far above the stars, which belongs to many mythologies, remains a matter of doubt; the biblical passages quoted in succeeding notes suggest the

> We well may liken to that laurel spray 15
> That from the heavenly eagle's golden seres
> Fell in the lap of great Augustus' wife;
> Which spray, once set, grew up into a tree
> Whereof were garlands made, and emperors
> Had their estates and foreheads crowned with them; 20
> And as the arms of that tree did decay,
> The race of great Augustus wore away,
> Nero being last of that imperial line,
> The tree and emperor together died.
> Religion is a branch, first set and blest 25
> By heaven's high finger in the hearts of kings,
> Which whilom grew into a goodly tree;
> Bright angels sat and sung upon the twigs,
> And royal branches for the heads of kings

major source of his images. The use of 'branch' is important in that it suggests lineal descendant: 'But there shall come a rod forth of the stock of Jesse, and a graff shall grow out of his roots' (Isa. xi.1). The tree of Jesse is well known from medieval art (N. Frye, *The Great Code*, p. 150), often being associated symbolically with the tree of life and the cross.

15. *that laurel spray*] As Ferguson points out, Chapman derived the legend of the laurel spray from Suetonius, *De vita Caesarum*, VII (Galba), who describes how an eagle dropped into Livia's lap a white hen with a sprig of laurel in its beak. Livia raised a brood of chickens from the hen and a grove of laurel from the sprig, from which the Caesars plucked laurels for their triumphs. At the end of Nero's reign, the grove withered and died. Ferguson suggests that Byron is using the story to cast doubts on the divine authority for Henry's kingship: 'Byron's application, which makes the tree stand for religion, is appropriate because the last of the Valois kings was the last true Catholic ruler, just as the laurel died with the last of Augustus' line.' (p. 235). Note ll. 45–8 below.

16. *seres*] claws, talons.

18. *set*] planted.

20. *estates*] thrones, canopies, other marks of pomp.

25–30.] Chapman's image of religion growing like a branch in the hearts of kings, which has been 'set' by God (in order to take hold) recalls Ezek. xvii. Here there is a contrast between two trees, one growing from a twig plucked by a colourful eagle from the top of a cedar of Lebanon, which is planted in a 'city of merchants' but is doomed to wither and die, and one which the Lord God 'will also take off the top of this high cedar, and will set it, and cut off the top of the tender plant thereof and . . . will plant it upon an high mountain and great', a tree which will flourish, bearing fruit and sheltering all the fowl of the air.

27. *whilom*] in time past.

Were twisted of them; but since squint-eyed Envy   30
And pale Suspicion dashed the heads of kingdoms
One 'gainst another, two abhorrèd twins
With two foul tails, stern War and Liberty,
Entered the world. The tree that grew from heaven
Is overrun with moss; the cheerful music   35
That heretofore hath sounded out of it
Begins to cease; and as she casts her leaves,
By small degrees, the kingdoms of the earth
Decline and wither; and look, whensoever
That the pure sap in her is dried up quite,   40
The lamp of all authority goes out

30. *squint-eyed Envy*] Bartlett notes several uses of this epithet for envy in Chapman's poems and traces it to Sylvester's translation of Du Bartas (1608 ed.), and a likely classical origin in Plutarch's *De invidio et odio* (Bartlett, p. 468).

31–2.] The long civil wars in France are suggested.

33. *Liberty*] licence, freedom from all restraints of law and custom. Parrott suggests that Chapman is referring to the liberty of rebellion against royal power claimed by extremists among both Catholics and Protestants in France and England at the time (p. 613). The conclusion of the speech glances sharply at Henry when condemning 'kings' revolts' against truth and loyalty, and no doubt also in the phrase 'playing both ways with religion', a reference to Henry's change from Protestantism to Catholicism and perhaps to the Edict of Nantes in 1598.

34–42.] In addition to the passage in Ezekiel, Chapman probably alludes to the dream of Nebuchadnezzar about a great tree 'in the midst of the earth ... and the height thereof reached unto heaven' (Dan. iv.7–8) and to Daniel's interpretation of its hewing down as the fall of Nebuchadnezzar's kingdom. Both passages picture the kingdoms of the earth as great trees which will wither and die or will be cut down, in contrast with the tree planted by God: 'And all the trees of the field shall know that I the Lord have brought down the high tree and exalted the low tree: that I have dried up the green tree, and made the dry tree to flourish ...' (Ezek. xvii.24). For the tree imagery, see E. A. S. Butterworth, *The Tree at the Navel of the Earth* (Berlin, 1970); medieval iconography also made much of the green tree and the dry tree.

35. *cheerful music*] The biblical passages describe the trees representing great kingdoms and the tree planted by God as harbouring the 'fowls of the heaven' but do not mention the unceasing songs of birds, as many of the myths of the world tree do (see Butterworth, p. 1).

40. *pure sap ... quite*] The biblical tree of life and the world tree have milk and honey issuing from their trunks and branches, or a river of pure water from their roots, a river which in Genesis becomes the four rivers of Eden. In Rev. xxii.1–2, the 'pure river of water of life' proceeds from the throne of God, but it is also associated with the tree of life and its fruits and leaves which 'serve to heal the nations with'.

   And all the blaze of princes is extinct.
   Thus, as the poet sends a messenger
   Out to the stage to show the sum of all
   That follows after, so are kings' revolts   45
   And playing both ways with religion
   Fore-runners of afflictions imminent,
   Which, like a chorus, subjects must lament.
D'Auvergne. My lord, I stand not on these deep discourses
   To settle my course; to your fortunes mine   50
   Are freely and inseparably linked,
   And to your love my life.
Byron.   Thanks, princely friend;
   And whatsoever good shall come of me,
   Pursued by all the Catholic princes' aids
   With whom I join, and whose whole states proposed   55
   To win my valour, promise me a throne,
   All shall be, equal with myself, thine own.

      [*Enter* LA BRUNEL.]

La Brunel. My lord, here is D'Escures, sent from the king,
   Desires access to you.

      Enter D'ESCURES.

Byron.   Attend him in.
D'Escures. Health to my lord the duke.
Byron.   Welcome, D'Escures.   60
   In what health rests our royal sovereign?

---

50. course; ... fortunes] *This ed.;* course ... fortunes; *Q1, Parrott.*   57.1. *Enter* LA BRUNEL] *Parrott.*

---

 43. *messenger*] Chapman may be thinking of the ghost, goddess or fury who foretells dire events at the beginning of several of Seneca's tragedies, or of the Elizabethan prologue as in *Doctor Faustus.* Cf. Hamlet's complaint about the players acting their dumb-show and the Prologue who enters immediately after: 'they'll tell all' (III.ii.137).

 48. *chorus*] The lamenting choruses of Senecan tragedies consisted of 'subjects', citizens of the state or captives.

 50.] Both the sense of the passage and the syntax seem to require the semicolon after 'course', rather than after 'fortunes' as Qq have it.

 55. *whose ... proposed*] whose entire estates or possessions having been put forward (one of Byron's typical exaggerations).

D'Escures. In good health of his body, but his mind
    Is something troubled with the gathering storms
    Of foreign powers, that as he is informed
    Address themselves into his frontier towns;   65
    And therefore his intent is to maintain
    The body of an army on those parts
    And yield their worthy conduct to your valour.
Byron. From whence hears he that any storms are rising?
D'Escures. From Italy; and his intelligence   70
    No doubt is certain that in all those parts
    Levies are hotly made; for which respect,
    He sent to his ambassador, de Vic,
    To make demand in Switzerland for the raising
    With utmost diligence of six thousand men;   75
    All which shall be commanded to attend
    On your direction, as the Constable,
    Your honoured gossip, gave him in advice,
    And he sent you by writing: of which letters
    He would have answer and advice from you   80
    By your most speedy presence.
Byron.   This is strange,
    That when the enemy is t'attempt his frontiers,
    He calls me from the frontiers. Does he think
    It is an action worthy of my valour
    To turn my back to an approaching foe?   85
D'Escures. The foe is not so near but you may come,
    And take more strict directions from his highness
    Than he thinks fit his letters should contain,
    Without the least attainture of your valour;
    And therefore, good my lord, forbear excuse   90
    And bear yourself on his direction,
    Who, well you know, hath never made design
    For your most worthy service where he saw
    That anything but honour could succeed.
Byron. I will not come, I swear.
D'Escures.   I know your grace   95
    Will send no such unsavoury reply.
Byron. Tell him that I beseech his majesty

---

72. *for which respect*] on account of which.
89. *attainture of*] stain to.

>   To pardon my repair till th'end be known
>   Of all these levies now in Italy.
> *D'Escures.* My lord, I know that tale will never please him,
>   And wish you, as you love his love and pleasure,
>   To satisfy his summons speedily,
>   And speedily I know he will return you.
> *Byron.* By heaven, it is not fit, if all my service
>   Makes me know anything; beseech him, therefore,
>   To trust my judgement in these doubtful charges,
>   Since in assured assaults it hath not failed him.
> *D'Escures.* I would your lordship now would trust his judgement.
> *Byron.* God's precious, y'are importunate past measure,
>   And, I know, further than your charge extends.
>   I'll satisfy his highness, let that serve;
>   For by this flesh and blood, you shall not bear
>   Any reply to him but this from me.
> *D'Escures.* 'Tis nought to me, my lord; I wish your good,
>   And for that cause have been importunate.
>   *Exit* D'ESCURES.
> *La Brunel.* By no means go, my lord; but with distrust
>   Of all that hath been said or can be sent,
>   Collect your friends and stand upon your guard;
>   The king's fair letters and his messages
>   Are only golden pills, and comprehend
>   Horrible purgatives.
> *Byron.*   I will not go,
>   For now I see th'instructions lately sent me,
>   That something is discovered, are too true,
>   And my head rules none of those neighbour nobles

---

98. *repair*] return.
th'end] the aim, objective.
100. *tale*] statement, with the suggestion of a piece of fiction.
104. *fit*] appropriate to the circumstances.
106. *doubtful charges*] uncertain responsibilities.
107. *assured assaults*] sure or certain attacks.
109. *God's precious*] by God's precious blood.
118.] This line suggests the watchword used by Essex and his friends just before Essex's attempted coup: see Appendix III.
120. *comprehend*] include.
122. *instructions*] information.
124–5.] These lines are puzzling. Parrott glosses: 'I am not one of those

That every pursuivant brings beneath the axe;   125
If they bring me out, they shall see I'll hatch
Like to the blackthorn that puts forth his leaf,
Not with the golden fawnings of the sun,
But sharpest showers of hail and blackest frosts:
Blows, batteries, breaches, showers of steel and blood   130
Must be his downright messengers for me,
And not the mizzling breath of policy.
He, he himself, made passage to his crown
Through no more armies, battles, massacres,
Than I will ask him to arrive at me;   135
He takes on him my executions,
And on the demolitions that this arm
Hath shaken out of forts and citadels,
Hath he advanced the trophies of his valour;
Where I in those assumptions may scorn   140
And speak contemptuously of all the world,
For any equal yet I ever found;
And in my rising, not the Sirian star
That in the Lion's month undaunted shines,

---

143. Sirian] *Parrott;* Syrian *Q1, Q2.*   144. month] *Parrott;* mouth *Q1, Q2.*

---

petty provincial nobles whom any king's messenger may lead unresisting to the scaffold.' Ferguson objects that Byron's statement is not an assertion of his superior dignity but rather: 'I see that the king has discovered something about me and *that* my head ranks no higher than the heads of ordinary nobles in his eyes' (p. 235).

    125. *pursuivant*] a royal messenger with power to execute warrants (*O.E.D.*).

    127. *blackthorn*] sloe or wild plum, a thorny shrub that bears white blossoms in early spring before the leaves.

    132. *mizzling*] drizzling, foggy, deliberately confusing.

    136. *executions*] destructive actions.

    140. *assumptions*] claims.

    143. *Sirian*] undoubtedly the correct reading (rather than the quarto 'Syrian') since the rising of Sirius was of such importance to the Egyptians and the Greeks in measuring out the year. Sirius rises before sunrise in July, the month in which the sun enters the zodiacal sign of the Lion. Schoell quotes Plutarch, *De solertia animalium* (974E), but there may well be other sources (p. 216).

    144. *month*] Q1's 'mouth' may be the result of a turned letter or a hasty assumption by the compositor that 'mouth' ought to follow 'lion', when 'undaunted' follows. Ray notes that there may be a confusion of animals: 'Sirius, known as the Dog Star, is situated in the mouth of the constellation Canis Major' (p. 440).

And makes his brave ascension with the sun,	145
Was of th'Egyptians with more zeal beheld	
And made a rule to know the circuit	
And compass of the year, than I was held	
When I appeared from battle, the whole sphere	
And full sustainer of the state we bear;	150
I have Alcides-like gone under th'earth	
And on these shoulders borne the weight of France:	
And for the fortunes of the thankless king,	
My father, all know, set him in his throne,	
And if he urge me, I may pluck him out.	155

Enter Messenger.

Messenger. Here is the President Janin, my lord,
    Sent from the king, and urgeth quick access.
Byron. Another pursuivant, and one so quick?
    He takes next course with me to make him stay:
    But let him in, let's hear what he importunes.   160
            [*Exit* LA BRUNEL *and Messenger.*]

Enter JANIN.

Janin. Honour and loyal hopes to Duke Byron!
Byron. No other touch me: say how fares the king?
Janin. Fairly, my lord; the cloud is yet far off
    That aims at his obscuring, and his will
    Would gladly give the motion to your powers   165

160.1. *Exit* LA BRUNEL] *Parrott; and Messenger | This ed.*

---

   149. *sphere*] equivalent to 'sustainer' since a sphere was supposed to support a planet or the fixed stars just as Byron believed that he supported the whole state of France.
   151–2.] Alcides or Hercules bore the heavens on his shoulders for Atlas while Atlas went to fetch the apples of the Hesperides.
   156. *President*] the title of an officer of state.
   159. *next course*] the nearest way.
   to . . . stay] to make him stay outside, cooling his heels. Parrott, however, suggests 'to make him wait', 'He' and 'him' referring to the king.
   160.1. Exit *LA BRUNEL*] La Brunel must go out at some point in order to make his re-entry at l. 225 below. But see l. 228n. below.
   163. *fairly*] brightly, as in 'fair' weather: note the following image linking the king with the sun.

  That should disperse it; but the means, himself
  Would personally relate in your direction.
Byron. Still on that haunt?
Janin.   Upon my life, my lord,
  He much desires to see you, and your sight
  Is now grown necessary to suppress,   170
  As with the glorious splendour of the sun,
  The rude winds that report breathes in his ears
  Endeavouring to blast your loyalty.
Byron. Sir, if my loyalty stick in him no faster
  But that the light breath of report may loose it,   175
  So I rest still unmoved, let him be shaken.
Janin. But these aloof abodes, my lord, bewray
  That there is rather firmness in your breath
  Than in your heart; truth is not made of glass
  That with a small touch it should fear to break,   180
  And therefore should not shun it; believe me,
  His arm is long and strong, and it can fetch
  Any within his will that will not come:
  Not he that surfeits in his mines of gold,
  And for the pride thereof compares with God,   185
  Calling, with almost nothing different,
  His powers invincible, for omnipotent,
  Can back your boldest fort 'gainst his assaults;
  It is his pride and vain ambition
  That hath but two stairs in his high designs –   190
  The lowest envy, and the highest blood –
  That doth abuse you, and gives minds too high
  Rather a will by giddiness to fall

---

 167. *relate ... direction*] declare in giving you direction or instructions.
 168. *haunt*] topic. Cf. *Revenge of Bussy*, I.ii.25: 'Still on this haunt'.
 174. *faster*] more firmly.
 178. *firmness ... breath*] loyalty in your speech.
 184ff.] No doubt Philip II of Spain was in the poet's mind (as in that of his audience), with his 'invincible' armada, his 'mines of gold' and his wide imperial claims. Philip III had succeeded his father in 1598 and was the Spanish king involved in the conspiracy which included Byron, Savoy and Fuentes, but he had not become the legendary figure his father had been. See *Trag.*, IV.ii.116ff.
 185. *compares with*] vies with, rivals.
 186. *with ... different*] with almost no distinction.
 191. *blood*] passion, high temper.

        Than to descend by judgement.
Byron.   I rely
    On no man's back nor belly; but the king   195
    Must think that merit, by ingratitude cracked,
    Requires a firmer cementing than words.
    And he shall find it a much harder work
    To solder broken hearts than shivered glasses.
Janin. My lord, 'tis better hold a sovereign's love   200
    By bearing injuries, than by laying out
    Stir his displeasure; princes' discontents,
    Being once incensed, are like the flames of Etna,
    Not to be quenched nor lessened; and be sure
    A subject's confidence in any merit   205
    Against his sovereign, that makes him presume
    To fly too high, approves him like a cloud
    That makes a show as it did hawk at kingdoms,
    And could command all raised beneath his vapour:
    When suddenly the fowl that hawked so fair   210
    Stoops in a puddle, or consumes in air.
Byron. I fly with no such aim, nor am opposed
    Against my sovereign; but the worthy height
    I have wrought by my service I will hold,
    Which if I come away, I cannot do;   215
    For if the enemy should invade the frontier,
    Whose charge to guard is mine, with any spoil,
    Although the king in placing of another
    Might well excuse me, yet all foreign kings

199. glasses] *Q1*; glass *Q2, Shepherd, Parrott.*

---

    195. *back nor belly*] support or maintenance (clothing, food).
    199. *glasses*] See proverbial expressions in Tilley, C814 (Shirley, 1633, 'And if she chance any way to crack her Venice glass, it will be not so easily soldered') and G134.
    201. *laying out*] exposing, in the sense of displaying and making much of (*O.E.D.*, 56g). Parrott suggests 'struggling, laying about one'; Ray glosses 'scheming'.
    205–11.] Cf. *Teares of Peace*: 'Your Actiue men, consume their whole lifes fire, / In thirst of State-height, higher still and higher, / (Like seeled Pigeons) mounting, to make sport, / To lower lookers on ...' (ll. 413–16).
    207. *approves*] proves.
    211. *Stoops ... puddle*] The hawk swoops down to its prey but the cloud melts in rain into a puddle.
    217. *spoil*] pillaging.

SC I]   THE TRAGEDY OF CHARLES DUKE OF BYRON   201

>   That can take note of no such secret quittance   220
>   Will lay the weakness here, upon my wants;
>   And therefore my abode is resolute.
> *Janin.* I sorrow for your resolution,
>   And fear your dissolution will succeed.
> *Byron.* I must endure it.
> *Janin.*   Fare you well, my lord.   225
>   [*Exit* JANIN.]
> *Byron.* Farewell to you.
>
>   *Enter* LA BRUNEL.
>
>   Captain, what other news?
> *La Brunel.* La Fin salutes you.   [*Giving letters.*]
> *Byron.* Welcome, good friend; I hope your wished arrival
>   Will give some certain end to our designs.
> *La Brunel.* I know not that, my lord; reports are raised   230
>   So doubtful and so different, that the truth
>   Of any one can hardly be assured.
> *Byron.* Good news, D'Auvergne; our trusty friend La Fin
>   Hath cleared all scruple with his majesty,
>   And uttered nothing but what served to clear   235
>   All bad suggestions.
> *La Brunel.*   So he says, my lord,
>   But others say La Fin's assurances
>   Are mere deceits, and wish you to believe
>   That when the Vidame, nephew to La Fin,
>   Met you at Autun to assure your doubts   240
>   His uncle had said nothing to the king

225. *Exit* JANIN] *Q2; not in Q1.*   227. *Giving letters*] *Parrott.*   230–2. I know ... assured] *Shepherd; set as prose in Q1.*

---

220. *quittance*] release (from duty).
221. *wants*] shortcomings.
224. *succeed*] follow.
228.] Byron's words of welcome sound as if La Brunel has arrived for the first time, bearing the letters of La Fin. However he has appeared before in this scene, bringing in D'Escures. Either these words are addressed to La Fin's letters as if La Fin were himself present, or Chapman intended a different person to enter at this point as messenger. In his directions to La Fin (*Trag.*, I.iii.96–7), the king had suggested that La Fin send his letters by some friend of Byron's or his brother-in-law (Ray notes a possible corruption in the incomplete l. 227 ending in a semi-colon.) See ll. 243–5 and n.

That might offend you, all the journey's charge
The king defrayed; besides, your truest friends
Willed me to make you certain that your place
Of government is otherwise disposed; 245
And all advise you, for your latest hope,
To make retreat into the Franch County.
Byron. I thank them all, but they touch not the depth
Of the affairs betwixt La Fin and me,
Who is returned contented to his house, 250
Quite freed of all displeasure or distrust;
And therefore, worthy friends, we'll now to court.
D'Auvergne. My lord, I like your other friends' advices
Much better than La Fin's; and on my life
You cannot come to court with any safety. 255
Byron. Who shall infringe it? I know all the court
Have better apprehension of my valour
Than that they dare lay violent hands on me;
If I have only means to draw this sword,
I shall have power enough to set me free 260
From seizure by my proudest enemy.

Exit [BYRON *with the rest*].

[ACT III SCENE ii]

[*Enter*] EPERNON, VITRY, PRÂLIN.

Epernon. He will not come, I dare engage my hand.
Vitry. He will be fetched then, I'll engage my head.
Prâlin. Come or be fetched, he quite hath lost his honour

261.1. BYRON *with the rest*] Parrott.

---

242. *offend*] wrong, hurt.

243–5.] These lines do not seem appropriate to La Brunel, Byron's captain, but rather to a friend from court who has brought the letters and verbal messages of warning.

247. *Franch County*] See *Consp.*, I.i.41n.

1. *engage*] pledge.

3ff.] Chapman makes use of a choral technique introduced in *Bussy* (V.ii.1ff.), which Jonson had also demonstrated in *Sejanus*, whereby characters withdraw momentarily from their dramatic roles to comment on the fortune and qualities of the central tragic figure. The device domesticates the classical chorus to the English stage tradition. In this example Prâlin makes a direct comment on Byron; Vitry and Epernon then generalise on human nature itself. Epernon's elaborate simile is satiric in tone and recalls Roiseau's

              In giving these suspicions of revolt
              From his allegiance; that which he hath won   5
              With sundry wounds and peril of his life,
              With wonder of his wisdom and his valour,
              He loseth with a most enchanted glory,
              And admiration of his pride, and folly.
Vitry. Why, did you never see a fortunate man   10
              Suddenly raised to heaps of wealth and honour,
              Nor any rarely great in gifts of nature,
              As valour, wit and smooth use of the tongue,
              Set strangely to the pitch of popular likings,
              But with as sudden falls the rich and honoured   15
              Were overwhelmed by poverty and shame,
              Or had no use of both above the wretched?
Epernon. Men never are satisfied with that they have;
              But as a man, matched with a lovely wife,
              When his most heavenly theory of her beauties   20
              Is dulled and quite exhausted with his practice,
              He brings her forth to feasts where he, alas,
              Falls to his viands with no thought like others
              That think him blest in her; and they, poor men,
              Court and make faces, offer service, sweat   25
              With their desires' contention, break their brains
              For jests and tales, sit mute and lose their looks,
              Far out of wit and out of countenance:
              So all men else do, what they have, transplant,
              And place their wealth in thirst of that they want.   30

30. that] *Q1*; what *Q2, Shepherd, Parrott.*

---

description of Byron at the archduke's court in *Consp.*, II.ii. However, later choral passages prepare for the tragic catastrophe more directly.

   8. *enchanted glory*] deluded boastfulness.

   9. *admiration ... pride*] wondering esteem given to his pride.

   12. *rarely*] exceptionally.

   14. *strangely*] astonishingly.

   pitch] the very highest point.

   18–30.] Cf. *Teares of Peace*: 'Others aduancements, others Fames desiring; / Thirsting, exploring, praysing, and admiring; / Like lewd adulterers, that their owne wiues scorne, / And other mens, with all their wealth, adorne.' (ll. 820–3).

   20. *theory*] contemplation, from Gk. θεωρία: viewing, a looking at.

   21. *practice*] familiarity, habitual manner of life.

   29–30.] All other men therefore transplant elsewhere what they possess, and place all their desire in what they do not have.

Enter HENRY, CHANCELLOR, VIDAME, D'ESCURES, JANIN.

Henry. He will not come. I must both grieve and wonder
    That all my care to win my subjects' love
    And in one cup of friendship to commix
    Our lives and fortunes, should leave out so many
    As give a man, contemptuous of my love   35
    And of his own good in the kingdom's peace,
    Hope, in a continuance so ungrateful,
    To bear out his designs in spite of me.
    How should I better please all than I do?
    When they supposed I would have given some   40
    Insolent garrisons, others citadels,
    And to all sorts increase of miseries,
    Province by province, I did visit all
    Whom those injurious rumours had dismayed,
    And showed them how I never sought to build   45
    More forts for me than were within their hearts,
    Nor use more stern constraints than their good wills
    To succour the necessities of my crown;
    That I desired to add to their contents
    By all occasions rather than subtract;   50
    Nor wished I that my treasury should flow
    With gold that swum in, in my subjects' tears;
    And then I found no man that did not bless
    My few years' reign, and their triumphant peace;
    And do they now so soon complain of ease?   55
    He will not come!

---

44. dismayed] *Parrott;* diswaide *Q1, Q2;* dissway'd *Shepherd, Ray.*   56.
He will not come] *Q2; Hen.* He will not come *Q1.*

    33.] Schoell (p. 217) notes Plutarch, *De Alexandri magni* (329C). The passage in Plutarch is a notable exposition of Alexander's hopes of uniting people of many cities and regions into one community, and hence is relevant to Chapman's portrait of Henry here and elsewhere in the play.
    37. *continuance*] persistence.
    38. *bear out*] support, confirm.
    40–54.] These lines follow closely Grimeston's description of Henry's tour through the provinces to allay fears and suspicions (p. 964).
    44. *dismayed*] Parrott's correction seems justified, though Shepherd, Phelps and Ray have kept the quarto 'diswaide' (as 'disswayed'), a possible coinage meaning 'swayed away from'.
    56.1. *Brother*] probably one of Byron's brothers-in-law, La Force or Saint

SC II] THE TRAGEDY OF CHARLES DUKE OF BYRON 205

Enter BYRON, D'AUVERGNE, Brother, *with others.*

Epernon. O madness, he is come!
Chancellor. The duke is come, my lord.
Henry. O sir, y'are welcome,
   And fitly, to conduct me to my house.
Byron. I must beseech your majesty's excuse
   That, jealous of mine honour, I have used   60
   Some of mine own commandment in my stay,
   And came not with your highness' soonest summons.
Henry. The faithful servant, right in Holy Writ,
   That said he would not come and yet he came:
   But come you hither, I must tell you now,   65
   Not the contempt you stood to in your stay,
   But the bad ground that bore up your contempt
   Makes you arrive at no port but repentance,
   Despair, and ruin,
Byron.   Be what port it will
   At which your will will make me be arrived,   70
   I am not come to justify myself,
   To ask you pardon, nor accuse my friends.
Henry. If you conceal my enemies, you are one,
   And then my pardon shall be worth your asking,
   Or else your head be worth my cutting off.   75
Byron. Being friend and worthy fautor of myself,
   I am no foe of yours, nor no impairer,
   Since he can no way worthily maintain
   His prince's honour that neglects his own;
   And if your will have been, to my true reason,   80
   Maintaining still the truth of loyalty,
   A check to my free nature and mine honour,

Blancart, and no doubt the 'brother' suggested by the king as a messenger to carry La Fin's letters (*Trag.*, I.iii.97). If he were the messenger, as suggested in *Trag.*, III.i.228n., it would be appropriate for him to return to court with Byron and D'Auvergne.

61. *commandment*] authority.
63. *faithful servant*] Henry may be adapting the parable in Matt. xxi.28 about the man who had two sons, one of whom refused to go to work in the vineyard but later went, and one who promised to go and did not go.
66. *stood to*] adhered to.
67. *bad ground*] evil foundation, i.e., Byron's conspiratorial activities.
76. *fautor*] protector.

   And that on your free justice I presumed
   To cross your will a little, I conceive
   You will not think this forfeit worth my head.   85
Henry. Have you maintained your truth of loyalty?
   When, since I pardoned foul intentions,
   Resolving to forget eternally
   What they appeared in, and had welcomed you
   As the kind father doth his riotous son,   90
   I can approve facts fouler than th'intents
   Of deep disloyalty and highest treason.
Byron. May this right hand be thunder to my breast
   If I stand guilty of the slend'rest fact
   Wherein the least of those two can be proved,   95
   For could my tender conscience but have touched
   At any such unnatural relapse,
   I would not with this confidence have run
   Thus headlong in the furnace of a wrath,
   Blown and thrice kindled, having way enough   100
   In my election both to shun and slight it.
Henry. Y'are grossly and vaingloriously abused;
   There is no way in Savoy nor in Spain
   To give a fool that hope of your escape,
   And had you not, even when you did, arrived,   105
   With horror to the proudest hope you had,
   I would have fetched you.
Byron.   You must then have used
   A power beyond my knowledge, and a will
   Beyond your justice. For a little stay

88–90.] *Parrott;* Resolving ... apperd in, / And ... son. *Q1.*

 85. *forfeit*] transgression.
 90.] Henry uses the parable of the prodigal son (Luke xv.11–32) to stress the fact that he forgave a repentant Byron on a previous occasion (*Consp.,* V.ii.107–10).
 91. *approve*] prove.
 93. *thunder*] a thunderbolt.
 99. *in*] into.
 100. *Blown and thrice kindled*] The suggestion is that Henry's wrath has been kindled before, blown with hot air like a furnace.
 101. *election*] free choice.
 shun and slight] avoid and ignore.
 102. *abused*] deceived.

SC II]   THE TRAGEDY OF CHARLES DUKE OF BYRON   207

> More than I used would hardly have been worthy 110
> Of such an open expedition;
> In which to all the censures of the world
> My faith and innocence had been foully foiled,
> Which, I protest, by heaven's bright witnesses
> That shine far, far, from mixture with our fears, 115
> Retain as perfect roundness as their spheres.

Henry. 'Tis well, my lord, I thought I could have frighted
Your firmest confidence: some other time
We will, as now in private, sift your actions
And pour more than you think into the sieve, 120
Always reserving clemency and pardon
Upon confession, be you ne'er so foul.
Come, let's clear up our brows: shall we to tennis?

Byron. Ay, my lord, if I may make the match.
The Duke Epernon and myself will play 125
With you and Count Soissons.

Epernon.   I know, my lord,
You play well, but you make your matches ill.

Henry. Come, 'tis a match.   *Exit.*

Byron.   How like you my arrival?

Epernon. I'll tell you as your friend in your ear.
You have given more preferment to your courage 130
Than to the provident counsels of your friends.

D'Auvergne. I told him so, my lord, and much was grieved
To see his bold approach, so full of will.

Byron. Well, I must bear it now, though but with th'head,
The shoulders bearing nothing.

---

113. foiled] *Q1, Q2;* soil'd *Shepherd.*

---

112. *censures*] judgements.
113. *foiled*] polluted.
116. *spheres*] the spheres in which the planets and other heavenly bodies revolve about the earth: a symbol of perfection, used in relation to his faith and innocence.
124. *make the match*] arrange the pairings for the game. Byron chooses Epernon as his partner, clearly as one whom he regards as a friend and a possible ally in a more serious match against Henry. Epernon admits Byron's skill in tennis but appears to warn him against his choice of antagonist and ally.
132–3.] D'Auvergne's comment about Byron's 'bold approach' is like that of many who warned Essex about his attitude toward Queen Elizabeth: see *Consp.*, V.i.53n.

Epernon. By Saint John 135
  'Tis a good headless resolution.
Exeunt.

135. *Saint John*] Saint John the Baptist, beheaded by Herod.

Act IV

ACT IV SCENE i

[*Enter*] BYRON, D'AUVERGNE.

Byron. O the most base fruits of a settled peace!
  In men, I mean; worse than their dirty fields,
  Which they manure much better than themselves:
  For them they plant and sow, and ere they grow
  Weedy and choked with thorns, they grub and prune,   5
  And make them better than when cruel war
  Frighted from thence the sweaty labourer;
  But men themselves, instead of bearing fruits,
  Grow rude and foggy, overgrown with weeds,
  Their spirits and freedoms smothered in their ease,   10
  And as their tyrants and their ministers
  Grow wild in prosecution of their lusts,
  So they grow prostitute and lie, like whores,
  Down, and take up, to their abhorred dishonours;

ACT IV SCENE i] ACTUS 4. SCENA I. *Q1*.   3. than] *Q2; not in Q1*.

1–28.] Parrott claims that this speech and Baligny's similar outburst in *The Revenge of Bussy* (I.i.32ff.) represent 'Chapman's view of the degeneration of England under the peaceful reign of James I' (p. 614). Yet both speeches are given a highly ironic context, Baligny being an informer searching out malcontents and Byron a conspirator against a just ruler. In dramatic terms, the lines fit Byron's character as a military hero, contemptuous of society and of authority and its flattery at court, though he is himself susceptible to gross flattery. But the passage goes beyond Byron's dramatic role, touching on a major theme evident in Chapman's *Teares of Peace* (1609), which Bartlett calls an 'anti-war poem', i.e., the conflict within man between spirit and passion, soul and body, which creates disorder in society. See Jacquot, pp. 223–6, and MacLure, pp. 69–77.

3. *manure*] cultivate.

9. *rude*] wild.

foggy] of grass, rank and coarse; of human bodies, bloated and flabby (*O.E.D.*, 1, 3).

11. *ministers*] officers of state.

13. *lie, like whores*] almost a proverbial expression, but the addition of 'down' in the next line alters the meaning.

14. *take up*] The phrase refers to sexual union but it also suggests 'taking up' profits, and diseases.

> The friendless may be injured and oppressed, 15
> The guiltless led to slaughter, the deserver
> Given to the beggar, right be wholly wronged
> And wrong be only honoured, till the strings
> Of every man's heart crack; and who will stir
> To tell authority that it doth err? 20
> All men cling to it, though they see their bloods
> In their most dear associates and allies
> Poured into kennels by it; and who dares
> But look well in the breast, whom that impairs?
> How all the court now looks askew on me! 25
> Go by without saluting, shun my sight,
> Which, like a March sun, agues breeds in them,
> From whence of late 'twas health to have a beam.
>
> *D'Auvergne.* Now none will speak to us; we thrust ourselves
> Into men's companies, and offer speech 30
> As if not made for their diverted ears,
> Their backs turned to us, and their words to others,
> And we must, like obsequious parasites,
> Follow their faces, wind about their persons
> For looks and answers, or be cast behind, 35
> No more viewed than the wallet of their faults.

Enter SOISSONS.

Byron. Yet here's one views me, and I think will speak.
Soissons. My lord, if you respect your name and race,
> The preservation of your former honours,
> Merits and virtues, humbly cast them all 40
> At the king's mercy; for beyond all doubt
> Your acts have thither driven them; he hath proofs

---

23. *kennels*] gutters.

23–4. *who dares ... impairs*] who dares look anything but cheerful even though weakened by such blood-letting among one's friends.

36.] Parrott notes that Phaedrus, *Fables* (IV, 10), is the source of the phrase 'the wallet of their faults' which cannot be viewed because it is hung on the back, but Schoell points out the probable direct source in Erasmus, *Adagia*, I.vi.90, 'Mantica in tergo' (p. 52). Shakespeare uses the image in *Troil.*, 'Time hath, my lord, a wallet at his back ...' (III.iii.145); the Shakespearean themes of Time's injuries and man's ingratitude are the substance of Byron's and D'Auvergne's speeches at this point.

wallet] bag or knapsack.

  So pregnant and so horrid that to hear them
  Would make your valour in your very looks
  Give up your forces, miserably guilty.   45
  But he is most loth, for his ancient love
  To your rare virtues, and in their impair,
  The full discouragement of all that live
  To trust or favour any gifts in nature,
  T'expose them to the light, when darkness may   50
  Cover her own brood, and keep still in day
  Nothing of you but that may brook her brightness:
  You know what horrors these high strokes do bring,
  Raised in the arm of an incensèd king.
Byron. My lord, be sure the king cannot complain   55
  Of anything in me but my true service,
  Which, in so many dangers of my death,
  May so approve my spotless loyalty,
  That those quite opposite horrors you assure
  Must look out of his own ingratitude,   60
  Or the malignant envies of my foes,
  Who pour me out in such a Stygian flood
  To drown me in myself, since their deserts
  Are far from such a deluge, and in me
  Hid like so many rivers in the sea.   65
Soissons. You think I come to sound you: fare you well.
               Exit.

  43. *pregnant*] significant, momentous.
  47. *in their impair*] in the weakening or loss of your fair virtues.
  50. *T'expose ... light*] to bring them (the proofs of Byron's treachery) into public view.
  52. *brook her brightness*] tolerate the full light of day.
  53. *high strokes*] strong acts of chastisement.
  58. *approve*] demonstrate.
  59. *assure*] affirm.
  62–5.] Who describe all my qualities and activities in a hellish flood to try to ruin me in my own deeds, since their own merits are far from being able to create such a deluge, and in any case are swallowed up by my vast achievements, as the ocean swallows up rivers.
  66. *sound you*] sound you out; also 'sound the depth of' after the images Byron has used of flood, rivers and sea.

Enter CHANCELLOR, EPERNON, JANIN, VIDAME, VITRY, PRÂLIN,
whispering by couples, etc.

D'Auvergne. See, see, not one of them will cast a glance
    At our eclipsèd faces.
Byron.   They keep all
    To cast in admiration on the king;
    For from his face are all their faces moulded.   70
D'Auvergne. But when a change comes, we shall see them all
    Changed into water, that will instantly
    Give look for look, as if it watched to greet us;
    Or else for one, they'll give us twenty faces,
    Like to the little specks on sides of glasses.   75
Byron. Is't not an easy loss to lose their looks
    Whose hearts so soon are melted?
D'Auvergne.   But methinks,
    Being courtiers, they should cast best looks on men
    When they thought worst of them.
Byron.   O no, my lord,
    They ne'er dissemble but for some advantage;   80
    They sell their looks and shadows, which they rate
    After their markets, kept beneath the state.
    Lord, what foul weather their aspects do threaten!
    See in how grave a brake he sets his vizard;

68–9.] *Parrott;* At ... faces; / They keepe ... King: *Q1.*   80. ne'er]
Shepherd; n'ere *Q1.*

68–75.] As Ferguson suggests, the whole passage is based on a metaphor of the king as the sun and the courtiers as clouds about the sun. 'Eclipsed faces' are faces upon which the sun does not shine; 'when a change comes' refers to a change in the royal weather which will turn clouds into rain and thus into pools that will 'give look for look', reflecting accurately the now sunlit faces of Byron and D'Auvergne; 'as if it watched' refers to the water in the pools waiting for them, like courtiers anxiously waiting to greet them. The weather imagery is carried on in ll. 83 and 91–2. In 'the little specks on sides of glasses', Chapman may be thinking of specks of liquid left in a drinking glass after it has been drained that reflect the drinker's face, or possibly flakes of reflecting silver at the edges of mirrors. The image of a liquid in a glass seems more likely in view of the watery imagery that has preceded it.

82. *after*] according to.

kept ... state] The buying and selling goes on close to the canopies and thrones of state.

84. *brake*] a vice or frame to hold anything steady, hence a fixed facial expression. Cf. *Bussy,* I.i.86–7.

vizard] mask, face like a mask.

Passion of nothing, see, an excellent gesture! 85
Now courtship goes a-ditching in their foreheads,
And we are fallen into those dismal ditches;
Why, even thus dreadfully would they be rapt
If the king's buttered eggs were only spilt.

Enter HENRY.

Henry. Lord Chancellor.
Chancellor.   Ay, my lord.
Henry.   And Lord Vidame. 90
         Exit [HENRY *with* CHANCELLOR *and* VIDAME].
Byron. And not Byron? Here's a prodigious change!
D'Auvergne. He cast no beam on you.
Byron.   Why, now you see
     From whence their countenances were copièd.

Enter the Captain *of Byron's guard with a letter.*

D'Auvergne. See, here comes some news, I believe, my lord.
Byron. What says the honest captain of my guard? 95
Captain. I bring a letter from a friend of yours.
Byron. 'Tis welcome then.
D'Auvergne.   Have we yet any friends?
Captain. More than ye would, I think: I never saw
     Men in their right minds so unrighteous
     In their own causes.
Byron.   See what thou hast brought. 100
     He wills us to retire ourselves, my lord,
     And makes as if it were almost too late.
     What says my captain: shall we go or no?
Captain I would your dagger's point had kissed my heart
     When you resolved to come.

90.1. HENRY ... VIDAME] *Parrott.*

---

86. *goes a-ditching*] digs ditches, furrows.
88. *rapt*] transported out of themselves. This interchange between Byron and D'Auvergne and the implied expressions and gestures of the courtiers on stage form a satiric picture of court life similar to passages in *Bussy, Revenge of Bussy* and *Chabot.*
98. *would*] want, desire.
99. *unrighteous*] false.
102. *makes*] makes out, alleges.

Byron.   I pray thee, why?   105
Captain. Yet doth that senseless apoplexy dull you?
    The devil or your wicked angel blinds you,
    Bereaving all your reason of a man,
    And leaves you but the spirit of a horse
    In your brute nostrils: only power to dare.   110
Byron. Why, dost thou think my coming here hath brought me
    To such an unrecoverable danger?
Captain. Judge by the strange ostents that have succeeded
    Since your arrival: the kind fowl, the wild duck,
    That came into your cabinet, so beyond   115
    The sight of all your servants, or yourself,
    That flew about, and on your shoulder sat,
    And which you had so fed and so attended
    For that dumb love she showed you, just as soon
    As you were parted, on the sudden died.   120
    And to make this no less than an ostent,
    Another that hath fortuned since confirms it:
    Your goodly horse, Pastrana, which the archduke
    Gave you at Brussels, in the very hour
    You left your strength, fell mad and killed himself;   125
    The like chanced to the horse the great duke sent you;
    And with both these, the horse the Duke of Lorraine
    Sent you at Vimy made a third presage
    Of some inevitable fate that touched you,
    Who, like the other, pined away and died.   130
Byron. All these together are indeed ostentful,
    Which by another like I can confirm:

---

106. *senseless apoplexy*] illness depriving one of sense and motion.
113. *ostents*] portents.
succeeded] followed.
114. *kind*] gentle.
wild duck] Parrott notes that Chapman followed Grimeston in this list of portents, including Grimeston's mistake about the bird: 'The original (*Matthieu*, vol. 2, p. 123) has "un oyseau qu'on appelle Duc". But the "Duc" is a sort of owl, a much more likely bird of ill omen than a wild duck.' (p. 615).
115. *cabinet*] private apartment.
116. *The sight of*] the experience of.
122. *fortuned*] occurred.
125. *left your strength*] abandoned your personal power.
128. *presage*] omen, warning.

SC II]   THE TRAGEDY OF CHARLES DUKE OF BYRON   215

> The matchless Earl of Essex, who some make,
> In their most sure divinings of my death,
> A parallel with me in life and fortune,   135
> Had one horse likewise that the very hour
> He suffered death, being well the night before,
> Died in his pasture. Noble happy beasts
> That die, not having to their wills to live;
> They use no deprecations nor complaints,   140
> Nor suit for mercy; amongst them the lion
> Serves not the lion, nor the horse the horse,
> As man serves man; when men show most their spirits
> In valour and their utmost dares to do,
> They are compared to lions, wolves and boars;   145
> But by conversion, none will say a lion
> Fights as he had the spirit of a man.
> Let me then in my danger now give cause
> For all men to begin that simile.
> For all my huge engagement, I provide me   150
> This short sword only, which if I have time
> To show my apprehender, he shall use
> Power of ten lions if I get not loose.   [*Exeunt.*]

[ACT IV   SCENE ii]

Enter HENRY, CHANCELLOR, VIDAME, JANIN, VITRY, PRÂLIN.

Henry. What shall we do with this unthankful man?
> Would he of one thing but reveal the truth,
> Which I have proof of, underneath his hand,
> He should not taste my justice. I would give

---

153. *Exeunt*] Phelps.

133. *Earl of Essex*] See *Intro.*, p. 2, and Appendix III. I have not been able to trace any source for this account of Essex's horse.
138–47.] These lines are based on several related excerpts from Plutarch's light-hearted 'Gryllus' or *Bruta animalia ratione uti* (987D–988D), as noted by Parrott and Schoell (p. 217), but they take on a more serious significance in Byron's speech.
139. *to their wills*] according to their conscious intentions.
140. *deprecations*] prayers to avert disaster (*O.E.D.*, 2).
146. *by conversion*] conversely.
150. *engagement*] encounter.

1–17.] Henry's speech is taken almost word for word from Grimeston.

>   Two hundred thousand crowns that he would yield   5
>   But such means for my pardon as he should;
>   I never loved man like him, would have trusted
>   My son in his protection, and my realm.
>   He hath deserved my love with worthy service,
>   Yet can he not deny but I have thrice   10
>   Saved him from death: I drew him off the foe
>   At Fountaine François, where he was engaged,
>   So wounded and so much amazed with blows,
>   That, as I played the soldier in his rescue,
>   I was enforced to play the marshal   15
>   To order the retreat, because he said
>   He was not fit to do it, nor to serve me.
> *Chancellor.* Your majesty hath used your utmost means,
>   Both by your own persuasions and his friends
>   To bring him to submission, and confess,   20
>   With some sign of repentance, his foul fault;
>   Yet still he stands prefract and insolent.
>   You have in love and care of his recovery
>   Been half in labour to produce a course
>   And resolution that were fit for him.   25
>   And since so amply it concerns your crown,
>   You must by law cut off what by your grace
>   You cannot bring into the state of safety.
> *Janin.* Begin at th'end, my lord, and execute,
>   Like Alexander with Parmenio.   30
>   Princes, you know, are masters of their laws,
>   And may resolve them to what forms they please,
>   So all conclude in justice; in whose stroke

---

25. that] *Q2;* what *Q1.*

    13. *amazed*] stunned.
    22. *prefract*] stubborn.
    24. *half in labour*] as if in childbirth.
    26. *amply*] widely.
    27. *grace*] favour, good will.
    29. *execute*] carry out the sentence.
    30. *Alexander with Parmenio*] Chapman draws this example from Grimeston. Alexander's execution of his trusted general, Parmenio, on suspicion and without trial was a well-known example of decisive action, though in Plutarch's account, also of possible error (*Life of Alexander*).

There is one sort of manage for the great,
Another for inferior: the great mother 35
Of all productions, grave Necessity,
Commands the variation; and the profit,
So certainly foreseen, commends the example.
Henry. I like not executions so informal,
For which my predecessors have been blamed: 40
My subjects and the world shall know my power
And my authority by law's usual course
Dares punish, not the devilish heads of treason,
But their confederates, be they ne'er so dreadful.
The decent ceremonies of my laws 45
And their solemnities shall be observed,
With all their sternness and severity.
Vitry. Where will your highness have him apprehended?
Henry. Not in the castle, as some have advised,
But in his chamber.
Prâlin.   Rather in your own, 50
Or coming out of it; for 'tis assured
That any other place of apprehension
Will make the hard performance end in blood.
Vitry. To shun this likelihood, my lord, 'tis best
To make the apprehension near your chamber, 55
For all respect and reverence given the place;
More than is needful to chastise the person
And save the opening of too many veins,
Is vain and dangerous.
Henry.   Gather you your guard,

---

34. *manage*] control or management (of the stroke of justice).
36. *productions*] what is produced, results.
37. *profit*] i.e., to the state.
39. *executions*] the carrying of judgements into effect.
informal] without the prescribed forms.
43-4.] Cf. Grimeston: 'that he hath power and authority sufficient to roote out by the forme of Iustice, not the Authors of such a Conspiracie, for they be Deuils, but the Complices and the instruments how terrible soeuer' (p. 968).
45. *decent*] proper.
55-6.] The Q punctuation separates l. 56 from l. 55 whereas the sense of the passage would seem to draw them together.
57. *chastise*] bring to punishment; possibly 'restrain' though *O.E.D.* gives no example of this usage before 1704.

218   THE TRAGEDY OF CHARLES DUKE OF BYRON   [ACT IV

>   And I will find fit time to give the word   60
>   When you shall seize on him and on D'Auvergne.
> *Vitry.* We will be ready to the death, my lord.
>   *Exeunt [except Henry].*
> *Henry.* O thou that govern'st the keen swords of kings,
>   Direct my arm in this important stroke,
>   Or hold it, being advanced; the weight of blood,   65
>   Even in the basest subject, doth exact
>   Deep consultation in the highest king;
>   For in one subject, death's unjust affrights,
>   Passions, and pains, though he be ne'er so poor,
>   Ask more remorse than the voluptuous spleens   70
>   Of all kings in the world deserve respect.
>   He should be born gray-headed that will bear
>   The sword of empire; judgement of the life,
>   Free state, and reputation of a man,
>   If it be just and worthy, dwells so dark   75
>   That it denies access to sun and moon;
>   The soul's eye sharpened with that sacred light,
>   Of whom the sun itself is but a beam,
>   Must only give that judgement. O how much
>   Err those kings, then, that play with life and death 80
>   And nothing put into their serious states
>   But humour and their lusts! For which alone
>   Men long for kingdoms, whose huge counterpoise
>   In cares and dangers could a fool comprise,
>   He would not be a king but would be wise.   85

62.1. *except Henry*] Parrott.

---

65. *Or ... advanced*] or hold it back when uplifted: a suggestion of the angel holding back Abraham's arm when he was about to sacrifice Isaac.
  weight of blood] importance of life.
68. *death's ... affrights*] terrors when death is unjust.
70. *remorse*] compassion.
  spleens] whims.
73–9.] The making of a judgement on the life, freedom and reputation of a man, if it is to be a just decision, does not proceed on the surface of the mind ('it denies access to sun and moon'), but must occur deep within the soul where truth is perceived by the divine light stemming from God.
81. *states*] states of mind.
82. *humour*] fancy.
83. *counterpoise*] balancing weight.
84. *comprise*] comprehend.

SC II]   THE TRAGEDY OF CHARLES DUKE OF BYRON   219

Enter BYRON *talking with the* Queen, EPERNON, D'ENTRAGUES,
D'AUVERGNE, *with another* Lady, [MONTIGNY *and*] *others
attending.*

    Here comes the man with whose ambitious head,
    Cast in the way of treason, we must stay
    His full chase of our ruin and our realm;
    This hour shall take upon her shady wings
    His latest liberty and life to hell.   90
D'Auvergne. [*Aside to Byron*] We are undone!
                                [Exit D'AUVERGNE.]
Queen.   What's that?
Byron.   I heard him not.
Henry. Madam, y'are honoured much that Duke Byron
    Is so observant. Some to cards with him:
    You four, as now you come, sit to primero,
    And I will fight a battle at the chess.   95
Byron. A good safe fight, believe me; other war
    Thirsts blood and wounds, and his thirst quenched, is
       thankless.
[*The Queen, Byron, D'Entragues, and Epernon play at cards;
       the King at the chess board with the Chancellor.*]
Epernon. Lift, and then cut.

85.2. MONTIGNY] *Phelps.*   91. *Aside to Byron*] *Parrott.*   91.1. *Exit*
D'AUVERGNE] *Phelps.*   97.1.] *This ed.;* Byron, *The* Queen, Epernon *and*
Montigny *play at cards Parrott.*

    87. *cast ... treason*] an ambiguous figure, possibly 'thrown in the way of
treason's advance'.
    stay] halt.
    91.1.] D'Auvergne must exit at some point since he is called back by the
king at l. 172 below; Byron answers the queen's question as if D'Auvergne had
already gone.
    93. *observant*] attentive.
    94. *primero*] 'a gambling card-game, very fashionable from about 1530 to
about 1640, in which four cards were dealt to each player, each card having
thrice its ordinary value' (*O.E.D.*).
    97.1.] The entry at l. 85.1 suggests that Byron enters with the queen,
Epernon with Mme D'Entragues, and D'Auvergne with another lady. When
the king suggests that 'You four, as now you come' should play at primero, it
seems likely he was referring to the first two couples. Parrott places Montigny
at the table since he takes part in the conversation at l. 156 below, but he may
well be an onlooker, like the Chancellor who rises to watch them when the king
leaves the chess board.

Byron. 'Tis right the end of lifting:
    When men are lifted to their highest pitch,
    They cut off those that lifted them so high.   100
Queen. Apply you all these sports so seriously?
Byron. They first were from our serious acts devised,
    The best of which are to the best but sports
    (I mean by best the greatest); for their ends,
    In men that serve them best, are their own pleasures.   105
Queen. So, in those best men's services, their ends
    Are their own pleasures. Pass.
Byron.   I vie't.
Henry.   I see't,
    And wonder at his frontless impudence.   *Exit* HENRY.
Chancellor. How speeds your majesty?
Queen.   Well; the duke instructs me
    With such grave lessons of mortality,   110
    Forced out of our light sport, that if I lose
    I cannot but speed well.
Byron.   Some idle talk
    For courtship' sake, you know, does not amiss.
Chancellor. Would we might hear some of it.
Byron.   That you shall;
    I cast away a card now, makes me think   115
    Of the deceasèd worthy King of Spain.

---

110. *mortality*] *Q1, Q2; morality Shepherd.*

---

   98. *Lift, . . . cut*] take up cards to decide who shall deal and then divide the pack. Parrott compares the punning on terms from card games with the similar but more elaborate scene from Heywood's *A Woman Killed with Kindness* (III.ii).

   right] truly.

   104. *ends*] goals, purposes of the sports.

   106-7.] The queen's reply is a witty rejoinder, suggesting that according to Byron the best men seek their own pleasures as their goals, whether in their services to 'sports' or to ladies.

   107. *vie't*] hazard a certain sum on the strength of one's hand.

   I see't] I wager an equal bet: an expression from card playing (*O.E.D.*, 13) but carrying the literal sense as well.

   108. *frontless*] unblushing, shameless.

   110. *mortality*] the condition of mortal life, i.e., life subject to death.

   116. *King of Spain*] Philip II, who had died in 1598. Byron's eulogy of Philip, enlarged from a brief statement in Grimeston (p. 968), has dramatic value in leading up to Montigny's interruption (also in Grimeston) concerning

Chancellor. What card was that?
Byron. The king of hearts, my lord,
  Whose name yields well the memory of that king,
  Who was indeed the worthy king of hearts,
  And had both of his subjects' hearts and strangers' 120
  Much more than all the kings of Christendom.
Chancellor. He won them with his gold.
Byron. He won them chiefly
  With his so general piety and justice;
  And as the little, yet great Macedon
  Was said with his humane philosophy 125
  To teach the rapeful Hyrcans marriage,
  And bring the barbarous Sogdians to nourish,
  Not kill their aged parents as before;
  Th'incestuous Persians to reverence
  Their mothers, not to use them as their wives; 130
  The Indians to adore the Grecian gods;
  The Scythians to inter, not eat their parents;
  So he with his divine philosophy,
  Which I may call his since he chiefly used it,
  In Turkey, India, and through all the world 135
  Expelled prophane idolatry, and from earth
  Raised temples to the highest; whom with the word
  He could not win, he justly put to sword.

Philip's refusal to spare his eldest son. Though appropriate enough to Byron's character, the speech has aroused controversy because of its length and eloquence on behalf of a king not highly regarded in Protestant England. Jacquot thinks the passage is part of Chapman's characterisation of Byron and not an indication of any conversion of Chapman to the Catholic cause nor of secret sympathy with it (p. 48). Parrott believes it to be typical of Chapman's defence of unpopular causes and cites Clermont's justification of the Massacre of St Bartholomew (*Revenge of Bussy*, II.i.199–234). E. D. Kennedy argues that the passage reflects Chapman's sympathy for James's peace-making activities, in particular his treaty with Philip III of Spain in 1604 ('James I and Chapman's Byron plays', *J.E.G.P.*, LXIV (1965), 687).

124. *Macedon*] Alexander the Great, 'little' because small in stature (Parrott).

125. *his ... philosophy*] In the *De Alexandri magni* from which Chapman derived these lines, Plutarch celebrates Alexander as a philosopher who profited from Aristotle's teaching and exemplified his philosophy not through words but through his civilising mission across the world (328C-E). A similar point is made about Philip in l. 134.

126. *rapeful*] given to rape.

Chancellor. He sought for gold and empire.
Byron.   'Twas religion
 And her full propagation that he sought;   140
 If gold had been his end, it had been hoarded
 When he had fetched it in so many fleets:
 Which he spent not on Median luxury,
 Banquets and women, Calydonian wine,
 Nor dear Hyrcanian fishes, but employed it   145
 To propagate his empire; and his empire
 Desired t'extend so that he might withal
 Extend religion through it, and all nations
 Reduce to one firm constitution
 Of piety, justice, and one public weal;   150
 To which end he made all his matchless subjects
 Make tents their castles and their garrisons;
 True Catholics, countrymen and their allies;
 Heretics, strangers and their enemies.
 There was in him the magnanimity –   155
Montigny. To temper your extreme applause, my lord,
 Shorten and answer all things in a word,
 The greatest commendation we can give
 To the remembrance of that king deceased
 Is that he spared not his own eldest son,   160
 But put him justly to a violent death,
 Because he sought to trouble his estates.
Byron. Is't so?
Chancellor. [*Aside to Montigny*] That bit, my lord, upon my
  life;
 'Twas bitterly replied, and doth amaze him.

---

163. *Aside to Montigny*] Parrott.

 139. *gold and empire*] Gold was inevitably associated with Philip II, as was the extension of Spanish empire throughout Central and South America; the treasure fleets from the West Indies (l. 142) had often been harried by English privateers.
 143–50.] from Plutarch's eulogy of Alexander's virtue in *De Alexandri magni* (342A): quoted by Parrott, p. 616.
 144. *Calydonian wine*] wine from Chalybon, a city in Syria. The variant spelling derives from Xylander's Latin and from the uncorrected Greek text.
 160. *eldest son*] Don Carlos, committed to prison by his father and killed there.
 164. *bitterly*] sharply, keenly.

SC II]   THE TRAGEDY OF CHARLES DUKE OF BYRON   223

The KING *suddenly enters, having determined what to do.*

Henry. It is resolved; a work shall now be done   165
  Which, while learn'd Atlas shall with stars be crowned,
  While th'Ocean walks in storms his wavy round,
  While moons at full repair their broken rings,
  While Lucifer foreshows Aurora's springs,
  And Arctos sticks above the earth unmoved,   170
  Shall make my realm be blest, and me beloved.
  Call in the Count d'Auvergne.

Enter D'AUVERGNE.

                                A word, my lord.
  Will you become as wilful as your friend,
  And draw a mortal justice on your heads
  That hangs so black and is so loth to strike?   175
  If you would utter what I know you know
  Of his inhuman treason, one strong bar
  Betwixt his will and duty were dissolved,
  For then I know he would submit himself.
  Think you it not as strong a point of faith   180
  To rectify your loyalties to me,
  As to be trusty in each other's wrong?
  Trust that deceives ourselves is treachery,

---

165. It is resolved] *Separate line in Q1.*   183. is] *Shepherd; in Q1, Q2.*

166–70.] This passage is translated from Seneca's *Oedipus* (ll. 504–8): the chorus proclaim that they will never cease worshipping Bacchus. Chapman has altered the first line from 'while the bright stars run' to the image of Atlas crowned with stars – presumably because he holds up the heavens on his shoulders. Atlas is 'learn'd' since he knows the secrets of the cosmos through the stars: see *Odysseys*, I, 88, and Chapman's gloss on the epithet given to Atlas (Parrott).
  168. *broken rings*] scattered circles of light.
  169. *Lucifer*] the morning star, Venus.
  Aurora's springs] the first appearance of dawn.
  170. *Arctos*] the constellation of the Bear or Ursa Major, but 'Arctos' was frequently used in Latin for the double constellation of Great Bear and Little Bear which never sets in the northern hemisphere and circles about the unmoved North Star.
  174. *mortal*] fatal, death-bringing.
  175. *hangs so black*] i.e., like a thunder cloud.
  177. *bar*] barrier.

        And truth that truth conceals, an open lie.
D'Auvergne. My lord, if I could utter any thought
        Instructed with disloyalty to you,
        And might light any safety to my friend,
        Though mine own heart came after, it should out.
Henry. I know you may, and that your faiths affected
        To one another are so vain and false
        That your own strengths will ruin you; ye contend
        To cast up rampires to you in the sea,
        And strive to stop the waves that run before you.
D'Auvergne. All this, my lord, to me is mystery.
Henry. It is? I'll make it plain enough, believe me!
        Come, my Lord Chancellor, let us end our mate.

              Enter VARENNES, *whispering to Byron.*

Varennes. You are undone, my lord.   *Exit.*
Byron.   Is it possible?
Queen. Play, good my lord: whom look you for?
Epernon.   Your mind
        Is not upon your game.
Byron.   Play, pray you, play!
Henry. Enough, 'tis late and time to leave our play
        On all hands. All forbear the room.
              [*Exeunt except Byron and Henry.*]
                        My lord,
Stay you with me. Yet is your will resolved
        To duty and the main bond of your life?
        I swear, of all th'intrusions I have made

---

189. faiths] *Shepherd;* faith's *Q1, Q2.*   194. mystery] *Shepherd;* misery *Q1, Q2.*   201.1 Exeunt ... Henry] *Parrott.*

---

   186. *instructed*] informed.
   189. *affected*] ostentatiously displayed.
   192. *rampires*] ramparts, dams.
   194. *mystery*] Q1's 'misery' makes sense, but Henry's reply makes it clear that Shepherd's correction to 'mystery' is justified.
   196. *mate*] checkmate. Henry uses the word for 'game of chess' but there is a hint also that he is about to take drastic action to prevent the placing of the king in check in Byron's game.
   203. *main bond*] major obligation, the allegiance Byron owes to the king. Henry wonders if Byron has abandoned duty and allegiance.
   204. *intrusions*] uninvited interventions.

Upon your own good and continued fortunes,	205
This is the last; inform me yet the truth,	
And here I vow to you, by all my love,	
By all means shown you, even to this extreme,	
When all men else forsake you, you are safe.	
What passages have slipped 'twixt Count Fuentes,	210
You, and the Duke of Savoy?	

Byron. Good my lord,
This nail is driven already past the head,
You much have overcharged an honest man;
And I beseech you yield my innocence justice,
But with my single valour, 'gainst them all   215
That thus have poisoned your opinion of me,
And let me take my vengeance by my sword;
For I protest I never thought an action
More than my tongue hath uttered.

Henry. Would 'twere true!
And that your thoughts and deeds had fell no fouler.   220
But you disdain submission, not rememb'ring
That, in intents urged for the common good,
He that shall hold his peace, being charged to speak,
Doth all the peace and nerves of empire break;
Which on your conscience lie. Adieu, good night. *Exit.*   225

Byron. Kings hate to hear what they command men speak:

---

210. *What ... slipped*] what communications have passed secretly.

213. *overcharged*] accused to excess.

215. *But ... valour*] The justice Byron asks is that he may be allowed to fight all his enemies at once, by himself.

220. *fell no fouler*] skin no more offensive (than the utterances of his tongue Byron has just mentioned). It might be argued that 'fell' is a 17th-century variant of 'fallen' and that 'fouler' is used adverbially as 'no more foully', but this seems less likely than the metaphor of a skin or hide made foul and ugly.

222. *intents*] purposes.

226, 228.] These lines are exact translations from Seneca's *Oedipus* (ll. 520 and 517) at the point where Creon has returned from necromancy with knowledge of the dreadful truth. Oedipus orders Creon to tell him everything he has learned and Creon replies thus. Chapman has reversed the context with considerable irony for those in the audience who knew Seneca's play. Henry is fully aware of Byron's treachery and pleads with him to confess, but Byron, in his ignorance of what Henry knows, arrogantly refuses, quoting Creon's lines in self-justification.

        Ask life, and to desert of death ye yield;
        Where medicines loathe, it irks men to be healed.

Enter VITRY *with two or three of the guard,* EPERNON, VIDAME
    following. Vitry lays hand on Byron's sword.

Vitry. Resign your sword, my lord. The king commands it.
Byron. Me to resign my sword? What king is he   230
    Hath used it better for the realm than I?
    My sword, that all the wars within the length,
    Breadth, and the whole dimensions of great France
    Hath sheathed betwixt his hilt and horrid point,
    And fixed ye all in such a flourishing peace!   235
    My sword that never enemy could enforce,
    Bereft me by my friends! Now, good my lord,
    Beseech the king I may resign my sword
    To his hand only.

Enter JANIN.

Janin. [*To Vitry*]   You must do your office;
    The king commands you.
Vitry.   'Tis in vain to strive,   240
    For I must force it.
Byron.   Have I ne'er a friend
    That bears another for me? All the guard?
    What, will you kill me? Will you smother here
    His life that can command and save in field
    A hundred thousand lives? For manhood sake,   245
    Lend something to this poor forsaken hand!
    For all my service, let me have the honour
    To die defending of my innocent self,
    And have some little space to pray to God.

239. *To Vitry*] Parrott.

---

  227. *desert*] reward, recompense.
  228. *loathe*] cause loathing.
  234. *Hath sheathed*] 'To sheathe the sword' is to put an end to war. Byron claims that with his sword he has put an end to all the wars throughout France.
    his] its.
    horrid] terrifying.
  236. *enforce*] overcome by violence.

SC II]   THE TRAGEDY OF CHARLES DUKE OF BYRON   227

Enter HENRY.

Henry. Come, you are an atheist, Byron, and a traitor,   250
    Both foul and damnable. Thy innocent self?
    No leper is so buried quick in ulcers
    As thy corrupted soul. Thou end the war
    And settle peace in France? What war hath raged
    Into whose fury I have not exposed   255
    My person, which is as free a spirit as thine?
    Thy worthy father and thyself combined
    And armed in all the merits of your valours,
    Your bodies thrust amidst the thickest fights,
    Never were bristled with so many battles,   260
    Nor on the foe have broke such woods of lances
    As grew upon my thigh, and I have marshalled –
    I am ashamed to brag thus; where envy
    And arrogance their opposite bulwark raise,
    Men are allowed to use their proper praise.   265
    Away with him.   *Exit* HENRY.
Byron.   Away with him? Live I,
    And hear my life thus slighted? Cursèd man,
    That ever the intelligencing lights
    Betrayed me to men's whorish fellowships,
    To princes' Moorish slaveries, to be made   270

---

256. which is] *Q1;* with *Shepherd, Parrott.*   263. where] *Q1;* but where *Parrott.*

250–66.] Henry's re-entry at this point and following speech are an addition to Grimeston's account.
    252. *quick*] alive.
    260. *bristled*] prickly with arms, like the stiffened bristles of an animal in a fight.
    262. *as grew ... thigh*] The wooden shaft of the lance was held in its rest against the thigh during a cavalry charge.
    263–5.] Schoell notes a passage in Plutarch's *Moralia: De sui laude* (541E), as an example of Plutarch's influence (p. 78).
    264. *opposite bulwark*] opposing rampart.
    268. *intelligencing lights*] stars carrying information about man's destiny. But there is also a suggestion in 'intelligencing' of the stars acting as spies: cf. *Consp.*, II.i.70.
    269. *whorish fellowships*] friendships ready to prostitute themselves for reward.
    270. *Moorish slaveries*] servitude as imposed by Moorish tyrants.

>   The anvil on which only blows and wounds
>   Were made the seed and wombs of others' honours;
>   A property for a tyrant to set up
>   And puff down with the vapour of his breath.
>   Will you not kill me?
> *Vitry.*   No, we will not hurt you;   275
>   We are commanded only to conduct you
>   Into your lodging.
> *Byron.*   To my lodging? Where?
> *Vitry.* Within the Cabinet of Arms, my lord.
> *Byron.* What, to a prison? Death! I will not go.
> *Vitry.* We'll force you then.
> *Byron.*   And take away my sword,   280
>   A proper point of force; ye had as good
>   Have robbed me of my soul. Slaves of my stars,
>   Partial and bloody! O that in mine eyes
>   Were all the sorcerous poison of my woes,
>   That I might witch ye headlong from your height   285
>   And trample out your execrable light.
> *Vitry.* Come, will you go, my lord? This rage is vain.
> *Byron.* And so is all your grave authority;
>   And that all France shall feel before I die:
>   Ye see all how they use good Catholics!   290
>   [*Exit* BYRON *guarded.*]
> *Epernon.* Farewell for ever! So have I discerned
>   An exhalation that would be a star

286. execrable] *Q2;* excrable *Q1.*   290.1. Exit BYRON guarded] *Parrott.*
291. discerned] *Shepherd;* desern'd *Q1;* decern'd *Ray.*

---

273. *property*] a piece of theatrical furniture, or perhaps a mere puppet (*O.E.D.*, 4, 5).
278. *Cabinet of Arms*] from Grimeston: a guarded storeroom for arms.
281. *A proper ... force*] a very apt element of force; 'point' refers also to the point of a sword (cf. 'at point': armed in readiness).
282. *Slaves of my stars*] Vitry and his guard are acting as slavish agents of the fatal influence of the stars.
283. *Partial*] biased, prejudiced.
284. *sorcerous*] carrying a spell as by sorcery.
285. *witch*] bewitch.
290.] Byron's cry as he is led out gives some support to the statements of others that he regarded himself as a scourge of the Huguenots: see *Trag.*, I.iii.1–3 and V.i.78–9; note also *Trag.*, I.iii.4 and n.
292. *exhalation*] meteor, thought of as a fiery vapour.

Fall, when the sun forsook it, in a sink.
Shoes ever overthrow that are too large,
And hugest cannons burst with overcharge. 295

[*Enter*] D'AUVERGNE, PRÂLIN *following with a guard.*

Prâlin. My lord, I have commandment from the king
 To charge you go with me, and ask your sword.
D'Auvergne. My sword, who fears it? It was ne'er the death
 Of any but wild boars. I prithee take it;
 Had'st thou advertised this when last we met, 300
 I had been in my bed and fast asleep
 Two hours ago. Lead, I'll go where thou wilt.
 Exit [*guarded.*]
Vidame. See how he bears his cross, with his small strength,
 On easier shoulders than the other Atlas.
Epernon. Strength to aspire is still accompanied 305
 With weakness to endure. All popular gifts
 Are colours that will bear no vinegar,
 And rather to adverse affairs betray
 Thine arm against them. His state still is best
 That hath most inward worth; and that's best tried 310
 That neither glories nor is glorified. [*Exeunt.*]

294. Shoes] *Q1;* Shows *Parrott.*   302.1. guarded] *Parrott.*   307. that] *Parrott;* it *Q1.*   309. is] *Q2;* his *Q1.*   311. Exeunt] *Q2.*

---

293. *sink*] pit.
294.] Parrott objects to the homeliness of the shoe image and reads 'shooes' as 'shows', though hesitantly; Ure accepts 'shoes' and notes the 'lapidary form' and 'neo-classic tone' of the Horatian echo from the *Epistles* I, x, 42–3 (*M.L.R.*, LIV (1959), 537–8). Ferguson had previously noted the reference to Horace as an illustration of the advantages of the middle estate (p. 236).
300. *advertised*] given notice of.
305–11.] Epernon and several others increasingly take on a choral role as the tragic catastrophe approaches.
307. *colours*] a painter's pigments, that work well with oil but not with vinegar and hence will not stand up to anything harsh or sour.
308–9.] Gifts that arouse popularity will betray your strength in standing up against 'adverse affairs'.
310. *best tried*] tested successfully.

Act V

ACT V SCENE i

[*Enter*] HENRY, SOISSONS, JANIN, D'ESCURES, [*with others*].

Henry. What shall we think, my lords, of these new forces
    That from the King of Spain hath passed the Alps?
    For which, I think, his lord ambassador
    Is come to court to get their pass for Flanders.
Janin. I think, my lord, they have no end for Flanders,   5
    Count Maurice being already entered Brabant
    To pass to Flanders, to relieve Ostend,
    And th'archduke full prepared to hinder him;
    And sure it is that they must measure forces
    Which, ere this new force could have passed the Alps,   10
    Of force must be encountered.
Soissons.   'Tis unlikely
    That their march hath so large an aim as Flanders.
D'Escures. As these times sort, they may have shorter reaches,
    That would pierce further.
Henry.   I have been advertised
    That Count Fuentes, by whose means this army   15
    Was lately levied, and whose hand was strong
    In thrusting on Byron's conspiracy,
    Hath caused these cunning forces to advance

ACT V SCENE i] ACTUS 5. SCENA I. *Q1*.   0.1. *with others*] *This ed.; cum aliis Q1.*   15. That] *Q1;* How *Q2, Shepherd, Parrott.*

1ff.] Chapman makes good use of the parallel passage in Grimeston (p. 971) to set forth the wider European context of Byron's conspiracy and suggest the dangers to France of Byron's contacts with Savoy and Fuentes. The scene also provides a necessary interlude between the arrest and the trial.
    6. *Count Maurice*] Maurice of Nassau, son of William the Silent (Parrott).
    7. *Ostend*] Ostend was besieged by the Spanish from 1601 to 1604. Maurice's attempt to relieve it, as Parrott notes, was unsuccessful.
    9. *measure forces*] try their strength against one another.
    11. *Of force*] of necessity.
    13. *sort*] turn out.
    14. *advertised*] given information.

SC I]   THE TRAGEDY OF CHARLES DUKE OF BYRON   231

    With colour only to set down in Flanders;
    But hath intentional respect to favour   20
    And count'nance his false partisans in Bresse
    And friends in Burgundy, to give them heart
    For the full taking of their hearts from me.
    Be as it will, we shall prevent their worst;
    And therefore call in Spain's ambassador.   25

Enter AMBASSADOR *with others.*

What would the Lord Ambassador of Spain?
Ambassador. First, in my master's name, I would beseech
    Your highness' hearty thought, that his true hand,
    Held in your vowed amities, hath not touched
    At any least point in Byron's offence,   30
    Nor once had notice of a crime so foul;
    Whereof, since he doubts not you stand resolved,
    He prays your league's continuance in this favour,
    That the army he hath raised to march for Flanders
    May have safe passage by your frontier towns,   35
    And find the river free that runs by Rhone.
Henry. My lord, my frontiers shall not be disarmed
    Till, by arraignment of the Duke of Byron,
    My scruples are resolved, and I may know
    In what account to hold your master's faith   40
    For his observance of the league betwixt us.
    You wish me to believe that he is clear
    From all the projects caused by Count Fuentes,
    His special agent; but where deeds pull down,
    Words may repair no faith. I scarce can think   45
    That his gold was so bounteously employed
    Without his special counsel and command:

36. Rhone] *Shepherd, Parrott;* Rhosne *Q1, Q2;* Rosny *Ray.*

   19. *colour*] pretence.
   20. *intentional respect*] deliberate aim.
   21. *his*] Byron's.
   36.] Grimeston wrote 'to haue the passage of the River of *Rhosne* free'. Q1 uses the same spelling but the phrase suggests that 'Rhosne' is a region or town rather than a river. Koeppel, as Parrott reports, thought Chapman had made a geographical blunder, but Parrott believes Chapman simply wished to fill out a line and did so rather carelessly.
   39. *scruples*] doubts.

These faint proceedings in our royal faiths
Make subjects prove so faithless. If, because
We sit above the danger of the laws, 50
We likewise lift our arms above their justice,
And that our heavenly Sovereign bounds not us
In those religious confines, out of which
Our justice and our true laws are informed,
In vain have we expectance that our subjects 55
Should not as well presume to offend their earthly,
As we our heavenly Sovereign; and this breach
Made in the forts of all society,
Of all celestial and humane respects,
Makes no strengths of our bounties, counsels, arms, 60
Hold out against their treasons; and the rapes
Made of humanity and religion
In all men's more than pagan liberties,
Atheisms and slaveries, will derive their springs
From their base precedents, copied out of kings. 65
But all this shall not make me break the commerce
Authorised by our treaties; let your army
Take the directest pass; it shall go safe.
Ambassador. So rest your highness ever, and assured
That my true sovereign loathes all opposite thoughts. 70
[*Exit.*]
Henry. Are our dispatches made to all the kings,
Princes and potentates of Christendom,
Ambassadors and province governors,
T'inform the truth of this conspiracy?
Janin. They all are made, my lord, and some give out 75
That 'tis a blow given to religion,
To weaken it in ruining of him
That said he never wished more glorious title
Than to be called the scourge of Huguenots.

---

70. loathes] *Q1;* hates *Q2.*   70.1. *Exit*] *Parrott.*

---

48. *faint proceedings*] half-hearted actions.
49. *so faithless*] faithless in the same manner.
52. *bounds*] limits.
54. *informed*] given their essential nature.
59. *humane respects*] human considerations.
79. *scourge of Huguenots*] Grimeston reports this phrase: cf. *Trag.*, I.iii.3n. and IV.ii.290.

Soissons. Others that are like favourers of the fault 80
  Said 'tis a politic advice from England
  To break the fearèd javelins both together.
Henry. Such shut their eyes to truth; we can but set
  His lights before them, and his trumpet sound
  Close to their ears; their partial wilfulness 85
  In resting blind and deaf, or in perverting
  What their most certain senses apprehend,
  Shall nought discomfort our impartial justice,
  Nor clear the desperate fault that doth enforce it.

Enter VITRY.

Vitry. The Peers of France, my lord, refuse t'appear 90
  At the arraignment of the Duke Byron.
Henry. The court may yet proceed; and so command it.
  'Tis not their slackness to appear shall serve
  To let my will t'appear in any fact,
  Wherein the boldest of them tempts my justice. 95
  I am resolved, and will no more endure
  To have my subjects make what I command
  The subject of their oppositions,
  Who evermore slack their allegiance,

82. fearèd] *Q1;* sacred *Q2, Shepherd, Parrott.*   88. impartial] *Q1;* imperiall *Q2.*

---

82. *fearèd*] There seems little reason for Q2's change to 'sacred' since 'fearèd' makes much better sense. 'Sacred' may be the Q2 compositor's misreading of the Q1 text: there are a number of apparently careless misreadings on the same sheet of Q2, particularly sig. o3r.

both together] Chapman alters from Grimeston's 'one after another' to point to the simultaneous arrest of Byron and D'Auvergne, as Koeppel and Parrott suggest. They would be regarded as 'fearèd javelins' because they wished to subvert the king's power and the English alliance.

84. *lights*] discoveries.

85. *partial*] biased, as opposed to 'impartial' in l. 88.

86. *resting*] remaining.

90–1.] Grimeston, following his source, observes that the peers had the right to appear, were called to appear, but did not choose to do so. There is no suggestion of the king's displeasure, merely: 'The Court forbeares not to proceed, notwithstanding their absence' (p. 974).

93–5.] Their slackness to appear shall not serve to hinder my determination to sit in judgement upon any crime where the boldest of them tempts my justice.

94. *let*] hinder.

    As kings forbear their penance. How sustain   100
    Your prisoners their strange durance?
Vitry.   One of them,
    Which is the Count d'Auvergne, hath merry spirits,
    Eats well and sleeps, and never can imagine
    That any place where he is, is a prison;
    Where on the other part, the Duke Byron   105
    Entered his prison as into his grave,
    Rejects all food, sleeps not, nor once lies down;
    Fury hath armed his thoughts so thick with thorns
    That rest can have no entry: he disdains
    To grace the prison with the slend'rest show   110
    Of any patience, lest men should conceive
    He thought his sufferance in the least sort fit;
    And holds his bands so worthless of his worth,
    That he impairs it to vouchsafe to them
    The least part of the peace that freedom owes it;   115
    That patience therein is a willing slavery,
    And, like the camel, stoops to take the load:
    So, still he walks; or rather as a bird
    Entered a closet, which unwares is made
    His desperate prison, being pursued, amazed   120
    And wrathful beats his breast from wall to wall,
    Assaults the light, strikes down himself, not out,
    And being taken, struggles, gasps and bites,

---

 112. least] *Parrott;* best *Q1.*   115. least] *Parrott;* best *Q1.*

---

 100. *forbear their penance*] spare or forgive them their penance (possibly 'their punishment').
 101. *strange*] unfamiliar.
 112. *sufferance*] patient endurance.
 least] Parrott assumes that the Q 'best' is a misprint for 'lest' both here and at l. 115, and corrects accordingly. The fault is probably due to a compositor's misreading of copy.
 113–15.] and considers his shackles so unworthy of his merit that he injures that merit to grant to them the least fraction of the peace that freedom acknowledges as due to merit.
 118. *still*] always, continuously.
 119. *closet*] small private room.
 unwares] unexpectedly.
 122. *light*] window.

SC I]   THE TRAGEDY OF CHARLES DUKE OF BYRON   235

    Takes all his taker's strokings to be strokes,
    Abhorreth food, and with a savage will   125
    Frets, pines and dies for former liberty.
    So fares the wrathful duke; and when the strength
    Of these dumb rages break out into sounds,
    He breathes defiance to the world, and bids us
    Make ourselves drunk with the remaining blood   130
    Of five and thirty wounds received in fight
    For us and ours; for we shall never brag
    That we have made his spirits check at death:
    This rage in walks and words; but in his looks
    He comments all, and prints a world of books.   135
Henry. Let others learn by him to curb their spleens,
    Before they be curbed, and to cease their grudges.
    Now I am settled in my sun of height,
    The circular splendour and full sphere of state
    Take all place up from envy: as the sun   140
    At height and passive o'er the crowns of men,
    His beams diffused and downright poured on them
    Cast but a little, or no shade at all,
    So he that is advanced above the heads
    Of all his emulators, with high light   145
    Prevents their envies, and deprives them quite. *Exeunt.*

---

    124. *strokes*] blows.
    133. *check*] stop short, wince (*O.E.D.*, 5).
    135. *comments*] expounds, makes a commentary upon.
    136–46.] Henry's final speech in the play is both a warning to other ambitious individuals who might seek to disturb the state, and a statement of confident assurance in the security of his throne. There is no hint of regret or loss with respect to Byron, though these were evident in earlier scenes; instead Chapman gives him a firm declaration of absolute power, using the metaphor of the sun at its height which Plutarch had used of Alexander and Cyrus (*De invidia et odio*, 538A: Schoell, p. 218).
    136. *spleens*] violent tempers.
    139.] Chapman often uses 'circle' and 'sphere' as symbols of completeness and perfection (Bartlett, p. 445). Schoell notes that Chapman may have drawn the idea from Erasmus's adage *Circulum absolvere* ('Commonplace Book', pp. 202–3).
    141. *passive*] apparently motionless.
    146. *Prevents*] anticipates, forestalls.
    deprives] empties, divests (of envies).

[ACT V SCENE ii]

Enter the CHANCELLOR, HARLAY, POTIER, FLEURY, *in scarlet gowns,*
LA FIN, D'ESCURES, *with other officers of state.*

Chancellor. I wonder at the prisoner's so long stay.
Harlay. I think it may be made a question
    If his impatience will let him come.
Potier. Yes, he is now well stayed: time and his judgement
    Have cast his passion and his fever off.   5
Fleury. His fever may be past, but for his passions,
    I fear me we shall find it spiced too hotly
    With his old powder.
D'Escures.   He is sure come forth;
    The carosse of the Marquis of Rosny
    Conducted him along to th'Arsenal   10
    Close to the river-side; and there I saw him
    Enter a barge covered with tapestry,
    In which the king's guards waited and received him.
    Stand by there, clear the place!
Chancellor.   The prisoner comes.
    My Lord La Fin, forbear your sight awhile;   15
    It may incense the prisoner, who will know
    By your attendance near us that your hand
    Was chief in his discovery, which as yet
    I think he doth not doubt.
La Fin.   I will forbear
    Till your good pleasures call me.   *Exit* LA FIN.
Harlay.   When he knows,   20

---

20. Harlay] Q2 (*Har.*); *Hen.* Q1.

1ff.] Chapman follows Grimeston closely in his account of the trial, though condensing the speeches of accusation and defence considerably for dramatic reasons.
    3. *impatience*] incomposure, lack of ability to endure.
    4. *stayed*] controlled (*O.E.D.*, 28).
    8. *powder*] powdered seasoning, also suggesting gunpowder and the explosive force of Byron's temper.
    9. *carosse*] caroche or carriage.
Marquis of Rosny] Duke of Sully, Henry's councillor and minister, whose name does not appear otherwise in the play.
    10. *Arsenal*] dockyard with military and naval stores.
    19. *doubt*] suspect.
    20. Harlay] Q1 gives *Hen.* as the speaker of these lines which occur at the

SC II]   THE TRAGEDY OF CHARLES DUKE OF BYRON   237

  And sees La Fin accuse him to his face,
  The court I think will shake with his distemper.

   Enter VITRY, BYRON, *with others and a guard.*

Vitry. You see, my lord, 'tis in the Golden Chamber.
Byron. The Golden Chamber! Where the greatest kings
  Have thought them honoured to receive a place: 25
  And I have had it. Am I come to stand
  In rank and habit here of men arraigned,
  Where I have sat assistant, and been honoured
  With glorious title of the chiefest virtuous;
  Where the king's chief solicitor hath said 30
  There was in France no man that ever lived
  Whose parts were worth my imitation;
  That, but mine own worth, I could imitate none,
  And that I made myself inimitable
  To all that could come after; whom this court 35
  Hath seen to sit upon the flower-de-luce
  In recompense of my renownèd service?
  Must I be sat on now by petty judges?
  These scarlet robes, that come to sit and fight
  Against my life, dismay my valour more 40
  Than all the bloody cassocks Spain hath brought
  To field against it.
Vitry.   To the bar, my lord.

---

top of a page, but the catch-word on the previous page is *Har.*, and so the misprint is clear. Q2 corrects to *Har.*

23. *Golden Chamber*] Grimeston describes this hall as 'the place whereas Strangers haue come to implore Iustice of the King; whereas great Kings haue held it an Honour to haue a place' (p. 974). Chapman gives to Byron the historian's comments on the significance of the place in relation to the fall of a great man.

27. *habit*] posture, appearance.

28. *assistant*] auxiliary (to the king).

30. *solicitor*] agent or official having charge of the king's interests (*O.E.D.*, 2b).

32. *parts*] qualities.

33. *but*] apart from.

36. *flower-de-luce*] fleur de lis, the heraldic device incorporated in the royal arms of France and presumably in this case on the throne in the hall of justice.

41. *bloody cassocks*] scarlet coats or cloaks of soldiers, but suggesting also the fighting qualities of the soldiers.

                          He salutes and stands to the bar.
Harlay. Read the indictment.
Chancellor.   Stay, I will invert,
    For shortness' sake, the form of our proceedings,
    And out of all the points the process holds   45
    Collect five principal, with which we charge you.
    1. First you conferred with one, called Picoté,
    At Orleans born and into Flanders fled,
    To hold intelligence by him with the archduke,
    And for two voyages to that effect   50
    Bestowed on him five hundred fifty crowns.
    2. Next you held treaty with the Duke of Savoy
    Without the king's permission, offering him
    All service and assistance 'gainst all men,
    In hope to have in marriage his third daughter.   55
    3. Thirdly you held intelligence with the duke
    At taking in of Bourg and other forts,
    Advising him, with all your prejudice,
    'Gainst the king's army and his royal person.
    4. The fourth is, that you would have brought the king 60
    Before Saint Katherine's Fort, to be there slain:
    And to that end writ to the governor,
    In which you gave him notes to know his highness.
    5. Fifthly, you sent La Fin to treat with Savoy
    And with the Count Fuentes of more plots   65

   43. *invert*] change, divert.
   45. *process*] the indictment mentioned in l. 43.
   46–66.] The five charges are almost identical with those listed by Grimeston, though Grimeston describes the payment (l. 51) as being one hundred and fifty crowns.
   49. *hold intelligence*] have communication.
   50. *voyages*] journeys.
   52. *held treaty*] conducted negotiations.
   57. *At ... Bourg*] The capture of the town of Bourg and of the fort of Ste Catherine were part of the very short and highly successful invasion of Savoy by France in 1600, a war not directly referred to in the play (*Consp.*, V.i.21n., V.ii.144 and 152). Byron commanded some of the French forces under Henry's close control.
   58. *prejudice*] hasty prejudgement (Lat. *praejudicium*).
   61. *Saint Katherine's Fort*] a fortress built by Savoy to menace Geneva; it was captured by Henry and destroyed.
   63. *notes*] Grimeston has 'tokens'.

Touching the ruin of the king and realm.
Byron. All this, my lord, I answer and deny.
　And first for Picoté: he was my prisoner,
　And therefore I might well confer with him;
　But that our conference tended to the archduke　　　70
　Is nothing so: I only did employ him
　To Captain La Fortune, for the reduction
　Of Seurre to the service of the king,
　Who used such speedy diligence therein
　That shortly 'twas assured his majesty.　　　75
　2. Next, for my treaties with the Duke of Savoy,
　Roncas, his secretary, having made
　A motion to me for the duke's third daughter,
　I told it to the king; who having since
　Given me the understanding by La Force　　　80
　Of his dislike, I never dreamed of it.
　3. Thirdly, for my intelligence with the duke,
　Advising him against his highness' army:
　Had this been true, I had not undertaken
　Th'assault of Bourg against the king's opinion,　　　85
　Having assistance but by them about me;
　And having won it for him, had not been
　Put out of such a government so easily.
　4. Fourthly, for my advice to kill the king,
　I would beseech his highness' memory　　　90
　Not to let slip, that I alone dissuaded
　His viewing of that fort, informing him
　It had good mark-men, and he could not go
　But in exceeding danger, which advice
　Diverted him; the rather, since I said　　　95
　That if he had desire to see the place

70. *tended to*] related to.
72. *Captain La Fortune*] Parrott describes La Fortune as 'a soldier in the civil wars of France who seized on the town of Seurre in Burgundy and held it, nominally for the League, against all attacks. Byron concluded a six years' truce with him, and after the Treaty of Vervins he was induced to surrender the town to the King' (p. 618).
78. *motion*] proposal.
80. *La Force*] Byron's brother-in-law.
83. *Advising ... against*] advising him to take action against.
89. *advice*] counsel, plan.

He should receive from me a plot of it,
Offering to take it with five hundred men,
And I myself would go to the assault,
5. And lastly, for intelligences held 100
With Savoy and Fuentes, I confess
That being denied to keep the citadel,
Which with incredible peril I had got,
And seeing another honoured with my spoils,
I grew so desperate that I found my spirit 105
Enraged to any act, and wished myself
Covered with blood.
Chancellor.   With whose blood?
Byron.   With mine own;
Wishing to live no longer, being denied
With such suspicion of me, and set will
To rack my furious humour into blood. 110
And for two months' space I did speak and write
More than I ought, but have done ever well;
And therefore your informers have been false,
And, with intent to tyrannise, suborned.
Fleury. What if our witnesses come face to face 115
And justify much more than we allege?
Byron. They must be hirelings, then, and men corrupted.
Potier. What think you of La Fin?
Byron.   I hold La Fin
An honoured gentleman, my friend and kinsman.
Harlay. If he then aggravate what we affirm 120
With greater accusations to your face,
What will you say?
Byron.   I know it cannot be.
Chancellor. Call in my Lord La Fin.

    97. *plot*] plan.
    103.] Historically, Byron did not capture the citadel of Bourg, though he took the town. The citadel was surrendered as a result of negotiations at the end of the war between Savoy and France (see l. 57n. above).
    109. *set will*] determined purpose.
    110. *rack*] torment, lacerate.
    114. *suborned*] bribed. It is Henry's intent to 'tyrannise' that is glanced at in Byron's phrase.
    117. *hirelings*] men acting for pay.
    120. *aggravate*] strengthen, make more heinous.

Byron.   Is he so near,
    And kept so close from me? Can all the world
    Make him a treacher?

                    Enter LA FIN.

Chancellor.   I suppose, my lord,   125
    You have not stood within, without the ear
    Of what hath here been urged against the duke;
    If you have heard it, and upon your knowledge
    Can witness all is true, upon your soul,
    Utter your knowledge.
La Fin.   I have heard, my lord,   130
    All that hath passed here, and upon my soul,
    Being charged so urgently in such a court,
    Upon my knowledge I affirm all true;
    And so much more, as, had the prisoner lives
    As many as his years, would make all forfeit.   135
Byron. O all ye virtuous powers in earth and heaven,
    That have not put on hellish flesh and blood
    From whence these monstrous issues are produced,
    That cannot bear in execrable concord
    And one prodigious subject, contraries;   140
    Nor, as the isle that of the world admired
    Is severed from the world, can cut yourselves
    From the consent and sacred harmony
    Of life, yet live; of honour, yet be honoured;
    As this extravagant and errant rogue   145
    From all your fair decorums and just laws
    Finds power to do; and like a loathsome wen
    Sticks to the face of nature and this court;
    Thicken this air, and turn your plaguey rage

---

125. *treacher*] traitor.
139. *execrable concord*] accursed harmony.
140. *prodigious subject*] abnormal or monstrous substance.
141. *the isle*] Great Britain.
143. *consent*] sympathetic agreement.
145. *extravagant*] roving beyond limits.
errant] downright (in the sense of 'arrant').
146. *decorums*] qualities of grace and order.
149. *Thicken*] make dense or opaque. Cf. *Mac.* 'Light thickens', (III.ii.50).
plaguey] plague-causing.

>   Into a shape as dismal as his sin; 150
> And with some equal horror tear him off
> From sight and memory; let not such a court,
> To whose fame all the kings of Christendom
> Now laid their ears, so crack her royal trump
> As to sound through it that here vaunted justice 155
> Was got in such an incest. Is it justice
> To tempt and witch a man to break the law,
> And by that witch condemn him? Let me draw
> Poison into me with this cursèd air,
> If he bewitched me and transformed me not; 160
> He bit me by the ear and made me drink
> Enchanted waters, let me see an image
> That uttered these distinct words: *Thou shalt die,
> O wicked king*; and if the devil gave him
> Such power upon an image, upon me 165
> How might he tyrannise, that by his vows
> And oaths so Stygian had my nerves and will
> In more awe than his own? What man is he
> That is so high but he would higher be?
> So roundly sighted but he may be found 170
> To have a blind side, which by craft pursued,
> Confederacy and simply trusted treason,
> May wrest him past his angel and his reason?
>
> *Chancellor.* Witchcraft can never taint an honest mind.
> *Harlay.* True gold will any trial stand, untouched. 175
> *Potier.* For colours that will stain when they are tried,
>   The cloth itself is ever cast aside.

---

154. *crack ... trump*] sound her royal trumpet.

155. *sound*] proclaim.

156. *got*] begotten.

157. *witch*] bewitch.

161ff.] These accusations of witchcraft come from Grimeston (pp. 976, 985).

162. *image*] figure of a person, made of wax or other substance.

167. *Stygian*] 'inviolable like the oath by the Styx, which the gods themselves feared to break' (*O.E.D.*, 1b).

170. *roundly sighted*] able to see all round.

172. *confederacy*] conspiracy.

173. *angel*] guardian angel, or good genius in the classical sense as Parrott suggests.

176. *tried*] tested.

Byron. Sometimes the very gloss in anything
    Will seem a stain; the fault not in the light,
    Nor in the guilty object, but our sight.   180
    My gloss, raised from the richness of my stuff,
    Had too much splendour for the owly eye
    Of politic and thankless royalty;
    I did deserve too much; a pleurisy
    Of that blood in me is the cause I die.   185
    Virtue in great men must be small and slight,
    For poor stars rule where she is exquisite;
    'Tis tyrannous and impious policy
    To put to death by fraud and treachery:
    Sleight is then royal when it makes men live,   190
    And if it urge faults, urgeth to forgive.
    He must be guiltless that condemns the guilty;
    Like things do nourish like, and not destroy them;
    Minds must be sound that judge affairs of weight,
    And seeing hands cut corrosives from your sight.   195
    A lord intelligencer? Hangman-like,
    Thrust him from human fellowship, to the deserts
    Blow him with curses. Shall your justice call
    Treachery her father? Would you wish her weigh
    My valour with the hiss of such a viper?   200
    What I have done to shun the mortal shame
    Of so unjust an opposition,
    My envious stars cannot deny me this,

---

180. Nor] *Q1;* Not *Q2.*

  178. *gloss*] surface lustre.
  181. *stuff*] the substance or fabric upon which the gloss is raised.
  182. *owly eye*] eye blinded by splendour, as the owl's eye is blinded by the light of the sun.
  184. *pleurisy*] excess.
  187. *poor stars rule*] bad fortune prevails.
  she] virtue.
  exquisite] cultivated to a high degree.
  190. *Sleight*] subtle dealing or policy.
  192ff.] Byron's string of aphorisms, uttered in the heat of his discomfiture, directs the hearer's or the reader's mind back to Henry's prayer and meditation as he comes to the decision that he must act (*Trag.*, IV.ii.63-85).
  195. *corrosives*] wasting or destroying agents.
  196. *intelligencer*] informer.
  199. *weigh*] a reference to the scales of the allegorical figure of Justice.

That I may make my judges witnesses,
And that my wretched fortunes have reserved   205
For my last comfort: ye all know, my lords,
This body, gashed with five and thirty wounds,
Whose life and death you have in your award,
Holds not a vein that hath not opened been,
And which I would not open yet again   210
For you and yours; this hand, that writ the lines
Alleged against me, hath enacted still
More good than there it only talked of ill.
I must confess my choler hath transferred
My tender spleen to all intemperate speech;   215
But reason ever did my deeds attend
In worth of praise and imitation.
Had I borne any will to let them loose,
I could have fleshed them with bad services
In England lately, and in Switzerland;   220
There are a hundred gentlemen by name
Can witness my demeanour in the first,
And in the last ambassage I adjure
No other testimonies than the seigneurs
De Vic and Sillery, who amply know   225
In what sort and with what fidelity
I bore myself, to reconcile and knit
In one desire so many wills disjoined,
And from the king's allegiance quite withdrawn.
My acts asked many men, though done by one;   230
And I were but one, I stood for thousands,
And still I hold my worth, though not my place.
Nor slight me, judges, though I be but one:
One man, in one sole expedition,

---

216. attend,] *Q2*; attend. *Q1*.

207. *gashed ... wounds*] Byron's numbering of his wounds here and at *Trag.*, V.iii.182, recalls the numbering of Coriolanus' wounds by Menenius and Volumnia where there is a slight contest over the exact number (II.i.136–47).
216. *tender spleen*] sensitive, easily affected temper.
217. *In worth of*] worthy of.
226. *sort*] manner.
230. *asked*] required, demanded.
231. *And*] even if; 'and' is a variant of 'an', meaning 'if' or 'even if'.
234–47.] The list of Pompey's victories is taken from Plutarch's *De fortuna*

Reduced into th'imperial power of Rome 235
Armenia, Pontus and Arabia,
Syria, Albania and Iberia,
Conquered th'Hyrcanians, and to Caucasus
His arm extended; the Numidians
And Afric to the shores meridional 240
His power subjected; and that part of Spain
Which stood from those parts that Sertorius ruled
Even to the Atlantic Sea he conquerèd.
Th'Albanian kings he from the kingdoms chased
And at the Caspian Sea their dwellings placed; 245
Of all the earth's globe, by power and his advice,
The round-eyed Ocean saw him victor thrice:
And what shall let me, but your cruel doom,
To add as much to France as he to Rome?
And, to leave justice neither sword nor word 250
To use against my life, this senate knows
That what with one victorious hand I took,
I gave to all your uses with another;
With this I took and propped the falling kingdom,
And gave it to the king; I have kept 255
Your laws of state from fire, and you yourselves
Fixed in this high tribunal, from whose height
The vengeful Saturnals of the League

244. the] *Q1*; their *Parrott*.

Romanorum, 324A (Schoell, p. 219). Plutarch's ironic conclusion ('then he was overcome by his own fate') is not in the play, but no doubt those in the audience who recognised the reference to Pompey would be aware of his destiny.

240. *meridional*] southern.

242. *stood*] extended.

Sertorius] leader of the Spanish revolt against Rome, he was murdered in 72 B.C.: see Plutarch's *Lives*.

246. *advice*] forethought, counsel.

248. *let*] hinder.

255–9.] Parrott describes the attack on the Parliament of Paris by the League in 1591 and the re-establishment of this parliament in 1594 by Henry, not by Byron. Chapman's audience might not recognise Byron's assumption of Henry's mantle in this particular case but would certainly link the boast with his other exaggerated statements in the play.

258. *Saturnals*] cold and gloomy leaders, born under the influence of Saturn, but probably also with a suggestion of the Saturnalia, the season of overthrowing of all order.

>   Had hurled ye headlong; do ye then return
>   This retribution? Can the cruel king, 260
>   The kingdom, laws, and you, all saved by me,
>   Destroy their saver? What, ay me! I did
>   Adverse to this, this damned enchanter did,
>   That took into his will my motion;
>   And being bankrupt both of wealth and worth, 265
>   Pursued with quarrels and with suits in law,
>   Feared by the kingdom, threatened by the king,
>   Would raise the loathèd dunghill of his ruins
>   Upon the monumental heap of mine:
>   Torn with possessèd whirlwinds may he die 270
>   And dogs bark at his murtherous memory!
> *Chancellor.* My lord, our liberal sufferance of your speech
>   Hath made it late, and for this session
>   We will dismiss you; take him back, my lord.
>   *Exit* VITRY *and* BYRON.
> *Harlay.* You likewise may depart.
>   *Exit* LA FIN.
> *Chancellor.*   What resteth now 275
>   To be decreed 'gainst this great prisoner?
>   A mighty merit and a monstrous crime
>   Are here concurrent; what by witnesses,
>   His letters and instructions, we have proved,
>   Himself confesseth, and excuseth all 280
>   With witchcraft and the only act of thought.
>   For witchcraft, I esteem it a mere strength
>   Of rage in him, conceived 'gainst his accuser,
>   Who, being examined, hath denied it all.
>   Suppose it true it made him false: but wills 285
>   And worthy minds witchcraft can never force.
>   And for his thoughts that brake not into deeds,
>   Time was the cause, not will; the mind's free act
>   In treason still is judged as th'outward fact.

260. *retribution*] recompense.
264. *motion*] power of movement or action.
270. *possessèd*] controlled by demons, lunatic.
275. *resteth*] remains.
281. *the ... thought*] the act of thought alone, thought rather than deed.
282. *strength*] intensity, violence.
288–9.] Cf. *Philotas*: 'The law, in treasons, doth the will correct / With like

If his deserts have had a wealthy share 290
In saving of our land from civil furies,
Manlius had so that saved the Capitol;
Yet for his after traitorous factions,
They threw him headlong from the place he saved.
My definite sentence, then, doth this import: 295
That we must quench the wild-fire with his blood
In which it was so traitorously inflamed,
Unless with it we seek to incense the land.
The king can have no refuge for his life
If his be quitted; this was it that made 300
Lewis th'eleventh renounce his countrymen,
And call the valiant Scots out of their kingdom
To use their greater virtues and their faiths
Than his own subjects, in his royal guard.
What then conclude your censures?
Omnes. He must die. 305
Chancellor. Draw then his sentence, formally, and send him;
And so all treasons in his death attend him. *Exeunt.*

[ACT V Scene iii]

Enter BYRON, EPERNON, SOISSONS, JANIN, VIDAME, D'ESCURES.

Vidame. I joy you had so good a day, my lord.
Byron. I won it from them all; the Chancellor

---

1. *Vidame*] Shepherd; *Vit. Q1.*

---

seuerenesse as it doth th'effect: ... To haue but will'd it, is to haue done the same.' (ll. 1498–9, 1502).
  289. *fact*] deed or crime.
  292. *Manlius*] Manlius saved the Capitol in Rome from the Gauls in 392 B.C. after being awakened by the legendary geese but was subsequently executed for his 'mutinies'.
  295. *import*] signify.
  296. *wild-fire*] a destructive fire liable to spread rapidly (i.e., his treachery).
  298. *incense*] consume with fire (*O.E.D.*, v., 2).
  300. *quitted*] set free, acquitted.
  301. *Lewis*] Louis XI reigned from 1461 to 1483. The comment about the Scots guard comes from Grimeston (p. 981) but may also be a compliment to Chapman's patron, Prince Henry, and his ancestry.
  305. *censures*] judgements, judicial sentences.

I answered to his uttermost improvements;
I moved my other judges to lament
My insolent misfortunes, and to loathe   5
The pocky soul and state-bawd, my accuser.
I made reply to all that could be said,
So eloquently and with such a charm
Of grave enforcements, that methought I sat
Like Orpheus casting reins on savage beasts;   10
At the arm's end, as 'twere, I took my bar
And set it far above the high tribunal,
Where like a cedar on Mount Lebanon
I grew, and made my judges show like box-trees;
And box-trees right their wishes would have made them,   15
Whence boxes should have grown, till they had struck
My head into the budget; but, alas,
I held their bloody arms with such strong reasons,
And, by your leave, with such a jerk of wit,
That I fetched blood upon the Chancellor's cheeks.   20
Methinks I see his countenance as he sat,
And the most lawyerly delivery
Of his set speeches: shall I play his part?

23.] *Enter Soiss: Esp. follows l. 23 in Q1 and l. 22 in Q2.*

---

3. *improvements*] condemnations (?): perhaps Chapman's formation of a noun from the obsolete verb 'improve' meaning 'blame, censure, condemn' (*O.E.D.* v., 1).

5. *insolent*] strange, unusual.

6. *pocky*] pock-marked, diseased.

9. *enforcements*] strong representations.

11. *bar*] In law, a bar is 'a plea or objection of force sufficient to arrest entirely an action or claim at law' (*O.E.D.*, 18). In the hall of justice it is also the bar to which the prisoner is called to answer the charges against him. Because of the physical effort suggested by 'arm's end' and 'bloody arms' in l. 18 there may also be a suggestion of the bar as 'a thick rod of iron or wood used in a trial of strength' (*O.E.D.*, 2).

14. *box-trees*] small evergreen trees or shrubs, often used in hedges, and insignificant when compared with a cedar of Lebanon or a pine tree (cf. *Sir Giles Goosecap*, III.ii.102–3).

16. *boxes*] There is no doubt some play on the word 'box' which can mean the box-tree, or the pale yellowish wood of the tree from which small boxes were made, or 'a blow or buffet' (*O.E.D.*, sb., 3).

17. *budget*] hangman's bag.

19. *jerk*] lit. a stroke with a whip, though also used fig. of sharp gibes and sallies of wit.

23.] Q1 has '*Enter Soiss: Espe.*' at the end of Byron's speech. Their entry

Epernon. For heaven's sake, good my lord!
Byron.   I will, i' faith.
   Behold a wicked man, a man debauched,   25
   A man contesting with his king, a man
   On whom, my lords, we are not to connive,
   Though we may condole; a man
   That *laesa majestate* sought a lease
   Of *plus quam satis*; a man that *vi et armis*   30
   Assailed the king, and would *per fas et nefas*
   Aspire the kingdom. Here was lawyer's learning!
Epernon. He said not this, my lord, that I have heard.
Byron. This or the like, I swear. I pen no speeches.
Soissons. Then there is good hope of your wished acquittal.   35
Byron. Acquittal? They have reason; were I dead
   I know they cannot all supply my place.
   Is't possible the king should be so vain
   To think he can shake me with fear of death?
   Or make me apprehend that he intends it?   40
   Thinks he to make his firmest men his clouds?
   The clouds, observing their aerial natures,
   Are borne aloft, and then, to moisture changed,
   Fall to the earth; where being made thick and cold
   They lose both all their heat and levity;   45
   Yet then again recovering heat and lightness,
   Again they are advanced, and by the sun

---

43. changed] *Shepherd;* hang'd *Q1, Q2.*

may well take place here, or a little earlier while Byron is speaking since Epernon must know what Byron has been saying. However I have left Q1's general entry (including Soissons and Epernon) at the beginning of the scene, since there is little reason for changing this.

   27. *connive*] look indulgently.
   29–31.] Byron adopts the conventional satiric view of the lawyer as one who speaks in a mish-mash of Latin and pompous English phrases, hardly applicable to the Chancellor, as Epernon points out: *laesa majestate*: treasonably, with harm to the ruler (and a Latin-English pun in 'lease'); *plus quam satis*: more than enough; *vi et armis*: by force and arms; *per fas et nefas*: through right and wrong.
   42. *aerial*] Clouds are closely related to air, one of the four elements, since they are hot and moist in their formation. The other elements are all mentioned in this passage.
   44. *thick*] dense.
   45. *levity*] lightness.
   47. *advanced*] raised (by the warmth of the sun).

>   Made fresh and glorious; and since clouds are rapt
>   With these uncertainties, now up, now down,
>   Am I to flit so with his smile, or frown?   50
> *Epernon.* I wish your comforts and encouragements
>   May spring out of your safety; but I hear
>   The king hath reasoned so against your life,
>   And made your most friends yield so to his reasons,
>   That your estate is fearful.
> *Byron.*   Yield t'his reasons?   55
>   O how friends' reasons and their freedoms stretch
>   When power sets his wide tenters to their sides!
>   How like a cure, by mere opinion,
>   It works upon our blood! Like th'ancient gods
>   Are modern kings, that lived past bounds themselves,   60
>   Yet set a measure down to wretched men;
>   By many sophisms they made good deceit,
>   And since they passed in power, surpassed in right.
>   When kings' wills pass, the stars wink and the sun
>   Suffers eclipse; rude thunder yields to them   65
>   His horrid wings, sits smooth as glass engazed,

---

66. engazed] *Q1;* englaz'd *Parrott.*

---

48. *rapt*] transported.
54. *most*] greatest.
57. *tenters*] frames for stretching cloth.
58. *opinion*] belief, expectation.
59. *It ... blood*] it affects our mettle.
59–72.] Byron's passionate outcry against 'power' and 'modern kings' may be compared with other passages in the double play, notably the 'idle and ridiculous kings' of *Consp.*, V.ii.5–21. Herford and Simpson refer to the famous passage quoted by Swinburne from *The Gentleman Usher* (V.iv.56–66) as an example of the 'note of republican sentiment' to be found in Chapman's plays. Commenting upon the possibility of Chapman being Jonson's collaborator in the lost first version of *Sejanus*, they point to a speech of Silius in the quarto (altered in the folio text III.302–10) which strikes a similar note and may be a remnant of Chapman's hand in the play: 'so soone, all best Turnes / With *Princes*, do conuert to inuries' (II, 4–5).
62. *sophisms*] specious arguments designed to deceive.
63. *passed*] surpassed.
64. *pass*] give judgement, pronounce.
66. *engazed*] Parrott corrects to 'englazed' but as Ferguson points out, glass can hardly be so described. 'Engazed', the intensive form of 'gazed', may possibly mean 'staring in surprise', on the model of 'agazed' (astounded, affrighted) and in parallel with 'amazed' in the next line (Ferguson, p. 236). The word remains a puzzle.

SC III]   THE TRAGEDY OF CHARLES DUKE OF BYRON   251

  And lightning sticks 'twixt heaven and earth amazed;
  Men's faiths are shaken, and the pit of Truth
  O'erflows with darkness, in which Justice sits
  And keeps her vengeance tied to make it fierce;   70
  And when it comes, th'increased horrors show
  Heaven's plague is sure, though full of state, and slow.
Sister. [*Within*] O my dear lord and brother! O the duke!
Byron. What sounds are these, my lord? Hark, hark, methinks
  I hear the cries of people.
Epernon.   'Tis for one   75
  Wounded in fight here at Saint Anthony's gate.
Byron. 'Sfoot, one cried 'the duke'! I pray harken
  Again, or burst yourselves with silence – no!
  What countryman's the common headsman here?
Soissons. He's a Burgonian.
Byron.   The great devil he is!   80
  The bitter wizard told me a Burgonian
  Should be my headsman: strange concurrences.
  'Sdeath, who's here?

    Enter four ushers bare, CHANCELLOR, HARLAY, POTIER,
      FLEURY, VITRY, PRÅLIN, *with others.*

       O then I am but dead.
  Now, now ye come all to pronounce my sentence.
  I am condemned unjustly: tell my kinsfolks   85
  I die an innocent; if any friend

73. *Within*] *Q2; not in Q1.* 83. dead.] *This ed.;* dead, *Q1.* 86–7.]
Parrott; I die an innocent: / If any ... sustainer *Q1.*

---

  67. *sticks*] stops. See *Bussy,* V.iii.193.
  68. *the pit of Truth*] As Parrott points out, there is an echo of this passage in Chapman's dedicatory epistle to Somerset, *Odysseys* (1614): '*Truth* dwels in Gulphs, whose Deepes hide shades so rich, / That *Night* sits muffl'd there, in clouds of pitch: / More Darke then Nature made her.'
  70.] Cf. the proverb: 'Mastiff grows the fiercer for being tied up' (Tilley, M742).
  72. *full of state*] solemn, dignified.
  73. *Sister*] Grimeston reports the lamentations of a woman; Chapman makes them into the cries of Byron's sister.
  77. *'Sfoot*] God's foot, an oath.
  80. *Burgonian*] Burgundian.
  81. *bitter*] baleful. Grimeston describes Byron's visits to La Brosse and to a magician in Paris (the bitter wizard) at the end of his account of Byron's career (pp. 993–4).
  83.1. *bare*] bareheaded.

    Pity the ruin of the state's sustainer,
    Proclaim my innocence. Ah, Lord Chancellor,
    Is there no pardon? Will there come no mercy?
    Ay, put your hat on and let me stand bare: 90
    Show yourself right a lawyer.
Chancellor.   I am bare;
    What would you have me do?
Byron.   You have not done
    Like a good justice, and one that knew
    He sat upon the precious blood of virtue;
    Y'ave pleased the cruel king, and have not borne   95
    As great regard to save as to condemn;
    You have condemned me, my Lord Chancellor,
    But God acquits me; he will open lay
    All your close treasons against him, to colour
    Treasons laid to his truest images;   100
    And you, my lord, shall answer this injustice
    Before his judgement seat: to which I summon
    In one year and a day your hot appearance.
    I go before, by men's corrupted dooms;
    But they that caused my death shall after come   105
    By the immaculate justice of the Highest.
Chancellor. Well, good my lord, commend your soul to him,
    And to his mercy; think of that, I pray.
Byron. Sir, I have thought of it, and every hour
    Since my affliction, asked on naked knees   110
    Patience to bear your unbelieved injustice;
    But you, nor none of you, have thought of him
    In my eviction; y'are come to your benches
    With plotted judgements; your linked ears so loud

---

91. right a] *Q1;* a right *Q2, Shepherd.*

 94. *sat*] sat in judgement.
 99. *close*] secret.
 99–100.] Byron claims that the Chancellor and the other judges have acted treasonably against God by pretending to speak for justice and right in order to give a plausible appearance to their treasons against God's true followers, himself and D'Auvergne.
 103. *hot*] quick.
 104. *dooms*] judgements.
 113. *eviction*] conviction.
 114. *plotted*] pre-arranged.
 linked] joined together, collaborating.

SC III]   THE TRAGEDY OF CHARLES DUKE OF BYRON   253

  Sing with prejudicate winds, that nought is heard   115
  Of all poor prisoners urge 'gainst your award.
Harlay. Passion, my lord, transports your bitterness
  Beyond all colour, and your proper judgement.
  No man hath known your merits more than I,
  And would to God your great misdeeds had been   120
  As much undone as they have been concealed;
  The cries of them for justice, in desert,
  Have been so loud and piercing that they deafened
  The ears of mercy, and have laboured more
  Your judges to compress than to enforce them.   125
Potier. We bring you here your sentence; will you read it?
Byron. For heaven's sake, shame to use me with such rigour;
  I know what it imports, and will not have
  Mine ear blown into flames with hearing it.
  [*To Fleury*] Have you been one of them that have
    condemned me?   130
Fleury. My lord, I am your orator: God comfort you!
Byron. Good sir, my father loved you so entirely,
  That if you have been one, my soul forgives you.
  It is the king, most childish that he is,
  That takes what he hath given, that injures me: 135
  He gave grace in the first draught of my fault,

---

130. *To Fleury*] Parrott.   131. *Fleury*] *Q1 (Flen.); Fle. Q2.*

---

 115. *prejudicate*] prejudiced, because the judgement has been decided beforehand.
 118. *colour*] excuse, show of reason.
 121. *undone*] not done.
 122. *in desert*] in terms of what they deserve.
 125. *compress*] repress, restrain.
 enforce] strengthen.
 130.] Grimeston has Byron asking this question of 'Roissy, Master of Requests' who does not appear in the play.
 131. Fleury] The English pamphlet 'A True and perfect Discourse of the practises and Treasons of Marshall Biron', published in London in 1602 and which Chapman may have known (see *Trag.*, V.iv.214n.), mentions Fleury as the judge who hesitated longer than the others over his decision: 'The same day the king was at the *Tuilleries*, and pressed hard to haue the matter growe to an end: Which had beene done at that time, but for *Monsieur de Fleury*, who refused to deliuer his opinion as then, excusing himselfe, because the houre was past. Wherupon hee was sent backe againe by water to the Bastill.' (pp. 17–18).
 orator] advocate.

And now restrains it: grace again I ask,
Let him again vouchsafe it: send to him,
A post will soon return. The Queen of England
Told me that if the wilful Earl of Essex   140
Had used submission, and but asked her mercy,
She would have given it, past resumption;
She like a gracious princess did desire
To pardon him, even as she prayed to God
He would let down a pardon unto her;   145
He yet was guilty, I am innocent:
He still refused grace, I importune it.
Chancellor. This asked in time, my lord, while he besought it,
And ere he had made his severity known,
Had, with much joy to him, I know been granted.   150
Byron. No, no, his bounty then was misery,
To offer when he knew 'twould be refused;
He treads the vulgar path of all advantage
And loves men for his vices, not for their virtues;
My service would have quickened gratitude   155
In his own death, had he been truly royal;
It would have stirred the image of a king

137. restrains] *Q2;* restaines *Q1.*   154. his] *Q1;* their *Q2.*   not] *Q2;* nor *Q1.*

---

138. *vouchsafe*] deign to grant.

139–47.] Byron's comparison of himself with Essex is closely drawn from Grimeston: 'The Queene of *England* told me that if the Earle of *Essex* would haue humbled himselfe and sued for grace, shee would haue pardoned him. Hee grewe obstinate and would neuer implore her mercy, taking from her all meanes to shew the effects. She like a generous Princesse desirying to pardon him, euen as she would that God should pardon her. He was guilty, I am innocent, he sued for no pardon for his offence. I craue it in mine Inocency.' (p. 984).

139. *post*] courier with the king's message.

142. *past resumption*] without any possibility of taking it back.

151. *misery*] miserliness (*O.E.D.*, 4)

153. *advantage*] superior position.

155–6. *quickened . . . death*] brought gratitude to life even when he was at the point of death.

157–8.] The carved figure of a king being moved by some kind of 'perpetual motion' machine, like the clocks described by Bacon in *The New Atlantis*, is Byron's metaphor for the true royalty of a king being aroused everlastingly, through the experience of a conspiracy like the one at Mantes and being saved in great danger from wolf-like enemies, as Byron had saved him. The conspiracy at Mantes and the siege of Amiens are mentioned by Grimeston.

> Into perpetual motion, to have stood
> Near the conspiracy restrained at Mantes,
> And in a danger that had then the wolf 160
> To fly upon his bosom, had I only held
> Intelligence with the conspirators,
> Who stuck at no check but my loyalty,
> Nor kept life in their hopes but in my death.
> The siege of Amiens would have softened rocks, 165
> Where, covered all in showers of shot and fire,
> I seemed to all men's eyes a fighting flame
> With bullets cut in fashion of a man;
> A sacrifice to valour, impious king,
> Which he will needs extinguish with my blood. 170
> Let him beware, justice will fall from heaven
> In the same form I servèd in that siege,
> And by the light of that he shall discern
> What good my ill hath brought him: it will nothing
> Assure his state; the same quench he hath cast 175
> Upon my life shall quite put out his fame.
> This day he loseth what he shall not find
> By all days he survives, so good a servant,
> Nor Spain so great a foe; with whom, alas,
> Because I treated am I put to death? 180
> 'Tis but a politic gloze; my courage raised me,
> For the dear price of five and thirty scars,
> And that hath ruined me, I thank my stars.
> Come, I'll go where ye will, ye shall not lead me.
>   [*Exit* BYRON.] 185

Chancellor. I fear his frenzy; never saw I man
    Of such a spirit so amazed at death.

---

173. discern] *Q2*; decerne *Q1, Ray*.   181. but] *Shepherd;* put *Q1, Q2*.
184.1. *Exit* BYRON] *Parrott*.   185–6.] *Parrott;* I feare his frenzie, / Never
... death. *Q1*.

---

  163. *stuck ... check*] had no scruples about any restraint or hindrance.
  168. *bullets*] cannon-balls.
  172. *form*] i.e., as a 'fighting flame'.
  175. *quench*] act of quenching (a fire). Cf. 'extinguish' in l. 170.
  180. *treated*] negotiated.
  181. *but*] Qq have 'put', probably a misreading because of 'put' in l. 180.
gloze] pretence, deceit.
  186. *amazed*] struck with terror.

Harlay. He alters every minute: what a vapour
   The strongest mind is to a storm of crosses!
                                                            Exeunt.
      Epernon, Soissons, Janin, Vidame, D'Escures [*remain*].
Epernon. O of what contraries consists a man!
   Of what impossible mixtures! Vice and virtue,   190
   Corruption and eternesse, at one time,
   And in one subject, let together loose.
   We have not any strength but weakens us,
   No greatness but doth crush us into air.
   Our knowledges do light us but to err,   195
   Our ornaments are burthens, our delights
   Are our tormentors, fiends that raised in fears
   At parting shake our roofs about our ears.
Soissons. O Virtue, thou art now far worse than Fortune;
   Her gifts stuck by the duke when thine are vanished,   200
   Thou brav'st thy friend in need: Necessity,

188.2. *remain*] *This ed.*; Manent *Q1*.

   191. *eternesse*] eternity.

   193–8.] The very similar passage in *The Teares of Peace* (ll. 676–83) which Parrott believes may have been the first draft of the lines in the play, though published in 1609, describes the harmony of the individual governed by true learning, and conversely the individual 'still out of tune' without such learning: 'And then, they haue no strength, but weakens them; / No greatnes, but doth crush them into streame; / No libertie, but turnes into their snare; / Their learnings then, do light them but to erre; / Their ornaments are burthens; their delights, / Are mercinarie, seruile Parasites, / Betraying, laughing; Feends, that raisde in feares, / At parting, shake their Roofes about their eares ...'.

   195. *knowledges*] acquaintance with various branches of learning.

   196. *ornaments*] adornments, qualities of beauty, grace or honour.

   199–204.] Soissons's contribution to the choral commentary is notably obscure, and much ingenuity has been expended in trying to clarify it. The Virtue/Fortune tension begins early in *The Conspiracy* in the argument between Savoy and Henry (*Consp.*, II.ii.89–108) and provides a dominant note in *The Tragedy*; it derives from Plutarch's *De Alexandri magni* (see *Trag.*, I.i.141 and n.). A paraphrase might read: 'Virtue left the duke even before Fortune, and now Virtue defies him in his greatest need. Necessity and Contempt, which used to attract Virtue's rewards and love, have abandoned Virtue as followers, in Byron's extreme distress. Virtue's power and comfort (in fortitude and wisdom) are mere dreams.'

   199. *Virtue*] nobility of spirit.

   201. *Necessity*] the condition of being totally under the control of circumstances.

|That used to keep thy wealth, Contempt, thy love,
Have both abandoned thee in his extremes;
Thy powers are shadows and thy comfort dreams.
Vidame. O real Goodness, if thou be a power, 205
And not a word alone, in human uses,
Appear out of this angry conflagration
Where this great captain, thy late temple, burns,
And turn his vicious fury to thy flame,
From all earth's hopes, mere gilded with thy fame; 210
Let Piety enter with her willing cross
And take him on it; ope his breast and arms
To all the storms Necessity can breathe,
And burst them all with his embracèd death.
Janin. Yet are the civil tumults of his spirits 215
Hot and outrageous: not resolved, alas,
Being but one man, render the kingdom's doom;
He doubts, storms, threatens, rues, complains, implores;
Grief hath brought all his forces to his looks,
And nought is left to strengthen him within, 220
Nor lasts one habit of those grievèd aspects:
Blood expels paleness, paleness blood doth chase,
And sorrow errs through all forms in his face.
D'Escures. So furious is he that the politic law

---

206. human] *Q1* (humaine); humane *Shepherd.*   217. render] *Q1, Q2;* under *Parrott.*

---

202. *Contempt*] the condition of being despised or disgraced.
206. *uses*] experience.
210. *mere gilded*] gilded only.
211. *willing cross*] See Matt. xvi.24.
214. *his embracèd death*] death that he willingly embraces.
216. *outrageous*] furious.
217.] The line may be corrupt. Parrott, following Deighton, conjectures 'under' for 'render' and extends the brackets to include the whole line; Loane reads 't'endure'. I prefer (hesitantly) to keep 'render', its subject being the 'civil tumults' of l. 215, which are 'not resolved, alas' and consequently bring to destruction that kingdom within one man where the tumults are taking place.
219. *looks*] facial expression.
221. *habit*] outward guise.
grievèd aspects] looks of grief.
223. *errs*] wanders.
224. *politic*] prudent.

Is much to seek how to enact her sentence: 225
Authority backed with arms, though he unarmed,
Abhors his fury, and with doubtful eyes
Views on what ground it should sustain his ruins;
And as a savage boar that, hunted long,
Assailed and set up, with his only eyes 230
Swimming in fire keeps off the baying hounds,
Though sunk himself, yet holds his anger up
And snows it forth in foam; holds firm his stand
Of battailous bristles; feeds his hate to die,
And whets his tusks with wrathful majesty: 235
So fares the furious duke, and with his looks
Doth teach Death horrors; makes the hangman learn
New habits for his bloody impudence,
Which now habitual horror from him drives,
Who for his life shuns death, by which he lives. 240
[*Exeunt.*]

[ACT V SCENE iv]

Enter CHANCELLOR, HARLAY, POTIER, FLEURY, VITRY, [PRÂLIN].

Vitry. Will not your lordship have the duke distinguished
From other prisoners? Where the order is

240.1. *Exeunt*] Parrott.   0.1. PRÂLIN] *Phelps.*

225. *is ... seek*] has much trouble seeking.
227. *Abhors*] shrinks back from.
228. *sustain*] carry the burden of.
230. *set up*] placed to fight.
with ... eyes] with only his eyes.
234. *battailous*] ready for battle.
238–9.] The duke's fury forces the hangman to learn new habits of behaviour in place of his usual impudence, new habits which his habituation to horror would normally drive from him; the fearful hangman, afraid for his life, delays the execution by which he gains his livelihood (an anticipation of the final scene).
240.1. Exeunt.] There is no *exeunt* in Qq at this point: the five choral characters may remain on stage while the rest come in, since D'Escures has a line to speak in the ensuing scene but no entry. However Parrott is probably right to indicate a change of locality to the place of execution by the conventional Elizabethan method of a general exit and a following entry. Since a scaffold is needed in the next scene, it must have been set up on the stage at this point or thrust forward, unless, as Wickham also suggests, it had been fixed on the stage throughout, along with throne and bar, in the tradition of the medieval mansions (*Early English Stages*, vol. II, pt. I (1963), pp. 314, 317).

SC IV]   THE TRAGEDY OF CHARLES DUKE OF BYRON   259

> To give up men condemned into the hands
> Of th'executioner: he would be the death
> Of him that he should die by, ere he suffered   5
> Such an abjection.
> *Chancellor.*   But to bind his hands,
>   I hold it passing needful.
> *Harlay.*   'Tis, my lord,
>   And very dangerous to bring him loose.
> *Prâlin.* You will in all despair and fury plunge him
>   If you but offer it.
> *Potier.*   My lord, by this   10
>   The prisoner's spirit is something pacified,
>   And 'tis a fear that th'offer of those bands
>   Would breed fresh furies in him, and disturb
>   The entry of his soul into her peace.
> *Chancellor.* I would not that, for any possible danger   15
>   That can be wrought by his unarmèd hands,
>   And therefore in his own form bring him in.
>
> *Enter* BYRON, [D'ESCURES,] *a Bishop or two, with all the guards,
>   soldiers with muskets.*
>
> *Byron.* Where shall this weight fall? On what region
>   Must this declining prominent pour his load?
>   I'll break my blood's high billows 'gainst my stars,   20
>   Before this hill be shook into a flat:
>   All France shall feel an earthquake. With what murmur

2–4. prisoners? ... executioner:] *Q1*; prisoners, ... executioner? *Parrott.*
17.1. D'ESCURES] *Ray.*

---

6. *abjection*] humiliation.
   But] only.
   15. *would not that*] would not wish that.
   17.1. *D'ESCURES*] No entry is given for D'Escures though he agrees to act on Byron's behalf at l. 143 below. His entry with Byron at this point is therefore justifiable. (See *Trag.*, V.iii.240.1n.) The 'Bishop or two' sounds like authorial vagueness, allowing the actors discretion as to numbers. At l. 23, the s.h. reads *Arch.*
   19. *prominent*] eminence or lofty hill. Cf. the Councillor's extended image of a 'mighty promontory' (*Consp.*, IV.i.190ff.).
   20–22.] Q punctuation does not indicate whether l. 21 should go more closely with l. 20 or with l. 22, either of which makes good sense. I have placed a colon after 'flat' simply to make a choice.
   22. *murmur*] muttered or indistinct complaint. Byron is suggesting that the shrinking of the world through his fall should provoke a noisier reaction.

This world shrinks into chaos!
Archbishop.   Good my lord,
    Forgo it willingly, and now resign
    Your sensual powers entirely to your soul.   25
Byron. Horror of death! Let me alone in peace,
    And leave my soul to me, whom it concerns;
    You have no charge of it; I feel her free,
    How she doth rouse and like a falcon stretch
    Her silver wings, as threatening death with death,   30
    At whom I joyfully will cast her off.
    I know this body but a sink of folly,
    The ground-work and raised frame of woe and frailty;
    The bond and bundle of corruption;
    A quick corse, only sensible of grief,   35
    A walking sepulchre, or household thief,
    A glass of air, broken with less than breath,
    A slave bound face to face to death, till death;
    And what said all you more? I know, besides,

---

23. *Archbishop*] Q1, Q2; *Bishop Parrott.*

23. Archbishop] Parrott notes that Grimeston records a visit of the Archbishop of Bourges to Byron during his imprisonment, though it was Garnier, the king's preacher and later Bishop of Montpellier, who attended Byron at his execution (p. 610). However Parrott's correction of the s.h. to 'Bishop' is not necessary.

24. *Forgo it*] i.e., the world.

26ff.] Grimeston reports that after the 'Diuines' had given him pious counsel, 'Hee then grewe into choller, swearing that they should suffer him in Peace, and that it concerned him only to thinke of his Soule, with the which they had nothing to do' (p. 987).

31. *cast her off*] let fly his soul, like a falcon, to prey on death.

32. *sink*] sewer or pit.

33. *ground-work*] foundation.
frame] structure.

34–8.] Cf. *The Teares of Peace*: 'This bond, and bundle of corruption; / This breathing Sepulcher; this spundge of grief; / This smiling Enemie; this household-thiefe; / This glasse of ayre; broken with lesse then breath; / This Slaue, bound face to face, to death, till death …' (ll. 1016–20).

34. *bond*] collection bound together.

35. *quick corse*] living corpse. Schoell notes that this phrase and the following 'walking sepulchre' are taken from Erasmus's *Adagia*: 'Vivum cadaver, vivum sepulchrum' ('Commonplace Book', p. 202).

38.] Chapman used this image several times, as in *The Teares of Peace* (noted above) and in *Bussy*, V.i.108–11. Virgil describes this horrific practice of the tyrant Mezentius in *Aeneid*, VIII, 485–8. 'Tyranny' and 'long in dying' (ll. 42–3) also seem to be echoes of the passage in the *Aeneid*.

SC IV] THE TRAGEDY OF CHARLES DUKE OF BYRON 261

    That life is but a dark and stormy night 40
    Of senseless dreams, terrors and broken sleeps;
    A tyranny, devising pains to plague
    And make man long in dying, racks his death;
    And death is nothing: what can you say more?
    I bring a long globe and a little earth; 45
    Am seated like earth betwixt both the heavens,
    That if I rise, to heaven I rise; if fall,
    I likewise fall to heaven; what stronger faith
    Hath any of your souls? What say you more?
    Why lose I time in these things? Talk of knowledge, 50
    It serves for inward use. I will not die
    Like to a clergyman, but like the captain
    That prayed on horseback, and with sword in hand,
    Threatened the sun, commanding it to stand;
    These are but ropes of sand.
Chancellor.   Desire you then 55
    To speak with any man?
Byron. I would speak with La Force and Saint Blancart.
Vitry. They are not in the city.

---

45. bring] *Q1, Q2*; being *Parrott.*   long] *Q1, Q2*; large *Parrott.*   58. Vitry] *Parrott; not in Q1, Q2.*   They ... city] *Parrott (from Grimeston); not in Q1, Q2.*

    45.] The reading as it stands is not very satisfactory but the suggested emendations are little better. 'Long globe' may be, as Henry Bradley suggests (Ferguson, p. 239), a version of Ovid's *longum caelum*, hence a reference to the vast sphere of the heavens; the 'little earth' is the small point at the centre of this sphere. 'Bring' may possibly be a compositor's misreading of 'being', as Parrott and others believe. If 'bring' is correct, the line suggests that Byron brings his own cosmos with him, his own sphere of the soul and his physical body like the earth within it – a microcosm of the universe. In l. 46, Byron places himself, his microcosm, at the centre with heaven above and heaven below (the Stoic cosmology made the earth the centre point of the universe). By freeing itself from the earthly elements of earth and water, his soul will rise according to the airy and fiery elements within it, and since heaven is below as well as above it, it can 'fall' to heaven as well as rise to it. See Ferguson for a full discussion (pp. 237–9).
    52. *the captain*] Joshua. The comparison is from Grimeston, p. 987.
    55. *These*] the hopes and prayers offered by the clergy.
    58.] There is no answer in the text to Byron's request to speak with La Force and Saint Blancart, his brothers-in-law, but the catchword at the bottom of the page (Q4r) is *Vyt.*, indicating that Vytry or Vitry is the next speaker. Parrott has supplied Vitry's speech from Grimeston: 'They tould him that they were not in the Cittie' (p. 988).

Byron.   Do they fly me?
    Where is Prevost, controller of my house?
Prâlin. Gone to his house i'th' country three days since.   60
Byron. He should have stayed here; he keeps all my blanks.
    O all the world forsakes me! Wretched world,
    Consisting most of parts that fly each other,
    A firmness breeding all inconstancy,
    A bond of all disjunction; like a man   65
    Long buried is a man that long hath lived;
    Touch him, he falls to ashes: for one fault,
    I forfeit all the fashion of a man.
    Why should I keep my soul in this dark light,
    Whose black beams lighted me to lose myself,   70
    When I have lost my arms, my fame, my mind,
    Friends, brother, hopes, fortunes, and even my fury?
    O happy were the man could live alone,
    To know no man, nor be of any known!
Harlay. My lord, it is the manner once again   75
    To read the sentence.
Byron.   Yet more sentences?
    How often will ye make me suffer death,
    As ye were proud to hear your powerful dooms?
    I know and feel you were the men that gave it,
    And die most cruelly to hear so often   80
    My crimes and bitter condemnation urged:

---

71. mind] *Parrott;* winde *Q1, Q2, Ray.*

    59. *controller*] household officer in charge of accounts.
    61. *blanks*] small coins, hence petty cash.
    65. *bond*] a uniting or cementing force.
    disjunction] separation.
    69–72.] translated from Seneca's *Hercules Furens* (ll. 1258–61) as Cunliffe and Parrott have noted. The quarto's 'winde' in l. 71 may be correct since Chapman elsewhere uses the word to mean 'breath', but in the context 'mind' in the sense of 'reason' makes better sense and also translates Seneca's 'mentem'. Hence I accept Parrott's correction. 'Cur animam in ista luce detineam amplius / morerque nil est; cuncta iam amisi bona: / mentem arma famam coniugem natos manus, / etiam furorem.'
    69. *dark light*] The sunshine of the king's favour and worldly success is paradoxically darkness and has caused him to lose himself. No doubt there is reference to well-known passages in Isaiah ix and lx in which the darkness of this world is contrasted with the light of spiritual reality.
    75. *manner*] customary procedure.

SC IV] THE TRAGEDY OF CHARLES DUKE OF BYRON 263

  Suffice it I am brought here, and obey,
  And that all here are privy to the crimes.
Chancellor. It must be read, my lord, no remedy.
Byron. Read if it must be, then, and I must talk.   85
Harlay. The process being extraordinarily made and examined
  by the Court and Chambers assembled –
Byron. Condemned for depositions of a witch,
  The common deposition and her whore
  To all whorish perjuries and treacheries!   90
  Sure he called up the devil in my spirits
  And made him to usurp my faculties:
  Shall I be cast away now he's cast out?
  What justice is in this? Dear countrymen,
  Take this true evidence betwixt heaven and you   95
  And quit me in your hearts.
Chancellor. Go on.
Harlay. Against Charles Gontaut of Byron, Knight of both the
  Orders, Duke of Byron, Peer and Marshal of France,
  Governor of Burgundy, accused of treason, a sentence was 100
  given the 22 of this month, condemning the said Duke of
  Byron of high treason, for his direct conspiracies against
  the King's person, enterprises against his state –
Byron. That is most false! Let me forever be
  Deprived of heaven, as I shall be of earth,   105
  If it be true: know, worthy countrymen,
  These two and twenty months I have been clear
  Of all attempts against the king and state.
Harlay. – treaties and treacheries with his enemies, being

---

100. treason, a sentence] *Parrott;* treason in a sentence *Q1.*

 86. *process*] summons or writ.
 89.] Byron calls the deposition 'common', like a common woman or prostitute, who is the 'whore' to a whole collection of 'perjuries and treacheries'.
 93. *cast out*] exorcised. Byron now claims that he is free of La Fin's devilish influence.
 96. *quit*] acquit.
 98–9. *both the Orders*] the order of St Michael, founded by Louis XI, and the Order of the Holy Ghost, founded by Henry III. Parrott notes that a member of the latter swore never to receive gifts or estates from foreign princes without permission.
 100.] A sentence does not accuse but it does condemn; hence the 'in' of Q1 is probably an interpolation.

Marshal of the King's army, for reparation of which crimes 110
they deprived him of all his estates, honours and dignities,
 and condemned him to lose his head upon a scaffold at the
 Greave –
Byron. The Greave? Had that place stood for my dispatch,
 I had not yielded; all your forces should not 115
 Stir me one foot; wild horses should have drawn
 My body piece-meal ere you all had brought me.
Harlay. Declaring all his goods, moveable and immoveable
 whatsoever, to be confiscate to the King; the Seigneury of
 Byron to lose the title of Duchy and Peer for ever. 120
Byron. Now is your form contented?
Chancellor.   Ay, my lord;
 And I must now entreat you to deliver
 Your order up; the king demands it of you.
Byron. And I restore it, with my vow of safety
 In that world where both he and I are one, 125
 I never broke the oath I took to take it.
Chancellor. Well, now, my lord, we'll take our latest leaves,
 Beseeching Heaven to take as clear from you
 All sense of torment in your willing death,
 All love and thought of what you must leave here, 130
 As when you shall aspire heaven's highest sphere.
Byron. Thanks to your lordship, and let me pray too
 That you will hold good censure of my life,
 By the clear witness of my soul in death,
 That I have never passed act 'gainst the king; 135
 Which, if my faith had let me undertake,

---

127. *Well*] Q2; *We'l* Q1.

---

 113. *Greave*] Place de la Grève, now the Place de l'Hôtel-de-Ville, often used as a place of public execution as well as for other public ceremonies. Grimeston and other contemporary historians note that the execution took place in a courtyard of the Bastille after friends of Byron had sent a plea to the king that he be not executed publicly. Chapman seems to have accepted this without specifying a particular place.
 121.] Are your formal requirements now satisfied?
 124. *safety*] salvation. Byron vows by the salvation he hopes for in that world beyond death where he and the king are equal.
 127. *Well*] Editors have accepted Q2's correction of 'We'l' to 'Wel'.
 128. *clear*] completely.
 133. *censure*] opinion.
 135. *passed*] executed, accomplished.

He had been three years since amongst the dead.
Harlay. Your soul shall find his safety in her own.
   Call the executioner!
                    [*Exeunt* CHANCELLOR *and* HARLAY.]
Byron. [*To D'Escures*]   Good sir, I pray,
   Go after and beseech the Chancellor   140
   That he will let my body be interred
   Amongst my predecessors at Byron.
D'Escures. I go, my lord.   *Exit.*
Byron.   Go, go! Can all go thus,
   And no man come with comfort? Farewell, world!
   He is at no end of his actions blest   145
   Whose ends will make him greatest, and not best;
   They tread no ground, but ride in air on storms
   That follow state and hunt their empty forms;
   Who see not that the valleys of the world
   Make even right with the mountains, that they grow   150
   Green and lie warmer, and ever peaceful are,
   When clouds spit fire at hills and burn them bare.
   Not valleys' part, but we should imitate streams
   That run below the valleys and do yield
   To every molehill, every bank embrace   155
   That checks their currents; and when torrents come
   That swell and raise them past their natural height,
   How mad they are and troubled! Like low streams
   With torrents crowned, are men with diadems.

137. He] *Parrott;* They *Q1, Q2.*   139.1. *Exeunt* ... HARLAY] *Parrott.*
139. *To D'Escures*] *This ed.*   158. streams] *Shepherd;* straines *Q1, Q2.*

137. *He*] The reading 'They' in Q1 does not make sense, unless Byron is thinking of the king and his supporters (so Ray). Parrott points to Grimeston's version for this correction: 'the King had not beene living three yeares since' (p. 988).
   145. *end*] conclusion or outcome.
   146. *ends*] goals (though also with some sense of the preceding).
   149–58.] There may be a distant recollection in these lines of *Timaeus*, v, where the priest describes how those dwelling on the mountains are sometimes destroyed by mighty fires while those living by rivers or the sea-shore are preserved, and similarly how the latter may suffer when great deluges swell the rivers into torrents.
   150. *make even right*] are made equal.
   153.] We should imitate, not the role of the valleys, but that of the streams.

Vitry. My lord, 'tis late; will't please you to go up? 160
Byron. Up? 'Tis a fair preferment: ha ha ha!
There should go shouts to upshots. Not a breath
Of any mercy yet? Come, since we must.
    [He mounts the scaffold.]

    [Enter Hangman.]

Who's this?
Prâlin.   The executioner, my lord.
Byron. Death, slave, down, or by the blood that moves me 165
I'll pluck thy throat out! Go, I'll call you straight.
Hold, boy, and this.
    [He casts his handkerchief and doublet to a boy.]
Hangman.   Soft, boy, I'll bar you that.
Byron. Take this then; yet I pray thee, that again;
    [He asks for the handkerchief back.]
I do not joy in sight of such a pageant
As presents Death; though this life have a curse, 170
'Tis better than another that is worse.
    [He blindfolds himself.]
Archbishop. My lord, now you are blind to this world's sight,
Look upward to a world of endless light.
Byron. Ay, ay, you talk of upward still to others,
And downwards look with headlong eyes yourselves. 175
Now come you up, sir.
    [The Hangman mounts the scaffold.]
                But not touch me yet;
Where shall I be now?
Hangman.   Here, my lord.
Byron.   Where's that?
Hangman. There, there, my lord.
Byron.   And where, slave, is that there?

163.1. *He ... scaffold*] Parrott.   163.2. *Enter* Hangman] *Parrott.*
167.1. *He ... boy*] Parrott.   168.1. *He ... back*] This ed.   171.1. *He blindfolds himself*] Parrott.   172. Archbishop] *Q1, Q2;* Bishop *Parrott.*
176.1. *The Hangman ... scaffold*] This ed.

---

162. *upshots*] the final shots in a match at archery. Byron claims there ought to be shouts from the crowd for the final shots of a match. An upshot is also a mark or end aimed at; an end, conclusion, or termination.
    163.1.] See Appendix I for Grimeston's account of this scene.
    175. *headlong*] with head foremost, as in falling; rash.

Thou seest I see not, yet speak'st as I saw.
Well, now is't fit?
Hangman.   Kneel, I beseech your grace,   180
   That I may do mine office with most order.
Byron. Do it, and if at one blow thou art short,
   Give one and thirty: I'll endure them all.
   Hold! Stay a little! Comes there yet no mercy?
   High Heaven curse these exemplary proceedings: 185
   When justice fails, they sacrifice our example.
Hangman. Let me beseech you I may cut your hair.
Byron. Out, ugly image of my cruel justice!
   Yet wilt thou be before me; stay my will,
   Or by the will of Heaven, I'll strangle thee!   190
Vitry. My lord, you make too much of this your body,
   Which is no more your own.
Byron.   Nor is it yours!
   I'll take my death with all the horrid rites
   And representments of the dread it merits;
   Let tame nobility and numbèd fools   195
   That apprehend not what they undergo
   Be such exemplary and formal sheep.
   I will not have him touch me till I will.
   If you will needs rack me beyond my reason,
   Hell take me, but I'll strangle half that's here,   200
   And force the rest to kill me. I'll leap down

---

179. speak'st] *Parrott*; I speake *Q1*.

---

179. *speak'st*] Parrott's emendation is sensible; the compositor seems to have inserted an additional 'I'.
  as I saw] as if I could see.
  183. *one and thirty*] perhaps with a recollection of his five and thirty wounds gained in battle.
  184. *Hold!*] The language suggests that Byron kneels at l. 182 and stands up again at this point, tearing the blindfold from his eyes. He seems to look for a messenger bringing a reprieve at l. 184 and obviously uses his eyes when addressing the hangman at l. 188 and later the soldier. (See Grimeston, pp. 990–1; Appendix I.)
  186. *sacrifice our example*] sacrifice us (who are innocent) as an example or deterrent.
  189. *stay*] await.
  194. *representments*] representations.
  197. *exemplary*] ready to serve as an example.
  formal] following form or custom.

> If but once more they tempt me to despair.
> You wish my quiet, yet give cause of fury:
> Think you to set rude winds upon the sea,
> Yet keep it calm, or cast me in a sleep   205
> With shaking of my chains about mine ears?
> O honest soldiers, you have seen me free
> From any care of many thousand deaths,
> Yet, of this one, the manner doth amaze me.
> View, view this wounded bosom: how much bound   210
> Should that man make me that would shoot it through!
> Is it not pity I should lose my life
> By such a bloody and infamous stroke?

Soldier. Now by thy spirit and thy better angel,
> If thou wert clear, the continent of France   215
> Would shrink beneath the burthen of thy death,
> Ere it would bear it.

Vitry.   Who's that?
Soldier.   I say well,
> And clear your justice: here is no ground shrinks;
> If he were clear, it would. And I say more,
> Clear, or not clear, if he with all his foulness   220
> Stood here in one scale, and the king's chief minion
> Stood in another, here: put here a pardon,
> Here lay a royal gift, this, this in merit
> Should hoise the other minion into air.

---

222. here] *Q1;* place *Parrott.*

210. *bound*] obliged, under a debt of gratitude.

214ff.] Grimeston recounts the effect upon the soldiers of Byron's appeal: 'At these wordes the teares fell from the souldiars eyes. All those of his profession sware by his Spirit, & by his good Angell, as the Ancients did by that of their Prince. The poorest souldiar was cherished by him, at the least he had some good words to assure him of his good liking.' (p. 990). This passage no doubt suggested to Chapman the interjection of the soldier in the play. In *A True and perfect Discourse*, there are two references to 'Roni' or 'Rosni' (Sully) as the king's 'great fauorite' and Byron's chief foe: 'The same morning there was also fastned a Placard vpon the pallace gate, which said, that to day shall Biron be executed to gratifie Rosny ...' (p. 18). In the play, the soldier's observation about 'the king's chief minion' may have some such source as this.

215. *clear*] free from guilt.
218. *clear*] demonstrate or prove.
224. *hoise*] lift upward.

Vitry. Hence with that frantic!
Byron. This is some poor witness 225
    That my desert might have outweighed my forfeit:
    But danger haunts desert when he is greatest;
    His hearty ills are proved out of his glances,
    And kings' suspicions need no balances;
    So here's a most decretal end of me, 230
    Which I desire, in me, may end my wrongs.
    Commend my love, I charge you, to my brothers,
    And by my love and misery command them
    To keep their faiths that bind them to the king,
    And prove no stomachers of my misfortunes, 235
    Nor come to court till time hath eaten out
    The blots and scars of my opprobrious death;
    And tell the earl, my dear friend of D'Auvergne,
    That my death utterly were free from grief
    But for the sad loss of his worthy friendship; 240
    And if I had been made for longer life,
    I would have more deserved him in my service,
    Beseeching him to know I have not used
    One word in my arraignment that might touch him,
    Had I no other want than so ill meaning. 245
    And so farewell for ever! Never more
    Shall any hope of my revival see me;
    Such is the endless exile of dead men.
    Summer succeeds the spring; autumn the summer;
    The frosts of winter the fall'n leaves of autumn; 250
    All these and all fruits in them yearly fade,

---

229. need] *This ed.;* needes *Q1*.

227. *desert*] worth.
228. *hearty ills*] misdeeds of the secret heart, of the inner man (*O.E.D.*, 'hearty', 4b).
230. *decretal*] decisive.
232. *brothers*] Byron's brothers-in-law, La Force and Saint Blancart.
235. *stomachers*] takers of offence or resentment (*O.E.D.* quotes this phrase).
245.] This awkward line seems to mean: 'Had I no other lack than such a bad intention'. As Parrott notes, Chapman misread a clause in Grimeston ('if it were not that he had more want than bad meaning') as referring to Byron rather than to D'Auvergne as intended. Grimeston's 'more want' is a reference to D'Auvergne's poverty (Parrott, p. 622).

And every year return: but cursèd man
Shall never more renew his vanished face.
Fall on your knees then, statists, ere ye fall,
That you may rise again: knees bent too late 255
Stick you in earth like statues. See in me
How you are poured down from your clearest heavens;
Fall lower yet, mixed with th'unmovèd centre,
That your own shadows may no longer mock ye.
Strike, strike, O strike! Fly, fly, commanding soul, 260
And on thy wings for this thy body's breath,
Bear the eternal victory of Death!

FINIS.

260. Strike ... strike! Fly ... soul] *set as two lines Q1, Q2.* 262.1. FINIS] *Q1.*

---

254. *statists*] those involved in political affairs.
258. *th'unmoved centre*] the unmoving centre of the earth and the universe in Stoic cosmology, where there are no shadows from the sun to mock those who are continually trying to climb higher.
260–2.] Cf. the image of the soul as a falcon ready to prey on death in *Trag.*, V.iv.28–30. The soul attains wings when it leaves the body, breathed out of the body like breath. 'The eternal victory of Death' is the victory over death and alludes to the well-known passage in 1 Cor. xv on immortality: 'Death is swallowed up into victory' (v. 54).
262.] There is no indication in Qq of the staging of the end of the play. Parrott argues for a 'tableau' ending, 'a curtain being drawn after the last line to conceal the figures of Byron kneeling on the scaffold and the hangman standing over him with his raised sword'. But he admits the difficulty of a scaffold, which Byron is required to mount, being placed in an alcove at the back of the stage or on the balcony (*M.L.R.* (Oct. 1908), pp. 63–4). Ray believes that a trick beheading may well have been staged, given Chapman's liking for realistic, often gruesome stage effects and the vogue for such beheadings in plays produced shortly after this (p. 571).
However the play ends with a splendid speech by Byron and no hint of any stage business, reaction from the spectators, or the carrying away of the body. The tone of the final speech is in keeping with the tone of the play as a whole; a theatrical trick at the end with its mingling of the horrifying and the ridiculous and no relief offered by choral characters or a person of authority seems highly unlikely. The conclusions of Chapman's other tragedies should be noted in this respect.
The staging of the final scene remains a problem. If as Wickham suggests (*Early English Stages*, vol. II, pt. 1 (1963), p. 314) a stage structure was brought in for the scaffold at the beginning of the final scene, it is possible that this structure had a curtain that could fall across it. The thud of the falling sword followed by a drum roll and solemn music for the departure of the remaining characters on stage would provide an ending appropriate to an epic tragedy.

APPENDIX I
Chapman and Grimeston

Chapman's only important source for the historical material of his double play was 'A General Inventorie of the History of France, From the beginning of that Monarchie vnto the Treatie of Vervins, in the year 1598. Written by Ihon de Serres. And continued vnto these Times, out off the best Authors which haue written of that Subiect. Translated out of French into English, by Edward Grimeston Gentleman. Imprinted at London by George Eld. 1607.' In the notes to the play there are indications of those passages where Chapman followed his source closely, and also of scenes greatly enlarged from a phrase or single sentence in Grimeston. It appears from his use of this material that Chapman, on this occasion, wished to give his play as much historical authenticity as possible.

The passages from Grimeston that follow have been selected to show, so far as a few brief examples can do so, how Chapman's characterisation of Byron and Henry depend on Grimeston's depiction of them (out of the French chronicles), how Chapman made Grimeston's vivid descriptions into drama and how he adapted Grimeston's view of Byron's tragic fall to the requirements of heroic tragedy.

(i) Summary of Byron's character: *The Conspiracy* I.i.59–82

This Marshall had goodly parts, communicable to fewe, his Valour was admirable, and happy in all his incounters; of an invincible Courage, infatigable and never tired with any toyle, continuing ordinarily fifteene dayes together on Horse-backe. He was not inclined to Voluptuousnesse, nor much to the love of Women, sober ynough, the which began to quench that furious humour, as Intemperancy & greatnesse increased, or that Rest did moderate his boyling passions. He was extremely Vaine-glorious, yea sometimes he would refuse his meate, and content himselfe with little to feede his Fantasie with Glory and Vanity. He was of a meane stature, Blacke, reasonable grosse, hollow eyd, and rough in speech and conversation. He was adventurous in War, Ambitious beyond all measure. The excesse of his Ambition made him to brave it without judgement. He became so presumptuous, as he thought that the King, nor *France* could not subsist without him. He was become ill-tounged, speaking ill of all the Princes, threatning the Parliaments, and the Officers of Justice, some with death, and to dispossesse others of their places. He was advanced from the meanest to the highest degrees of Honour; of a simple Souldiar, hee became a Captaine, then a Colonell, afterwards Admirall and Marshall, and in the ende Lieutenant of the Kings Armies, and in his Heart he aspired to be Duke of *Burgundy*, Son in Lawe to the Duke of *Savoy*, and Nephew to the King of *Spaine*. (p. 992)

(ii) Visit to La Brosse: *The Conspiracy* III.iii

After the death of his elder Brother, his father caused him to be called Baron of *Biron* & brought him to Court, where at the first he had a quarrell with the Lord of *Carency* . . . the which was ended by a Combat of three against three . . . . The Duke of *Espernon* got his pardon, the which was confirmed through the credit which his father had then in Court. Some say that being thus in trouble, he went disguised like a Carrier of Letters, unto one *la Brosse* a great Mathematician whom they held to be skilful in casting of Nativities, to whom he shewed his Nativity, drawn by some other. And dissembling it to be his, he said *it was a Gentlemans whom he served & that he desired to know what end that man should have.* La Brosse having rectified this figure, said unto him, *That he was of a good house, & no elder then you are,* said he to the Baron, asking him if it were his? the Baron answered him, *I wil not tell you: But tel me* (said he) *what his Life, his meanes, & end shal be.* This good old man who was then in a little Garret which served him for a Study, said unto him, *My Son, I see, that he, whose Nativity this is shall come to great Honours, by his industry and Millitary valour, and may be a King, but there is a* CAPUT ALGOL *which hinders it. And what is that* (said the Baron of *Biron*?) *Aske me not* (said *la Brosse*) *what it is. No* (said the Baron) *I must know it.* In the end he sayd unto him; *My Son, it is, that he wil do that which shall make him loose his Head.* Wherupon the Baron (as they report) did beat him cruelly, & having left him halfe dead he went downe, & carried away the Key of the Garret dore, whereof he bragged when he was gone. (p. 993)

(iii) Henry's hesitation and Byron's arrest: *The Tragedy* IV.ii.59–229

The King having done walking, invited the Duke of *Biron* to play; they entred into the Queenes Chamber. The Count of *Auvergne* passing by the Duke at the entry of the Doore, sayd unto him in his Eare, *We are undonne.* There played at Primero, the Queene, the Duke of *Biron* (upon whom all the mischeefe must fall,) and two others. The King played at Chesse, and in playing did acte the part of Ulisses, going and comming to give order to his affayres. It appeared that his Spirit was troubled with a waighty action. He entred into his Cabinet, being perplexed with two contrary Passions, doubtful whereunto he should yeeld. The Love which he had borne to the Duke of *Biron*, the knowledge he had of his Valour, and the remembrance of his services, made him to reject all thoughts of Justice, and to intreat him, as *Licurgus* had done him that put out his Eye. On the other side, feare of trouble in his Estate, and the apprehension of the execrable effects of so unnaturall a Conspiracy, accused his Clemency of cruelty, which preferred the private before the publike. He praied unto God to assist him with his holy Spirit, to pacifie the Combat which he felt in his soule, and to fortefie him with a holy resolution, to that which should be for the good of his People, over whom he commanded by his onely Grace. His praier being ended, all difficulties which troubled him were dispersed, and he fully resolved to deliver the Duke of *Biron* into the hands of Justice, if he might not otherwise draw the truth from him of his bad attempts. They continued play still, the King taking the Queenes place sometimes, attending the end of his resolutions. The Count of Auvergne was retyred, The King sent for him, and walked up & down the chamber whilest the Duke of *Biron* drempt of nothing but his Game. *Varennes* Lieutenant of his Company, making a shewe to take up his Cloake, told him in his eare, *That he was undon.* This word troubled him so, as he neglected his Game. The Queene observed it and told him, *That he had misreckoned himselfe to his owne losse:* The King said; *That they had plaied ynough, commanding every man to retire.* He entred into his Cabinet, & commanded the Duke of *Biron* to enter with him, whose Health or Ruine depended upon an answer pleasing to his Majesty. Who willed him once for all to declare what he had done with the Duke of *Savoy*, & the Count of *Fuentes*, and that he should assure himselfe, his Clemency should be greater then his fault. The Duke of *Biron* who beleeved that he deserved Death that demanded Life, had not the Heart to humble himselfe, nor the Tongue to crave pardon. He answered the King more boldly then ever, *That they had overprest an Honest man, and that he never had any other desseigne, then that which he had sayde. I would to God it were so,* replyed the King, *but you will not tell it mee: Adieu, Good night.*

As he goes out off the Cabinet, and had past the chamber doore, he met with *Vitry*, who layes his hand upon his Sword, and demands it of him by the Kings commandment. (pp. 968–9)

(iv) The execution: *The Tragedy*, V.iv.162–201

His Judgement being read, the Preachers perswaded him to call to God for helpe, and not to thinke any more on Earth, but to yeeld his Soule to the immortal disposition of the Creator, and to leave his bodie to that which Justice had decreed. He asked what he should doe, and takes his hand-kercher with the which he blinds his eyes, asking the Execusioner where he should set himselfe: He answered him, there my Lord, there: And where is that? Thou seest that I see nothing, and yet thou shewest mee as if I did see plainely: and therewith being in choller, he pulled away his hand-kercher to see: He blinded his eyes againe, and for that it is a kind of grace to be soone dispatcht, and a great crueltie to languish in the expectation of a paine, he commanded the Executioner to make an end. He desired to die standing, according to the advise of *Vespasian*. The Executioner answered him that hee must kneele, that hee might doe nothing out of Order. No no, said the Duke of *Biron*, *if thou canst not doe it at One, give Thirtie. I will not stirre.* They prest him to kneele, and hee obeyed, willing the Executioner to dispatch, then he start up sodainly againe, casting his eyes upon the Executioner, and looking upon the standers by, hee asked if there no mercy: It was imagined, that either hee would have layd hand uppon the Executioners sword, or that hee presumed that when he should be readie to receive the fatall stroake they would bring him his pardon, and that the King would doe him no other harme then feare him, as *Papirius Cursor* did one of his souldiars for breaking of his ranke. The Executioner intreated him to suffer him to cut his heire. At that word he grew into choller againe, he unbanded himselfe, and sware that if he toucht him hee would strangle him. You may see in two persons, two extreame passions. Feare retyred the Executioner within himselfe. Choller transported the Duke of *Biron* beyond himselfe. The one trembled for feare, the other for rage. *Voisin* sayd unto him, *that he had too much care of his bodie, which was no more his owne.* He turned to him in choller with an oath, saying, *I will not have him touch mee, so long as I shall bee living: If they put mee into choler, I will strangle halfe the company that is here, and will force the rest to kill mee, I will leape downe if you thrust me into dispaire.* His colour did rise and shewed a distemperature in his face. Those that were uppon the scaffold went downe. The Executioner remayned amazed, fearing death more then he that was to die. (pp. 990–1)

(v) The tragic fall

Such was the ende of the Duke of *Biron*. There is no Calme but hath a Storme: one would have said to have seene him at the height of his prosperities; *That he had fixed a Nayle on Fortunes wheele, that it might not turne*, and yet he is sodainly cast downe. There past but one night, betwixt his Glory and his Ruine. This Flower being so sodainely blowne, the first Northern winde did wither it, and carry it away. His Honours and Greatnesse were the meanes to ruine him, like unto *Absolons* long Hayre, by the which hee was hanged. King *Lewis* the 11. did alwayes say; *That Pride carried Ruine behinde him*, A Heart which knowes from whence the good comes which it injoyeth, is alwayes an enemy to Pride. So there is but a moment betwixt Glory and Ruine. Great Trees are long in growing, but are rooted up in an instant. And it is true, if the Duke of *Biron* had had a Brayne, he had not lost his Head, and had not brought it into the handes of his Princes Justice, whom hee had so much offended. (p. 992)

APPENDIX II A

Letter from the French ambassador, Antoine Lefèvre de la Boderie to Pierre Brulart de Puisieux, Marquis de Sillery, 8 April 1608

From a manuscript in the *Bibl. Nat.* printed by J. J. Jusserand, *M.L.R.*, VI, 203, and by E. K. Chambers, *Eliz. Stage*, III, 257–8. The translation is my own, checked by Professor J. A. Curtis of the University of Toronto.

> About mid-Lent those very actors whom I had had barred from playing the history of the late Marshal de Biron, noting all the court to be away, did so nonetheless, and not only that but introduced into it the Queen and Madame de Verneuil, the former treating that lady very ill verbally and giving her a slap on the face. Having been informed of this some days after the event, immediately I went to see the Earl of Salisbury and made a complaint to him that not only were those members of the troupe contravening the prohibition made against them but they were adding to it things not only more serious but which had nothing to do with the Marshal de Biron and furthermore were all false, at which in truth he showed great anger. And at once he sent orders to arrest them. However only three were found, who were at once put into prison where they are still; but the principal culprit, the author, escaped. A day or two before, they had slandered their King, his mine in Scotland,[1] and all his Favourites in a most pointed fashion; for having made him rail against heaven over the flight of a bird and have a gentleman beaten for calling off his dogs, they portrayed him as drunk at least once a day. Having learned this, I thought he would be angry enough against the said players without my making him any more so and that it would be better to attribute their punishment to the irreverence they had shown him than to what they might have said of the afore-mentioned Ladies, and for that reason I decided to say no more about it but simply consider what they did. When His aforesaid Majesty was here, he showed himself greatly annoyed with the scoundrels and commanded that they be punished and especially that a diligent search be made for the author. What is more, he forbade the further performance of any plays whatsoever in London, to lift which prohibition four other companies which are still there are already offering a hundred thousand francs, which could well restore permission to them: but at the very least this will be

---

1. *his mine in Scotland*] Sometimes 'sa mine d'Escosse' is translated as 'his Scottish mien' (see Andrew Gurr, *The Shakespearean Stage 1574–1642*, p. 36), but Sir Thomas Lake's letter to Lord Salisbury, quoted by Chambers (*Eliz. Stage*, III, 53–4) makes it clear that the players had offended 'in ye matter of ye Mynes and other lewd words': perhaps a reference to James's handling of monopolies for silver mines in Scotland.

on condition that they should no longer perform any modern histories nor speak of contemporary affairs on pain of death. If I had believed that there had been any particular incitement in what the aforesaid players had said, I should have made a stronger protest; but having every reason to think the opposite, I thought it best not to stir up matters any further and to leave it to the aforesaid King to take revenge in his own right. Nevertheless if you judge, Monsieur, that I have not done enough, it is not too late.

APPENDIX II B
The Dobell letters

Bertram Dobell, 'Newly discovered documents of the Elizabethan and Jacobean periods', *The Athenaeum* (1901), 23, 30 March, 6, 13 April; from a manuscript now Folger 420423.

> Sr – Not wearie of my Shelter, but uncertaine why the forme of the cloude still hovers over me, when the matter is disperst, I write to intreate your resolution; And all this tyme have not in this sort visted you, for feare I should seeme to give spurrs to your free disposition; But now (least imagininge me hotter of my libertie than I am, you should thinke me unhowsde, and not to have presented you with my first thankfull Apparence) I thought good to send out this dove; And thoughe I am put, by the Austeritie of the offended tyme to this little pacience, yet can I not be so thanklesslye jelouse of the knowing judgment from whence your actions proceede to retaine any thought of youre favours Repentaunce; or neglect of their extension in the safe retreat: when your daungerous charge for me was so resolute and worthie. I am the same I was when you thought me worthie of youre vertuous kindnes; and will ever remaine (whatsoever I may be)
> Wholy yours in all affectionate Requitall. For his right worthie and exceedinge good frend Mr Crane: Secretorie to my Lord Duke of Lennox.
> *(Ath.* 6 April 1901, p. 433)

> Sr – I have not deserv'd what I suffer by your austeritie; if the two or three lynes you crost were spoken; my uttermost to suppresse them was enough for my discharge: To more then which no promysse can be rackt by reason; I see not myne owne Plaies; nor carrie the Actors Tongues in my mouthe; The action of the mynde is performance sufficient of any dewtie, before the greatest authoritie, wherein I have quitted all your former favors. And made them more worthie then any you bestowe on outward observers; if the thrice allowance of the Counsaile for the Presentment gave not weight enoughe to drawe yours after for the presse, my Breath is a hopeles adition; if you say (for your Reason) you know not if more then was spoken be now written no, no; nor can you know that, if you had bothe the Copies, not seeing the first at all: Or if you had seene it presented your Memorie could hardly confer with it so strictly in the Revisall to discerne the Adition; My short reason therefore can not sounde your severitie: Whosoever it were that first plaied the bitter Informer before the french Ambassador for a matter so far from offence; And of so much honor for his maister as those two partes containe, perform'd it with the Gall of a Wulff, and not of a man: And theise hautie and secrett vengeances taken for Crost, & officious humors are more Politique than Christian; which he that hates will one day discover in the open ruyne of their Auctors; And though they be trifles he yet laies them in Ballance (as they concern Justice, and bewray Appetites to the greatest Tyrannye) with

the greatest; But how safely soever Illiterate Aucthoritie setts up his Bristles against Poverty, methinkes yours (being accompanied with learning) should rebate the pointes of them, and soften the fiercenes of those rude manners; you know Sr, They are sparkes of the lowest fier in Nature that fly out uppon weaknes with every puffe of Power; I desier not you should drenche your hand in the least daunger for mee: And therefore (with entreatie of my Papers returne) I cease ever to trouble you.

By the poore subject of your office for the present.

(*Ath.* 6 April 1901 p. 433)

APPENDIX III

Byron and the Essex Conspiracy

There are several incidents and touches of characterisation and language in *The Conspiracy and Tragedy of Byron* which may have recalled to a contemporary audience the fall of Essex and its remarkable similarities to the fall of Byron. The two direct references to Essex are both placed in the mouth of Byron: one is the story of Essex' horse (*Trag.*, IV.i.133–8) for which no source has been found; the other is Byron's account of what Queen Elizabeth told him at their meeting about the refusal of Essex to beg for mercy (*Trag.*, V.iii.139–42), a passage taken from Grimeston. In the apparently much-altered scene of Byron's embassy to Elizabeth, there is no direct mention of Essex, although Elizabeth warns Byron about the dangers of ambition, particularly the ambition of a subject who aspires to a throne (*Consp.*, IV.i.128–43). According to Parrott, Koeppel wondered whether the original uncensored scene contained the striking passage from Pierre Matthieu (not in Grimeston) which describes Elizabeth showing Byron the heads of traitors, including that of Essex, on the battlements of the Tower, but Parrott thinks this highly unlikely (p. 607).

One scene which probably set up resonances occurs when Byron draws a pistol after the king has laughed at him, and is forcibly restrained by D'Auvergne from attacking the king, an episode only hinted at in Grimeston (*Consp.*, V.i.154ff.) At least part of the audience would have been reminded of the occasion when Queen Elizabeth gave Essex 'a cuffe on the eare' for turning his back contemptuously upon her. According to Camden, he laid his hand upon his sword and had to be restrained by the Lord Admiral (*Annals*, 3rd ed., 1635, p. 493, year 1598). Essex, like Byron, was forgiven by his sovereign, and yet continued on his course, using bold and defiant language in spite of the warnings of his friends (Camden, p. 552).

At several points in *The Tragedy*, Chapman stresses Henry's desire to use mercy rather than harsh punishment should Byron show any sign of submission. He would almost certainly have known Bacon's report in his *Apologie* (1604) of Elizabeth's repeated statements that her proceedings against Essex should be '*ad castigationem, & non ad destructionem*' and '*ad reparationem* and not *ad ruinam*' (pp. 42, 51). Both the Henry of the play and the Elizabeth of contemporary accounts lament the ingratitude of followers whom they had showered with honours and raised to almost the highest place in the kingdom.

There may be rather more doubt about relating the La Fin of the plays to the Henry Cuffe of history, but there are several intriguing parallels. Cuffe, who was Essex's secretary, did not betray him to the queen but he did, according to the Earl's own deposition, instigate his treasons. The descriptions of Cuffe that survive suggest a man who gained the confidence of his master by cunning and subtle means and through his 'turbulent' nature encouraged him toward fatal action. He was also known as a scholar, though not apparently with any reputation for magic. Sir Henry Wotton describes him thus:

> There was amongst his nearest attendants, one *Henry Cuffe*, a man of secret Ambitious ends of his own, and of proportionate Counsels smothered under the habit of a Scholar, and slubbered over with a certain rude and clownish fashion, that had the semblance of integrity.
> (*Reliquiae Wottonianae*, 4th ed., London, 1685, p. 54)

And Bacon writes of him in *A Declaration of the Practises & Treasons* (1601) 'a base fellow by birth, but a great scholler, and indeede a notable Traytor by the booke, being otherwise of a turbulent and mutinous spirit against all superiours ...' (sig. D2v). Chapman may have used certain of Cuffe's qualities in his development of the character of La Fin, particularly in *The Conspiracy*.

In *The Tragedy*, there is one scene in which the link with Henry Cuffe may be remembered: the dramatic confrontation between Byron and La Fin during Byron's trial (*Trag.*, V.ii.125). In *A Declaration*, there is a record of the confrontation between Essex and Cuffe, described by Sir Thomas Egerton and his fellow signatories in 'Particularities of that which passed ...'. After his trial, Essex requested that he be allowed to speak to Cuffe, 'his Secretary':

> Against whom hee vehementlie complained vnto vs, to haue bene a principall Instigator to these violent courses, which he had vndertaken. Wherein he protested, that he chieflie desired that he might make it appeare, that he was not the onely perswader of these great offences, which they had committed: .... This request being granted him, and *Cuffe* brought before him, hee there directly and vehemently charged him. And amongst other speaches vsed these words: Henry Cuffe, call to God for mercy, and to the Queene, and deserue it, by declaring trueth. For I, that must now prepare for another world, haue resolued to deale clearely with God, and the world: and must needes say this to you; You haue bene one of the chiefest instigators of me, to all these my disloyal courses, into which I haue fallen.
> (sig. Q3r, Q3v)

One may see in the two confrontations parallel moments of high passion and a desire in the two accused to blame lesser men for stirring them up to wrongful deeds.

The clearest echo in the Byron plays of actual language associated with the Essex conspiracy occurs in *The Tragedy* when La Brunel advises Byron not to return to court but rather 'Collect your friends and stand upon your guard' (III.i.118). This seems an inocuous enough phrase until it is remembered 'That my Lord would stand upon his guard' was the password of Essex and his friends just before the attempted coup. Reported in *A Declaration* as 'a kind of cipher and watchword amongst his friends and followers' (sig. D3v), it must have been widely known.

The letter of Essex to Sir Thomas Egerton after the incident of the cuff on the ear did not reach public attention until Camden published the second part of the Annals in 1625, though Camden notes that it had been 'divulged with advisement by his friends' so that there is a possibility that Chapman had seen it. It was written 'stomachfully', Camden notes, to the Lord Keeper who had advised Essex to apologise to the queen. Though it cannot be shown to have had a direct influence on the speeches Chapman gives to Byron, Camden's version of the letter is of great interest in relation to the links we have been examining between Essex and Byron:

> The Queenes heart is obdurate, What I owe as a Subiect I know and what as an Earle, and Marshall of England: to serve as a servant and a slave I know not: If I should acknowledge my selfe guilty, I should be iniurious to the truth, and to God the author of truth. I have received wounds all my bodie over. Having received this scandall, flatly it is impietie to serve. Cannot Princes erre? Can they not wrong their Subiects? Is any earthly power infinite? (*Annals*, 3rd ed., 1635, p. 494, year 1598)

Even in Camden's Latin, the letter has the very ring of Byron's passionate outbursts in Chapman's play. Like Essex, Byron proclaims his innocence and declares his service to the state in terms of the number of his wounds. He contests the authority of kings over free-born individuals, asking 'who will stir / To tell authority that it doth err?'

(*Trag.*, IV.i.19–20)

Glossarial Index to the Commentary

Most of the words in this glossary are given in their uninflected forms unless the inflected form has a particular significance. An asterisk indicates that the annotation referred to supplements information given by the *O.E.D.* The abbreviations '*C*' and '*T*' refer to *The Conspiracy* and *The Tragedy* respectively; '*Ep.*' to the Epistle, and '*Prol.*' to the Prologue.

Abhor, *T.* V.iii.227
abider, *C.* I.i.105
abiding, *C.* II.ii.220
abjection, *T.* V.iv.6
aboding, *C.* III.ii.215
absolute, *C.* I.ii.94 (cf. *C.* I.ii.102; *C.* IV.i.110)
accent, *C.* I.ii.49
addition, *C.* I.ii.65
adust, *C.* II.ii.43
advertise, *T.* IV.ii.300
aerial, *T.* V.iii.42
affectation, *C.* III.iii.18
affected, *C.* II.i.71 (cf. *T.* IV.ii.189)
affection, *C.* I.i.20
Alcides, *C.* II.ii.93; *T.* III.i.151
Alexander, *T.* IV.ii.30; *T.* IV.ii.124
all-inclining, *C.* IV.i.210
altitude, *C.* IV.i.79
amaze, *C.* III.ii.94
ambassage, *C.* I.i.89
apprehension, *C.* III.iii.31
approve, *T.* III.i.207
Arctos, *T.* IV.ii.170
argosy, *C.* II.ii.68
arras, *C.* III.i.50
arsenal, *T.* V.ii.10
artificial, *T.* II.i.77
aspect, *C.* I.i.174; *C.* III.iii.122
aspire, *C.* II.i.35 (cf. *C.* II.i.46)
assured, *C.* II.ii.113
asterism, *C.* III.i.8
Atlas, *T.* IV.ii.166–70
attainture, *T.* III.i.89
attractive, *C.* I.ii.6
Aurora, *T.* IV.ii.169

Back nor belly, *T.* III.i.195
balloon, *C.* V.ii.156
bar, *T.* V.iii.11
barbarous, *C.* II.i.168

bays, *C.* III.ii.256
battailous, *T.* V.iii.234
battery, *C.* I.I.106
besom, *C.* III.ii.236
bewray, *C.* I.i.178
bitter, *T.* V.iii.81
blackthorn, *T.* III.i.127
blank, sb., *T.* V.iv.61
blessed, *T.* I.ii.26
blood, *T.* I.i.137
bloody houses, *C.* III.iii.122
blue, *C.* III.iii.81
bond, *T.* V.iv.34 (cf. *T.* V.iv.65)
botcher-up, *C.* V.i.35
bound, adj., *T.* V.iv.210
bound, sb., *C.* I.ii.195
box, *T.* V.iii.16
box-tree, *T.* V.iii.14
brack, *C.* V.i.36
brake, *T.* IV.i.84
brass, *C.* III.ii.70
bravery, *T.* I.i.37
breach, *Prol.* 5
breathe, *C.* I.ii.71
bristled, *T.* V.iii.260
broad terms, *C.* V.i.53
brooding up, *T.* I.ii.31
brook, vb., *C.* II.i.171
budget, *T.* V.iii.17
bullet, *T.* V.iii.168

Cabinet, *C.* II.i.3 (cf. *T.* IV.i.115; *T.* IV.ii.278)
Calydonian, *T.* IV.ii.144
Camillus, *T.* I.ii.36
camp, *T.* I.i.9
capital, *T.* II.ii.211
Caput Algol, *C.* III.iii.52
career, *C.* II.ii.203
carosse, *T.* V.ii.9
carriage, *C.* V.ii.235
carve, *C.* I.ii.98
cassock, *T.* V.ii.41
cast, *C.* III.iii.39
—— off, *T.* V.iv.31

Catiline, *C.* I.ii.15
censure, vb., *C.* III.ii.293
——, sb., *T.* V.ii.305
centre, *C.* I.i.161; *C.* I.ii.47
change, *C.* I.ii.27
chaos, *C.* III.ii.16 (cf. *T.* I.ii.30)
character, *C.* I.i.170
charge, *C.* II.ii.128
*chastise, *T.* IV.ii.57
check, vb., *T.* V.i.133
—— at, *C.* IV.i.27
chief sway, *C.* I.i.6
choler, *C.* II.ii.43
chorus, *T.* III.ii.48
chymical philosophers, *C.* I.i.53
close with, *C.* II.i.49
closet, *T.* V.i.119
Colchis, *C.* III.iii.89
colour, vb., *C.* I.i.144
——, sb., *T.* IV.ii.307
comment, vb., *T.* V.i.135
comparative, *C.* V.i.88
compare, *C.* II.ii.229
competence, *C.* IV.i.142
composition, *C.* V.ii.198
compress, *C.* I.ii.38 (cf. *T.* V.iii.125)
compression, *C.* III.i.66
conceit, *T.* II.i.62 (cf. *C.* IV.i.203)
concept, *C.* III.i.56
conclusions of estate, *T.* III.i.5
conclusive, *C.* IV.i.93
concord, *T.* V.ii.139
condition, *C.* I.i.30
confessed, *C.* IV.i.101
conformed, *C.* IV.i.185
confusion, *C.* III.iii.76
conjuration, *T.* I.ii.2
conjure, *T.* I.iii.67
connive, *T.* V.iii.27
conscience, *C.* III.i.2
consort, sb., *C.* III.ii.230

283

contain, C. III.ii.59
content, sb., C. I.i.211
contention, C. II.ii.108
continence, C. III.ii.279
continent, C. III.ii.49 (cf. C. IV.i.222)
continuance, T. III.ii.37
continuate, C. I.ii.142
controller, T. V.iv.59
conversion, T. I.ii.23
convince, C. II.ii.108
corrosive, sb., T. V.ii.195
corrupted, C. IV.i.196
corse, T. V.iv.35
counsel, C. I.i.50
countenance, C. I.i.9 (cf. C. I.i.126)
counterfeit, C. III.ii.164
counterpoise, T. IV.ii.83
crack, vb., T. V.ii.154
crystal, C. IV.i.40 (cf. C. V.i.129; T. I.i.97)
cuckoo, C. III.ii.60
cullis, C. III.ii.17
curiously, C. V.i.99
curry, C. V.ii.161
Curtian, C. III.ii.65
curvet, C. V.i.9
Cyclop, C. III.ii.97

Dauphin, C. IV.i.160
decession, C. I.ii.94
decipher, C. I.i.160
decorum, T. V.ii.146
decretal, T. V.iv.230
deeds of heart, C. I.i.44
defy, C. I.i.178
deprecation, T. IV.i.140
deprive, T. V.i.146
desert, sb., C. I.ii.97
despite, C. I.ii.66 & 68
dild C. V.ii.257
diminutive, C. V.i.87
disjunction, T. V.iv.65
dissolution, C. III.i.30
dissolve, C. I.ii.28
distance, T. I.ii.24
distill, C. IV.i.80
division, T. II.i.35
doctrinal, C. II.ii.78
doctrine, C. I.i.172
drift, C. I.i.22

Earth, C. V.ii.47
ease, vb., C. III.ii.260
eaten, C. IV.i.205
—— down, C. I.ii.162
effeminate war, T. II.i.56
Egyptian, C. II.i.147
Elean, C. V.ii.52
element, C. II.iii.43
embraced, T. V.iii.214
embrue, C. III.ii.77
empery, C. I.i.208

enchanted, T. III.ii.8
endure, C. III.ii.183
enforce, C. I.ii.60
enforcement, T. V.iii.9
engage, T. III.ii.1
*engazed, T. V.iii.66
entitle, Ep. 11
entreaty, C. I.ii.200
envy, vb., C. III.iii.10
equity, C. I.i.148
errant, T. V.ii.145
estate, T. III.i.20
eternesse, T. V.iii.191
event, C. II.i.40
eviction, T. V.iii.113
excitement, T. I.iii.98
execrable concord, T. V.ii.139
execution, T. III.i.136 (cf. T. IV.ii.39)
exemplary, T. V.iv.197
exhalation, T. IV.ii.292
expert, C. I.ii.107
express, C. III.ii.159
expuate, C. II.i.101
expugner, C. I.i.105
exquisite, T. V.ii.187
extravagant, T. V.ii.145

Fact, C. II.ii.53; T. V.ii.289
faction, C. I.ii.56
fairly, T. III.i.163
false fire, C. IV.i.175
fautor, T. III.ii.76
fell, adj., C. III.iii.81
—— sb., T. IV.ii.220
feral, C. III.ii.224
fighting sulphur, C. II.ii.48
figure, sb., T. III.iii.39
—— vb., T. II.i.128
fire, C. IV.i.175
fit, adj., C. I.i.93
—— vb., C. I.i.91
flaming crystal, C. V.i.129
flood, Prol. 23
flourish, C. I.ii.134
flower-de-luce, T. V.ii.36
fly, C. I.i.204
flying, C. II.i.49
foggy, T. IV.i.9
force, sb., C. I.ii.157
—— vb., C. I.i.186
forfeit, sb., T. III.ii.85
form, sb., C. I.i.29 (cf. C. I.ii.35; C. I.ii.118)
formal, T. V.iv.197
Fortune, T. I.i.141
foul, adv., C. III.ii.97
fowling, C. II.ii.37
friendly livers, C. III.ii.86
front, sb., C. IV.i.197
—— vb., C. III.ii.247

frontless, T. IV.ii.108
fume, C. III.i.13
fury, C. III.ii.252 (cf. T. I.i.57)

Gait, C. I.ii.143
gall, vb., C. I.ii.19
garb, C. III.ii.19
gate, C. I.ii.194
generous, Ep. 11
genial, C. I.ii.17
gird, C. I.ii.110
girdle, C. I.ii.206
give it charge, C. II.ii.128
globe, T. V.iv.45 (cf. C. I.i.36)
glorious, C. I.i.71 (cf. C. II.ii.135
gloss, C. I.i.29
gloze, T. V.iii.181
god of light, T. I.ii.89
gossip, T. I.iii.64
grace, C. I.i.66 (cf. C. IV.i.62
graceful, C. II.ii.23 (cf. Ep. 21)
gravity, C. III.ii.154
ground, C. II.ii.221 (cf. C. IV.i.205)
—— stream, C. IV.i.90
—— work, T. V.iv.33
grove, C. II.ii.124
guardlike, C. II.i.11

Habit, C. I.ii.84, 89 (cf. C. IV.i.73)
halcyon, T. I.i.120
handle, sb., C. III.iii.26
—— vb., C. III.ii.159
handsel, C. II.i.145
hanger, C. I.ii.206
happy, C. I.i.62
harbour, T. IV.i.82
haunt, T. III.i.168
hawk, vb., T. II.i.21
headlong, T. V.iv.175
headstall, C. V.i.7
heart, C. I.i.44 (cf. C. I.i.152)
—— and marrow, C. I.i.8
hearty ills, T. V.iv.228
hieroglyphic, C. II.ii.78
hireling, T. V.ii.117
hoise, T. V.iv.224
hold, C. I.ii.33
holy fury, C. III.ii.252
hopeless, C. II.ii.24
horrid, T. IV.ii.234
horse-fair, C. V.i.127
hot, T. V.iii.103
house, C. III.iii.122
humanity, C. IV.i.57
humorous, C. II.i.122
humour, C. II.i.101 (cf. T.

INDEX

I.ii.19)
*hunt down, C. V.ii.133–4
Hymen, C. I.ii.24

Ill-aboding, C. III.ii.215
illustrate, *Prol.* 14 (cf. C. IV.i.72)
image, T. V.ii.162
imaginous, C. III.i.52
imp, vb., C. III.ii.255
impair, sb., T. IV.i.47
impatience, T. V.ii.3
impious counting, C. V.ii.159
imposition, C. I.ii.132
impression, *Ep.* 6 (cf. T. I.ii.48)
*improvement, T. V.iii.3
incense, vb., T. V.ii.298
inclination, C. III.iii.6
incompose, T. I.ii.26
indifferent, C. I.i.139
infanta, C. I.i.33
infatigable, C. V.ii.164
infernal, C. I.ii.114
influence, C. IV.i.79
inform, T. V.i.54
informal, T. IV.ii.39
ingenious, T. III.i.4
insolent, T. V.iii.5
insultation, C. II.i.55
intelligence, T. I.i.40
intelligencing, C. II.i.70 (cf. T. IV.ii.268)
intendment, T. I.ii.3 (cf. T. I.iii.43)
intentional respect, T. V.i.20
intercession, C. I.ii.174
intrusion, T. IV.ii.204
invert, T. V.ii.43

Jar, T. II.i.19
jerk, T. V.iii.19
judgement, C. V.ii.64
junket, C. II.ii.6
Juno, C. II.ii.93

Kennel, T. IV.i.23
knowledges, T. V.iii.195

Last, sb., C. III.ii.258
lasting, C. I.i.29
laurel spray, T. III.i.15
law, C. I.i.125
lay out, T. III.i.201
leer, C. III.ii.253
levity, T. V.iii.45
liberty, T. III.i.33
licentiate, C. I.i.145
lie at, C. V.ii.238
light, T. V.i.84 (cf, T. V.i.122)

lingering, C. I.i.26
litigious, C. I.i.98
liver, C. III.ii.86
loathe, T. IV.ii.228
long globe, T. V.iv.45
long-tongued, C. I.i.22
loose, C. II.i.123
Lucifer, T. IV.ii.169
lure, C. III.i.67

Make, C. I.ii.135
malignant, C. III.iii.122
Manlius, T. V.ii.292
mansion, C. I.ii.161
manure, T. IV.i.3
mark, sb., C. II.ii.230
——, vb., C. III.ii.273
marrow C. I.i.8
mate, T. IV.ii.196
melancholy choler, C. II.ii.43
member, C. I.ii.58
memory, C. III.ii.182
mere, C. III.ii.15
meridional, T. V.ii.240
messenger, T. III.i.43
mind, C. I.i.133
minion, C. II.i.141
misconstruction, C. I.i.144
misery, T. V.iii.151
mizzling, T. III.i.132
monology, C. III.ii.61
moonshine, C. III.ii.231
mortal, C. I.ii.55
most stranger, C. V.ii.190
motion, T. V.ii.78

Nap, vb., C. III.ii.256
nature, C. I.ii.92 (cf. C. I.ii.94)
nectar, C. III.ii.257
noblesse, C. I.i.149
nostril, C. III.iii.15
numerous, C. I.ii.46 (cf. T. I.ii.58)

Object, sb., C. III.ii.277
obsequious, C. III.ii.189
observant, T. IV.ii.93
*observation, C. I.ii.201
obtain, C. III.ii.1
occasion, C. IV.i.51
odds, C. II.ii.118
offend, T. III.i.242
Ophir, C. II.i.148
opposition, C. V.ii.122
orator, T. V.iii.131
organ hose, C. V.ii.241–2
ornament, T. V.iii.196
Oros, C. III.ii.155
ostent, T. IV.i.113
out-buy, C. IV.i.177

outrageous, T. V.iii.216
overcharge, T. IV.ii.213
overmatch, T. I.i.123
overnight, C. V.ii.160
overplus, C. I.i.140
overreach, C. II.i.41
oversee, C. IV.i.202
owly eye, T. V.ii.182

Pace, sb., C. I.ii.142
pageant, C. V.i.110
parcel, T. II.i.68
Parmenio, T. IV.ii.30
partial, *I.* IV.ii.283
pash, C. II.ii.154
pass, T. I.i.148 (cf. T. V.iii.64)
passage, C. I.i.109
—— of spleen, C. I.i.42
passenger, C. IV.i.193
passive, T. V.i.141
Pelides, C. II.i.151
penance, C. I.ii.69 (cf. T. V.i.100)
penny-prick, T. II.i.48
pension, C. I.i.39
physic, C. I.i.93
physiognomy, C. III.ii.130
piece out, C. V.i.141
Pierian, C. II.i.84
pitch, sb., C. III.iii.92
pity, C. III.iii.84
plaguey, T. V.ii.149
plate, C. I.ii.205
Plato, C. II.ii.213
pleurisy, T. V.ii.184
plotted, T. V.iii.114
plummet, T. III.ii.2
——, golden, T. I.iii.10
ply, C. II.ii.70
pocky, T. V.iii.6
pole, C. IV.i.28
policy, C. II.i.64; C. IV.i.55; T. I.iii.13
politic, C. I.i.86; C. III.i.27
potato, C. III.ii.16
powder, T. V.ii.8
practice, C. II.i.16 (cf. T. III.ii.21)
prefer, C. II.i.165
prefract, T. IV.ii.22
pregnant, T. IV.i.143
prejudicate, adj., T. V.iii.115
prejudice, T. V.ii.58
presage, T. IV.i.128
prescribe, *Ep.* 9
presence, C. III.ii.21
presentment, *Ep.* 9; C. III.ii.117
president, T. III.i.156
press, sb., *Prol.* 8; T. II.i.65

——, vb., C. V.ii.125
prevent, C. V.ii.8
primero, T. IV.ii.94
privation, C. I.ii.85
process, T. V.ii.45 (cf. T. V.iv.86)
prodigious, C. III.ii.225
—— subject, T. V.ii.140
progeny, C. II.ii.16
projection, C. I.i.54
prominent, sb., T. V.iv.19
property, C. V.i.110 (cf. T. IV.ii.273)
propose, C. V.ii.199
purchase, sb., C. I.i.127
——, vb., C. III.ii.175
purfle, C. III.ii.121
pursuivant, T. III.i.125
pursy regiment, C. I.i.131

Quarter, T. I.i.25
quench, sb., T. V.iii.175
quick corse, T. V.iv.35
quit, C. I.i.126
quite, vb., C. III.i.87
quittance, T. III.i.220

Rack, vb., T. V.ii.110
rampire, T. IV.ii.192
rapeful, T. IV.ii.126
rapt, C. III.iii.138
reach, C. II.i.98
recompense, C. V.i.101
rectify his habit, C. IV.i.73
regiment, C. I.i.131
register, sb., C. V.i.130
reiter, C. II.ii.124
religious, C. III.ii.88
relish, T. II.i.34
remedy of pity, C. III.iii.84
remonstrate, C. V.i.131
representment, T. V.iv.194
resemble, C. IV.i.104
resolve, T. I.iii.40
respect, sb., T. V.i.20 (cf. C. III.ii.283; T. V.i.59)
——, vb., C. V.ii.1
rest, C. I.i.10
retreat, sb., C. I.i.113 (cf. C. II.i.25)
rite, C. I.i.124 (cf. C. I.ii.57)
roundly sighted, T. V.ii.170
royal man, C. III.i.31
—— quarter, T. I.i.25
rude, C. II.ii.201
rule, C. I.i.52

Safety, T. V.iv.124
Saturnal, T. V.ii.258

scape, C. I.ii.74 (cf. C. II.ii.21)
school T. III.i.2
scope, C. III.ii.99
seated, C. II.ii.87
Sebastian, C. II.i.159
secure, C. I.i.193
—— pace, C. I.ii.142
see it, T. IV.ii.107
Semele, C. I.ii.37
sense, C. IV.i.181
senseless, C. I.ii.58 (cf. T. IV.i.106
sententious, T. I.ii.59
seres, T. III.i.16
Sertorius, T. V.ii.242
shadow, C. III.ii.149
shoot off, C. IV.i.175
shot, T. I.ii.12
show, sb., C. II.i.169
sighted, T. V.ii.170
sightly, C. III.iii.92
sincere earth, C. V.ii.47
sink, T. IV.ii.293 (cf. T. V.iv.32)
Sirian, T. III.i.143
site, C. II.ii.71
sleight, T. V.ii.190
*slight, C. V.i.85
smoke our practices, C. II.i.16
sod, adj., C. IV.i.114
solicitor, T. V.ii.30
something-stooping, C. III.ii.146
sometimes, C. III.ii.192
soothe, C. I.i.75
soothed, adj., C. IV.i.54
sophism, T. V.iii.62
sorcerous, T. IV.ii.284
sort, C. II.ii.161 (cf. C. V.i.88)
sound, vb., C. II.ii.57
sparing, C. IV.i.30
speed, C. III.ii.192
spent, C. III.ii.218
spersed, C. III.ii.105
sphere, T. III.i.149; T. III.ii.116
spirit, C. I.i.9 (cf. C. I.i.58; C. II.ii.147)
spleen, C. I.i.42 (cf. C. V.ii.65; T. IV.ii.70)
spoil, sb., T. III.i.217
spot, C. I.ii.7
spring, vb., C. I.i.202
spur, C. III.iii.129
squadron, C. V.ii.160
squint-eyed Envy, T. III.i.30
stand attractive, C. I.i.6
state, C. I.i.68 (cf. C. I.i.68; T. IV.i.82)
statist, T. V.iv.254

statuary, C. III.ii.142
stay, vb., T. IV.ii.87
still, vb., C. II.ii.83
stomacher, T. V.iv.235
stoop, C. I.ii.182
strange affections, C. I.i.20
stroke, C. III.ii.220
stuff, C. I.i.29 (cf. C. I.ii.35)
Stygian, C. V.ii.46 (cf. T. V.ii.167)
subject, T. V.ii.140
suborn, T. V.ii.114
substance, C. I.ii.93
substantial, T. II.i.112
sudden, sb., C. III.ii.221
sufferance, C. I.i.44
suit of tapestry, C. I.ii.208
sulphur, C. II.ii.48
sumpture, C. III.ii.213
superstitious, C. II.i.163
supportance, C. I.i.128
suppose, C. IV.i.180
surcharge, C. II.ii.193
sway, C. I.i.6
swinge, C. V.ii.214
Switzer, C. II.i.166

Table, T. II.i.2.2
take, C. III.ii.135
tapestry, C. I.ii.208
tenter, T. V.iii.57
theory, T. III.ii.20
thicken, T. V.ii.149
thirst, Prol. 19
tickle, adj., C. II.ii.236
tough, T. I.ii.19
toward, Ep. 2
tract, C. III.ii.121
treacher, T. V.ii.125
treen, C. II.ii.233
triumph, C. I.i.23
tumultuous, C. V.ii.65
tuned, C. III.ii.257
turn, T. I.ii.17

Ulysses, C. II.i.52
undone, T. V.iii.121
unmoved centre, T. V.iv.258
unsettled blood, T. I.i.137
unwares, T. V.i.119
upshot, T. V.iv.162
use, vb., C. I.ii.63
uttermost, C. I.ii.175

Valour, C. I.i.62 (cf. C. II.i.25)
vapour, C. II.ii.47
vein, C. I.i.100
vie it, T. IV.ii.107

virtue, *C.* I.ii.47
vizard, *T.* IV.i.84
voluble, *C.* III.ii.147
vouchsafe, *C.* V.ii.142, 148
voyage, *C.* I.i.47
vulgarly, *C.* III.ii.233

Wallet, *T.* IV.i.36
want, sb., *T.* III.i.221
weigh, *C.* I.i.35
whilom, *T.* III.i.27
wide, *T.* I.i.51
wild-fire, *T.* V.ii.296
wind, sb., *T.* I.ii.45

winter of shot, *T.* I.ii.12
witch, vb., *C.* I.i.154
worthy, *C.* I.i.61 (cf. *T.* I.iii.33)
wring, *C.* I.i.11